IRAQ ARCHAEOLOGICAL REPORT

ARTEFACTS OF COMPLEXITY:
TRACKING THE URUK IN THE NEAR EAST

Edited by J.N. Postgate

BRITISH SCHOOL OF ARCHAEOLOGY IN IRAQ

ISBN 0–85668–736–7

Printed in the United Kingdom
at the University Press, Cambridge

Table of Contents

Preface

The papers in this volume all derive from the authors' contributions to a conference with the same title held in Manchester in November 1998. In addition to the 11 papers whose written version is included here we heard contributions from Johannes Boese on Tell Sheikh Hassan, Robyn Stocks and Jane Moon on Bahrain, and Holly Pittman on Uruk glyptic, and the proceedings were introduced and summed up in stimulating fashion by Andrew Sherratt standing in at short notice as our external moderator.

* * * *

The late 4th Millennium in South Mesopotamia is universally known as the "Uruk Period" because it is at Uruk that the German excavations have exposed the most remarkable manifestations of this complex society, in the shape of architecture and artefacts, and of the social order expressed most tellingly in the invention and development of cuneiform script. Although it is evident that many other south Mesopotamian settlements shared in this culture, at the major urban centres the Uruk Period levels tend to be buried under metres of later occupation, so that the best known contemporary site is the small town at Tell Uqair, and even at Uruk itself our knowledge of the period is largely confined to the exceptional agglomeration of public architecture. Within Iraq, therefore, many aspects of the Uruk Period remain poorly known and understood.

In recent decades, however, artefacts and indeed entire settlements which look as though they have been transported on a magic carpet from South Mesopotamia have been uncovered in places as far apart as the Mahi Dasht in Iran and the Euphrates in South-eastern Turkey. Some of these settlements seem to be entire new foundations, which it is hard not to attribute to traders or colonists from the south. Others have sectors within them which suggest that there was an "Uruk enclave" within a pre-existing local settlement, while further afield the Uruk presence may be reflected solely in certain characteristic artefacts. The conference at Manchester brought together a combination of presentations on some of the most significant individual sites with regional surveys of the Levant and Egypt, placing emphasis on the artefactual evidence and its interpretation. Several of our contributors had also recently participated in a School of American Research Advanced Seminar on the Uruk period organized by Mitchell Rothman in Santa Fe, which focussed rather on more abstract issues. We are very grateful to them for agreeing to revisit the period from a different angle, and hope that the present volume will form a useful contrasting approach to the Uruk. The proceedings of the Santa Fe conference are due to appear in November 2001 under the title *Uruk Mesopotamia and its Neighbors: Cross-cultural interactions in the era of state formation*, edited by Mitchell Rothman (Santa Fe: SAR Press).

* * * *

The conference was co-sponsored by the British School of Archaeology in Iraq and the University of Manchester, and we are very grateful to the British Academy for their subvention towards the cost of bringing speakers from abroad. For the smooth running of the conference and accommodation we are very grateful to our colleagues in Manchester, in particular Stuart Campbell, joint organizer of the conference, to the staff and students of the Department of Art History and Archaeology, to Elizabeth Healey and the staff of Ashburne Hall, and to Honor Giles who administered the conference with gentle efficiency. This volume was initially typeset by Anna Lethbridge, and the illustrations scanned and edited by Gary Reynolds Typesetting.

* * * *

Two final remarks to the user of the volume. Maps of Uruk sites will be found in the articles of Rothman (p. 53), Stein (p. 156), and Philip (p. 207). In the Index of sites references to these maps are listed first in italics. The indices are intended to be comprehensive for proper names. It is hoped that the lists of ceramic, chronological and general terms will be found helpful, but completeness and consistency is not achievable. Note in particular that site names may feature not only in the index of sites but also in the sections on pottery and/or time spans.

Nicholas Postgate

Contributors

Virginia Badler   123 Buck Lane, Haverford, PA 19041
                         vbadler@central.cis.upenn.edu

Govert van Driel   Talen en Culturen van het Nabije Oosten, Rijks Universiteit Leiden
                         Postbus 9515, 2300 RA Leiden

Marcella Frangipane   Dipartimento di Scienze Storiche, Archeologiche e Antropologiche
                         dell'Antichità
                         Università di Roma "La Sapienza", Via Palestro 63, 00185 Roma

Renate V.Gut   Institut für Orientalische Archäologie und Kunst
                         Martin-Luther-Universität Halle-Wittenberg
                         Brandbergweg 23c, 06099 Halle / Saale

Hans J. Nissen   Institut für Vorderasiatische Altertumskunde, Freie Universität Berlin
                         Hüttenweg 7, 14195 Berlin

Joan Oates   McDonald Institute for Archaeological Research, University of Cambridge
                         Downing Street, Cambridge CB2 3ER

Edgar Peltenburg & Fiona Stephen
                         Department of Archaeology, University of Edinburgh
                         Old High School, Edinburgh EH1 1LT
                         E.Peltenburg@ed.ac.uk

Graham Philip   Department of Archaeology, University of Durham
                         South Road, Durham DH1 3LE
                         Graham.Philip@durham.ac.uk

Mitchell S. Rothman   College of Arts and Sciences, Social Science Division
                         Widener University, One University Place, Chester, PA 19013-5792

Gil Stein   Anthropology Department, Northwestern University
                         1810 Hinman Avenue, Evanstown, IL 60208
                         g-stein@northwestern.edu

Toby Wilkinson   Christ's College
                         Cambridge CB2 3BU

URUK: KEY SITE OF THE PERIOD AND KEY SITE OF THE PROBLEM

Hans J. Nissen

This conference has been one of several within a short period of time to focus on the Uruk period. Undoubtedly, this is due to the specific importance of this period as the one which saw the consolidation of the early Mesopotamian civilization; yet, an additional reason may be a general dissatisfaction resulting from the fact that in spite of concentrated efforts these conferences never succeed in leading to a general agreement on chronology and the general context. Every so often someone else gets frustrated and in spite of previous failures has the idea that there ought to be a solution — eventually leading to the call for another conference.

Apart from the normal problems resulting from the inadequacy of any archaeological material, I maintain that in this case the basic problem rests with the inadequacy and sometimes misrepresentation of the information available from the key site Uruk and the failure to get the basic problems of the site disentangled.

The first part of this paper is trying to do just that, ending, however, in not more than a big CAVEAT! Yet, although Uruk proves to be one main source of the problems, the site nevertheless remains the main site which we have to turn to if we want to see a large early urban place functioning. The second part, then, will scrape together all the bits and pieces of information on the short period of time of Archaic Level IVa which we happen to know best. Instead of giving the normal composite picture for 'Late Uruk' a snap-shot is intended for this very latest phase of the Uruk period.

URUK: KEY SITE OF THE PROBLEM

Part of the problem is that all primary information on Uruk has been, and to some extent still is, given in such a manner that no one is encouraged to or would be able to question its validity. In this context, it is telling that none of the excavators ever gave a full and general account of the work done in Uruk; a useful but somewhat dry attempt to disentangle the Archaic Eanna levels is found in Eichmann (1989). And indeed it will be difficult to give a full summary going beyond presenting architectural plans and catalogues of finds because except for the preliminary reports, there just is nothing available except the plans and the find registers — and, of course, the finds themselves. Though there is a need for a critical evaluation of the work in Uruk in general I will limit

myself to evaluating the reliability of pottery published from the Archaic levels in Uruk; it is there that our problems arise.

A rough sketch of the course of the excavation of those levels we are concerned with here will serve as an introduction both to the problem section and the narrative part.

Despite the fact that remains of that same period have been uncovered at a number of sites, Uruk retains its position as the site with the largest exposure and the most important finds, because of the relatively easy and large scale accessibility of remains of this period, resulting from the history of that city during her early periods (Fig. 1).

As a result of the shrinkage of both the city and its central area following the enormous expansion during the early years of the 3rd millennium, large parts of the former central areas had been left open, only eventually to be resettled by private houses in the 8th/ 7th centuries BC. Thus building remains of the late 4th and early 3rd millennium were encountered almost immediately beneath the houses of the 1st millennium BC. Those houses, built of baked bricks, were easy to excavate, and after their removal an area of almost 6 ha was available for an extensive recovery of the early remains.

The remains of the uppermost early levels dubbed Archaic Levels I through III in Eanna, in addition were heavily damaged by erosion (Fig. 2). These levels resembled each other since a platform intended to receive a temple, on top of which nothing remained, marked the center of the central area, surrounded by buildings of apparently lesser prestige, with one exception: the so-called pisé-building (Stampflehmgebäude) which although sometimes preserved to a height of 3 meters did not pose too many stratigraphic problems, and thus again was removed relatively easily; both its purpose and its history and exact stratigraphic position remain enigmatic (Boehmer 1991; Finkbeiner 1991a; Siewert 1991). Ongoing exposure revealed that this situation was the result of a comprehensive re-organization of the central area of Uruk following the situation in Level IV when the entire area within the early temenos wall had been used for major and some minor public buildings without any apparent central feature (Fig. 3). It was relatively easy to reach this pre-reorganization level, which by then had become the focus of attention anyway because it had

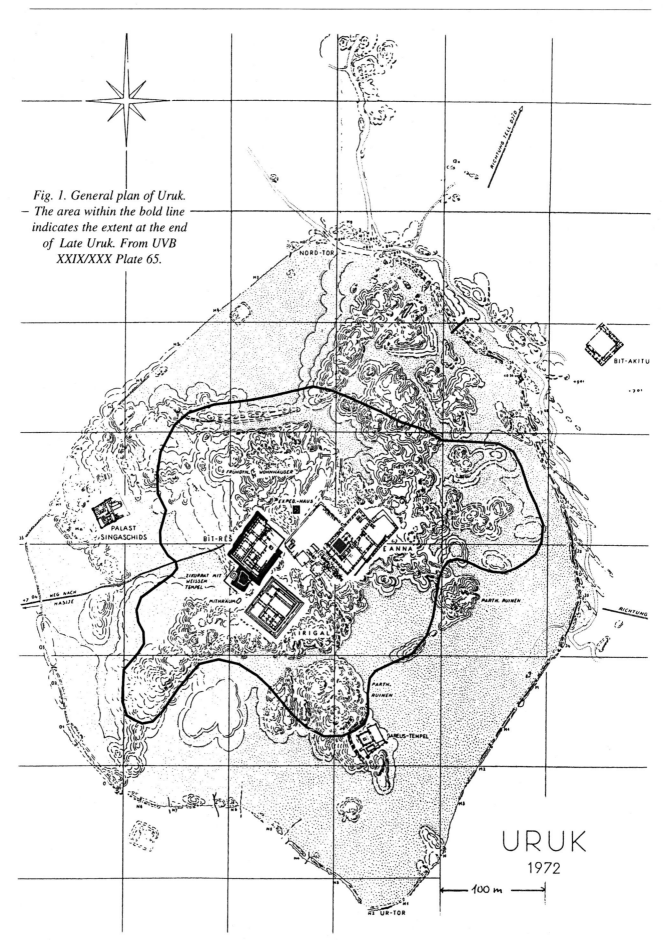

Fig. 1. General plan of Uruk. – The area within the bold line indicates the extent at the end of Late Uruk. From UVB XXIX/XXX Plate 65.

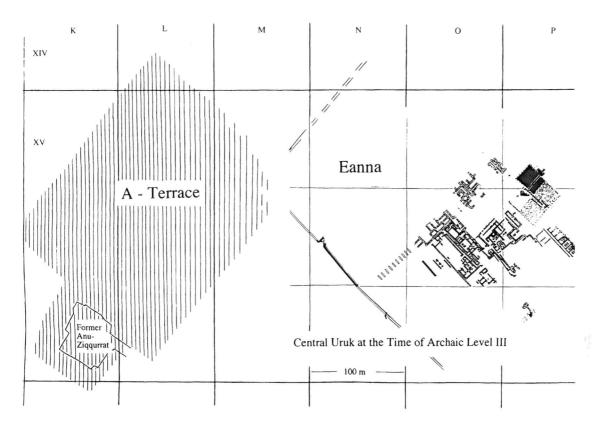

Fig. 2. Plan of the central area of Uruk during Eanna Archaic Level III. Author's original based on UVB X, Abb. 2 and UVB XX Plate 30.

turned out to be associated with the occurrence of the earliest clay tablets with true writing (UVB II, 43ff.).

This rearrangement of the architecture after Archaic Level IV was taken as the dividing line between two main cultural phases, and since by that time efforts were made to design a general system of chronological subdivisions, Level III was called after the site of Ğemdet Naṣr while IV was assigned to the end of a period called after Uruk itself (Potts 1986). In due course, in addition to hundreds of the earliest tablets several hundreds of lumps of clay with impressions of magnificently decorated cylinder seals, some objects of major art, and ensembles of buildings remarkable for both their plans and their size were recovered from this level.

Uruk had been started as the third excavation of the German Oriental Society after Babylon and Assur, all run by historians of architecture. Unlike Babylon and Assur, howev-

er, with their firm context in well known historical periods, the excavations in Uruk from an early point on opened a door into an unknown context. This turned out to pose problems which the architects were not equipped to deal with. None of them was trained in methods of prehistoric research and while some of the early directors would admit that pottery could be a useful tool for dating

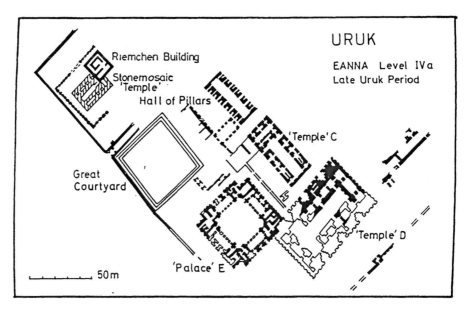

Figure 3. Plan of the buildings of Eanna Archaic Level IVa. Author's original.

and comparative purposes, Lenzen as the one who was longest in office was explicitly opposed to this approach and consequently during his long years of directorship, attention was only paid to pottery if it were complete vessels, or if the sherds happened to be decorated. While architecture was meticulously recorded, and tablets and seals were given due attention, pottery was explicitly neglected in most cases. This happened to create most of the problems when it comes to linking Uruk with the contemporary outside world. Furthermore, the pioneering work of Falkenstein's on the first 620 of the oldest clay tablets (Falkenstein 1936) seemed to suggest that once the tablets could be read, they would throw enough light on the period to make it redundant to question archaeological material of allegedly inferior value like pottery or animal bones. This critical view may sound strange, since after all, there does exist a pottery sequence from the so called deep sounding in Uruk, which everyone is referring to. But exactly this is the center of the problem, because this sequence is not what it pretends to be.

The general neglect of pottery in the Uruk excavations could have continued, but all of a sudden,

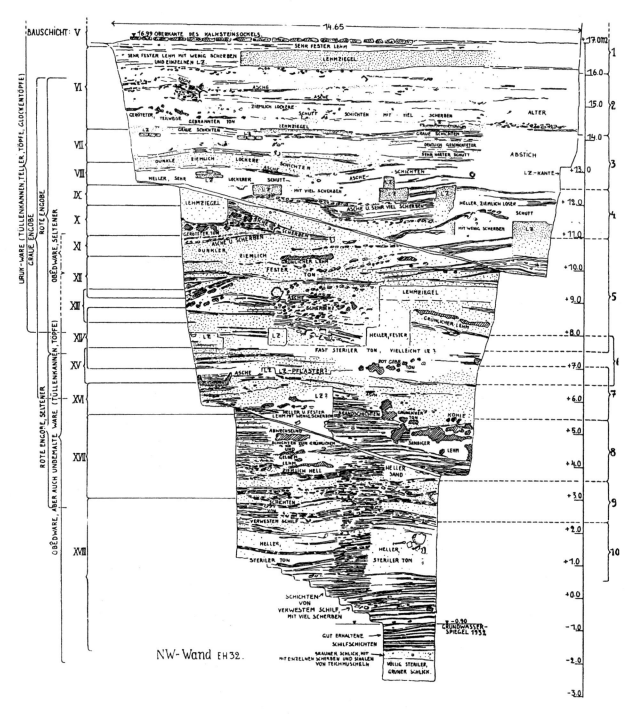

Fig. 4. Section of the deep sounding. From UVB IV Plate 2.

Mesopotamian archaeology, and the excavators of Uruk in particular, were confronted with the finds from Habuba Kabira, and shortly thereafter from Tell Kannas and Jebel Aruda on the Euphrates in modern Syria (for literature cf. Algaze, 1993). Findings of unmistakable Uruk-period affiliation turned up in large quantities, within a presumed alien environment. Immediately questions arose as to the nature of relations with Uruk-period Babylonia, and in particular as to the exact temporal relation. The Uruk crew was caught by surprise and was unprepared to enter a meaningful dialogue. Instead, no one interfered, if only by cautioning, when people started using the pottery sequence of the Uruk deep sounding as the point of reference. It is at this point when the second part of the problem began. But first let us check the reliability of the pottery from the deep sounding.

People had noticed before that on the pottery plates for the Archaic Levels I - III of the Uruk sequence (von Haller, 1931, Taf. 20 B and C) items were included which undoubtedly were of much later date, and, secondly, questions were raised whether more material might be available than published. While this question was never answered, at least most of the published sherds themselves were found in the reserves of the Berlin museum. Subsequently, the sherds were re-studied, re-drawn and re-published (Sürenhagen, 1986 and 1987). However, this publication of Sürenhagen's did not change the basic message, and the validity of the pottery sequence was not only not challenged but strengthened - in particular, he did not even try to question the completeness of the material.

In order to understand the basic problems one has to know that the deep sounding had only been started after the Level V building, the so-called Limestone Temple, had been cleared already to its floor level. The site of one of the large courtyards of that building was chosen (Eichmann 1989, 39f.; Beilage 25). Consequently, the lower levels encountered there received designations from VI on. Altogether 13 lower levels could be distinguished using floors or walls as dividers (von Haller 1931 Taf. 2; Eichmann 1989, Beilage 4; here: Fig. 4).

This meticulous recording of occupational traces contrasts with the kind of information on the other finds. To be sure, the publication gives us a rich collection of pottery (von Haller 1931); but nowhere do we find information on whether this constitutes everything found, or only a selection. In fact the much wider range of pottery shapes and finishes recorded than for other parts of the Uruk excavation led and still leads readers to believe that every sherd was kept. But while from assemblages from other sites we know that certain types were more numerous than others, the assemblages of the Uruk deep sounding resemble more a mean section, giving one example for each 'type' only.

Two examples may suffice: one is provided by the type 'cup with strap handle' which in other Late Uruk contexts (for example, Nippur: Hansen 1965, 202 fig. 6;

203 fig 10; Susa: Le Brun 1978, fig. 28; Chogha Mish: Delougaz and Kantor 1996, Pl. 95-97) is reported as quite frequent, while from the deep sounding for all Late Uruk levels, i.e. levels IV through VIII, only 2 examples are published (von Haller 1931, Taf. 18, Cu; Dv).

The other example concerns the so-called Bevelled Rim Bowls. While from all other sites of Uruk date we know that mass-produced types like bevelled rim bowls, or early conical cups sometimes account for half, or even more, of the total sherd count (Delougaz and Kantor 1996, 49-50), we find only one single Bevelled Rim Bowl depicted within the deep sounding plates, and this is for Level XII (von Haller 1931 Taf. 18A c); none of these bowls appears for the levels when elsewhere they occur in massive numbers. The answer is that still in my time in Uruk any of these sherds would be met with 'we have seen them before', and be thrown away. It is my firm conviction that the pottery tables of the deep sounding represent a selected sample only.

This is true anyway for anything depicted for Level V and above because as mentioned, the sounding was started only below the floor of V. Everything given for Level V and upwards is either material from another trench in Eanna (the so-called 'Sägegraben', again republished by Sürenhagen (1987), or a selection of sherds found over the entire area of Eanna which had been ascribed to one of these levels mostly by non-archaeologists. To add the final point: the task of publishing the pottery was entrusted to the architect von Haller. No wonder, therefore, that good 2nd millennium sherds are found among the pottery depicted for Levels IV or III.

The failure to see these basic problems started to have consequences when the excavators of the newly found sites in Syria started comparing their pottery assemblages with the Uruk sequence in order to establish temporal links. The presence, and even more the absence, of features from the Uruk pottery assemblages as represented in the plates of the deep sounding were taken as authoritative when it came to close dating. One of the last and most unfortunate examples is Sürenhagen's correlation of the Habuba assemblage with Uruk Levels VI and VII, on account of the alleged absence of bevelled rim bowls from Levels V and IV in Uruk (Sürenhagen 1993)!

This may sound like academic dogmatism, but in fact, it pulls the carpet from under our feet: with the pottery sequence of the Uruk deep sounding shown to be unreliable we have nothing to substitute for it. The Nippur deep sounding is not published in full (Hansen 1965), and the Abu Salabikh sequence is not long enough. To be sure, there are other items from Babylonian excavations which could be used for dating purposes, like seals or writing tablets, but they either do not occur in the areas outside of Babylonia, or not in a way to be used for comparative purposes. With pottery being the only reliable means of correlation we therefore have to face the fact, that at a point when Uruk — and Babylonia — from all we know would seem to be the most obvious point of reference for this period, details do not allow us to use it as such.

Unfortunately, this is not end of the problems with the material from Uruk. When people talk about Uruk-period Uruk, one often gets the feeling that they are not aware of the totally disparate amount and kind of evidence. In fact, almost everything we ascribe to the (Late) Uruk period — whether architecture, or seals, or writing, or art — originates from the short phase of Level IVa. Only very little is known of Levels IVb and c, and even less of Level V, and almost nothing of the lower levels. Our habit to speak of the Late Uruk period having seals, art and writing, is stretching the evidence because it is only for architecture that we have evidence for the IVa building principles reaching back as far as level VI. If we want to avoid unfounded assumptions we have to keep those phases which have yielded little more than pottery apart from Level IVa with the abundance of information I am going to talk about later on.

A final misunderstanding derives from the fact that the excavators treated those rubbish layers containing the tablets and sealings as if this rubbish originated from the buildings underneath. As has been stated over and over by the excavators themselves, all the magnificent buildings were found totally emptied. The reason behind it is, that from all our evidence, these buildings were not destroyed but apparently were carefully dismantled down to wall stumps of about 50 cm in height. The cleaned areas between these stumps then were filled with bricks from the demolished walls, in order to create huge terraces which eventually were used as foundation platforms for the next building. In other places, for instance between former buildings, larger depressions had to be filled before reaching the intended height. In these cases, rub-

bish from somewhere else was brought to the spot in order to level the ground before the spreading of the terrace. It was these rubbish layers which in addition to pottery, bones and ashes contained the tablets with archaic writing, and the sealings. Contrary to the opinion of the excavators the rubbish was not connected to the building on top of which it was found. The proof for this departure from the excavators' assertion is provided by adjoining fragments of the same tablets found in totally different rubbish complexes (Green, Nissen 1987, 24-25).

If any dates can be given to these objects found in the rubbish, it is the date of their final dumping which can be encircled only in those cases where the rubbish stra-

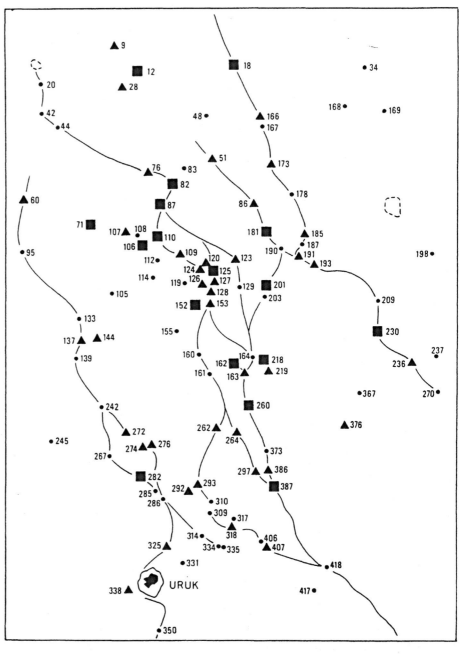

Fig. 5. Warka Survey map of the Late Uruk period. Author's original.

tum is sealed by a superimposed structure which itself is tied into the stratigraphic sequence. Consequently, all allegedly dated objects from Uruk have to be re-examined as to whether they belong to this category.

Of these cases, only one example should be mentioned here, the sealed clay bullae, which outside of Uruk have been found at many places in Syria/SE Anatolia as well as in Susiana. Their peculiar appearance suggests a specific purpose making it unlikely that they emerged independently. Thus their appearance could be an ideal temporal anchor, putting all find spots within a narrow bracket of time. The evidence from most of the other sites points to a date before the final phase of the Late Uruk period. Unfortunately, these bullae were found in Uruk in a pit sealed by a structure of Level III date. The situation of finds in Uruk therefore cannot be used for a close dating within the Late Uruk period, excluding their use for establishing a close link between Uruk and the other sites.

As mentioned before, Uruk period levels have nowhere been uncovered on either a comparable scale, or representing the full sequence. Thus no other material is available which could at least help straighten the Uruk mess. Since there is no hope for quick remedy in Uruk or Babylonia, the only way out is to turn the tables: all efforts should be put into establishing a close net of correlations and crossdatings between the sites outside of Babylonia, into which one day the Babylonian sequence may be tied.

URUK AT THE TIME OF ARCHAIC LEVEL IVA

Taking advantage of this new situation I feel free to concentrate on the material from Uruk itself, treating it as a self-contained universe, without constantly paying attention whether and to what degree its development can be linked to the outside world. As a matter of course, it is understood that this approach is justified only as long as this internal net of correlations within the outside world has not been established. It goes without saying that this approach does not mean a digression from our basic concept, that both development and importance of Uruk cannot be fully understood unless its relation with the neighboring areas is considered.

Before turning to the main topic, I should like to mention another point adding to the notion of complexity. Except for short interludes, up to the end of the Parthian period, Uruk and her hinterland had always been watered by a branch of the Euphrates. During the Sasanian period, however, the Euphrates changed its bed to the modern position and barely touched the westernmost fringes of the old agricultural area. Fallen desert since, this area, especially north and east of Uruk, provides an opportunity to investigate large stretches of land whose surface had not been touched since centuries. Only altered by wind erosion which in fact even enhances the potential of finding items of archaeological importance on the surface, this area around Uruk proved to be an ideal ground for applying methods of archaeological surface surveying.

It was another stroke of luck that particularly for the Uruk period it was possible to locate more than 100 sites of all sizes in the countryside of Late Uruk date. However, none of them came even close to the probable size of Uruk of 250 ha, leaving Uruk undoubtedly the largest and most important site of the area. Since for this survey, antedating any of the subsequent investigations in Syria and Southeast Anatolia, only the material from Uruk was available for establishing the pottery sequence, the nomenclature had to follow the guidelines derived from Uruk. Though later findings, for instance from Abu Salabikh, could suggest that a distinction could have been made between Middle and Late Uruk, the basis did not exist yet. Since the survey operated on the principle of diagnostics for each period and since no full collections could be kept, the evidence does not allow a revision.

Though the first part of my paper has conveyed a rather pessimistic outlook as to the reliability of the information from Uruk there is enough material available to venture giving a sketch of the situation in Uruk during the Late Uruk period. Unless explicitly mentioned, however, this sketch will refer only to Archaic Level IVa.

According to the surface survey of the site (Finkbeiner 1991b), the dense coverage with Late Uruk pottery extends over an area of at least 250 ha, or 2.5 square kilometers (cf. Fig. 1). As a rule of thumb we came to use a ratio of 100 to 200 inhabitants per ha of inhabited area. Unfortunately, the preoccupation with the central areas never left time to investigate private quarters in Uruk. Thus any more refined approach to population figures is excluded. If from these 250 ha we deduct 50 for the public areas, streets etc. we end up with between 20.000 and 40.000 inhabitants of Uruk around 3200 BC. N. Postgate has even calculated that we might have to reckon with 500 per ha (Postgate, 1994). But even the lower figures may suffice to give an impression of the many and complex problems of organization connected with such size.

To stay with the organization for a minute, I would like to refer to the results of the survey of the hinterland (Fig. 5). In the sectors north and east of the city — because of swamps and cultivation west and south were inaccessible for the same kind of archaeological investigation — more than 100 settlements could be located which by their surface pottery can be shown to have been inhabited in the Late Uruk phase. In size they range from less than 1 ha to more than 20. Furthermore they are arranged in such a manner that one could imagine several small settlements relating each to a larger one. Obviously, one cannot expect them to be arranged to follow the theoretical pattern of settlement systems of Christaller's when he formulated the central place theory (Christaller, 1934), but there are enough elements visible to finally reconstruct a four-tier system of settlements with Uruk at the very top.

The idea of the central place theory is that within an array of settlements, one of them would attract those organizational functions which everyone needed but which are too specialized to be sustained in every small village. A central place by definition would be the home of central functions which are on a higher level of complexity. To control these functions or to enhance them, needs a higher socio-economic competence and organizational abilities. The more tiers a system has the higher the degree of specialization, the more complex the situation of the society, and the higher the competence necessary to keep everything under control (Johnson, 1977). Quite obviously, the top of a four-tiered system required a very high level of competence in various fields, of which I may mention here only the one directly connected to the city-hinterland relation.

As a matter of course, the inhabitants of the city, are not able to produce all of their food. For instance, if we assume that the 40,000 inhabitants had to grow their own barley, an area of 70 square kilometers of intensively cultivated land would have been needed, or an area of 5 km radius from the city limits. However, part of that land was already occupied by villages. Another part seems to have consisted of swamps which existed well into the next period (Adams, Nissen 1972, p. 25 with fig. 12). Consequently, we should assume that part of the food supplies had to be delivered to the city by the hinterland. Unfortunately, there is no information in the texts on how this could have been organized. Most probably, this system was very precarious and prone to be disturbed, and yet it just had to be kept functioning short of creating food problems in the city.

But back to the city itself. Possibly the city grew out of two settlements on either side of the Euphrates which then would have flowed right through the center of later Uruk. Because of later overburden, there is no evidence available. The assumption, then, is based on the existence of the two main cultic installations, 'Anu' and Eanna facing each other in the center of Uruk; on the assumption of tensions between the two, as a result of which one of them ('Anu') was totally withdrawn from sight by the very end of Late Uruk (Nissen, 1972); and on the later tradition which keeps the memory of the old, venerable name of Kullaba for Uruk or a part of it without specifying its location. In a country criss-crossed by rivers, crossing-points are important points of aggregation; it should not be unusual to find twin settlements on either side of such a crossing; for examples within the Uruk hinterland see Adams, Nissen 1972 fig. 11. Although both parts would long have been joined by the time of the Late Uruk period, with the Euphrates divided into two courses on either side of the city limits, the difference must have been still visible, as from all information we have, the western part of the city was about 4 m lower on the average than the eastern part. As the most vivid remains, there survived two central areas in the center of the city, known as Eanna in the east and the so called Anu district in the west.

Of the two, Eanna is much better known because over the next couple of thousand years it remained the

cultic center of the city, re-arranged by Urnammu shortly before 2000 BC in form of a Ziqqurrat with surrounding courtyards and buildings. The Late Uruk ensemble was much larger and probably covered an area of 8-9 ha, of which close to 6 hectares have been uncovered. It stood out in height by two meters from the surrounding eastern part of the city area and presented an almost even surface, sloping down towards the southern corner. As far as it has been investigated the area was occupied by a number of major buildings of up to 1500 square meters of floor space, interspersed with small special structures, remains of older cultic structures, open spaces and a square water basin with sides 50m long. Unless a central building is still hidden in the unexcavated area, these buildings and structures seem to have served either a number of different functions, or a pattern of consecutive functions. None can claim from size or arrangement to have been more important than the others.

At this point it should be stressed already that none of the structures in any way resembles buildings destined for any kind of economic activities.

Much less is known about the western center because right after the end of the Uruk period part of a complete reorganization of the central areas consisted of the erection of a huge platform which was supposed to engulf the old central building of the Western part. Since this terrace remained in use for unknown purposes and later was even taken as the foundation for the enormous building complex of the Bit Resh, a large temple complex of Seleucid times, the larger part of that old western center remains inaccessible. Fortunately, we happen to know what probably was the oldest central structure, a high terrace of 11 m in height, with a temple on top, known as the White Temple, which may have risen a further 6-7 meters. The impression must have been a totally different one from Eanna, with that White Temple standing as a landmark to be seen from afar.

Going on to talk on the level of complexity, it would be easiest to expand on what we know from the archaic tablets. But it would be unfair against all my colleagues who do not control this kind of material, and if I understood the topic of this conference correctly, the idea was also to probe into the question of to what extent it is possible to talk about complexity when we have only archaeological material available. In fact, this is the issue for all other sites except Uruk. Before turning to the texts, I therefore would like to restrict myself to discussing the archaeological evidence for complexity. If this is accepted then three items remain to be discussed: pottery, a workshop area, and the cylinder seal.

With my remark on the normal attitude in Uruk towards pottery it is quite obvious that there never was pottery collected which would be suited for any kind of technical analysis or a study of the production process. In our context, remarks on pottery therefore have to be limited to two issues: the use of the true potter's wheel and the mass appearance of the bevelled rim bowls.

Until not too long ago it was held that what distinguishes Uruk pottery from Ubaid pottery, apart from largely being undecorated, is that Uruk pottery was made on the wheel, and that it was the only one for which this new tool was used. With new evidence pouring in from Syria and Southeast Anatolia this may not be the case any more as other contemporary kinds of pottery also seem to be produced the same way. But this does not affect my argument which then would be valid for the other complexes too.

The idea is that a new tool, or a new technical process is an answer to a challenge, or the other way around, without challenge no new technical device. One may derive an idea on the kind of challenge from comparing the new with the old situation and ask for the advantages of the new process over the old one (Nissen, 1989). In our case, the advantages are that the use of the fast wheel undoubtedly serves to speed up the process of pottery production. This could be answering two problems. On the one hand this could be a compensation for a decrease in the number of people employed in pottery production, as one of the results of the increasing professionalization of the crafts. On the other hand, or in addition, it could be an answer to an increasing demand, be it because of population growth or because of a growing diversification of types within the average household. Only the sheer population growth would be neutral in the sense of our question, while both other points are elements of an increase in complexity.

Fig. 6. Bevelled Rim Bowl. Author's original.

Much has been written on the issue of the Bevelled Rim Bowls (Fig. 6; summarized in Millard 1988), and although I am still holding on to my idea of these bowls being designated to issue the daily barley rations to large numbers of people, this is only part of the argument here. The main point is its massive appearance — Chogha Mish (Delougaz and Kantor 1996, 49-50) —, and its uniform size. Whether destined for rations, votive offerings (Mallowan, 1933, 168), yoghurt (Delougaz, 1952, 127f.) or bread (Millard, 1988), they served one limited purpose for an unlimited number of cases. If the Bevelled Rim Bowls were for bread, it would mean that either bread would be distributed in large quantities, requiring a cen-

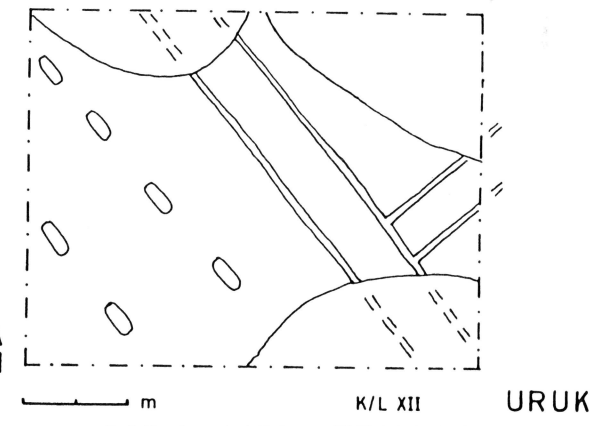

Fig. 7. Plan of excavation in Uruk squares K/L XII. Author's original.

Abb. 1

Abb. 2

Abb. 3

Abb. 4

Abb. 5

Fig. 8. Drawing of some cylinder seal impressions of Late Uruk. From Lenzen 1949, Abb. 1.

tral agency, or bread would be made by private bakers but in uniform weight, and again it would require a central agency controlling the compliance with the standard. At any rate, the existence of Bevelled Rim Bowls by the millions as in Babylonian or Susiana sites does indicate a high level of complexity.

Next is the case of a workshop within Uruk. Since I used this example quite often before (Nissen, 1988, 90f.), I may be allowed to restrict myself to a short reference (Fig. 7). A number of parallel long troughs and accompanying oval holes were found dug into a gently sloping surface, everything exposed to high temperatures. The troughs and the pits still contained ashes. Although nothing pointed to the nature of their purpose, I proposed that it may have been a metal-melting plant, where in the absence of larger crucibles small amounts of metal were molten in each of the pits, and then poured into the preheated troughs where they would join and flow into the direction of something like a foundry. People have argued that metal couldn't possibly stay liquid, but specialists support my proposal.

Anyway, in this context my argument is not connected to what was done there, but I am interested in the organization. Because it seems obvious that something was done simultaneously at each of the pits in direction of the troughs. This is a case of bundling of labor which is considered to be an advanced kind of division of labor. One may go one step further and assume that supervisors were necessary to keep the work on the troughs under control, and might even think of a higher level of coordination should the idea of a foundry hold. We will see in a minute that such hierarchization is present in the texts.

My last archaeological sample is the cylinder seals. As mentioned earlier, the Uruk material does not give a clear answer as to the earliest occurrence (Fig. 8). Attempts by M. A. Brandes (1979) and R. M. Boehmer (1999) following H. J. Lenzen (1949) to assign some seal impressions an early date in the Uruk sequence have to be dismissed: the rubbish including the seal impressions dates from the same time as the building underneath - rejected above-, while Boehmer (1999) in addition ignores the principle that rubbish can only be dated in very loose terms, and only if superimposed by a stratigraphically dated structure (Green and Nissen 1987, 21ff.). In fact, the oldest firmly dated specimens may date back to Level IVc, since there is vague reference to seal impressions found on or between the stones of the limestone temple of Level V. All the evidence from other sites tells us that cylinder seals must be older, however, and I would not hesitate to accept a dating to Level VI or VII times.

No matter at what time, but certainly when the cylinder appears then it is a sudden affair of almost entirely replacing the old stamp seal. If we want to know the reason we should ask for the advantages the cylinder had over the stamp. Two come to mind immediately: much larger surfaces can be provided with an impression of the seal, and more complex and encompassing themes can be applied to the seal. Taking for granted that seals always had played a role as a controlling device in economy we may ask what these two new elements may have been a reaction to.

The function of a seal always had rested on the possibility to recognize the owner of the seal through its design and thus to know who would take sanctions against any improper treatment of the sealed item. Stamp seals offer a limited space for design variation, and thus only limited possibilities to create unmistakable patterns which is necessary if the aim is to identify the owner. If the provision of a larger space for seal designs was a reason for the cylinder seal, this could be an answer to a growing need to enlarge the range of distinguishable designs. Two possible explanations come to mind: one, growth in the number of people who were engaged in economic matters and needed an unmistakable seal. The other one derives from the observation that within a small community a code with minute differences may be acceptable but with the enlargement of the range of economic activities to include even unknown partners it becomes more important to have strong code differences.

The latter argument could also be used in the case of the second main difference to the stamp. While earlier it was held sufficient to know who applied the seal in order to safeguard the sealed object, the sealing of the total surface by means of the cylinder seal adds another quality of security: any breakage of the sealed surface would be noticed immediately because the relief could not be restored. Now, it is not only the authority of the seal owner protecting the item but also the impersonal total coverage. If this provision was intended, it again could argue for an expansion of the range of economic life beyond the limits where it was based on personal acquaintance.

Whatever reason was responsible we will never know, but the cylinder seal probably succeeded rather quickly because it provided solutions to several problems. These problems were all connected with the economic situation, and no matter which one we chose to have been the driving force, they all argue for an expansion of the economy, both in volume and in the number of people involved as well in the range in the geographical sense.

To return to our topic: if already the frequent use of the stamp seal in connection with some kind of centralization as in Ubaid period Tell Abade speaks for a rather complex administrative situation, then certainly the advent of the cylinder seal marks a considerable increase in complexity.

Finally the first script. Again so much has been written on the earliest writing (Nissen, Damerow, Englund 1993) that I may be allowed to limit myself to a number of comments, both on a more general level and specific to the topic.

It may not need to be reiterated that the existence of a writing system is a sign par excellence of complexity, but it is worthwhile to recall the probable course of events which ultimately led to the appearance of writing. This is especially so, because we get another argument for a period of increasing complexity which we derived already from the discussion of the other items.

Some points may briefly be recalled in advance. On the problem of the dating of the first emergence of writing I can only repeat myself: the earliest tablets can be assigned a terminus ante quem date of IIIc, leaving as date for their manufacture the time of Level IVa, not excluding a slightly earlier date (Green and Nissen 1987, 50).

We have no idea on the original place of their employment. True, the contents of a number of the administrative documents can be read as part of a centralized economic administration, taking in enormous quantities of food stuff and other goods, and distributing them to offices and individuals, but this does not necessarily require that all tablets belonged to that sphere. I cannot help developing the feeling that the fact that nearly all tablets were found within the limits of Eanna plus the prevailing ideas on a centralized temple economy extracted from later sources have prevented us (including myself) from asking inconvenient questions.

There is more reason to question the Archaic Texts being a true sample. Wherever levels of the Archaic period date have been reached outside of Eanna (squares OXI-XII; UVB V, 13ff.; K/L XII: Nissen 1970;

Archaische Siedlung: UVB XIX) at least one Archaic tablet has been found. The almost exclusive provenience of the tablets from Eanna may thus be nothing else but reflecting the area of exposure: 60.000 square meters of Eanna against a total of approximately 25 square meters for all the other trenches!

And finally, we have not been able so far even to suggest where both the storage and the controlling may have taken place. Unless one assumes all these structures to have been located in the still unexcavated areas, there is just no structure within Eanna to accommodate such activities. The longer I am confronted with this problem the less am I excluding the possibility that this area may have been outside of Eanna. As I mentioned already, the rubbish used for these layers in Eanna must have been brought there from a central dump area where all the garbage from the occasional cleaning of the stores and offices had been brought, including the expired tablets and sealed items.

But let us return for a moment to the question of the origin of writing. As in previous cases, we should start by asking what it was an answer to. Among the close to 5000 archaic tablets and fragments from Levels IVa and III we do not have a single one which would not belong to the main big groups of documents of economic administration on the one side, and lexical lists on the other side. Specifically, from its overwhelming use as a means of economic control there can be no doubt that it answered to new needs in the economic system. If we are asking for precursors, then we should be looking for arrangements which may have fulfilled that task before, only on a more restricted level. Since apart from all the connotations which we usually attribute to writing, writing certainly is the most universal means of information storage, it is worthwhile to look for older kinds of information storage.

As such we met the sealing technique already which is nothing but a system to store information on the seal owner. Like seals we know from the Neolithic of another system of storing numbers or quantities by means of clay tokens which according to different numerical values took on different shapes (Schmandt-Besserat 1992).

These are simple but effective systems, simple because they allowed only one item of information to be stored at the same time. For thousands of years this apparently was held sufficient, only in the course of the Late Uruk development do we recognize attempts to enlarge the storage capacity. Two features come to mind: the sealed clay bullae and the sealed numerical tablets. In the first case, a certain number of clay tokens representing a certain number was wrapped into a ball shaped clay envelope whose surface was entirely imprinted with one or more cylinder seals. This way the same device allowed to store information on the number and on the person responsible at the same time. The same is true for the sealed numerical tablets, consisting of clay slabs supplied with indentations standing for numbers; the surface of the tablet then would be fully covered by cylinder seal impressions.

I take these items for indications that the older systems of information storage were not found sufficient anymore, and that more encompassing systems were looked for, in order to control the problems of a growing economy. In all cases discussed so far, these are substantial changes in the daily routine, and I would suggest that unusual pressure must have mounted before such changes are introduced. I further assume that the search to come up with better devices went on on a broad front, until finally someone had the idea of a script, which because of the ongoing search immediately was recognized by everyone as the final answer.

I took some time to expand on this issue because it fits nicely what we have suggested before, that the Late Uruk saw some severe changes towards more complexity, raising problems which needed to be answered, at least on the level of economy, but we will see in a moment that it probably encompassed all aspects of society.

Though this sounds like a straight forward development, there is one big problem: the evidence from Uruk does not allow us to substantiate this course of events. As I mentioned before, find circumstances in Uruk do not enable us to be in any way more precise on the earliest occurrence of cylinder seals, sealed bullae and numerical tablets than assigning them to the Late Uruk.

Short of reporting on details of the administrative documents, I would just like to mention one basic observation. It seems that the administrators' task was only to keep track of what entered the stores and what left them. It looks as if it was secondary to them, where things came from and where they finally went, but as if they were primarily interested in keeping control over what actually was in store, calculated as the entries minus the exits. Possibly they needed these figures for planning purposes as is shown by one tablet where they calculated how much seed had to be retained for so large a field (Nissen, Damerow, Englund, 1993, fig. 51.).

To our dismay that means that we should not expect to get any information on where the goods came from and how this procurement was organized. This cuts out any hope that we might get some information on the relation of Uruk to its hinterland from the texts. Likewise we should not expect too much information on who received allotments, or wages, as once the goods had left the stores it was not a matter of interest anymore. The closest we get is a tablet of Level III date which lists enormous amounts of barley distributed to four high officials (Nissen, Damerow, Englund 1993, fig. 34). Yet these amounts are much too high to be intended for their personal use. It seems more likely, therefore, that these amounts were meant to be distributed to the employees of that office. How this would have worked, and primarily, what the amount was for each individual recipient remains unaccounted.

This, by the way, is a good example of the need to limit our expectations, because we are constantly confronted with the observation that writing was used very economically. That means that everything considered common knowledge would not be noted. In fact, it is only the unusual information being documented, rendering it extremely difficult for us to understand these texts because as a matter of course we have no command over what was normal knowledge by that time.

The last, but to my mind, the most important point is not provided by the administrative documents but by one of the lexical lists I referred to earlier. About 15% of all the archaic texts belong to this kind where words and concepts belonging to the same semantic family are listed one after the other in consecutive lines. There are lists of trees and wooden objects, of metal objects, of animals according to kind, and of place names. Altogether we have identified 16 such lists which each follow a fixed order throughout their many copies. These lists have not only been copied over and over at the same time but also over many centuries. The last time that we find copies of such lists retaining exactly their original

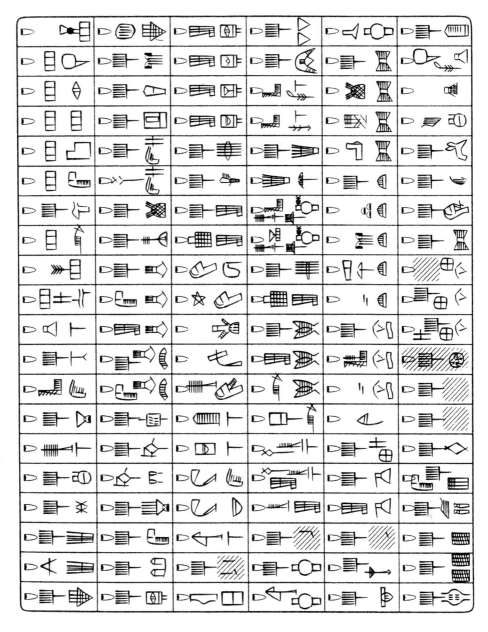

Fig. 9. Reconstructed text of the Lú A list. From Englund and Nissen 1993, Abb. 4.

sequence of entries, is the Akkadian period, when the lists existed already for almost 1000 years. There is a strong probability that these texts formed an essential part of the school curriculum.

The most famous one of these lists to judge from the number of both contemporary and later copies is a list of titles and professions (Englund, Nissen 1993, 14-19. Nissen, Damerow, Englund, 1993, 110f; Selz 1998, 294ff.; here: Fig. 9). To be sure, of this text also we understand only a fraction, but there is enough to let us be sure of several points. First of all, the entries are arranged according to rank. This is shown by the repeated occurrence of lines in the text when the second element would be repeated through two or more lines, but in the first line always be combined with the sign GAL which we know

to mean 'big'. The corresponding element in the next line varies and may be 'small', or 'son', or 'younger brother'. We take it to mean that within a trade or craft named by the repeated sign there is differentiation between ranks.

If this were the rationale behind the arrangement, then the first line of the list should be the most important or highest rank. Unfortunately, the sign combination we read NÁM-EŠDA is not known from later sources as title of an high official, but fortunately people continued copying this list until it was not understood anymore, when the necessity arose to translate some of these terms into everyday language. Thus someone compiled a dictionary around 2000 years later, and translated our NÁM:EŠDA with *šarru*, then the word for king (Selz 1998, 300-1).

Accepting then that the list starts with the title of the highest official of the polity we get a clue to the meaning of the next lines, all a combination with the word NÁM standing for 'leader', or 'head of...'. As second elements we meet 'the city', 'law', 'barley', 'the plow' and 'the work force'. It takes little imagination to assume that this list reads almost like a directory of heads of departments with the heads of the city administration, of the law department, of the plowmen, of the food department and of the labor department.

Of course, this is all tentative and I am sure that we will have to revise our current ideas in a number of cases. But several things probably will remain valid. On the one hand, this is a vivid picture of a strictly hierarchically organized administration, if not society. And this seems not only to be true for the higher ranks but also for the level of crafts; it matches with what I said in conjunction with the workshop in Uruk.

Secondly, I cannot but assume not only that this list reflects the situation at the time of the first writing but also that this is an established system already by that time. I am inclined to think that these were structures which again like in the other cases had evolved as an answer to something. And I would not hesitate to put the responsibility on the same increase in the level of complexity which we had encountered before as a major driving force.

Two additional points seem especially worth mentioning. One concerns conflicts and their management. It certainly is true that for most of human history we have no direct information on that important aspect of human life. Even in writing anything dealing with conflict management shows up relatively late in the record. And yet, it is totally inconceivable that conflicts and conflict management were not a major issue of society, from the appearance of sedentary life at the latest. One reason for the lack of information seems to be that it probably always has been a field of relatively few but firm rules with a set of sanctions which would not need to be fixed. In addition, unfortunately, it is impossible to think of any kind of archaeological setting which would be able to give us any clues as to kind and level of conflict management.

It would be totally misleading, however, to assume that early societies didn't know how to deal with conflicts. I am referring specifically to an article of Greg Johnson's on scalar stress, when he was able to show using ethnography that group-size and amount and level of conflicts are systemically and inseparably interconnected (Johnson 1982). Apparently, there are thresholds of size which let the level of conflicts rise exponentially. Johnson talks about 300 people being one of these thresholds above which the level of conflicts necessitates an established manner of dealing with them.

I don't want to expand on this important issue, and just ask the rhetorical question whether it is conceivable that a group of at least 20,000 could live together without a set of rules and sanctions. And to my mind, this even requires an agency which would not only administer these rules and sanctions but also see to their application. I am not surprised at all, therefore, to find very high in our titles list someone who I modernistically call the head of the law department (Nissen 1999b).

The last point concerns the observation that none of the understandable entries of the list has to be affiliated in any way with a cultic function. Although at this point I am not yet ready to propose a complete anti-model to the prevailing one which sees Archaic Uruk as an early counterpart of Late Early Dynastic Lagash, i.e. as an early example of a temple-run and -centered city-state, I see none of the arguments surviving which had been used for this model.

At the end of this survey of what we know about IVa-Uruk, Uruk emerges as a very powerful polity, based on a highly complex social structure as well as a strong economy, with a strong political leadership, which can use its accumulated wealth to import everything deemed necessary: all kinds of colored stones for jewelry, seals, works of art and vessels from the Zagros mountains; metal from an unknown source, and certainly also timber from the mountains. Its sheer economic power certainly made it a difficult neighbor, although we don't know anything about external conflicts. What is used sometimes as a sign for warfare, the so called prisoner scenes on cylinder seals, to my mind speak more for the existence of internal conflicts, as there are no efforts made to differentiate between the 'soldiers' and the 'prisoners'.

There remains one point on the agenda, as otherwise all arguments would be kept hanging in the air. Repeatedly, I have referred to a growing complexity as the driving force behind the development of cylinder seals, the writing system, or the emergence of political institutions. Since I have repeatedly elaborated on this topic (Nissen 1988; 1999a), I may be allowed briefly to summarize what I see as the ultimate cause for this change.

From the joint surveys of lower Mesopotamia we derive the clear statement that by the Ubaid period this plain had been sparsely settled, that by Early Uruk we find a major increase in the number of settlements starting from the northern end of the plain, and that by the Late Uruk, especially in the middle and southern part of the plain we see a settlement density of totally unparalleled dimensions. In the hinterland of Uruk the number of settlements rises from 11 to more than 100 early in the Late Uruk. In addition, not only is Uruk, with at least 250 ha, many times larger than the largest settlements known from the previous period, but within the hinterland of Uruk there are several sites larger than Susa or Chogha Mish during the Ubaid.

To my mind, the opportunity to settle this extremely large and fertile plain of lower Mesopotamia within a relatively short period of time had the consequence of creating a population density of totally unknown dimensions. While all solutions to the new problems rested on earlier accomplishments, the new quality and dimension of the problems prompted the emergence of institutions on a much higher level than before. It is the total of these answers which we summarize when we talk about the Early Urban Civilization. The higher level of competence and flexibility of dealing with complex problems acquired during these processes becomes the main asset when Babylonia over the next couple of centuries is confronted with fundamental problems which might have thrown off balance a less settled society.

As I mentioned at the beginning, Uruk remains the main supplier of information if we want to reconstruct the fascinating history of the early urban phase; nevertheless, we have to admit that Uruk remains unique for the time being. Much effort - in particular on the Mesopotamian side - will be needed before we can tie that close net necessary if we want to understand what was going on in the Ancient Near East during the Uruk period.

REFERENCES

Adams, R. McC., H. J. Nissen, 1972. *The Uruk Countryside*, Chicago.

Algaze, G., 1993. *The Uruk World System*, Chicago.

Boehmer, R. M., 1991. Lugalzagesi, der Bauherr des Stampflehmgebäudes in Uruk, in: *Bagh. Mitt.* 22, 165-174.

Boehmer, R. M., 1999. *Uruk: Früheste Siegelabrollungen*, Mainz.

Brandes, M. A., 1979. *Siegelabrollungen aus den archaischen Bauschichten in Uruk-Warka*, Wiesbaden.

Christaller, W., 1934. *Die zentralen Orte Süddeutschlands*, Jena.

Delougaz, P. P., 1952. *Pottery from the Diyala Region*, Chicago.

Delougaz, P. P. and H. J. Kantor, 1996. *Chogha Mish I*, Chicago.

Eichmann, R., 1989. *Uruk: Die Stratigraphie, Grabungen 1912-1977 in den Bereichen 'Eanna' und 'Anu-Ziqqurrat'*, (=AUWE 3), Mainz.

Englund, R. K., H. J. Nissen, 1993. *Die Lexikalischen Listen der Archaischen Texte aus Uruk*, Berlin.

Falkenstein, A., 1936. *Die Archaischen Texte aus Uruk*, Leipzig.

Finkbeiner, U., 1991a. Die Kleinfunde aus dem Stampflehmgebäude und dessen Datierung, in *Bagh. Mitt.* 22, 11-23.

Finkbeiner, U., 1991b. *Uruk: Kampagne 35-37, 1982-84, Die archäologische Oberflächenuntersuchung* (Survey), Mainz.

Green, M. W., H. J. Nissen, (unter Mitarbeit von P. Damerow, R. K. Englund), 1987. *Zeichenliste der Archaischen Texte aus Uruk*, Berlin.

Haller, A. von, 1931. Die Keramik der archaischen Schichten von Uruk, in: *UVB 4* Taf. 20 B and C.

Hansen, D. P., 1965. The Relative Chronology of Mesopotamia II, in: R. W. Ehrich, *Chronologies in Old World Archaeology*. Chicago, 201-213.

Johnson, G. A., 1977. Aspects of Regional Analysis in Archaeology, in: *Annual Review of Anthropology* 6, 497-508.

Johnson, G. A., 1982. Organizational Structure and Scalar Stress, in: C. Renfrew (Hrsg.), *Theory and Explanation in Archaeology*, New York (1982) 389-421.

Le Brun, A. 1978. Le Niveau 17B de l'Acropole de Suse (Campagne de 1972), in: *Cahiers de la DAFI* 9, 57-154.

Lenzen, H. J., 1949. Die Tempel der Schicht IV in Uruk, in: *ZA* 49, 1-20

Mallowan, M. E. L., 1933. The Prehistoric Sondage of Nineveh 1931-1932, *Liverpool Annals of Archaeology and Anthropology* XX, 168.

Millard, A. R., 1988. The Bevelled Rim Bowls: Their Purpose and Significance, in: *Iraq* 50, 49-57.

Nissen, H. J., 1970. Uruk/Warka: Grabung in den Quadraten K/L XII, in: *Bagh. Mitt.* 5, 101-191

Nissen, H. J., 1972. The City Wall of Uruk, in: P. Ucko, R. Tringham, G. W. Dimbleby (Hrsg.), *Man, Settlement, and Urbanism*, London, 793-798

Nissen, H. J., 1988. *The Early History of the Ancient Near East, 9000-2000 B.C.*, Chicago.

Nissen, H. J., 1989. The Ubaid Period in the Context of the Early History of the Ancient Near East, in: E. F. Henrickson, I. Thuesen (Hrsg.), *Upon this Foundation: The Ubaid Reconsidered*, Copenhagen, 245-255.

Nissen, H. J., 1999a. *Geschichte Alt-Vorderasiens*. München.

Nissen, H. J., 1999b. Konflikt und Konfliktlösung im frühschriftlichen Babylonien, in: B. Böck, E. Cancik-Kirschbaum, Th. Richter (eds.), *Munuscula Mesopotamica (Festschrift Renger)*. Münster.

Nissen, H., J. P. Damerow, R. K. Englund, 1993. *Archaic Bookkeeping*, Chicago.

Postgate, J. N., 1994. How many Sumerians per Hectare? — Probing the Anatomy of an Early City, in: *Cambridge Archaeol. Journal* 4,1, 47-65.

Potts, D. T., 1986. A Contribution to the History of the Term Ǧamdat Nasr, in U. Finkbeiner, W. Röllig (Hrsg.), *Ǧamdat Nasr: Period or Regional Style?*, Wiesbaden, 17-32.

Schmandt-Besserat, D., 1992. *Before Writing, I-II*, Austin.

Selz, G. J., 1998. Über mesopotamische Herrschaftskonzepte, in: M. Dietrich and O. Loretz (eds.), *dubsar anta-men* (Festschrift W. H. Ph. Römer). Münster.

Siewert, H. H., 1991. Die Architektur des Stampflehmgebäudes, in: *BaghM.* 22, 2-11.

Sürenhagen, D. 1986. Archaische Keramik aus Uruk I: *Bagh.M.* 17, 7-95.

Sürenhagen, D. 1987. Archaische Keramik aus Uruk II: *Bagh.M.* 18, 1-92.

Sürenhagen, D. 1993. The Relative Chronology of the Uruk Period: New Evidence from Uruk-Warka and Northern Syria. In: *Bull. of the Canadian Soc. for Mesopotamian Studies.* 25, 57-70.

Wickede, A. von, 1990. *Prähistorische Stempelglyptik in Vorderasien*, München.

UVB = Uruk, Vorläufige Berichte (Preliminary Reports)

THE SIGNIFICANCE OF THE URUK SEQUENCE AT NINEVEH

Renate V. Gut

THE DEEP SOUNDING

When in Neo-Assyrian times Sennacherib chose to make Nineveh his new centre, he chose not only a famous city and a strategically situated location, but a site that had a long past. Already by then Nineveh's history went back for more than 5000 years. Through excavations undertaken in the late twenties and early thirties, and mainly through a Deep Sounding right in the centre of Kuyunjik, it became clear that Nineveh was occupied almost continuously from the Hassuna through to the Ninevite 5 period, that is from the seventh to the mid-third millennium BC.

This paper focuses on what Nineveh's long prehistoric sequence can contribute to our knowledge of the Uruk period in northern Mesopotamia. I hope to show that the Nineveh Deep Sounding still deserves our attention, and should not be dismissed as a pioneering but outdated venture in the archaeology of the ancient Near East. Up to this day, Nineveh's long sequence of prehistoric occupation has not been paralleled, and many modern excavations which could supersede it – or parts of it – are still unpublished. The evidence cited below is set out in much greater detail in my re-study of prehistoric Nineveh (Gut 1995).

Nineveh is situated in northern Iraq, on the left bank of the Tigris river, opposite the modern town of Mosul. By the seventh century BC it included two large mounds, Kuyunjik and Nebi Yunus, and was surrounded by a city wall enclosing an area of more than 700 hectares. For Uruk Nineveh, only Kuyunjik, the larger of the two mounds, concerns us. Other related sites include Tepe Gawra, Grai Resh, Tell al-Hawa, Qalinj Agha in a suburb of Erbil, some of the rescue excavations in the Eski-Mosul Dam Project above Eski Mosul, and Tell Brak in north-eastern Syria.

Uruk levels at Nineveh were uncovered during four seasons of excavation conducted by R. Campbell Thompson from 1927 to 1932 (Thompson, Hutchinson 1929, 1931; Thompson, Hamilton 1932; Thompson, Mallowan 1933). They were the last excavations at Nineveh on behalf of the British Museum, and were located near the centre of the mound, which is here at its highest, some 30 m above bedrock. The area is close to the temple of Nabû which Campbell Thompson had identified in 1905, and in between the South-West and North

Palaces where Layard and others began excavation in the nineteenth century (Thompson 1934: fig. 1).

Campbell Thompson's first season of 1927-8 was aimed at clearing the site of the temple of Nabû, and did not produce prehistoric material. From 1929 on, he concentrated on two areas. In squares A-H (Thompson, Hutchinson 1931: pl. 39) there was a building which he first called Shalmaneser's palace, but later published as the palace of Ashurnasirpal; he dated it to the Neo-Assyrian period, though it was probably later. The second area comprised squares I to YY, the site of the temple of Ishtar, known from the texts, which was his main objective for the third and fourth seasons (Thompson, Hamilton 1932: pl. 90). Not all of the grid letters are indicated on the plans published by Campbell Thompson, but luckily a sketch by him has survived (Gut 1995: fig. 4), and the location of all the squares can be established (fig. 1). There was no grid system for the whole mound; the excavators simply assigned a new letter whenever they opened a new square.

Unfortunately, not much of the temple of Ishtar remained. The remains more or less consisted of a solid foundation platform of unbaked mudbricks, which had cut into Ninevite 5 levels and rested directly upon the Late Uruk level. These early levels formed the summit of an unusually high prehistoric mound. The slope of this mound was clearly visible in the sections to the northwest of the mudbrick platform, as can be seen in another sketch by Campbell Thompson (fig. 2). The prehistoric mound still determined the shape of Kuyunjik in the first millennium BC, as it accounts for the significant difference in height between the temple of Ishtar and the much lower temple of Nabû.

During Campbell Thompson's second and third seasons there were superficial investigations of the prehistoric mound, virtually as a by-product of the search for Assyrian buildings and inscriptions, although two test-pits in squares H and N were dug down to a depth of around 14 m. The Late Uruk level was exposed on a large scale, but no building structures were found, due mainly to the fact that the excavators dug too fast and failed to trace unbaked mudbrick walls. All we can safely say from the notebooks is that the published buildings, notably the so-called Vaulted Tombs, were not themselves prehistoric; they were merely built into the early levels, and rested upon them. However, cylinder seal impressions and part of a numerical tablet (Collon, Reade 1983), as well as masses of bevelled-rim bowls and other typical Late Uruk vessels (Thompson, Hamilton 1932: pl. 61), leave no doubt about the date and importance of the site.

In the fourth season a proper Deep Sounding was dug down from the highest point of Kuyunjik in square MM, with the aim of identifying all the different prehistoric levels and reaching the very first occupation of Nineveh (pl. 1 a-b). This sounding was supervised and published by Max Mallowan, Campbell Thompson's assistant in the fourth season. Bedrock was finally reached after eleven weeks, at a depth of 25 m (or 80 feet as measured by the excavators), which may be compared with a depth of 3 m (10 feet) in square MM for the overlying remains of historical cultures.

Remains of the Uruk period occupy 12 m of this sequence, and it is the sheer length of it that is most significant. It enables us to establish a continuous chronological framework from the end of the Ubaid through to Ninevite 5. Each of the many phases is characterised by distinct pottery types. They not only allow us to securely correlate Nineveh and other Uruk sites in northern Iraq, such as Tepe Gawra (Speiser 1935; Tobler 1950; Rothman 1988), Grai Resh (Lloyd 1940), Qalinj Agha (Hijara 1973; Gut 1996) and Tell Mohammed Arab (Roaf 1983, 1984), but also to date Uruk material from unstratified contexts and surface surveys with much more precision than currently assumed.

Material available from Campbell Thompson's and Mallowan's excavations is scarce. It includes some of the pottery itself, some objects, the excavation notebooks, sketches drawn inside the notebooks, and several photographs, but there are no measured plans or sections. The sherds and objects are usually marked in pencil or crayon with the approximate depths at which they were found. Most of the archives and material from the Deep Sounding are accessible at the British Museum (Department of the Ancient Near East).

The Deep Sounding is special, in that we know much more about the non-academic side, since it is mentioned in the autobiographies of Max Mallowan and Agatha Christie (Mallowan 1977; Christie 1977). From them we learn that Campbell Thompson was not at all happy spending his limited budget on a pit where no cuneiform tablets could be obtained, which had become dangerously deep, and where no end was in sight even at 21 m below the surface (fig. 3). Mallowan reports how Thompson tried to argue that the workmen would not want to work there because they could not earn as much bakshish as they could digging elsewhere in historic levels; Mallowan countered, however, by paying them bakshish for painted potsherds. At -63 feet, at a stage when the letter reproduced as fig. 3 was being written to a sponsor of the excavations, the top of the Halaf level had just been reached, and 15 feet full of painted Halaf, Samarra and Hassuna pottery were still to come. Campbell

Thompson's estimate of a water level at -90 feet clearly shows that he had already guessed that much. Although afraid of heights, Campbell Thompson bravely climbed down to the bottom of the deep sounding once every day, but surely must have rejoiced when in the first days of 1933 virgin soil was reached and the black hole was completely filled back in.

Two of the photographs of the Deep Sounding show burials in early Uruk levels (pl. 1 c-d). They are annotated in Mallowan's handwriting. The urn from pot burial pl. 1 c, or a very similar one, is now in the Ashmolean Museum (inv. no. 1932 1172). Two other photographs show groups of pottery. One is interesting as it includes two of the earliest bevelled-rim bowls found (pl. 2a). Another is a photograph of the more complete pots found during the fourth season, unfortunately out of focus; not all of these vessels are from the Deep Sounding — the three pots on the left are Uruk in date, the others Ninevite 5 (pl. 2b).

Mallowan's Deep Sounding was the first attempt to establish a chronological scheme for prehistoric Assyria (fig. 4). He divided it into five levels or stages and named them Ninevite 1 to 5 from bottom to top. Only Ninevite 3 and 4 concern us here. They cover the fourth millennium BC, that is the Uruk period, or Gawra period as it is often called in northern Iraq. Ninevite 1 and 2b date to the Hassuna period, and Ninevite 2c to the Halaf period. The top level, Ninevite 5, actually gave its name to an archaeological period, although the pottery only occurs in northern Iraq and north-eastern Syria, and the term should be restricted to that area. Already then, at the time of excavation, it was clear that there was one lengthy gap in the occupation of the settlement, during the Ubaid period between Ninevite 2c and 3.

The table in fig. 5 indicates what pottery still exists from the Deep Sounding, classified and listed according to depth, with the earliest periods and wares at the top. From this table, two things are obvious. First, there is what one might call the 'bakshish-effect': namely, that sherds have been kept mainly from the bottom and top of the Deep Sounding, as these are periods with predominantly painted pottery. In contrast, the long Ninevite 3-4 sequence is characterised by undecorated pottery, and is therefore under-represented. Even from these strata, because of Mallowan's own aesthetic preferences, it is primarily the decorated sherds that have been kept, including all stray out-of-context Hassuna and Samarra sherds. Secondly, it is obvious that of all the periods into which Mallowan divided the sequence, only the Ninevite 5 pottery group coincides with his Ninevite 5 phase. The subdivision of Ninevite 3 and 4 is very complex, and is discussed below. Ninevite 4 itself, which runs from approximately -31 to -20 feet, represents the Late Uruk period, with pottery which we know from Habuba Kabira, Uruk and Susa.

The pottery from Ninevite 3 and 4 is not only under-represented in the actual number of sherds that have been kept, but also in Mallowan's publication (Thompson, Mallowan 1933). A further drawback, and probably the more important one, lies in the way the pottery has been published. Many of Mallowan's drawings lack adequate profiles or fail to indicate diameters. It is therefore impossible to determine size and shape. Some plates in the publication are confusing, as they employ different scales, or show pottery from several levels (fig. 6). Undecorated sherds without a special feature such as a spout or lug fared worst: if published at all, the reproduction was often an inked version of a sketch in the notebook, as are all the sherds on fig. 7. It is in fact the publication that has concealed many of the results, and has prevented the excavators of other sites from linking their material with Nineveh.

THE SEQUENCE
The following discussion will concentrate on the many phases into which the Uruk sequence at Nineveh can be divided, and will focus on the early phases, as the Late Uruk period is much better understood from other sites. It will not deal with the Halaf and earlier material, nor with the subsequent Ninevite 5 material.

Reoccupation after the Halaf period
When was Nineveh reoccupied after the Halaf period? The clues are deeply hidden in the published report, but there are good indicators. One of them is sherd fig. 8.1. It is small, fairly thick-walled, and scarcely curved, and it is mainly the pattern that links it with U-shaped pots from Gawra XII, which in turn link it with so-called 'sprig ware', also very typical of Gawra XII (fig. 8.2-5). Both patterns also occur on pots of different shapes (fig. 8.6-8). Other indicators are sherds fig. 8.9 and 11, the former being most likely the same type as one of the Gawra XII bowls whose interior had only been painted on one side (fig. 8.10). Fig. 8.12 is another one that has a direct parallel at Gawra XII (fig. 8.13). These sherds all come from -64, which is the top layer of the Halaf settlement, apparently already disturbed unless sherds fell from above during the excavation (pl. 3a).

Apart from these stray sherds of Gawra XII types, there are some greenish, dark-painted sherds from Nineveh (Gut 1995: nos. 770-782) which indicate that the reoccupation took place already during the late Ubaid period, during Gawra XIII. They again come from the upper Halaf level, and from Lower Ninevite 3.

Lower Ninevite 3
Next there are the Ninevite 3 sherds which were found *in situ*. Ninevite 3 runs from -62 to approximately -31 feet. At a depth of -45 to -50 feet the excavators had to install higher steps, and consequently we do not have many sherds from these depths. Excluding these strata, it is possible to divide the pottery into three groups: Lower, Middle and Upper Ninevite 3. The first group comes from approximately -59 to -50 feet. Two of the painted sherds

(fig. 9.1-2, pl. 3 b-c) can be directly compared to vessels fig. 9.3-4 from Gawra XI-IX. Other painted Nineveh sherds confirm this correlation (Gut 1995: nos. 793, 796, 798, 799; cf. Tobler 1950: nos. 408, 412, 433, 521, 523, 525), but, for the reasons given above, it could not have been deduced from the published report alone (pl. 3 c). A plan of Tepe Gawra level IX (fig. 10) may give an indication of what Nineveh may have looked like at that time.

One of the most characteristic pottery profiles of Lower Ninevite 3 belongs to bowls with an inwardly bevelled rim. One of them is fig. 7.33. Its depth is given as -24 feet, which indicates a Late Uruk date, but two arrows in Mallowan's personal copy of the excavation report tell us that it was published with the wrong provenance, and that this bowl came from somewhere around -50 to -58 feet. Such bowls are frequently sketched in the notebook (fig. 11.1-7), with the proper depth but the wrong alignment, and it is only the last in the series (fig. 11.7) which is more appropriately aligned. The description of it says: 'Bowl or flat dish, section might be read the other way, i.e. horizontally'. Only one undecorated specimen has been kept (fig. 11.8), along with several others decorated either with two or three dark brown blobs just beneath the rim, or with a wide red band on the inside (fig. 11.9-12, pl. 3d). Two of the vessels with the blotches are hidden in the publication (fig. 6.5, 15 = fig. 11.11, 13).

Complete examples of this bowl type from Tepe Gawra have either round bases or a small ring base (fig. 11.14-16). In Tepe Gawra these bowls were found alongside chaff-tempered, crudely made flat-based bowls, which too can be found among Mallowan's Nineveh sketches (fig. 11.17-23). They are related to the Anatolian and North Syrian Coba bowls, and probably are the forerunners of the Uruk bevelled-rim bowls, although they are not made in a mould.

Another piece of the same date is a small painted sherd (fig. 6.1 = fig. 12.1) which belongs to an otherwise unpainted group of pottery, described in the notebook as highly characteristic of Lower Ninevite 3, although Mallowan published only the two latest examples, found at -32 feet (fig. 7.30-31). They are shown here in a new drawing (fig. 12.2-3), alongside the three other examples from Lower Ninevite 3, and two examples from the bottom of the test trench in square H (fig. 12.4-8). This hand-made but delicate ware, burnished on the outside, is best known from Qalinj Agha, where it is misleadingly called 'Proto-Ninevite 5 ware' (fig. 12.9-12). That the top four levels at Qalinj Agha match with lower Ninevite 3, however, and are much earlier than Ninevite 5, is confirmed by other types common at both sites, such as the rim profiles on fig. 12.13-25 and fig. 12.26-44. Mallowan did not publish the Nineveh examples, and in his notebook always calls them 'peculiar'. The relationship between Qalinj Agha and Nineveh is also confirmed by jar rims from Qalinj Agha, which have their best parallels at Nineveh in previously unpublished pottery from the lowest levels in Campbell Thompson's test trench H (fig. 12.45-49, 50-54).

Finally, some other examples kept from the Lower Ninevite 3 phase of the Deep Sounding, and also very typical of Gawra XI-IX, are fig. 13.1-5 (fig. 13.4 = pl. 3 e). Fig. 13.1 and 2 are burnished hole-mouth jars with a reddish-brown surface or slip.

Not found at Nineveh, or more probably not kept though surprisingly not recorded, are the double-rimmed pots which are commonly found at Gawra XI-IX sites. On the other hand there is a very noticeable absence at Nineveh of two distinctive pottery types, both of which are present at Tepe Gawra and Qalinj Agha. These are small cups with flaring ribbed rims (fig. 13.6-9), of which a singular piece with a folded rim is best known (fig. 13.9), and a very typical kind of decorated pottery, the so-called 'Gawra impressed ware', which has either impressed or applied decoration (fig. 13.10-15).

Although their absence at Nineveh could be pure chance, a re-analysis of the published Gawra XI-IX pottery surprisingly confirms that there are indeed two chronological phases, of which the Gawra impressed ware and the painted ware are good indicators (fig. 14). Whereas most of the undecorated pottery types seem to run through, the decorated types clearly occur in stages: U-shaped pots and 'sprig ware' are limited to Gawra XII, Gawra impressed ware to Gawra XIA to c. XA, and the painted ware to Gawra c. XA to IX.

This new subdivision is further confirmed by two sites in the Eski-Mosul Dam Project, neither fully published yet. Tell Musharifa or Mishrife (Fujii, Oguchi 1987; Oguchi 1987) has all the types that are present at Nineveh (fig. 13.16); it is a single period site, with three distinct architectural layers, which all produced this kind of pottery. Most of what is published from the Polish excavation at the 'Early Uruk' site of Tell Rafaan (Bielinski 1987), on the other hand, can be classified as 'Gawra impressed ware' (fig. 13.17). A further confirmation of this subdivision, if needed, is Thalathat II (Egami 1959), which also only has the later material. We can therefore safely say that Lower Ninevite 3 dates only to the latter part of Gawra XI to IX.

Middle Ninevite 3
The next group in the Deep Sounding, Middle Ninevite 3, is characterised by a burnished grey ware (pl. 4a), described by Mallowan as the most typical feature of the whole of Ninevite 3, although it is limited to a depth of -45 to approximately -39 feet.[1] It comes in two very distinctive shapes: club headed bowls (fig. 15.1-6) and club headed jars (fig. 15.7-10), including burial urns such as the one now in Oxford (fig. 15.11). Apart from the burial urn, and one grey ware bowl profile hidden on the plate with the inked sketches (fig. 7.16), the only other still existing sherd that was published from Middle Ninevite 3 is a small burnished grey ware bowl (fig. 15.12). Once again it is a wrongly aligned notebook sketch that has been used for the publication.

The site with which we can best link the grey Ninevite 3 pottery is the large building of Grai Resh level II (Lloyd 1940: 18, fig. 7.7,9; cf. Lloyd 1948: 43). It also turned up in trench LP at Tell al-Hawa (Ball et al. 1989: 39f., fig. 28.32-41), in level 4a of area S 17 and the cemetery at Khirbet Hatara in the Eski-Mosul area (Negro 1998: fig. 2.19-22[2]; Fiorina 1997: fig. 29 and presumably figs. 33, 40), and in the niched Uruk temple at Tell Hammam et-Turkman in northern Syria (Akkermans 1988: 307, pl. 105.81,83,84, pl. 107.101, pl. 108.102-104). At Grai Resh as well as at Khirbet Hatara, the burial urns were covered with the bowls.

Hardly any pottery from this phase apart from the grey ware has been kept, but to judge from Mallowan's sketches, many types seem to have continued from Lower into Middle Ninevite 3, e.g. the bowls with inwardly bevelled rims which now seem to have a more rounded rim than before (fig. 15.13, pl. 3d).

It is at some time during the Middle Ninevite 3 phase that bevelled-rim bowls appear for the first time in small numbers. By the Late Uruk period they have become a mass-produced vessel and were found in such great numbers that Campbell Thompson feared that 'if these miserable bowls represent all that is to be found' he would not find future sponsors for his excavations. In the Deep Sounding, they seem to start at around -40 feet. Mallowan describes the early ones as 'possibly a little less squat than the latest examples thereof' (Gut 1995: 58). They were found at Grai Resh, but not at Tepe Gawra or Tell Hammam et-Turkman. At Uruk they start as early as Uruk XII (Sürenhagen 1986: 17).

It is nevertheless most likely that Gawra VIII links up with the Middle Ninevite 3 phase, rather than with Lower Ninevite 3. But as hardly any pottery from Gawra VIII has been kept and published, we have to rely on Speiser's description of it: '... extensive comparative material from other sites is lacking ... It will not surprise therefore to learn that clear and significant ceramic connections with Gawra VIII are found only in prehistoric Nineveh, stage III. These are, however, unmistakable. I shall not dwell on the grey burnished and grey-slip wares of Gawra; the former are more common in Nineveh III than they are on our site ... The resemblance in shapes is far more conclusive' (Speiser 1935: 152). Gawra VIII A ended in a 'conflagration that had reduced the buildings of VIII A to masses of fused clay', and 'many of the buried rooms were thus preserved to a height of three metres' (Speiser 1935: 182). Tepe Gawra then remained unoccupied for a long time.

Upper Ninevite 3
With Upper Ninevite 3, we are clearly approaching the kind of Uruk pottery that is commonly known. The pieces we have can be dated fairly securely to the Middle Uruk period, roughly levels X to VII at Uruk. They occur at a depth of approximately -37 to -31 feet. Small spouted vessels with straight spouts close to the rim (fig. 6.7-8 = fig. 16.1-2), a combed ware sherd which is included twice

on Mallowan's plate (fig. 6.10 and 12 = fig. 16.3), and the first four-lugged jars, still crudely made (fig. 6.13 = fig. 16.4³, fig. 16.5-7), are all typical, as are the first examples of pseudo-reserved slip, and the first examples of pottery made on a fast wheel (pl. 4b).

Incised and combed sherds are the type fossils for Upper Ninevite 3 (fig. 16.8-15, pl. 4 c-e). All have close parallels at Uruk, especially the combed pottery in grey fabric. This is almost identical to pieces from the Uruk Deep Sounding now in Berlin (e.g. Sürenhagen 1986: 36 no. 161, 37 no. 180⁴), and differs from the combed pottery known from Syria which is combed horizontally rather than vertically, and often with well spaced bands (e.g. Boese 1995: 260 fig. 3 bottom). Also very typical for Upper Ninevite 3 are chaff-tempered pots or casseroles, three of which have been kept plus the base of a fourth which was probably used as a lid (fig. 17.1-4, pl. 4 f). They were found at a slightly higher level than the combed grey ware, in the uppermost Ninevite 3 and lowest Ninevite 4 strata.⁵

Apart from the examples shown, pottery from this phase again exists in the form of sketches only, which imply that many undecorated types, for instance angular bowl rims and carinated bowls, appear in Upper Ninevite 3 and continue into Lower Ninevite 4, but we have to leave this question open. Tepe Gawra was abandoned by now, and there is no other known northern Iraqi site to replace it. Only Tell al-Hawa still shows comparable pottery, but this comes from a surface survey and not from excavation.

Ninevite 4 and the transition to Ninevite 5
Finally, the Ninevite 4 stage and the transition to Ninevite 5 may be illustrated briefly with pottery mainly not from the Deep Sounding but from the previous seasons.⁶ Nineveh is the only site currently known in northern Iraq where Ninevite 4 or the Late Uruk period is represented, in contrast with the situation in contemporary Syria where it is more abundant, and in contrast to the succeeding Late Uruk phase of Tell Mohammed Arab which is attested at many sites in northern Iraq.

Most distinctive for the Late Uruk period are bevelled-rim bowls (fig. 17.5); a type of beaker (fig. 17.6); conical cups with string-cut bases (fig. 17.7), the earlier ones with a small spout or lip (Gut 1995: no. 1502, pl. 131 e); small four-lugged pots (fig. 17.8, though this one is probably slightly later); red-slipped four-lugged jars (fig. 17.9); incised four-lugged jars (fig. 17.10); and drooping spouts (fig. 17.11, this jar comes from underneath the Vaulted Tombs). Almost all these vessels come from the squares on the north-western side of the temple of Ishtar. To judge from the pottery kept, the excavations east of the temple did not reach Late Uruk levels proper. They were abandoned in levels which we now recognise, thanks to the rescue excavations in the Eski-Mosul Dam area, as two intermediate phases between Late Uruk and Ninevite 5.

The earlier of these two phases is the last one to be considered here. It is best known from Tell Mohammed Arab (Roaf 1983, 1984), but also from Tell Karrana 3 (Wilhelm, Zaccagnini 1993). Bevelled-rim bowls, red-slipped pottery and four-lugged jars continue during this phase, though in small numbers. Miniature Uruk vessels and coarsely made conical bowls are also typical (fig. 17.12-13). Shapes which already anticipate Ninevite 5 pottery occur for the first time. Incised four-lugged jars continue as well, with a more rounded profile and a more fugitive decoration which is no longer limited to the shoulder of the jars. The most characteristic new features are vessels painted in red, often with cross-hatched triangles; small jars with two opposed, doubly pierced lugs; and four-lugged jars with a raised rib instead of the former rope-like incisions; and jars with vertical raised ribs instead of lugs (fig. 17.14-15 and Gut 1995: fig. 30 a-b, fig. 31 e-f, pl. 132 a). These two-lugged jars and ribbed vessels, with different patterns, continue in the later of the two phases, as attested at Nineveh (Thompson, Hamilton 1932: pl. 59.25; Gut 1995: fig. 30 c-e, nos. 1093-1094, pl. 132 c, d) and Tell Karrana (Wilhelm, Zaccagnini 1993: pl. 23.145, pl. 28.257).

CONCLUSIONS
Mallowan's 12 m deep Ninevite 3-4 sequence can be divided into four chronological phases: Lower, Middle and Upper Ninevite 3, and Ninevite 4 (fig. 18). These four phases cover almost the entire length of the Uruk/Gawra period, excluding the lower and upper limits, to which I shall return. Ninevite 4 is Late Uruk in date and serves as a chronological fixed point.

Perhaps the best result of the reassessment is that for the first time we can correlate Tepe Gawra and Nineveh without resorting to speculation. Lower Ninevite 3, at a depth of roughly -59 to -50 feet, matches the later part of Gawra XI-IX. This shows how early the Gawra sequence must be: material corresponding to Gawra IX is followed by at least two phases, before we reach Late Uruk Ninevite 4. In other words, at Nineveh material resembling that of Gawra IX lies 6 m deeper than the earliest Ninevite 4 stratum. We can therefore safely say that the material assemblage of Gawra XI-IX does not represent a local northern Mesopotamian culture of Middle or Late Uruk date, but rather an earlier chronological stage.

The earlier phase of Gawra XI-IX is not represented in the Deep Sounding at Nineveh, though it may have been elsewhere on Kuyunjik, as we have some stray sherds of Gawra XII and Gawra XIII date, which indicate that after the Halaf period Nineveh was reoccupied already by Late Ubaid times.

At the other end of the Uruk sequence, Nineveh proves that the Late Uruk phase of Tell Mohammed Arab is later than Late Uruk proper. At Tell Mohammed Arab, where this phase was first found, the term 'Late Uruk' was used in inverted commas, but Mohammed Arab Late

Uruk material was soon generally seen as another local phenomenon contemporary with the 'real' Late Uruk sites. At Nineveh, pottery of the Mohammed Arab 'Late Uruk' phase was mixed up with Ninevite 5, but in all the squares excavated it never comes from the Ninevite 4, or Late Uruk, level.

The many phases resulting from the combination of Tepe Gawra, Mallowan's Ninevite 3 and 4, and Tell Mohammed Arab necessitate a new terminology, as there is a limit to the use of Early, Middle and Late. Even if we follow Perkins and attribute Gawra XII to the Ubaid period, which is very reasonable, we are left with six phases for the Uruk period in northern Iraq. Three of these are earlier than the Middle Uruk Upper Ninevite 3. Only the uppermost of these three, Middle Ninevite 3, which links up with Grai Resh II, is roughly comparable to Eanna XII-IX, or Early Uruk in southern Iraq. I have therefore chosen the previously synonymous terms Gawra and Uruk as chronological terms, restricting the term Uruk to only those phases which can be directly compared with Early to Late Uruk in the South, and using Gawra for the two early phases for which Tepe Gawra is the type site (fig. 18, fig. 19; cf. Gut 1995: 233 Tab. 22). I think it likely that the two Gawra phases are earlier than Early Uruk in the South (Gut 1996: 11), but as the Ubaid-Uruk transition in southern Iraq is hardly known, this must remain hypothetical. And if we presume that Gawra VIII dates to the earliest Uruk phase this is no contradiction, because the ceramic repertoire of Gawra VIII is not known, and Gawra VIII would not be referred to as a type site.

When this scheme was created in 1990, Uruk in northern Mesopotamia was generally divided into two phases, or three phases at most. The classification of a site as Early or Late Uruk was highly confusing, and often contradictory. For this reason I tried to avoid the terms Early, Middle and Late Uruk, and chose letters instead (i.e. Gawra A, B and Northern Uruk A, B, C and D). Almost invariably the first question that was asked was how these new phases correlated with the South, which is why, when it came to publication, I have added Early, Middle, Late and Terminal Uruk in brackets, although a proper investigation into this question is needed (Gut 1995: 287 Tab. 30). In my view, letters — or alternatively figures — have the advantage that they allow for further subdivision, which no doubt will be needed in the future.

Architecture and artefacts other than pottery, mostly from sites other than Nineveh, confirm the many phases of this new sequence, but need to be re-studied in the light of the new chronological scheme. Best known are the stamp seals of the Gawra and earliest Uruk phases, which are gradually replaced by cylinder seals from Middle Uruk times onwards. Also noteworthy are the hut symbols made of clay, which are common in the Gawra phases, and the eye idols made of stone that seem to be typical for the earlier Uruk phases, Northern Uruk A and B.

A possible disadvantage of the proposed scheme lies in the subdivision of a period that should basically be considered as one. On the other hand, I am proposing that terms which already exist should be used in a much more precise temporal context. The separation of the Gawra material emphasises its regional character, and allows a relative dating independent from the sequence of the South.

I do not think that the recently proposed Late Chalcolithic 1-5 terminology (cf. Rothman, this volume) is a satisfactory alternative. The term Chalcolithic is best restricted to a terminology which uses Neolithic, Chalcolithic, and Early Bronze Age. Besides, in northern Iraq we can distinguish not five, but six phases, two Gawra and four Uruk, though this does not mean that there have to be six everywhere. In south-eastern Anatolia, for instance, the artefacts that follow after the Late Chalcolithic/Late Uruk period cannot be classified as Terminal Uruk: they represent the earliest phase of the succeeding local Early Bronze Age.

It is important to realise that northern Mesopotamia is not a single entity during the Uruk period, and we should first concentrate on independent chronological schemes for the different areas. The painted pottery with the blobs of Gawra X-IX, for instance, is absent at Tell Brak and the Khabur sites in north-eastern Syria, but occurs at Norşun Tepe, Tepecik and Tülintepe in the Altinova (Gut 1995: 230 n. 606). On the other hand, the Mohammed Arab 'Late Uruk' phase is restricted to northern Iraq and north-eastern Syria, and is not known from west of Tell Brak, or from Turkey. We need to establish regional sequences before we can compare.

With the ceramic type-fossils of the combined Nineveh and Gawra sequence, sites of the Uruk period in northern Iraq and north-eastern Syria can be dated fairly securely. The last two tables give the earlier sites on fig. 20, the later ones on fig. 21. Even without going into detail, it is obvious that the majority of these sites was occupied during the earlier phases. Of all the many sites inhabited in the Gawra period, few remained in use during the Northern Uruk A phase, and hardly any — only Nineveh and Tell al-Hawa — during the Northern Uruk B phase. Only Nineveh continued to exist during the Late Uruk and Terminal Uruk phase into Ninevite 5. Many small sites, however, which are not listed here, were newly founded either during the Terminal Uruk phase or the Ninevite 5 period. Likewise, in north-eastern Syria, many sites in the Khabur basin existed during the Gawra B or Northern Uruk A phase, but very few afterwards. Again, only Tell Brak was continuously occupied right into post-Uruk levels.

Nineveh and Tell Brak are exceptional, in that the Late Uruk settlement was located on a high mound which was continuously occupied. Normally, sites of the Gawra and Uruk periods seem to have occupied new, or lower, locations, and were frequently abandoned after a short time. I think that the principal reason why we have so few Middle and Late Uruk sites is not a question of whether they are colonies (they are not), but a change in the actual pattern of settlement: they are inconspicuous, preferably somewhere in the flats, and often eroded, as at Umm Qseir. Even Habuba Kabira-South was well disguised before excavation: only the many bevelled-rim bowls were noticed by the excavators who started digging first on the main mound (Strommenger, Sürenhagen 1970: 59).

It is no wonder, therefore, that in the surveys that have been conducted, Uruk sites are not numerous, and are likely to have been missed. Which means that we are at the end of the beginning, rather than at the beginning of the end, of understanding Uruk in the North.

---

[1] It is distinctly different and much commoner than the grey ware of the Lower Ninevite 3 strata.

[2] Judging by the published pottery, level 4a of area S 17 at Hatara should date to the Middle Ninevite 3 phase (Northern Uruk A, see below), followed by level 5b which is Terminal Uruk (Northern Uruk D) or Transitional Ninevite 5 in date, and level 5a, Early Ninevite 5 period. Since the excavators date level 4a to the Late Uruk period, this could be levelling fill.

[3] Found at a depth of -36 feet according to Mallowan's notebook vol. II, p. 79.

[4] Combing not indicated nor mentioned.

[5] The so-called Middle Uruk phase of Tell Brak (TW 13; see Oates this volume, p. 111 and 115) only equates with the uppermost Ninevite 3 and lowest Ninevite 4 strata. At Nineveh, the conical bowls with a small pouring lip which are typical for TW 13 (cf. Oates this volume, p. 115) are only attested in the lower Ninevite 4 strata, i.e. they are an Early Late Uruk type. See below.

[6] For colour photographs see Gut 1995: pls. 131-133.

REFERENCES

Akkermans, P.M.M.G., 1988. The Period V pottery. In: M.N. van Loon (ed.), *Hammam et-Turkman* I: 287-349. Istanbul & Leiden.

Ball, W., Tucker, D., Wilkinson, T.J., 1989. The Tell al-Hawa project: archaeological investigations in the North Jezirah 1986-87. *Iraq* 51: 1-66.

Bielinski, P., 1987. Tell Raffaan and Tell Rijim 1984-85: preliminary report on two seasons of Polish excavations in the Saddam Dam Project area. In: Republic of Iraq, Ministry of Culture and Information, State Organization of Antiquities and Heritage (ed.), *Researches on the Antiquities of Saddam Dam Basin Salvage and other Researches*: 13-19. Baghdad.

Boese, J., 1995. *Ausgrabungen in Tell Scheikh Hassan I: Vorläufige Berichte über die Grabungskampagnen 1984-1990 und 1992-1994.* Schriften zur Vorderasiatischen Archäologie 5. Saarbrücken.

Christie, A., 1977. *An Autobiography.* London.

Collon, D., Reade, J., 1983. Archaic Nineveh. *Baghdader Mitteilungen* 14: 33-41.

Egami, N., 1959. *Telul eth-Thalathat, Vol. I: The Excavation of Tell II, 1956-1957.* Tokio.

Fiorina, P., 1997. Khirbet Hatara — La stratigrafia. *Mesopotamia* 32: 7-61.

Fujii, H., Oguchi, H., 1987. Tell Mašrafa. In: K. Nashef, Ausgrabungen und Geländebegehungen, Irak (II), *Archiv für Orientforschung* 34: 188-192.

Gut, R.V., 1995. *Das prähistorische Ninive. Zur relativen Chronologie der frühen Perioden Nordmesopotamiens.* Baghdader Forschungen 19. Mainz.

- 1996. Zur Datierung der "Proto-Ninive 5"-Ware von Qalinj Agha. *Baghdader Mitteilungen* 27: 1-12.

Hijara, I., 1973. Excavations at Tell Qalinj Agha (Erbil), fourth season 1970. *Sumer* 29, Arabic section: 59-80.

Lloyd, S., 1940. Iraq Government soundings at Sinjar. *Iraq* 7: 13-21.

- 1948. Uruk pottery. *Sumer* 4.1: 39-51.

Mallowan, M.E.L., 1977. *Mallowan's Memoirs.* London.

Negro, F., 1998. Khirbet Hatara (Eski Mossul), livelli 4a-5b-5a: La ceramica. *Mesopotamia* 33: 29-145.

Oguchi, H., 1987. Tell Musharifa. In: Republic of Iraq, Ministry of Culture and Information, State Organization of Antiquities and Heritage (ed.), *Researches on the Antiquities of Saddam Dam Basin Salvage and other Researches:* 49-55. Baghdad.

Roaf, M., 1983. A report on the work of the British Archaeological Expedition in the Eski Mosul Dam Salvage Project. *Sumer* 39: 68-82.

- 1984. Excavations at Tell Mohammed 'Arab in the Eski Mosul Dam Salvage Project. *Iraq* 46: 141-156.

Rothman, M., 1988. *Centralization, Administration and Function at Fourth Millennium B.C. Tepe Gawra, Northern Iraq.* University Microfilms, Ann Arbor.

Speiser, E.A., 1935. *Excavations at Tepe Gawra,* Vol. I. Philadelphia.

Strommenger, E., Sürenhagen, D., 1970. Die Grabung in Habuba Kabira-Süd. *Mitteilungen der Deutschen Orient-Gesellschaft* 102: 59-71.

Sürenhagen, D., 1986. Archaische Keramik aus Uruk-Warka. *Baghdader Mitteilungen* 17: 7-95.

Thompson, R. Campbell, 1934. The buildings on Quyunjik, the larger mound of Nineveh. *Iraq* 1: 95-104.

Thompson, R. Campbell, Hamilton, R.W., 1932. The British Museum excavations on the Temple of Ishtar at Nineveh, 1931-32. *Liverpool Annals of Archaeology and Anthropology* 19: 55-116.

Thompson, R. Campbell, Hutchinson, R.W., 1929. The excavations on the Temple of Nabu at Nineveh. *Archaeologia* 79: 103-148.

- 1931. The site of the Palace of Ashurnasirpal at Nineveh, excavated in 1929-30 on behalf of the British Museum. *Liverpool Annals of Archaeology and Anthropology* 18: 79-112.

Thompson, R. Campbell, Mallowan, M.E.L., 1933. The British Museum excavations at Nineveh, 1931-32. *Liverpool Annals of Archaeology and Anthropology* 20: 71-186.

Tobler, A.J., 1950. *Excavations at Tepe Gawra,* Vol. II. Philadelphia.

Wilhelm, G., Zaccagnini, C., 1993. *Tell Karrana 3, Tell Jikan, Tell Khirbet Salih.* Baghdader Forschungen 15. Mainz.

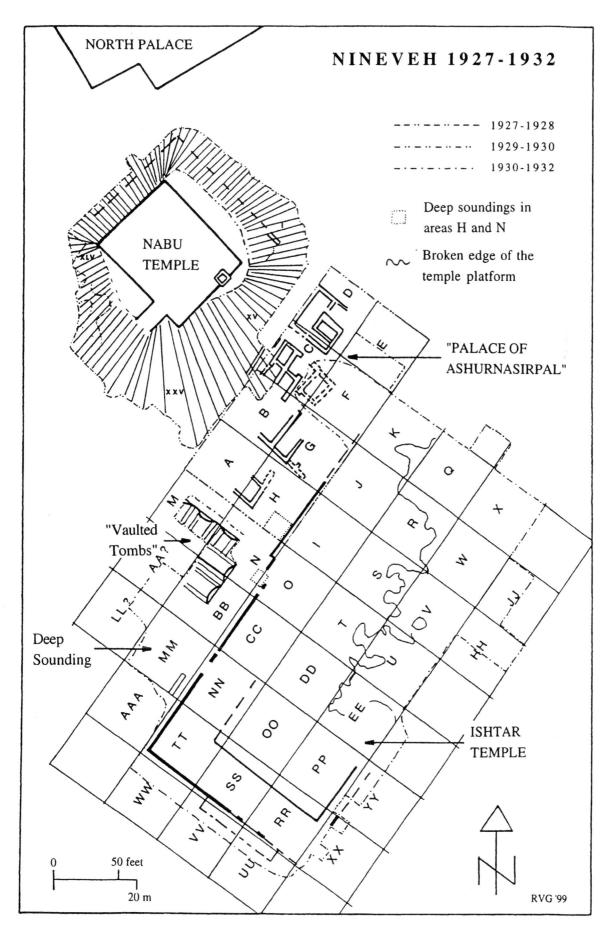

Fig. 1. Composite plan of areas excavated during 1927-1932 in the centre of Kuyunjik

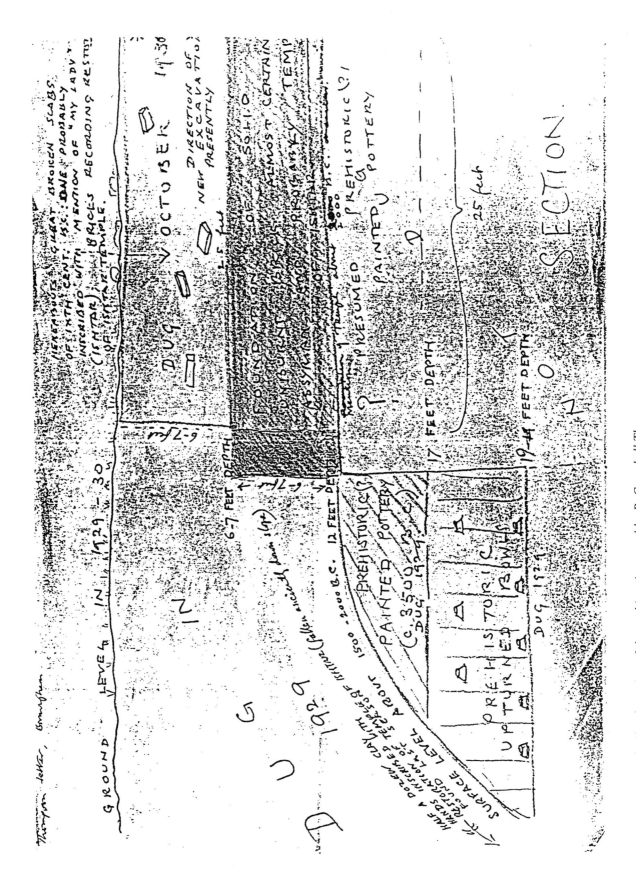

Fig. 2. Sketch section of the prehistoric mound by R. Campbell Thompson

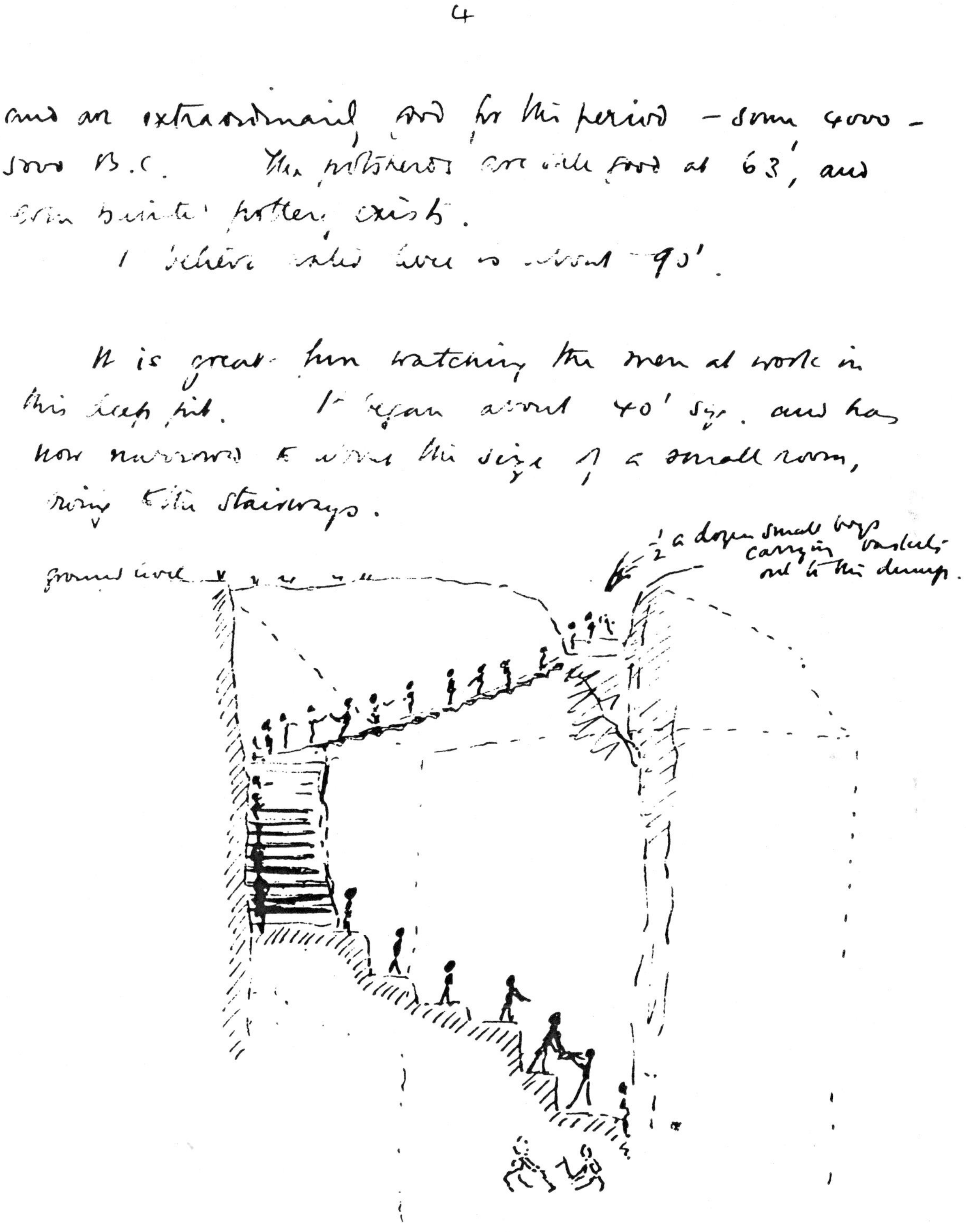
4

and an extraordinary find for this period — some 4000–5000 B.C. The potsherds are still found at 63', and even painted pottery exists.

I believe virgin soil is about 90'.

It is great fun watching the men at work in this deep pit. It began about 40' sq. and has now narrowed to about the size of a small room, using little stairways.

ground level
½ a dozen small boys carrying baskets out to the dump.

Fig. 3. R. Campbell Thompson's sketch of the Deep Sounding, from a letter to a sponsor of the excavations

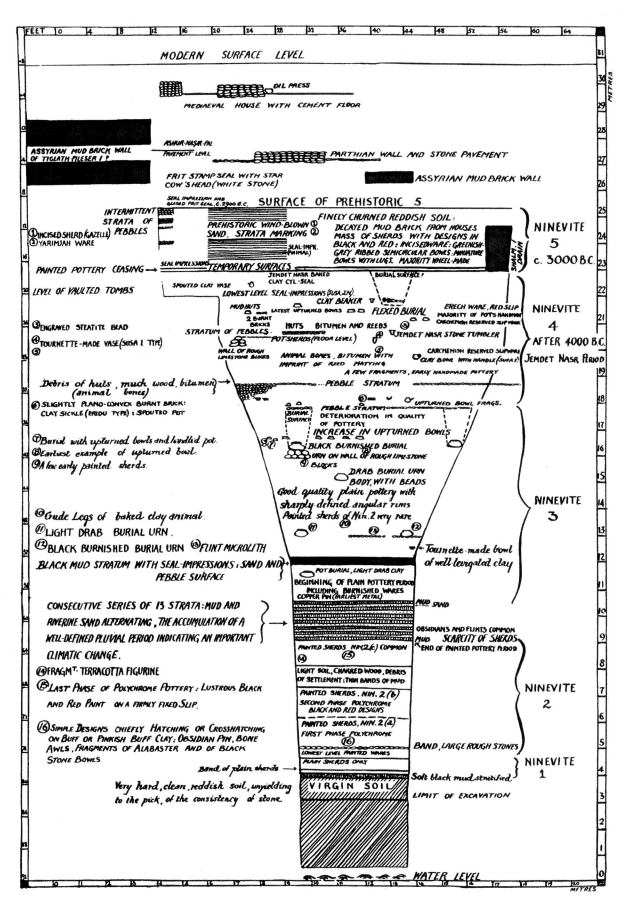

Fig. 4. Schematic section through the Deep Sounding (Thompson, Mallowan 1933, pl. 73)

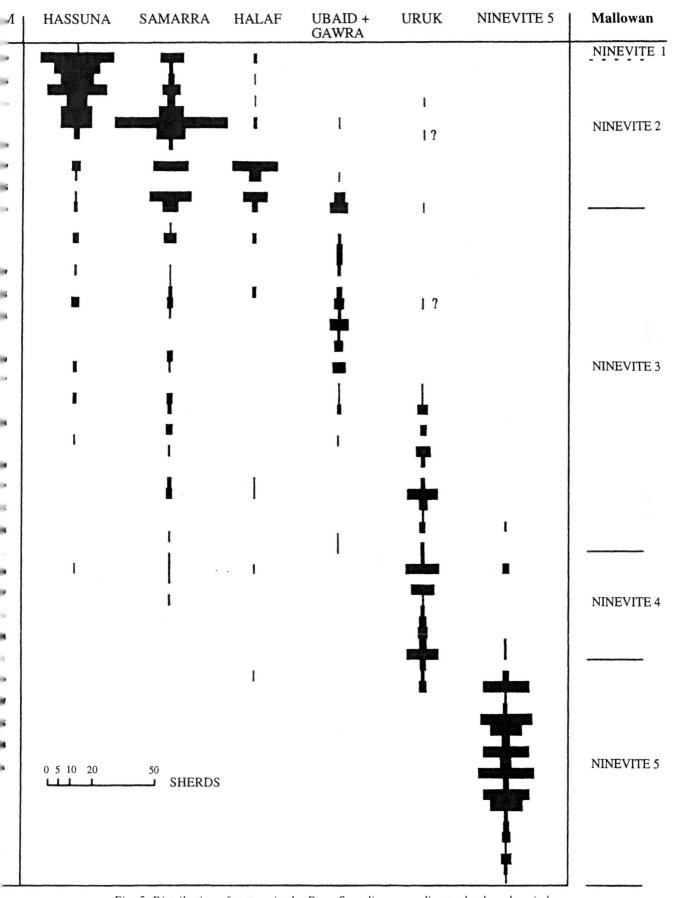

Fig. 5. Distribution of pottery in the Deep Sounding according to depth and period

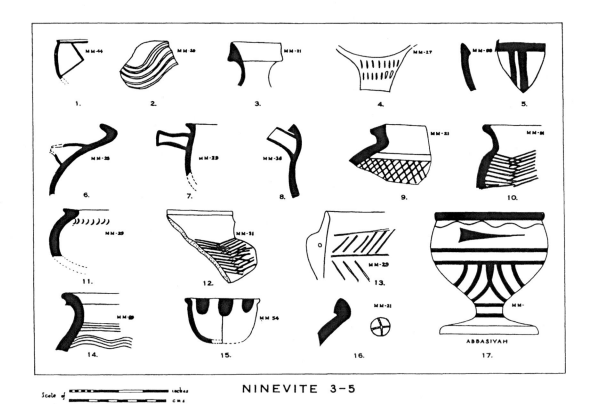

NINEVITE 3-5

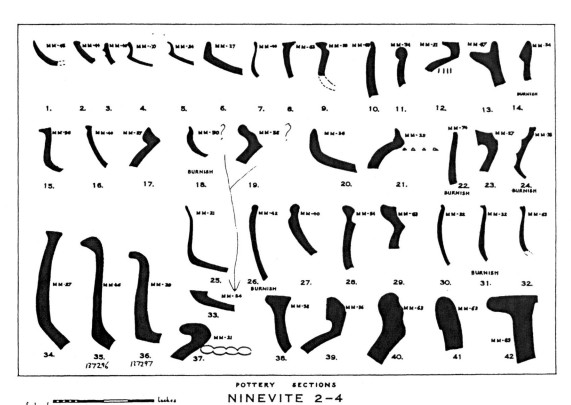

POTTERY   SECTIONS
NINEVITE 2-4

Fig. 6 (top). Thompson, Mallowan 1933: plate 50

Fig. 7. Thompson, Mallowan 1933: plate 49

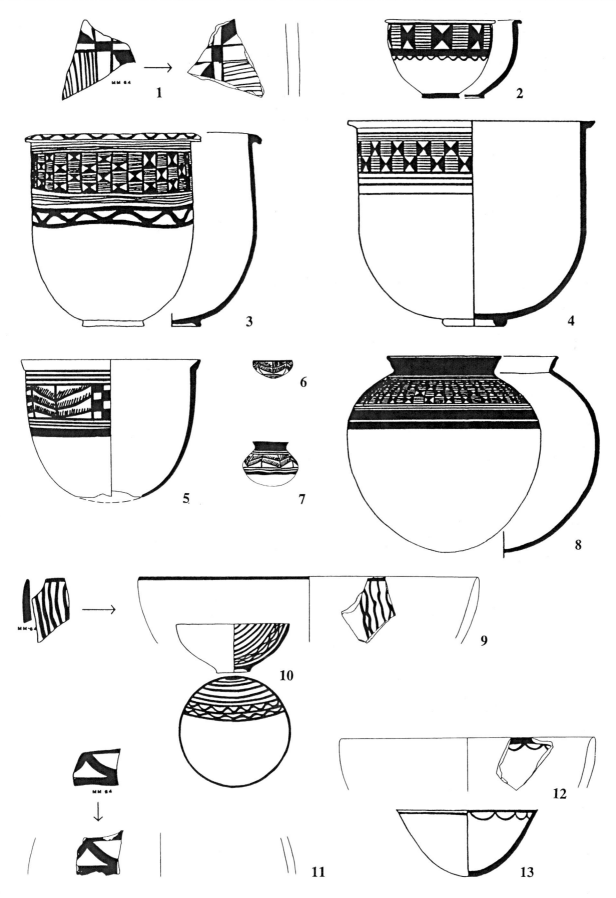

Fig. 8. Terminal Ubaid pottery from Nineveh (nos. 1, 9, 11-12) and Tepe Gawra (nos. 2-8, 10, 13).
Scale 1:4, except nos. 2-8, 10, 13 at scale 1:8

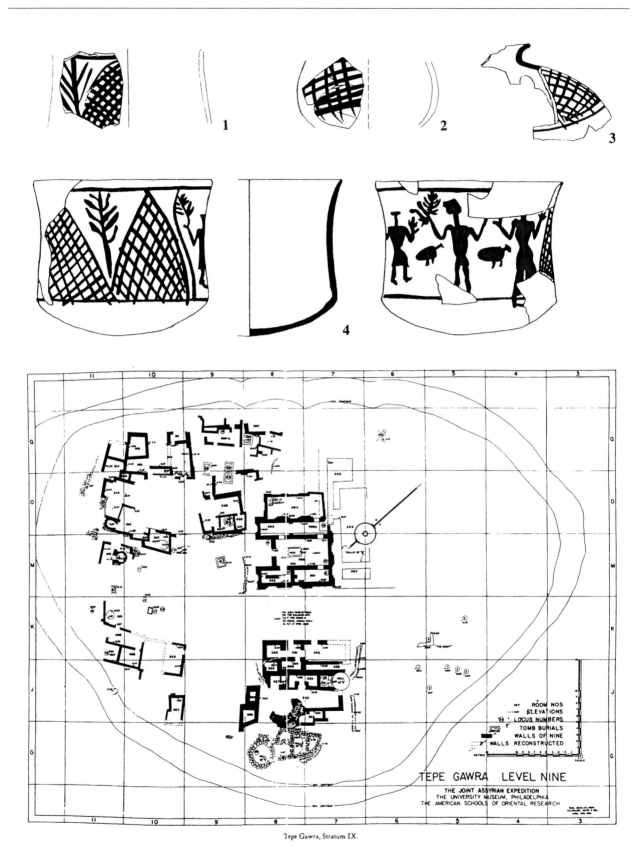

Fig. 9. *Painted pottery of the Gawra period from Lower Ninevite 3 (nos. 1-2) and Tepe Gawra (nos. 3-4). Scale 1:4*

Fig. 10. *Plan of Tepe Gawra level IX*

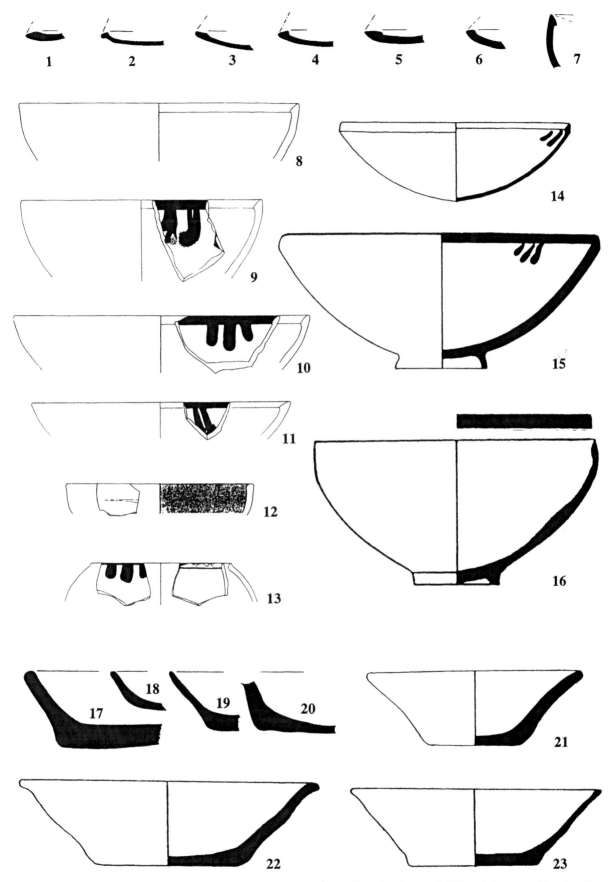

Fig. 11. Bowls and a jar with inwardly bevelled rim from Lower Ninevite 3 (nos. 1-13) and decorated bowls of the same type from Tepe Gawra (nos. 14-16); flat based bowls from Lower Ninevite 3 (nos. 17-20) and Tepe Gawra (nos. 21-23). Scale 1:4, except nos. 1-7 and 17-20 which are sketches by Mallowan (scale not known)

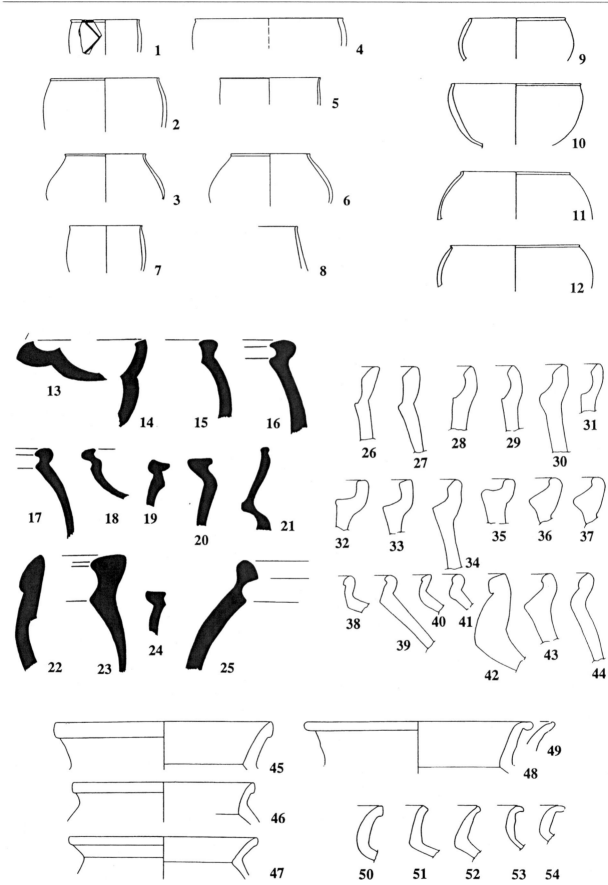

Fig. 12. Cups of the Gawra period (so-called 'Proto-Ninevite 5 ware') from the Nineveh Deep Sounding (nos. 1-6), from Nineveh, test trench in area H (nos. 7-8), and from Qalinj Agha (nos. 9-12); jar rims of the Gawra period from Nineveh (nos. 13-25, 45-49) and Qalinj Agha (nos. 26-44, 50-54). Scale 1:4, except no. 8 and Mallowan's sketches (nos. 13-25), scale not known; scale of the Qalinj Agha examples uncertain (1:4?)

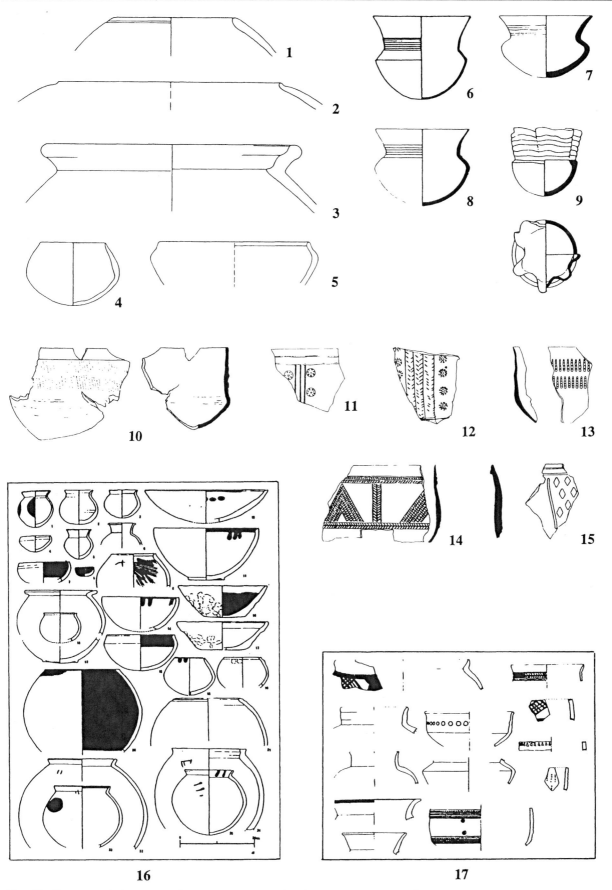

Fig. 13. Gawra period pottery: characteristic examples from Lower Ninevite 3 (nos. 1-5, Gawra B phase), from Tepe Gawra (Gawra A phase, nos. 6-15), from Tell Musharifa (no. 16, Gawra B phase) and Tell Rafaan (no. 17, mostly Gawra A phase). Scale 1:4, except no. 16 at 1:10, no. 17 at 1:5

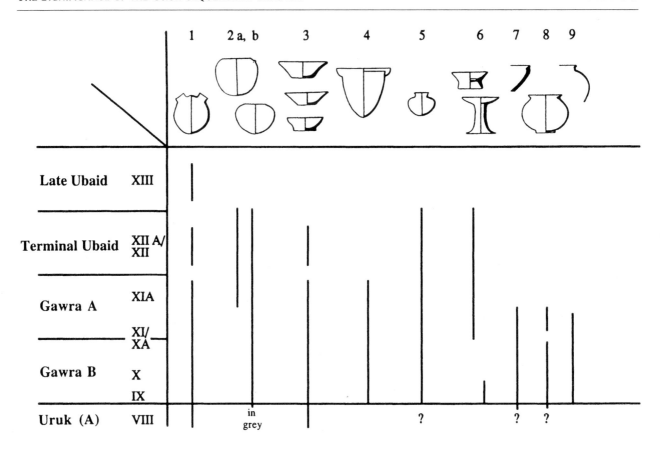

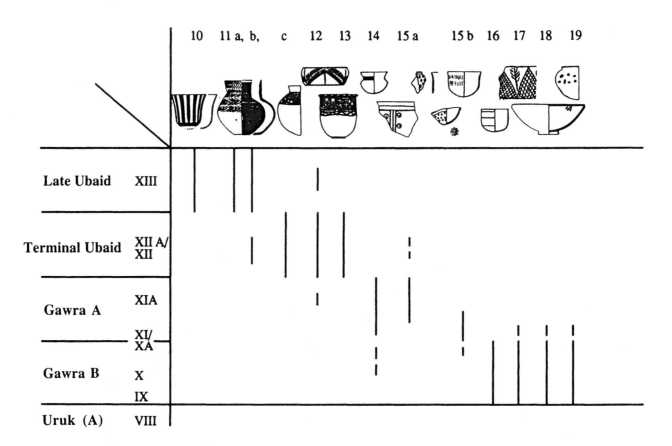

Fig. 14. Tepe Gawra: occurrence of pottery types in the Late Ubaid, Terminal Ubaid and Gawra phases

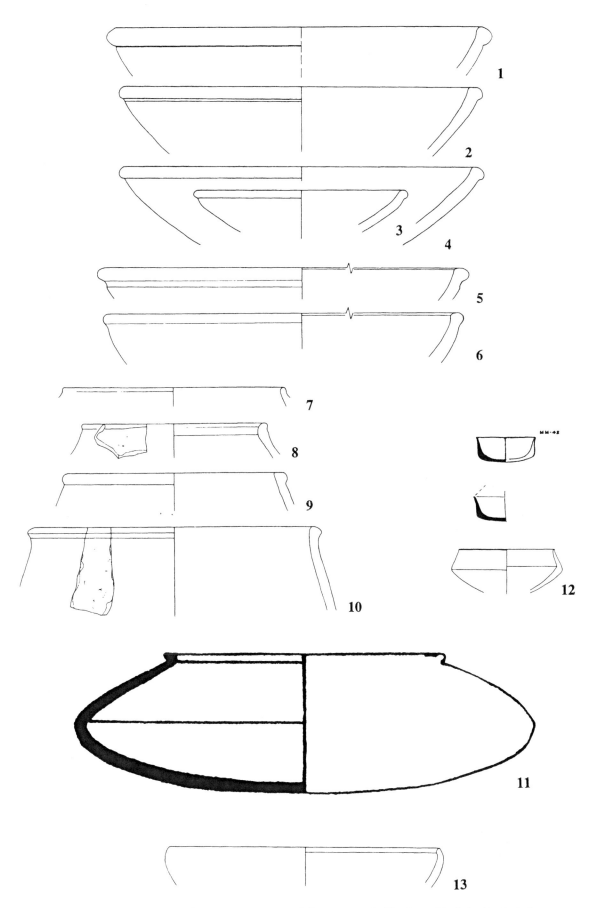

Fig. 15. Burnished grey ware from Middle Ninevite 3 (Northern Uruk A). Scale 1:4

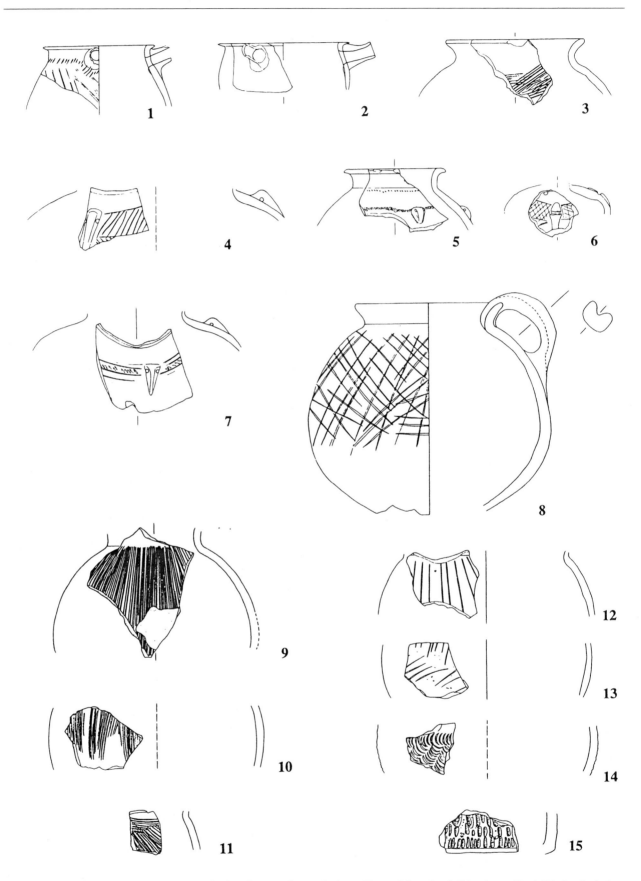

Fig. 16. Spouted, four-lugged, combed and incised vessels from Upper Ninevite 3 (Northern Uruk B). Scale 1:4

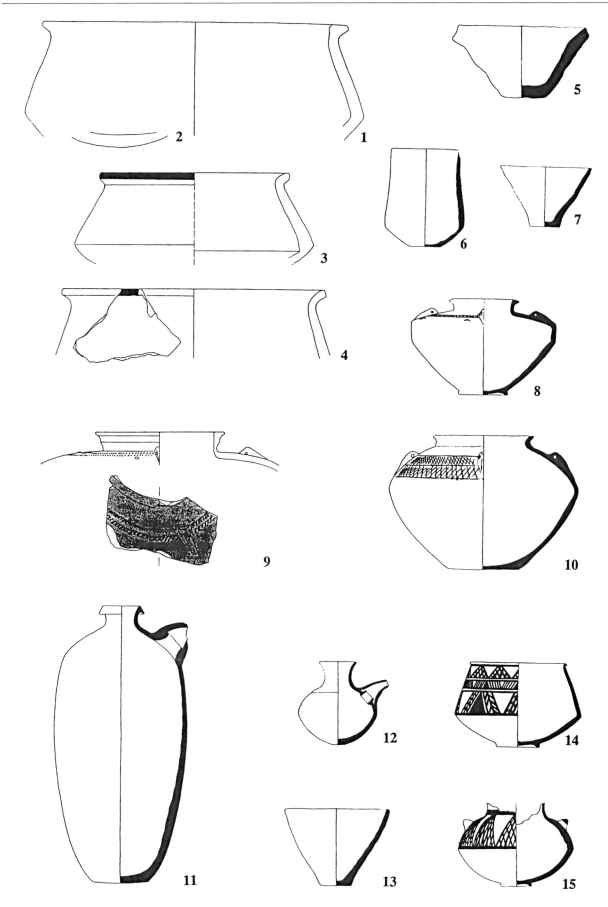

Fig. 17. Casseroles from Upper Ninevite 3 and Lower Ninevite 4 (Northern Uruk B/C) and typical examples of Late Uruk and Terminal Uruk pottery from areas other than the Deep Sounding, except no. 9 from Ninevite 4. Scale 1:4

MM	Mallowan divisions and designations	Proposed new subdivisions and designations		"Period"
-80		*(Ninevite 0)* *Proto-Hassuna* *Ninevite 1* *Early Hassuna*		
-78 -75	Ninevite 1	Ninevite 2a	Transitional Early – Late Hassuna	Hassuna
-72	Ninevite 2a			
	Ninevite 2b	Ninevite 2b	Late Hassuna	
-67		=========== ? ==		
-63	Ninevite 2c	Ninevite 2 c	Early to Middle Halaf	Halaf
		==============		
-60		*Late Ubaid* *Terminal Ubaid*		Ubaid
		=========== ? ==		
	Ninevite 3	Lower Ninevite 3	Gawra B (Gawra XA - IX)	Gawra
-45				
-37		Middle Ninevite 3	Northern Uruk A	
-31		Upper Ninevite 3	Northern Uruk B	Uruk
-20 -18	Ninevite 4	Ninevite 4	Northern Uruk C (Late Uruk)	
	Ninevite 5	*"Mohammed Arab Late Uruk" or Terminal Uruk*		
		"Transitional Ninevite 5"		
		Ninevite 5 Ninevite 5		Ninevite 5
-6				

Fig. 18. Sequence of levels in the Deep Sounding at Nineveh. The figures on the left represent depths below datum, in feet. In the central column, occupations only attested through occasional sherds and notebook references are indicated by italics, and breaks in occupation by broken lines

NINEVEH		TEPE GAWRA	QALINJ AGHA	GRAI RESH	PERIOD (Gut 1995)
Hiatus		(XIV)	.	.	LATE
(-64)	(2c/	XIII	.	.	UBAID
		XIIA	.	.	TERMINAL
-60	3)	XII	.	.	UBAID
?		XIA	VI	VII?	GAWRA A
		XI			
		XA			
-59	3	X			GAWRA B
-45		IX	I	III	
	3	VIIIC			NORTHERN URUK A
		VIIIB		II	
-37		VIIIA			
-31	3				NORTHERN URUK B
-20	4				NORTHERN URUK C (Late Uruk)
-19	(5)	intrusive in VIIIA (?)			NORTHERN URUK D (Terminal Uruk)
-18 -16	(5)	intrusive in VII			TRANSITIONAL NINEVITE 5
-15 0	5	intrusive in VIIIA, VII, IV			NINEVITE 5
		VI		I	"AKKADIAN"

Fig. 19. Correlation of Nineveh, Tepe Gawra, Qalinj Agha and Grai Resh

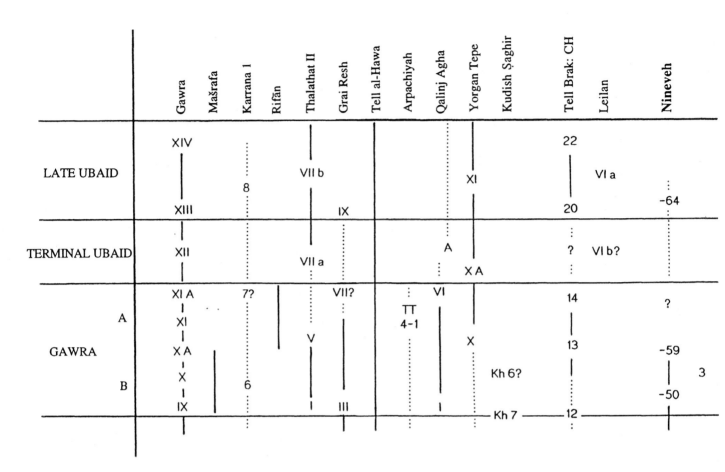

Fig. 20. Sites of the Late Ubaid, Terminal Ubaid, Gawra A and Gawra B phases

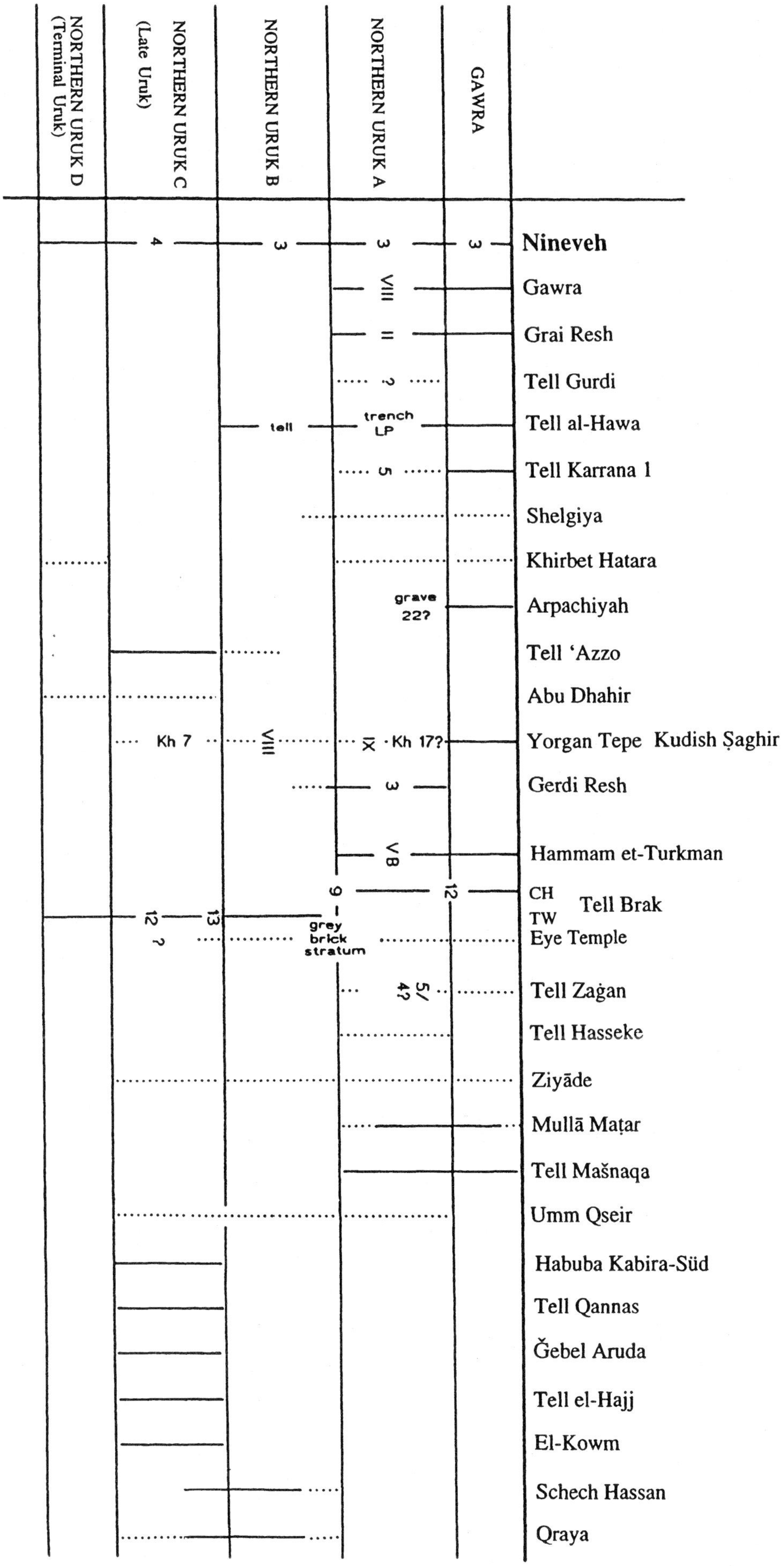

Fig. 21. Northern Mesopotamian sites of the Uruk period

NORTHERN URUK D (Terminal Uruk)	NORTHERN URUK C (Late Uruk)	NORTHERN URUK B	NORTHERN URUK A	GAWRA	
	4	3	3	3	**Nineveh**
			VIII		Gawra
			II		Grai Resh
			?		Tell Gurdi
		tell	trench LP		Tell al-Hawa
			5		Tell Karrana 1
					Shelgiya
					Khirbet Hatara
			grave 22?		Arpachiyah
					Tell 'Azzo
					Abu Dhahir
	Kh 7	VIII	IX · Kh 17?		Yorgan Tepe Kudish Ṣaghir
			3		Gerdi Resh
			VB		Hammam et-Turkman
	12	13	9	12	CH Tell Brak
	?		grey brick stratum		TW Eye Temple
			5/ 4?		Tell Zaġan
					Tell Hasseke
					Ziyāde
					Mullā Maṭar
					Tell Mašnaqa
					Umm Qseir
					Habuba Kabira-Süd
					Tell Qannas
					Ǧebel Aruda
					Tell el-Hajj
					El-Kowm
					Schech Hassan
					Qraya

43

The 90' pit looking E.
Men passing up baskets

1a

331) The 90' pit looking W

1b

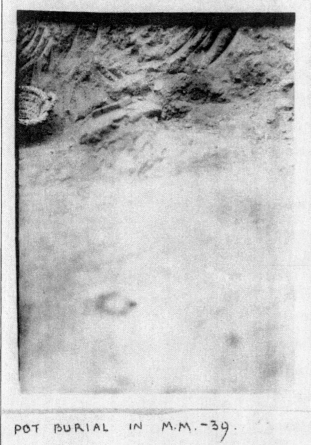

POT BURIAL IN M.M.-39.

1c

POT BURIAL SMASHED NOT LONG AFTER
IT HAS BEEN DEPOSITED BY THE WEIGHT
OF SOIL SUPERIMPOSED WITHIN IT WAS
FOUND THE SKELETON OF A GIRL(?) IN HER
TEENS AND A NUMBER OF BLACK AND
WHITE STEATITE BEADS M.M.-43

1d

S.E. END OF PIT: GROUP OF FOUR BAKED
CLAY POTS IN POSITION INCLUDING TWO
'UPTURNED' BOWLS. ASSOCIATED WITH THEM
ANIMAL BONES AND CHARKED WOOD. MM -37.

Pl. 1a, b. The Deep Sounding

Pl. 1c. Deep Sounding: burial at -39 feet

Pl. 1d. Deep Sounding: burial at -43 feet

Pl. 2a. Deep Sounding: group of pots at -37 feet

Pl. 2b. Deep Sounding: group of pottery

2a

2b

3a   3b

3c

3d

3e

Pl. 3 a. Terminal Ubaid sherds from the
Deep Sounding

Pl. 3 b-c. Painted sherds from Lower
Ninevite 3 (Gawra B phase)

Pl. 3 d. Decorated bowls and cups of
the Gawra period (Gawra B phase) with
inwardly bevelled rim; and grey ware
bowl of the Northern Uruk A phase
with inwardly bevelled rim (lower right)

Pl. 3 e. Cup of the Gawra period from
Lower Ninevite 3 (Gawra B phase)

4a

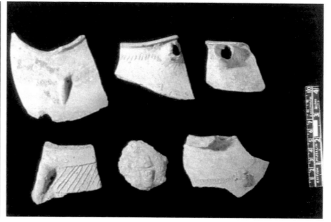

4b

4c

Pl. 4a. Burnished grey ware from Middle Ninevite 3 (Northern Uruk A phase)

Pl. 4b. Spouted and four-lugged vessels from Upper Ninevite 3 (Northern Uruk B phase)

Pl. 4c. Incised grey ware vessel from Upper Ninevite 3

4d

Pl. 4d. Combed grey ware sherds from Upper Ninevite 3

Pl. 4e. Combed, incised and impressed sherds from Upper Ninevite 3

Pl. 4f. Casseroles from Upper Ninevite 3/ Lower Ninevite 4

4f   *4e*

ILLUSTRATION SOURCES

Fig. 1: Gut 1995: fig. 5;

fig. 2: ibid., fig. 25;

fig. 3: letter by R. Campbell Thompson to Sir Charles Hyde (Birmingham City Museum);

fig. 4: Thompson, Mallowan 1933: pl. 73;

fig. 5: Gut 1995: Tab. 5b;

fig. 6: Thompson, Mallowan 1933: pl. 50;

fig. 7: ibid., pl. 49;

fig. 8.1: Thompson, Mallowan 1933: pl. 43.24 = Gut 1995: no. 785;

fig. 8.2-3: Tobler 1950: nos. 262, 278;

fig. 8.4: Speiser 1935: no. 18;

fig. 8.5-8: Tobler 1950: nos. 275, 243, 311, 308;

fig. 8.9: Thompson, Mallowan 1933: pl. 43.20 = Gut 1995: no. 787;

fig. 8.10: Tobler 1950: no. 247;

fig. 8.11: Thompson, Mallowan 1933: pl. 43.5 = Gut 1995: no. 789;

fig. 8.12: Thompson, Mallowan 1933: pl. 45.15 = Gut 1995: no. 788;

fig. 8.13: Tobler 1950: no. 238;

fig. 9.1: Thompson, Mallowan 1933: pl. 45.19 = Gut 1995: no. 795;

fig. 9.2: Gut 1995: no. 797;

fig. 9.3-4: Tobler 1950: nos. 524, 398;

fig. 10: ibid., pl. 2;

fig. 11.1-7: Gut 1995: nos. S 255-259, S 328-329;

fig. 11.8: ibid., no. 810;

fig. 11.9-13: ibid., nos. 800, 802, 801, 807, 804;

fig. 11.14-15: Tobler 1950: nos. 375, 383;

fig. 11.16: Speiser 1935: no. 5;

fig. 11.17-20: Gut 1995: nos. S 250-253;

fig. 11.21-23: Tobler 1950: nos. 371, 370, 367;

fig. 12.1: Gut 1995: no. 825;

fig. 12.2-3: ibid., nos. 827, 826;

fig. 12.4-8: ibid., nos. 822-824, 1480-1481;

fig. 12.9-12: Gut 1996: fig. 1 g, i, o, n;

fig. 12.13-25: Gut 1995: nos. S 312-S 322, S 324, S 449;

fig. 12.26-44: Hijara 1973: pl. 20.2-20;

fig. 12.45-49: Gut 1995: nos. 1482-1486;

fig. 12.50-54: Hijara 1973: pl. 21.17-21;

fig. 13.1-4: Gut 1995: nos. 817, 813, 816, 820;

fig. 13.5: ibid., no. 839 = Thompson, Mallowan 1933: pl. 51.11;

fig. 13.6-15: Tobler 1950: 386-388, 390, 519, 514-515, 517-518, 520;

fig. 13.16: Oguchi 1987: fig. 14 = Fujii, Oguchi 1987: fig. 112;

fig. 13.17: Bielinski 1987: fig. 5;

fig. 14: Gut 1995: Tab. 21;

fig. 15.1-10: Gut 1995: nos. 848, 853-862;

fig. 15.11: Thompson, Mallowan 1933: pl. 51.12;

fig. 15.12: Thompson, Mallowan 1933: pl. 51.13 = Gut 1995: no. S 436 = ibid., no. 840;

fig. 15.13: ibid., no. 811;

fig. 16.1-15: ibid., nos. 892-893, 871, 886, 885, 889, 887, 863, 866-867, 869, 872-874, 879;

fig. 17.1-4: ibid., nos. 881-884;

fig. 17.5-8: Thompson, Hamilton 1932: pl. 61.26, 8, 27, 20;

fig. 17.9: Gut 1995: no. 916;

fig. 17.10-15: Thompson, Hamilton 1932: pl. 61.1, 16, 18, 29, pl. 53.15, pl. 55.9;

fig. 18: Gut 1995: Tab. 29;

fig. 19: Gut 1996: Tab. 1;

fig. 20-21: Gut 1995: Tab. 25, Tab. 27.

Pl. 1 a, b: Gut 1995: pl. 138 c, d;

pl. 1 c: ibid., pl. 139 d;

pl. 1 d: ibid., pl. 139 f;

pl. 2 a: ibid., pl. 139 e;

pl. 2 b: ibid., pl. 140 b;

pl. 3 a: ibid., nos. 787-789, 785;

pl. 3 b: ibid., no. 795;

pl. 3 c: ibid., nos. 793, 792, 794, 799, 798, 797, 796;

pl. 3 d: ibid., nos. 806, 804, 803, 809, 802, 811;

pl. 3 e: ibid., no. 820;

pl. 4 a: ibid., nos. 856, 861, 852, 860, 851, 849, 862, 855, 854;

pl. 4 b: ibid., nos. 887, 892, 893, 886, 889, 885;

pl. 4 c: ibid., no. 863;

pl. 4 d: ibid., nos. 869, 870, 866, 867, 868;

pl. 4 e: ibid., nos. 879, 871, 872, 874;

pl. 4 f: ibid., nos. 882, 884, 883, 881.

Photographs by courtesy of the Trustees of the British Museum.

TEPE GAWRA: CHRONOLOGY AND SOCIO-ECONOMIC CHANGE IN THE FOOTHILLS OF NORTHERN IRAQ IN THE ERA OF STATE FORMATION

Mitchell S. Rothman

INTRODUCTION

The period from the end of the fifth millennium B.C. to the end of the fourth millennium, the 'Uruk' in southern Mesopotamia and 'Late Chalcolithic' in northern and eastern Mesopotamia, is of interest for three inter-related reasons. First, states — these are societies with a high degree of social, political, and economic complexity -- evolved in the alluvial south of the region (see Wright 1994, 1977, Johnson 1973, Rothman 1994a, Stein 1994). At the same time societies in almost every part of the region increased in the elaboration of their political control mechanisms, in the expansion of economic specialization, and in general, in the heterogeneity of their social structures (see Stein 1998). Second, as part of this increasing complexity, cities — by this I mean truly urban systems, not merely sites with large agglomerations of people (Blanton 1976) — evolved. Third, the level of interaction between societies in *all* parts of the region increased dramatically. Not only was contact increased South-to-North, but also East-West in the Late Chalcolithic world. As Gordon Childe has written (1974), this was surely a revolutionary period.

Of the three reasons, the third, increased interaction, is by far the most controversial and is largely the subject of debate in this volume and elsewhere (Rothman, ed., in press and 1989, Algaze 1989, 1993, Stein 1990, Rothman 1993). However, this fourth millennium period is hardly the first time such interaction had occurred among parts of the Greater Mesopotamian region. In the preceding 'Ubaid Period large areas of northern, southern, eastern, and western Mesopotamia shared stylistic similarities in artifacts and probably deeper currents of cultural thought and action (Algaze 1993, J. Oates 1993, see Henrickson and Thuesen 1989, Hole 1983). In spite of talk of an 'Uruk Collapse,' interaction certainly did not stop at the beginning of the third millennium B.C. The quantities of metal goods found in Early Dynastic and Proto-Elamite sites in the South certainly indicate that an active exchange system continued to function.

The big questions that remain for us to discuss, research, and interpret are the following:

1. Over what period of time did these interactions increase?
2. What is the nature of the increased interaction? Is a higher level of cultural interaction based on exchange? Is it based on migration? Is it based on colonization in the sense of the Greek colonies, where people from a common homeland move into a new and to them foreign territory (Schwartz 1988b), or colonization in the sense of empire with cultural and economic domination of one society over another?
3. How did these interactions, whatever they are, affect the speed and direction of evolution in *each* of the societies involved?

Clearly, these are rather big questions, which no one project, nor even the sum of current excavations and surveys, can completely answer. In continuing our discussion of these questions, I start in my own analysis here with a number of assumptions. First, the processes we are discussing evolved over a long period of time. As Henry Wright often points out, the period we are discussing for ancient Mesopotamia is about the length of time between William the Conqueror and today in English history. Second, I assume that the different sub-regions within Mesopotamia experienced different kinds and degrees of interaction and evolved differing reactions to those contacts over this tremendously long span of time. These contacts also occurred over an ecologically diverse and geographically extensive area. Third, I assume that the reactions, that is, adaptations are always local (Rothman 2000). In other words, pre-existing, local conditions, to some degree, explain how interaction was received and how it affected local societies. Even if the interactions between any two sets of societies were the same initially, the results that we as archaeologists can see may be very different. No simple formula can predict the same local results if the same outside influence, even imperial rule, is applied. The contrast of British colonial rule in India, Africa, and the Middle East validate this argument. Therefore, even if, for example, Southern stylistic elements appear in a number of different places, the explanation for what that means socially, economically, and politically may be quite different.

TEPE GAWRA

For my part I will discuss one small, seemingly odd, yet very important site in the piedmont zone of northeastern Mesopotamia. Tepe Gawra remains important despite the

Fig. 1. Hajji Firuz Tepe, Iran, Pisdeli Period (left). Tepe Gawra Phase XI Seal 7-114 (right).

fact that the site's excavation was completed over 60 years ago. It is important, because a largely unbroken sequence of superimposed towns ranging from approximately 4300 to 3700 B.C. was recovered. It is also significant, because the excavators were able to open large horizontal exposures of the site; for levels VIII, IX and X they excavated the entire town (Speiser 1935, Tobler 1950, Rothman 1988, in press a). We can therefore speak of the whole range of functions that are archaeologically attested for the site.

Gawra sits in the northeast corner of modern Iraq, 30 kilometers north and east of the Tigris at Mosul/Nineveh. Although sterile soil has never been reached, it probably was first occupied in the Neolithic. The site has a propitious location in a rainfall agricultural zone by a perennial spring and sits at the intersection of a number of ecological zones. Hunting must have been quite good, as was access to arable land and pasture in the immediate area. Gawra is also located along a critical pass through the Jebel Maqlub into the highlands of Western Iran. Similarities between Gawra and northwestern Iranian sites like Geoy Tepe and Pisdeli period sites south of Lake Urmia are illustrated by the amazing commonality of pottery and seal designs of the early fourth millennium B.C. (Fig. 1). This commonality may be

B.C.		North Syria			Upper Euphrates			Tigris		Southern Mesopotamia
3,000						Arslantepe		Mohammad	Nineveh	
	LC5	Habuba K	Sheikh	Brak	Hassek	VIA		Arab	(Gut)	Late Uruk
		Jebel Aruda	Hassan 4	TW 12				Late Uruk	Späturuk	
									Ninevite 4	
						↑				
						Arslantepe			L: 31-20	
3,400			Sheikh	Brak		VII	Hacinebi		Norduruk	Late
	LC 4	↑	Hassan	TW			B2	Tepe Gawra	B	Middle
			5-7	13	Leilan			hiatus	L: 37-31	Uruk
					IV		Hacinebi			
3,600		Qraya					B1	Tepe Gawra	Norduruk	Early
			Sheikh	Brak				VIII	A	Middle
	LC 3	↕	Hassan	TW					L: 45-37	Uruk
			8-10/13	14-17	Leilan			Tepe Gawra		
3800					V			IX-X	Gawra	
		Hammam et							B	
		Turkman					Hacinebi	Tepe Gawra		
		VB		Brak			A	XI/XA	L: 59-45	Early
4000	LC 2			TW	hiatus?					Uruk
				18-19					Gawra A	
4200		Hammam et						Tepe Gawra		
		Turkman				Arslantepe		XIA/B	hiatus?	
	LC 1	VA				VIII		Tepe Gawra		Post 'Ubaid
		Hammam et			Leilan			XII	L: 60	
	Pre	Turkman		. .	late			Tepe Gawra		End 'Ubaid
	LC	IVD			VIb			XIIA/XIII		

Table 1. SAR Chronological Framework (partial). Copyright: Algaze, D'Altroy, Frangipane, Nissen, Pittman, Pollock, Rothman, Schwartz, Stein, and Wright.

related to exchanges between northern Iran and Mesopotamia. Herrmann (1968) asserts that Gawra played a major role in exchanges of lapis lazuli and other materials, which were transported over the Iranian Plateau from Afghanistan early in the fourth millennium B.C. Stylistic connections also exist with sites in the Jazira, the Khabur triangle, and in an arc across the Turkish highlands toward Norşuntepe.

The levels of Gawra that are relevant here are levels XII, the two phases of level XIAB, two phases of level XI/XA, level X, level IX, level VIII (C, B, A). As I will explain below, after redoing the architectural stratigraphy of these levels, it became clear that an earlier phase than is illustrated in Tobler for XIA (1950: plate VI) existed, and the plans of XII and XIA are conflated. Also, as Forest proposed (1983), Charles Bache's notes indicate, and my stratigraphic analysis demonstrates, phases XA and XI shared a number of large buildings on the edges of the mound, and are not completely separate architectural levels. In addition, a conflation of separate levels XIIA and XII has created some confusion in the analysis of the LC1 period at Tepe Gawra. The chronological span of these levels currently appears to be 4,300 to 3,700 B.C., calibrated.

The area around Tepe Gawra has never had a modern survey, but there are contemporaneous sites of similar small size within Gawra's area. Many of these sites probably fell within Gawra's orbit, as I will discuss below (see Fig. 2).

CHRONOLOGY

As I have already said, one of the first issues we must address before we can explain the nature and effects of intra-regional interaction is that of time. Although the necessity of doing this seems obvious, we have been trying to come to grips with the chronology of this region for some time, and we still have more research to do before resolving it to most scholars' satisfaction. What is striking to me, however, is that there is more agreement on the general outline of the chronology than most people will admit.

The problem is often related to terminology or too great a focus on one site as the chronological yardstick for the entire region. What, for example, is 'Late Uruk' or 'Northern Middle Uruk' in absolute terms. If one chooses a particular site to be the basis of a regional or even sub-regional chronology, which one would it be? What criteria could one use? If the criterion were the quality of stratigraphic recovery or sampling, few sites would qualify. In spite of the excellent work of Gut (1995), Mallowan and other excavators clearly did not collect their material with the same care as modern excavators do. Mallowan himself admits (1933)[1] that he did not excavate the site using modern stratigraphic techniques, and let the pottery dictate the naming (i.e. the stratigraphy) of chronological horizons. Even if he had followed modern archaeological methodology, he clearly did not

save a representative sample of all strata. As Gut pointed out at Manchester, Ninevite V painted pottery is represented by a much, much larger collection than is the less 'pretty' plainware pottery of the fourth millennium. The same is true of Gawra[2] and of Uruk/Warka. If the criterion were representativeness of the region, again few sites would qualify. Sub-regional variation makes it difficult to relate one sub-region precisely with the next (Lupton 1996; Rova in press). Neither Gawra, Nineveh, Kurban Höyük, Leilan, nor Hacinebi are so inclusive that they can be related to all other sites. The one possible exception is Tell Brak, whose TW excavations are very promising, but it is a small excavation area in a huge site. The sample from TW may therefore be somewhat unrepresentative, even of Brak. In general, focusing too much on one site can lead to a scheme that does not work for other sites. The otherwise thoughtful analysis of Trufelli (1997) suffers from this problem, because of the long Arslantepe VII period. He necessarily conflates time according to that site's stratigraphy (see Table II).

The framework that I will use here to analyse the chronology of Gawra is one developed by a group who met in Santa Fe two years ago (Rothman, ed. in press). In building that chronology we thought it is a mistake to base chronological schemes on any single site. At the School of American Research we built a skeleton for our chronology on the one currently available absolute dating method, radiocarbon analysis (Wright and Rupley in press) and modified it according to artifact style comparisons. We also sought a nomenclature that was purely chronological. This avoids the confusion between the 'Uruk' period and the 'Uruk' culture. We evolved a framework using LC1-5. We chose LC (Late Chalcolithic) as a recognizable, and yet purely chronological term.

As Gut (1995) writes, it is possible to refine these categories even further. Gut and I, for example, feel LC2 can be split into early and later sub-phases for the Jazira and piedmont of modern northeastern Iraq (her Gawra A and B). However, it was our determination in Santa Fe to construct a truly regional chronology in order to discuss the very intra-regional interactions that are at the heart of the 'Uruk Phenomenon.' My personal preference would be to follow our Classical archaeology colleagues and construct a purely chronological scheme; e.g., 7th century B.C. for the Phrygians, or in our case 4300-4100 B.C. for LC1 or 3300-3000 B.C. for LC5, but few of my colleagues agree with this idea.

Whatever scheme we use, however, if one compares the School of American Research scheme to Gut's (1995) recent analysis for Northern Mesopotamia alone, one finds amazing overlap. LC1 is in effect her Spät 'Obeid, LC2 her Gawra A and B, LC3 her Uruk A, LC4 her Uruk B (and C?) and LC5 her Uruk C, that is, Spät Uruk and Enduruk, although I think her examples for Uruk C all are at the very end of the Late Uruk Period or even the beginning of Ninevite V/ Early Bronze 1, as

	Schwartz in press	Oates Brak	Truffeli 1997	Umm Qseir	Rova	Gawra Rothman	Gut 1995
LC 5 *Late Uruk*	tall bottles w/ droop spouts, tablets continuation of Classic Uruk types	*Late Uruk* TW 11-12 Habuba material Uruk VI/V	*Late Chalcolithic III Late phase* Continuity of chaff faced wares Increase in grit tempered wares Many southern Uruk types.			*Late Uruk* Mixed with Ninevite V, Gawra VIII sub-VI/ VII	*Uruk C* Fine mineral wares,4 lug jars; Conical cups; Early reserved slip, etc.
LC 4 *Late Middle Uruk*	thin walled conical cups with pour rims, carinated bowls with spouted rims incised 4 lug jars w/red slip and applique pellets .tall necked jars with everted ledge or bead rims.	*Middle Uruk* TW 13 Local Chalcolithic wares like Sheikh Hassan Qraya, etc.	*Late Chalcolithic II Middle phase* Wheel made open jars & bowls elaborated necks on jars large jars coarse flint scraped bowls Fine chaff			hiatus	*Uruk B* End Uruk gray ware Earliest reserve slip Fast wheel or hand-made Incised x-hatched, spouted bowls
LC 3 *Early Middle Uruk*	Chaff-faced wares: casseroles hammer head bowl corrugated rim jars first Bevel rim bowls Late Amuq F	*Northern Middle Uruk* TW 14-17 Fine and chaff local Chalcolithic [Gawra VIII?]	tempered w/ red orange slip.	*LC III* carinated bowl hammer rim platter casserole corrugated rim jar	*LC Phase 2* Chaff-faced wares: casseroles hammer head bowl Beveled rim bowls	*Middle Uruk* VIII-IX Wheel-made green gray ware Earliest cylinder seals Flat base jars In-curved bowls slightly flare rim to bead rim casserole	*Uruk A* Unpainted, fast wheel made ; Beveled rim bowl Nin 3 grayware Vessels with thickened flat rims Globular jars
LC 2 *Early Uruk* late .... early	chaff faced wares Coba bowls angle neck jars hole mouth bowls stamped applique incised blob paint channel rim ** bowls	*Northern Early Uruk* TW 18- Gawra XIA-IX Large quantity in CH	*Late Chalcolithic I Early phase* Ubaid-like painted types. Earliest gray ware, slipped & burnished. Chaff-tempered wares w/ flint scraping slow wheel	*Late Chalcolithic I I* stamped incised applique carinated beaker inner ledge rim bowl channel rim blob paint	*LC Phase 1* Wide flower pots double mouthed jars channel rim bowls stamped applique incised blob paint x-cross painted triangles carinated beaker red burnished, beaker/tumblers,	*Early Uruk* XA-IX Smooth Wide flower pots double mouthed jars channel rim bowls blob paint x-cross painted triangles (late sprig wares) carinated beakers 3 line paint cup XIAB-XA cannon spouts, stamped applique incised vessels; tumblers; gray ware; hole mouth; coarse WFP *; channel rim ** bowls; bow tie paint	*Gawra A/B* All: WFP* Channel rim** *Gawra B* Inner ledge bowls Globular jars Blob paint Short neck jar w/ paint Beakers w/paint Fugitive red paint and x-cross triangles *Gawra A* Double mouth pot; large hole mouth pots; Impressed ware tumblers
LC 1 *Post Ubaid*	painted black on red ware, sprig ware Coba bowls	*Post or Terminal Ubaid* Sprigware Sealing wax ware Gawra XII CH in Eye Temple area		*LCI* Coba bowl (sic) sprig ware u shaped pots hole mouth panel pattern (sic)	*Late-Final Ubaid* Coba bowls	*Transitional Ubaid/Uruk* XII sprig ware stands extended base coarse chaff bowls	*Terminal Ubaid* Sprig ware Jars w/ painted bands; U-shaped jars; ring based jars; early double mouth pots
Ubaid 4		*Late Ubaid* CH 18/19-22	*Late Ubaid*	*Coba* bowl *panel pattern*		**Late Ubaid** XIIA/XIII painted bowls, broad lines, triangles closed bowl, internal ledge painted beakers U shaped bowls	

Table II. Various Chronological Schemes for Northern Mesopotamia.

Rova (in press) also argues. We as archaeologists have gotten ourselves so confused by the plethora of new terms and by wishing to force everything into the old terminology that we fail to see even where we agree.

As a way to understand the commonalities of the various schemes, Table II lists the various modern analyses with the ceramic markers for each period. The various schemes highlight the chronologies of the North along the Euphrates, in the Khabur, and in the piedmont toward the East.

As far as Gawra is concerned, I think Gut is right for the most part. Gawra began its 'fourth millennium' B.C. history with Level XII at about 43-4200 BC calibrated and ended when VIIIA burned or was burned *before* Ninevite IV. Gawra was surely in some kind of hiatus long before Habuba Kabira, Jebel Aruda, Arslantepe VIA, Tell Brak TW12, and Godin V were at their height between about 3300-3050 B.C.

As anyone who has read my earlier analyses will note (Rothman 1988, 1993), this represents a change in my assessment of the Gawra chronology. I have had (and

to some degree continue to have) problems with Gawra VIII. In earlier analyses I started with the axiom that there is no major stratigraphic hiatus from XII to VIIIA. I still believe this is true, based on a new stratigraphic analysis I made of the site (Rothman 1988, in press a). Some of the wares from VIII — there are many more than Gut acknowledges — would seem to have parallels with eggshell wares and other types that appear quite late in the millennium, and at the same time there are wares that are very consistent with a much earlier date. It is this confusion that causes Trufelli in a new analysis (1997: 26, Table I) to push XIA-X back in time from earlier assessments and yet place Gawra VIIIA parallel in time to Arslantepe VIA, post Ninevite IV, Tell Brak TW 11-10, which I have always argued is impossibly late. In order to explain this seeming discrepancy in the past, I argued for the stylistic conservatism of Gawra's residents (Rothman 1993). In other technologies, such as metallurgy, this conservatism seems clear (V. Pigott, personal communication). However, the lengthening of the Uruk Period and the much earlier appearance of wheel-made pottery and

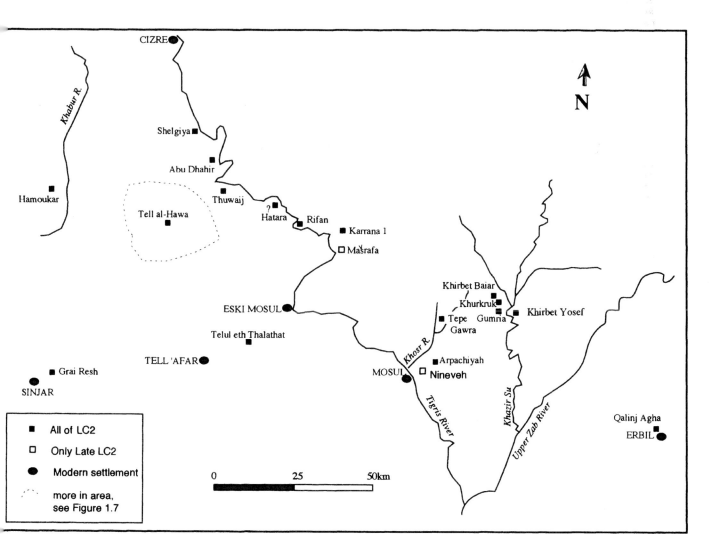

Fig. 2. LC 2, Early Uruk Period.

beveled rim bowls in the North may permit me to overcome this seeming discrepancy and put Gawra XII-VIIIA in a time frame which takes account of its continuous occupation and stylistic parallels.

Gawra XIIA and XII, LC1; Late and Terminal Ubaid
Much of the difficulty of dating the earliest phase discussed here is a conflation of two distinct levels, XIIA, which is a continuation of the 'Ubaid 4 period level XIII, and XII, in which the first signs of the transition to the distinctive pottery of the fourth millennium began. XII fits within the LC1, Terminal 'Ubaid, or even Early Uruk Period. XIIA and XII are clearly distinctive in stratigraphic terms (see Fig. 3).

Figure 3 is what I call a schematic section. It is a ten meter wide section running east and west about in the middle of the north-south axis of the mound. There were no such sections drawn. With the help of some little paper 'chits' and original pencil architectural plans I have drawn these sections, revised the site plans published by Speiser (1935) and Tobler (1950), and built my own chronology. We must remember that Speiser, although one of the great philologists of his day, was not a trained archaeologist,[1] and Tobler was the site photographer for the Speiser seasons when only VIII, a bit of IX, and small pieces of earlier fourth millennium B.C. levels were excavated. Our 'hero' is Charles Bache, who supervised

the third, fourth, fifth and seventh seasons. His so-called chits were notes taken on 5,000 artifacts, assigning them to a precise three-dimensional location, often with clues as to the nature of the fill in which they were buried. Using chits and original notes from Mueller, the architect on site (but not the draftsman of the final published plans), I constructed schematic sections by drawing an imaginary line through the square and placing any buildings cut by this line in their stratigraphic place.

As you can see from the schematic section from squares 3M to 7M (Fig. 3), after XIII a few architectural remains of a level XIIA remain near the site's edges (see Tobler 1950, plate X). Again, these are distinct architectural levels. In the following Table III the illustrated pots from Tobler's volume are divided into those from XII, those in graves, and those from XIIA.

In stylistic terms this means that the pottery of XIIA is mostly painted, but the ceramics of XII have many fewer painted forms than XIIA and XIII. A typical painted pot of XIIA (Fig. 4, i) has good parallels with Hammam et Turkman IVD (Fig. 4, h), which its excavator places in the last Ubaid period (Akkermans 1988). As with Mallowan, 85 percent of the level XII sherds Gawra excavators saved are painted. Of whole pots, however, 88 percent (n=89) are unpainted and 12 percent (n= 12) were painted (Rothman in press a: artifact catalogue). This trend toward plain pottery is thought of as typical of the

Level		XIIA		Grave	Below	XII		Level	XII
Tobler Plate#	Field Number	Tobler Plate #	Field Number			Tobler Plate #	Field Number	Tobler Plate #	Field Number
235	6-244	270	5-1745	238	6-291	287	6-270	237	4-1140
236	6-282	273	6-332 g	248	6-251	288	6-235	240	5-1740
239	5-1682	276	6-286	249	6-456	290	5-1754	242	5-1663
241	5-1709	281	5-1757	250	6-35	291	6-54	243	6-589
246	6-36	283	4-1231	257	6-306	292	6-255	244	6-213
247	6-314	289	6-499	259	6-253	296	6-38	245	5-1388
252	7-272	293	5-1693	262	6-259	297	6-252	251	5-1144
253	6-311	313	6-355	264	6-268	298	5-1611	258	6-120
254	no #	314	5-1660	268	6-327	299	5-1761	260	4-713
255	6-316	317	6-307	269	5-1584	300	6-338	261	5-1241
256	6-316	318	6-601	274	5-1752	301	6-322	267	5-1618
263	6-277	319	6-72	275	5-1572	302	6-121	271	5-1758
265	6-591	320	4-1230	277	5-1718	303	5-1569	272	5-1568
266	6-283	322	6-310	278	6-269	304	5-1763	294	6-594
		323	6-245	279	6-261	305	6-336	295	6-618
		325	5-1665	280	6-339	306	6-254	307	4-1145
		326	6-392	282	5-1685	308	6-279	310	6-201
				284	5-1686	309	6-155	311	6-588
				285	6-138	315	5-1723	312	5-1623
				286	5-1728	316	5-1553	321	5-1523
								327	5-1436

Table III. Assignment of XII and XIIA pots from Tobler to provenience.

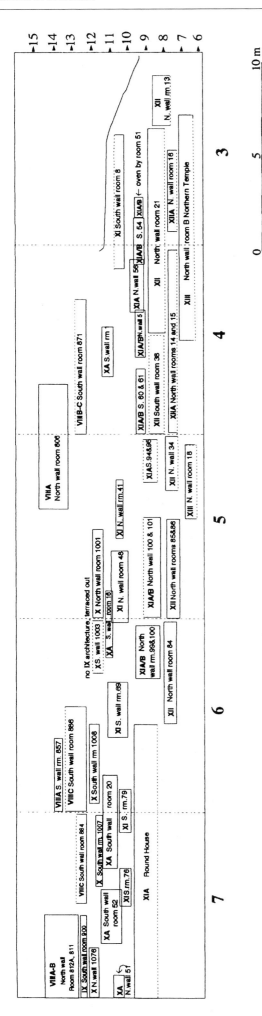

Fig. 3. Tepe Gawra, Schematic Section (partial) M squares.

Late Chalcolithic Period and its Southern parallel, the early Uruk Period. The one exception is so-called sprig ware (Fig. 4, n, o, p)[4] and the first appearance of cross-hatched triangles under the rim or neck (Fig. 4, j, l), which remains common across the North for another 5 or 600 years (e.g., Leilan V (Schwartz 1988b, figure 61, 12)). This same design continued into LC 2/3 (Fig. 6, g, h, q; Fig. 8, a, f; Fig. 9, p) and into LC5 or classic Uruk as an incised design.

A chronologically sensitive type, the so-called Coba bowls, provide a way of distinguishing some of these earlier phases from later ones. Confusion of terminology — what fits into the category of Coba bowls and in another category of coarse chaff-faced wares, Wide Flower pots — obscures the distinction.[5] From Gawra and elsewhere I see four distinct types. The 'true' Coba bowl is a high-sided flint-scraped bowl of the Late Ubaid or Terminal Ubaid. It is found in the Euphrates Basin at sites like Değirmentepe and Hammam et Turkman IVD, but, as Rova (in press) notes, not in the East. Mellaart (1981: Fig. 202) correctly places Coba bowls at the Ubaid/ 'Uruk' (LC1) boundary. However, there are at Gawra three varieties of these open, chaff tempered, flint-scraped crude bowls, which are chronologically sensitive. The first is an extended base variety, which ends after Gawra XII (Fig. 4, c, d, e, and f). Clear parallels are found to Norşuntepe J/K 17 and Leilan VIb (Schwartz 1988: figure 65, 4). These are, in effect, the eastern versions of the Coba bowl. The second variety is the Wide Flower Pot. These, too, are very crudely made, chaff-tempered bowls, in ware much like beveled rim bowls, but not in their shape. They flare more than the earlier deep based varieties. This third type appears earliest in XII (Fig. 4, g) and continues at Gawra through level XA (Figs. 6, n; 8, j), in other words, early LC2. The final variety in shape is identical to the previous forms (Wide Flower Pots), but is made with less chaff, and is smoothed, perhaps turned on a tournette (Fig. 9, n and o). This fourth type is typical of Gawra IX and VIII. Wide Flower Pots appear also at Umm Qseir Late Chalcolithic II, Telul eth Thalathat VIIIa, Musharifa in the Eski Mosul area, in Arslantepe VII (Fig. 6, k, l, m, and j respectively), as well as at Brak and other sites. The description of the Umm Qseir Flower Pot appears to link it chronologically to the latest Wide Flower Pots, although I do not know the precise characteristics of the others illustrated.

Other types that appear in Level XII at Gawra are included among the types in Table II. For example, ring base jars (see Fig. 4, q) from Gut (1995: 291), stands or braziers from Gawra and Norşuntepe J/K 17 (Fig. 4, r, s), etc. U-shaped pots are found only in graves at Gawra, but can be associated with Tepe Gawra XII and this temporal phase, as Gut proposes (1995:291).

Other categories of artifacts appear for the first time in XII: hut statues and typical LC2 appliqué rosettes and a slab-constructed, 'bubbled' — I believe these are what Oates calls 'wax' — ware. In seal design, XII fits a LC1 date (Pittman in press), although von Wickede (1990:159) had some trouble drawing a typical XII seal style, because he sees elements of XIII and also XIA[B] styles mixed within it.

Gawra XIAB to IX, LC2, Early Uruk, Gawra A/B.
The levels of LC2, Gut's Gawra A/B, or Early Uruk are fairly uncontroversial chronologically. For Gawra, this phase encompasses levels XIAB, XI/XA, X, and much if not all of IX. As I mentioned above, both Gut and I see early and late (Gawra A and B) LC2 phases. These phases run from about 4100-4050 B.C. and 4050-3800 B.C.

The most distinctive wares of Gawra A or early LC2 are the impressed and appliqué wares, either comb impression, rosettes, or triangles (Fig. 5, a-l). Wares on which these designs are impressed include those with the slab made, creamy white-gray wares (Fig. 5, a and h), orange, gritty wares, reddish gray wares, almost all with high grit, sand, or lime tempering.

Other wares show some continuity from level XII. Some ring base jars continue (e.g. Fig. 5, o; Fig. 6, g), mostly painted ones. Also, excavators found wide flaring neck jars (Fig. 4, m; Fig. 5, s and t).

Other types from this early LC2 period include short, angle necked jars (Fig. 5, p, q, r), hole mouth jars (Fig. 6, a, b, c), channel or double rim vessels (Fig. 6, d, e, f, i), tumblers and beakers (Fig. 6, o, p, q, r; Fig. 8, b, c). Double mouthed jars, which first appeared in Gawra XII with the mouths very close together and flared out like an example from Brak (Fig. 7, e), are also a marker of LC2 (Fig. 7, f, g; also three mouth version in Fig. 9, s). A motif of black painted bow ties is associated with this period (Fig. 6, r, s; also see Schwartz 1988b: Fig. 61, 8 of the Leilan V period). A rarely mentioned, but clear marker of early LC2 are rounded bowls with spouts that look like cannons (Fig. 5, m, n; and Leilan V, Schwartz 1988b: Fig. 61, 6). These spouted bowls are at times painted or burnished, and tend to be grit rather than chaff tempered. Another small, beaded rim, straight spouted bowl with thick reddish slip is found late in the early LC2 at Gawra and at Tell Brak in the CH 13-14 provenience (Fig. 7, a, b). Some unique elements of this earlier phase, such as a large incense burner from phase XI of level XI/XA should find parallels at some point (Fig. 7, k). Taken together these early LC2 types are the ones cited by Gut (1995: 291) and Tomita (1998: Fig. 84).

Perhaps the only real controversy of the early LC2 for Tepe Gawra is more a stratigraphic than a purely chronological one. Forest (1983) proposes that the Round House of XIA was built very early in his Restitution 1. Many of the other building blocks from Tobler's XIA plan were part of level XI and then XA. The schematic sections show this (Fig. 3 to some degree shows this, although the section from K is clearer (Rothman in press a: Fig. 5)). What Forest saw are not problems at all. In fact, the Round House was built late, not early, in XIA/B and there was an earlier phase of this level, which I call XIB, before the Round House was built.

The later, Gawra B phase of LC2 is marked by a continuation of some older forms, but also a variety of new ones. A series of bowls and small jars are notable for paint design of two or three blobs of dark paint off the edge (Fig. 7, l, m, o, p, q, r, s, t; Fig. 9, r.). The distribution of this type is quite wide in the eastern steppe and in the hilly country of modern southeastern Turkey. Its earliest appearance at Tepe Gawra is in phase XA of Level XI/XA, and it is not seen again after Level IX. Carinated cups (Fig. 8, a, g, h, n, o) are also common. Some of these are tournette made, but others, especially the pointed cups of Gawra X and IX appear fast wheel thrown. Small jars with potter's marks are also found (Fig. 7, i, j). In general the tempering and surface treatment of the 'local wares' of Arslantepe VII are quite different certainly from those of Gawra, but the shapes are very reminiscent (see Frangipane 1993: figures 9 and 10). Globular jars (Fig. 8, l), which Gut (1995:291) cites as a marker of her Gawra B period, are common (Fig. 8, l; fig 9, a-d, q). Levels X and IX are marked by a sprig motif, slightly different than the earlier, XII style, usually with a single sprig rising between crosshatched triangles (Fig. 8, a, d, f). Similar wares are found at Nineveh and Norşuntepe. More parallels are also evident with sites like Grai Resh (Fig. 9, j, k).

LC 2/3, Uruk A, Early Middle Uruk.
Chronologically, this leaves some of IX, but mostly Gawra VIII and its three phases VIIIC, B, and A. I agree with Gut and my earlier assessment that VIII is a continuation of IX in many ways, but not completely. I would not, nor ever have, put VIII as late as Arslantepe VI A (Trufelli 1997). Because of the inexperience of Speiser as an excavator and because of early problems with registration, this critical level is very problematic. In the past I have assigned these three phases to the Middle Uruk, just peeking into the Late Uruk (Rothman 1988, 1993). Of course, at the time we all saw the beveled rim bowl as a marker of the Late Uruk period and the so-called Uruk Expansion. Most scholars of this period now see now see the beveled rim bowl as a marker of the early Middle Uruk Period, that is, LC3 (Schwartz, in press, Gut 1995, Rova in press, etc.). Most now see the 'Uruk Expansion' as a very slow process begun during the LC3, and proceeding through two or three quite different stages, ending with Habuba Kabira and Jebel Aruda.

The pottery of Gawra VIII certainly continues to have markers of the late LC2 or Gawra B, such as Wide Flower Pots type 3 (Fig. 9, n), jars with painted, crosshatched triangles (Fig. 9, p), and multiple mouth jars (Fig. 9, s). Starting with IX and continuing into VIII, however, many fast wheel made ceramics, mostly those classified as green-gray ware by Speiser (1935) were recovered. Other indicators of a LC3 date include a wheel-made, carinated shape parallel to a funnel from

Brak TW 16 in Gawra IX (Fig. 9, f, g). The bead rim bowls of Hammam et Turkman Vb, which Gut (1995: 256-59) includes in her Uruk A phase, and which Rova refers to as a possible replacement for Wide Flower Pots, are present at Gawra already in Level IX (Fig. 9, h). Gray ware vessels, another marker of the Uruk A for Gut is present at Gawra and Hammam et Turkman Vb (e.g., Fig. 9, l, m). Other wares also indicate a late LC2 or LC3 date for these levels at Tepe Gawra. They include bowls with an inner ledge (Fig. 10, h, i, j), bowls with corrugated upper surfaces (Fig. 10, a, b, c), bowls with in-flaring rims (Fig. 10, k, l), fine bowls with tapered in-turned rims (Fig. 10, m, n), large flat bottom jars (Fig. 10, o, p), and globular jars with spouts (Fig. 10, q, r). In the last form, the rim itself is less thickened than in the Nineveh samples. In addition, carinated, flaring rim cups (Fig. 10, d, e) and small carinated bowls (Fig. 10, f, g) appear to indicate early forms at Tepe Gawra that would develop into Middle Uruk forms at Nineveh and Sheikh Hassan. Another early confusion about the date of Tepe Gawra resulted from a terrace cut down from level VI of the Akkadian Period through level VII. My analysis of level VII indicates that it is in fact a series of levels largely destroyed by the terracing and leveling of the occupants of Gawra VI (Rothman in press b). Pottery from these levels is of Ninevite V date. A typical pot of this later, badly stratified period is a small carinated, high sided, wheel turned, hard-fired bowl (Fig. 10, t). Its parallels are in the terminal Uruk or Uruk/Ninevite V levels of Mohammad Arab (Fig. 10, u) or very late Norşuntepe J/K 18/19. Gawra VIII must have burned long before that period. The whole corpus of chaff-faced wares—casseroles, hammerhead bowls, corrugated rim bowls, platters, and beveled rim bowls— that typify the north-western Mesopotamian LC3 never appear at Gawra.

Seals and sealings from Gawra VIII indicate a similar date to ceramics. Pittman (in press) writes:

> In the region of the upper Tigris, there is precious little evidence for this early Middle Uruk phase ... It is, however, significant that Gawra VIII is dated to the Early Middle Uruk Period on the basis of ceramics. If this is indeed correct, there is a new composition introduced in this period which comes to be important in later Uruk glyptic that is strongly associated with the southern traditions. One of the compositions is cross-necked animals. The crossing of animal necks is common on seals from Uruk and Susa in the Late Uruk Period. It is very likely that this composition was developed in the last stages of the Ubaid stamp seal tradition seen at Gawra VIII and then borrowed by southern seal makers. Another composition that appears here for the first time is the tête bêche organization of animals.... Finally, in Gawra VIII two fragments of what may be bone cylinders drilled with random patterns may be the northern version of the baggy style cylinder.... Hacınebi Tepe level B1 produced a small but interesting collection that displays connections to Gawra VIII, to Brak and to northern Anatolian glyptic styles.

It is therefore clear that Gawrans were aware of the Southern culture, if not Southerners, during the earliest organized incursions of Southerners in the LC3.

After the early part of the LC3, Gawra was abandoned for the first time in 6-700 years. The chronology thus constructed makes sense in terms of a consistent relative dating of sites in northern, especially northeastern Mesopotamia. Our analysis began in the transitional Ubaid/Uruk, or LC1 Period at about 4300 BC and ended in the earlier LC3, later in the 3700s.

GAWRA AND THE URUK EXPANSION

This new dating of Gawra XII to VIII has serious implications for our understanding of the interaction of North and South in Mesopotamia and on the currently most often cited explanation of the 'Uruk Expansion' by Algaze (1989, 1993, in press). Algaze explains the spread of classic Uruk styled artifacts as a process of cross-cultural interaction, which begins in the LC3 and reaches its height in LC5, before collapsing at about 3,000 B.C. As became clear in the discussion in Santa Fe, this process of increasing contact happened in three general stages. The first at the beginning of the LC3 represents increased contact for the purposes of exchanging goods, especially those lacking in the South. Some merchants may have gone northward, or intermediaries may have tapped into existing trade routes, sending more goods southward than had been the case before. This initial phase is followed by a period of trading outposts founded and lived in by Southerners among Northern Late Chalcolithic populations in LC4. The 'colony' or better trading post (*karum*?) at Hacınebi may be a classic example of this second stage (Stein 1999). These outposts are semi-autonomous neighborhoods within Northern settlements. Evidence from Hacınebi indicates that the trading communities may have been made up mostly of men, who were responsible for their own up-keep (see Stein, ed. 1999). They grew their own crops using traditional Southern methods, including baked clay sickles. For those who deny the presence of actual Southerners, I would ask the following question. Why would any Northerner with easy access to high quality chipping stone and a long tradition of chipped stone sickles rely on undoubtedly inefficient clay sickles? Parenthetically, excavators also found clay sickles at Nineveh in the deep sounding at stratum 35 (Mallowan 1933: Plate LXXI). Stratum 35 is parallel in time to the Hacınebi B2 Southern community. The final stage is the development of major Southern cities in the Euphrates Basin at Habuba Kabira Süd/Tell Qannas and Jebel Aruda.

The heart of Algaze's explanation of this process can be summarized as follows (Rothman in press c):

> In my opinion, Algaze's thesis brings together three elements in trying to explain a pattern of the spread of clearly Southern Uruk artifact styles and the presence of physical Southerners in the North and East, the steppes and hilly country, of Greater Mesopotamia. The first (Algaze this volume) is that once a society of the complexity of the

state evolves in the southern alluvium, one of the core processes that is catalyzed because of the very nature of all states is geographical expansion, in this case to garner the natural resources its leaders and citizens value. In doing so, a series of networks based largely on trade developed. In generating these new networks the more administratively elaborated societies of the South generated a World System. Algaze asserts that the Southerners received raw materials, which they processed. Manufactured goods made from these raw materials certainly were distributed though Southern economic systems, and also presumably traded back to Northern and Eastern polities in some undetermined amounts. Therefore, members of Northern and Eastern societies were classic colonists in an economic sense. By sending, in modern economics terminology, non-valued added raw materials to the South and receiving value added goods manufactured in the South, development was catalyzed primarily in the South, but not in the North. This is the essential concept of Wallerstein's World Systems (Peregrine 1996: 3).

The North, according to Algaze, was therefore an underdeveloped, politically unsophisticated periphery, where Southerners from the developed core could quickly move in without force of arms and overwhelm simple economic and political systems. In my mind there are many serious theoretical and interpretive flaws in this Uruk Expansion Theory, including the assertion that the system collapsed completely. I will not repeat all those points here, as they are covered elsewhere (Rothman 1993, in press c).

What I will discuss are the developments specifically within Tepe Gawra and its sub-region in the eastern Jazira, and Iraqi piedmont (including the new work in the Eski Mosul area). I will argue that the new chronology for Gawra that I, and with slight variations Gut (1995), Rova (in press), and Tomita (1998) now propose implies an unexpectedly high level of economic and political development in the North before the increased contact of the LC3-5 periods. Some call this period Pre-Contact (e.g. Lupton 1996), but I do not as all evidence I have seen indicates long and continuous contact millennia before the LC3.

In fact, I argue that the Uruk Expansion represents an increase in economic exchange, which benefited leaders in the North and South, as well as groups of entrepreneurs and craftsmen in both areas. That is to say, this process was not one of dominance or colonialism. Clearly, increasing demand in the South for metals and high quality chipping stone to be used in tool and weapon making, and for other raw materials used in building or as markers of status impelled traders to move northward. The lack of movement southward is not a sign of underdevelopmental or political impotence. Why would Northerners with their access to rich natural resources want to migrate southward?

This increased exchange created new opportunities for expanding networks of interaction. For newly instituted leadership organizations, both in the states of the South and the increasingly complex chiefdoms of the North, this interchange offered an opportunity for gaining advantage and political security. As I wrote above, the fourth millennium B.C. was one of revolutionary changes in governance, economic structure, and ideology. The kings we see in the glyptic of Uruk/Warka and Susa were not members of long-established dynasties, nor did they rule after long traditions of state governance. The same could be said of the leaders in the North at sites like Arslantepe. Many of the older social groupings continued. Organizations like the 'city,' a council of some kind and guilds of merchants and other occupations competed with rulers (Oppenheim 1977:95-125). Leaders were therefore at risk from various groups within their own polities. They must have evolved strategies, given the limits on their authority imposed by the opposition of other groups, to benefit and maintain themselves politically and economically.

What the evidence from Gawra XII to VIII shows is a series of new strategies among the members of the community to garner influence and establish control. These strategies illustrate the complexity of economic and political systems in this part of Mesopotamia before the LC3. They also illustrate why the strategies of leadership groups would change once opportunities of increased exchange with new markets presented themselves in the early LC3.

In a recent article a group of Americanist anthropological archaeologists (Blanton, Feinman, Kowalewski, and Peregrine 1996, Blanton 1998) proposed an approach to this problem of strategy and its social consequences, which is useful here (also see Rothman and Peasnall 1999). They argued that these strategies tend to fall into two general categories: corporate and exclusionary. In the corporate strategy leaders emphasize their role in promoting the common good. The storing of foodstuffs in anticipation of a drought by the Pharaoh in Egypt in the Biblical Joseph story is an example of this. The exclusionary strategy emphasizes the amassing of wealth or political authority by 'elites', forcing them to distinguish themselves symbolically from others in their society. One of the best ways to establish an exclusionary strategy is by building a network of exchange outside of one's local polity. According to Blanton _et al_, there are two sources of authority and influence, objective — this is embodied in the control of external sources of material wealth or control of production — and knowledge-based or ideological. The control of production and storage of goods as a basis for power is evidenced at Arslantepe VI A (Frangipane 1997). In many early complex societies leaders associate themselves with the gods. The utility for fourth millennium rulers to do so is obvious. The Mesopotamian gods were considered to be providers (Jacobsen 1976: Chapter 2); in other words, they both were seen as having a corporate strategy, which is closer to a kinship model, and yet were distinct and superior to ordinary humans in authority, status, and possessions, part of an exclusionary strategy.

Gawra illustrates the evolving strategies of its residents through a series of changes before the Uruk Expansion. Because we have very large exposures of these levels, and because of Bache's chits, we can in many cases reconstruct activity areas by mapping artifacts across space and in a surprising number of cases by determining the nature of their provenience.

What I propose is the following. Before the end of the 'Ubaid Period, Gawra was more than a self-enclosed agricultural community. The temples of level XIII — they actually never stood all together but were built one after another — were clearly the focus of more than just the people living on the Gawra mound. Temples have been recovered at a series of Ubaid and LC1 and 2 period sites: Qalinj Agha (Abu al Soof 1968), Nuzi (Starr 1939), Grai Resh (Lloyd 1940). This indicates that in the sparsely occupied piedmont and eastern Jazira many small communal centers based on religious ritual had been formed.

Level XII, however, yielded no temple, although one might exist in the half of the mound not excavated.[6] This time is parallel to Susa A with its rank marking artifacts and the 'massif' presumably with temples and storehouses (Hole 1983). The remains of Gawra XII are typified by a series of parallel large, probably two-story buildings with the same layout. Each, including the largest, the so-called White Room building, has a large central room or *mittelsaal* like the traditional Anatolian *salon*. They are all multi-functional spaces with evidence of cooking, of craft and agricultural tools, and religious artifacts. A large number of burials, especially of young children and infants are found under the floors of each. This together I interpret as evidence of extended family dwellings, also found in the Late 'Ubaid at Tell Madhhur and Abada (Roaf 1984). Two elements mark Gawra XII as more than a village. There are two large buildings which appear to be grain storage facilities, each with broken sealings and a seal and each with piles of the precursor to the beveled rim bowl, the Wide Flower Pot. These ceramic forms are associated with ration systems, that is, corporate strategies. The other is a series of rooms near the entryway with an area of bins behind for sorting items, presumably craft goods, including items of imported lapis, gold, and obsidian blades found in the small storerooms. Evidence of administration, seals and sealings, is present, but it seems to be quite diffuse. A second set of strategies may have presented itself long before any Uruk Expansion proposed by a modern scholar. That strategy is the centralized storage of grain, and the production of luxury or utilitarian goods for exchange off the mound, not for subsistence. Note that many of the materials of these exchange goods came from a long distance trading network - gold, obsidian, chlorite soft stone, and lapis lazuli.

Gawra XIB and XIA seem quite similar to XII. The notable change is that grain storage moved into a different multi-function building, the Round House, toward the end of that level's occupation. The Round House along with a defensive tower and the way buildings at the edge formed a continuous wall, speaks of a violent time with competition.

Gawra XII was burned. In XII dead bodies were found in the street with stones in their backs. The Round House and a significant part of the site was also burned at the end of XIA. Clearly, the functions of Gawra in this terminal 'Ubaid (LC 1) and early LC2 periods were sufficiently specialized and noteworthy to create the competition that led to their demise. XIA/B and XII were quite similar in town plan and in functional specialization, although smaller houses appear for the first time at Gawra in XIA.

In Figure 2, a site distribution map of the LC2 period, note that Nineveh seems to have had none of the typical early LC2 wares. Gut (1995:268) wrote that this may be due to the small size of the stratigraphic trench, but she now accepts this hiatus (this volume, p.20). Without occupation at Nineveh the central role of Gawra in the time from XIA/B to XA makes some sense.

The next major step in the evolution of complexity is evidenced in phase XI of level XI/XA. A large temple was built with its entrance facing out east into the countryside and hills, not into the interior of the town. The craft activities evidenced in XII and XIA/B, including thread spinning, cloth making, stone tool knapping, wood carving, and small clay object making, continued. In Gawra XI/XA these activities become centralized. A separate wood working shop, weaving shop, and area for firing small religious objects were performed in special-function buildings or areas. A public building whose purpose seems largely administrative was also built. Houses were now small, not the multi-room extended family houses of XII, whose form seems transmogrified into the form of public buildings. What is most striking is that the distribution of seals and sealings is almost exclusively in the specialized buildings, and the topic of seals used for the temple is distinct from that of the administrative and crafts shops (Rothman 1994b).

Gawra X and IX represent a new strategy for the administrators of Gawra. If XII and XIA/B concentrated on grain storage and luxury good production, and XI/XA on craft manufacturing and religion, X and IX were focused largely on religion. The same craft activities continue to be present on the Gawra mound, but they are dispersed. The temple and a large administrative building dominate the site. Interestingly it is at this period when the clearest signs of social stratification emerge in the graves of Gawra X. Remains of administrative activity concentrate around the two main functions of the town.

This same pattern is even more emphasized in Gawra VIII. VIII was occupied after the first incursions of Southerners into the North. Leaders were clearly mobilizing labor for some purpose. In a side room of the so-called West Temple (Speiser 1935), excavation records note the remains of 'decimeters of grain' and a photograph shows a large pile of Wide Flower Pots stacked up in the same room. A new hierarchical level in administration seems to have been added represented by a central warehouse[7] and the seals which direct material from the warehouse to all the other institutions. However, added to religion to was a new production trade — obsidian blades. Large blocks or cores were imported to Gawra during level VIII, and most of the blades show no signs of use wear. Also, a centralized warehouse was built in VIIIB with manufactured goods more than foodstuffs. When one thinks of the large collection of obsidian blades in the later Riemchengebäude at Uruk/Warka, the desirability of this trade southward is evident.

It is in Gawra VIII that we see one kind of reaction to increased contact. Certainly, some symbolic reference is made to the outside world, especially in seals design (Pittman quoted above). At the same time, many of the traditional motives and traditional ways of doing things remain. I have tried to trace where the painted pottery of Gawra in LC2 and 3 is found. I am not ready to say I have the pattern clear, but it seems that this almost Ubaid style is found in primary or secondary contexts associated with temples, public buildings, or shrines. This may indicate a kind of ideological power, which references the past. These same designs re-appear in the Ninevite V period and were clearly known, remembered, and associated with the local culture.

Another indicator of reaction to contact at Gawra is the administrative system of level VIII. Remember, in XI different spheres of activity seem to be controlled by groups using different subjects. For the first time in VIII, persons using one seal, the bull, dog, and snake, seem to control goods going into the warehouse and then out to each and every other major institution. In fact, by VIIIA there are very few domiciles on the mound.

A number of years back I and James Blackman of the Smithsonian Institution attempted to measure the size of the network of exchange that Gawrans were involved with (Rothman and Blackman 1990). We ran a series of neutron activation analyses on the clay used in Gawra sealings. We also were able to get sealings from the Mallowan excavation at Nineveh and from Arpachiyah. For the time from XI/XA to IX every sealing was made from clay of amazing homogeneity, what I called Gawran clay. This clay is not from the same source as the sealings from Nineveh or Arpachiyah were. The only times when clay from sources other than Gawran clay was found

were in XII and XIA during the period of luxury good production and lapis importation, and again in VIII. This suggests that either the geographical sphere in which Gawran leaders functioned was larger or that Gawrans had come into contact with other groups, some of whom may have permitted them to develop more elaborated, hierarchical administrative structures.

Throughout this long period of time, in fits and starts, economic and administrative complexity increased. As the leadership seems to have moved toward a more exclusionary or network strategy, did they mark their distinct and superior status in public show? They did. Interments were in simple loose graves, in vessels, with a sidewall, in cists, pisé and libn brick tombs (Rothman and Peasnall 1999; Peasnall, in press). Libn tombs are the ones with the richest grave goods. As time passed, there was increasing bifurcation into the simplest and most elaborate types, and increasing child burials in elaborate tombs. In XII-XI grave goods consisted of a few pots and the odd object. The artifacts found in tomb 109, dug from level X, include 1 marble jar, 1 oolite jar, 1 alabaster bowl, 4 gold rosettes, 285 gold studs, bangles, beads and crescents, 3 gold and lapis eye ornaments, 110 electrum beads, 428 lapis beads and rings, 1 lapis seal, 2 obsidian blades, etc., etc. This certainly is impressive for this far corner of the piedmont. Clearly, high rank was being signified.

What the data from Tepe Gawra XII to VIII appear to show is an unexpectedly complex society economically and administratively before the increased contact with the South. This belies the idea that Southerners could merely take over the exchange networks of the North in LC3-5 without force of arms. Certainly, evidence from Tell al-Hawa (Ball *et al.* 1989), Samsat (Lupton 1996:73f.), and Arslantepe (Frangipane in press, 1997) suggest that the same was true after Gawra was abandoned in LC3. In fact none of these sites was abandoned in the 'Uruk Collapse' (Lupton 1996).[8] Rather, these same centers appear to grow after the so-called collapse (Lupton 1996). The evidence from Gawra VIII also seems to indicate that far from being overwhelmed by early contact, increased opportunity to exchange goods to the South increased the complexity of administration and functions at a small center like Gawra. We have a lot more to learn about this period, and we have to look at our older assumptions and theories again.

[1] Mallowan writes (1933: 129-30), "Although the general evidence presents us with a coherent and orderly series, we cannot lay claim to establishing precise lines of demarcation between the levels — there was an unfortunate absence of well-defined building levels."

[2] It is an irony of early attempts at finer field recording that I can tell you the precise location of close to four hundred baskets of pottery recovered from the site, but have no idea what was in any of the baskets.

[3] According to a letter I received from Cyrus Gordon, part of the Gawra team, Speiser had a tendency to illness, and was rarely on the site during excavation (Rothman 1988: 45).

[4] Tobler mistakenly placed a sprig ware pot in XIII.

[5] A recent article on the Late Chalcolithic (Gülçer 2000) highlights this problem, as she equates everything from Gawra XII-IX with LC1 Norşuntepe J/K 17 because of the presence of 'Coba' bowls.

[6] See Rothman in press a and Rothman and Peasnall 1999 for more detail.

[7] Note the similarity of the VIIIB-A warehouse and the later building at Sheikh Hassan.

[8] Rather than an abandonment, an EB1 town with a wall may follow the palace/temple complex (Frangipane, personal communication).

REFERENCES

Abu al-Soof, B., 1969. Excavations at Tell Qalinj Agha (Erbil), Summer, 1968. *Sumer* 25:3-42

Akkermans, P.M.M.G., 1988. An Updated Chronology for the Northern Ubaid and Late Chalcolithic Periods in Syria: New Evidence from Tell Hammam et-Turkman. *Iraq*: 109-145.

Algaze, G., 1989. The Uruk Expansion: Cross-cultural Exchange in the Early Mesopotamian Civilization. *Current Anthropology* 30 (5): 571- 608.

- 1993. *The Uruk World System.* Chicago: University of Chicago Press.

Ball, W., 1997. Tell Shelgiyya: an Early Uruk 'Sprig Ware' Manufacturing and Exporting Centre on the Tigris. *Al-Rafidan* XVIII: 93-104.

Ball, W., Tucker, D., and Wilkinson, T.J., 1989, The Tell al-Hawa Project: Archaeological Investigations in the North Jazira 1986-87. *Iraq* LI: 1-66.

Blanton, R., 1976. Anthropological Studies of Cities. *Annual Review of Anthropology* 5: 249-64.

- 1998. Beyond Centralization: Steps Toward a Theory of Egalitarian Behavior, in Feinman, G. and Marcus, J., eds. *Archaic States.* pp. 135-172. Santa Fe: SAR Press.

Blanton, R., Feinman, G., Kowalewski, S., and Peregrine, P., 1996. A Dual-Processual Theory for the Evolution of Mesoamerican Civilization. *Current Anthropology* 37(1): 1-14.

Boese, J., 1995. *Ausgrabungen in Tell Sheikh Hassan.* Vol I. Saarbrücken: Saarbrücker Druckerei und Verlag.

- 1995/96. Tell Sheikh Hassan in Nordsyrien: eine Stadt des 4 Jahrtausends v. Chr. am Euphrat. *Nürnberger Blätter zur Archäologie* Heft 12: 157-172.

Brown, T. Burton, 1951. *Excavations in Azarbaijan, 1948.* London: John Murray.

Childe, V. G., 1974. The Urban Revolution, in J. Sabloff and C.C. Lambert-Karlovsky, eds., *The Rise and Fall of Civilizations*, pp. 6-14. Menlo Park, CA: Cummings Press.

Egami, N., 1959. *Telul eth Thalathat Report I: excavation of Tell II 1956-7.* Tokyo: Yamakawa Publishing Co.

Esin, U., 1972. Tepecik Excavations 1970. *Keban Project Activities 1970.* Pp. 149-160. Ankara: METU

- 1983. Zur Datierung der vorgeschichtlichen Schichten von Değirmentepe bei Malatya in der östlichen Türkei. In Boehmer, R.M. and H. Hauptmann, eds., *Beiträge zur Altertumskunde Kleinasiens* (Bittel Festschrift). pp 175-190. Mainz: von Zabern.

Forest, J.-P., 1983. *Les pratiques funéraires en Mésopotamie du 5e millénaire au début du 3e, étude de cas.* Memoire 19. Paris: Editions Recherche sur les civilisations.

Frangipane, M., 1997. A 4th-Millennium Temple/Palace Complex at Arslantepe-Malatya. North-South Relations and the Formation of Early State Societies in the Northern Regions of Greater Mesopotamia. *Paléorient* 23/1:45-73.

- 1994. The Record Function of Clay Sealings in Early Administrative Systems as seen from Arslantepe-Malatya, in *Archives Before Writing*, P. Ferioli, E. Fiandra, G. Fissore, and M. Frangipane, eds. pp.125-37. Rome: Scriptorium.

- 1993. Local Components in the Development of Centralized Societies in Syro-Anatolian Regions, in Frangipane, M. *et al.*, eds. *Between the Rivers and Over the Mountains*, pp. 133-62. Rome: Università di Roma.

Gülçer, S., 2000. Norşuntepe: die chalkolithische keramik (Elazığ/Ostanatolien) in C. Marro, H. Hauptmann, eds., *Chronologies des Pays du Caucase et de l'Euphrate aux IVe-IIIe millénaires.* pp. 375-418. Paris: De Bocchard.

Gut, R., 1995. *Das Prähistorische Nineve.* Mainz: Verlag Philipp von Zabern.

Hauptmann, H., 1972. Die Grabungen auf dem Norşun-Tepe 1970. *Keban Project Activities 1970.* pp. 103-122. Ankara: METU.

- 1976. Die Grabungen auf dem Norşun-Tepe 1972. *Keban Project Activities 1972.* pp. 71-108. Ankara: METU.

- 1979. Die Grabungen auf dem Norşun-Tepe 1973. *Keban Project Activities 1973.* pp. 61-96. Ankara: METU.

- 1982. Die Grabungen auf dem Norşun-Tepe 1974. *Keban Project Activities 1974-5.* pp. 41-94. Ankara: METU.

Henrickson, E. and Thuesen, I., (eds.), 1989. *Upon this Foundation - the 'Ubaid Reconsidered.* Carsten Niebuhr Foundation Publication 10.

Herrmann, G., 1968. Lapis Lazuli: Early Phases of its Trade. *Iraq* XXX(1): 21-57.

Jacobsen, T., 1976. *The Treasures of Darkness.* New Haven: Yale University Press.

Johnson, G., 1973. *Local Exchange and Early State Development in Southwestern Iran.* Ann Arbor: University of Michigan Museum of Anthropology Anthropological Paper no. 51.

Lloyd, S., 1940. Iraqi Government Soundings at Sinjar. *Iraq* VI: 13-21.

Lupton, A., 1996. *Stability and Change. Socio-political Development in North Mesopotamia and South-East Anatolia 4000-2700 B.C.* Oxford: BAR International Series 627.

Mallowan, M., 1933. The Prehistoric Sondage of Nineveh, 1931-32. *Annals of Archaeology and Anthropology* 20: 127-77.

Mellaart, J., 1981. The Prehistoric Pottery from the Neolithic to the Beginning of the E.B. IV. In *The River Qoueiq, North Syria and Its Catchment.* J. Matthers, ed. Pp. 131-319. BAR International Series 98. Oxford.

Oates, D. and J., 1993. Excavations at Tell Brak 1992-93. *Iraq* LV: 155-99.

- 1994. Tell Brak: a Stratigraphic Summary 1976-1993. *Iraq* LVI: 167-176.

Oates, J., 1985. Tell Brak: Uruk Pottery from the 1984 Season. *Iraq* XLVII: 175-86.

- 1993. Trade and Power in the Fifth and Fourth Millennia BC: new evidence from Northern Mesopotamia. *World Archaeology:* 24/3: 403-422.

Oguchi, H., 1987. Tell Musharifa. *Researches on the Antiquities of Saddam Dam Basin Salvage and Other Researches.* pp. 49-54. Baghdad: Republic of Iraq Ministry of Culture and Information.

Oppenheim, A. L., 1977. *Ancient Mesopotamia.* Chicago: University of Chicago Press.

Peasnall, B., in press. Appendix A. Burials, in M. Rothman, *Fourth Millennium B.C. Tepe Gawra.* Philadelphia: University of Pennsylvania Museum Publications.

Peregrine, P., 1996. Introduction: World-Systems Theory and Archaeology, in Peregrine, P. and Feinman, G. 1996. *Pre-Columbian World Systems.* pp. 10. Madison: Prehistory Press.

Pittman, H., in press. Mesopotamia in the Era of State Formation: Interregional Relations reflected through Glyptic Evidence, in M. Rothman, ed., *Uruk Mesopotamia and its Neighbors: Cross-cultural Interactions and their Consequences in the Era of State Formation.* Santa Fe: SAR Press.

Reimer, S., 1989. Tell Qraya on the Middle Euphrates. *Paléorient* 15/1: 284.

Roaf, M., 1984. The Stratigraphy and Architecture of Tell Madhhur. *Sumer* XLIII (1/2): 110-26.

- 1998. A Group of Pottery from Mohammad Arab Period I, in *About Subartu* IV, I., M. LeBeau. Pp. 131-149. Turnhout Belgium: BREPOLS.

Rothman, M. S., in press a, *Tepe Gawra: the evolution of a small, prehistoric center in Northern Iraq.* Philadelphia: University of Pennsylvania Museum Publications.

- in press b, Tepe Gawra, in Fleming, S. , Stech, T. , and Pigott, V. (eds.), *Mesopotamian Metals Project* volume II. Philadelphia: University of Pennsylvania Museum Publications.

- in press c, The Tigris Piedmont and Eastern Jazira in the Fourth Millennium B.C. *Uruk Mesopotamia and its Neighbors: Cross-cultural Interactions and their Consequences in the Era of State Formation.* Santa Fe: SAR Press.

- 1988. *Centralization, Administration and Function at Fourth Millennium B.C. Tepe Gawra, Northern Iraq.* Ph.D. thesis. University of Pennsylvania.

- 1993. Another Look at the Uruk Expansion from the Zagros Piedmont, in M. Frangipane *et al.* (eds.), *Between the Rivers and Over the Mountains*, pp.163-76. Rome: Università di Roma La Sapienza.

- 1994a. Evolutionary Typologies and Cultural Complexity, in *Chiefdoms and Early States in the Near East: The Organizational Dynamics of Complexity*, edited by G. Stein and M. S. Rothman, pp. 1-10. Monographs in World Prehistory 18. Prehistory Press, Madison, WI.

- 1994b. Seal and Sealing Findspots, Design, Audience and Function in Ferioli, P., Fiandra E., Fisore, G. and Frangipane, M., editors. *Archives Before Writing.* pp. 97-121. Università di Roma.

- 2000. Environmental and Cultural Factors in the Development of Settlement in a Marginal, Highland Zone, in L.E. Stager, J.A. Greene, and M.D. Coogan, *The Archaeology of Jordan and Beyond: Essays in Honor of James A. Sauer*. Pp. 429-43. Winona Lake, Ind: Eisenbrauns.

Rothman, M.S., (ed.), 1989. Out of the Heartland: The Evolution of Complexity in Peripheral Mesopotamia During the Uruk Period: Workshop Summary. *Paléorient* 15/1: 279-290.

- in press. *Uruk Mesopotamia and its Neighbors: Cross-cultural Interactions and their Consequences in the Era of State Formation*. Santa Fe: SAR Press.

Rothman, M.S. and Blackman, M.J., 1990. Monitoring Administrative Spheres of Action in Late Prehistoric Northern Mesopotamia with the Aid of Chemical Characterization (INAA) of Clay Sealings, in Miller, N., editor. *Economy and Settlement in the Near East*. pp 19-45, MASCA Supplement, University Museum.

Rothman, M.S. and Peasnall, B., 1999. Societal Evolution of Small, Pre-state Polities: the Example of Tepe Gawra in Northern Mesopotamia. *Paléorient* 25/1:101-114.

Rova, E., in press. A Tentative Synchronization of the Local Late Chalcolithic Ceramic Horizons of Northern Syro-Mesopotamia. *Mesopotamia*.

Schwartz, G., in press. Syria and the Uruk Expansion. In *Uruk Mesopotamia and its Neighbors: Cross-cultural Interactions and their Consequences in the Era of State Formation*. M. Rothman, ed. Santa Fe: SAR Press.

- 1988a. *A Ceramic Chronology from Tell Leilan: Operation 1*. Yale Tell Leilan Research, Volume 1. New Haven and London: Yale University Press.

- 1988b. Excavations at Karatut Mevkii and Perspectives on the Uruk/Jemdet Nasr Expansion. *Akkadica* 56:1-41.

Speiser, E. A., 1935a. *Excavations at Tepe Gawra. Vol. I*. Philadelphia: University of Pennsylvania Press.

Starr, R. F. S., 1939. *Nuzi. Volumes I and II*. Cambridge, Mass: Harvard University Press.

Stein, G., 1990. Comments on G. Algaze: The Uruk Expansion: Cross Cultural Exchange in early Mesopotamian Civilization. *Current Anthropology* 31(1): 66-67.

- 1994. The Organizational Dynamics of Complexity. In *Chiefdoms and Early States in the Near East: The Organizational Dynamics of Complexity*, edited by G. Stein and M. S. Rothman, pp. 11-22. Monographs in World Prehistory 18. Prehistory Press, Madison, WI.

- 1998. Heterogeneity, Power, and Political Economy. *Journal of Archaeological Research* 6(1): 1-44.

- 1999. *Rethinking World Systems*. Tucson: University of Arizona Press.

Stein, G. (ed.), 1999. The Uruk Expansion: New Perspectives from Hacinebi, Hassek Höyük, and Tepe Gawra. *Paléorient* 25/1.

Tobler, A., 1950. *Excavations at Tepe Gawra*. Vol. II, Philadelphia: University of Pennsylvania Press.

Tomita, T., 1998. Late Chalcolithic Chronology in Syria and Northern Mesopotamia. In *Excavations at Tell Umm Qseir in Middle Khabur Valley, North Syria*. Tsuneki, A. and Miyake, Y., eds. Pp. 197-201. University of Tsukuba

Trufelli, F., 1997. Ceramic Correlations and Cultural Relations in IVth Millennium Eastern Anatolia and Syro-Mesopotamia. *Studi Miceni ed Egeo-Anatolici* 39/1:5-33.

Tsuneki, A. and Miyake, Y., 1998. *Excavations at Tell Umm Qseir in Middle Khabur Valley, North Syria*. University of Tsukuba.

Wickede, von A., 1990. *Prähistorische Stempelglyptik in Vorderasien*. München: Profil Verlag.

Wright, H.T., 1977. Toward an Explanation of the Origin of the State, in *Explanation of Prehistoric Change*, J. Hill, ed. Albuquerque: University of New Mexico Press. pp. 215- 230.

- 1994. Prestate Political Formations, in G. Stein and M. Rothman, eds., *Chiefdoms and Early States in the Near East*. pp. 67-84. Wisconsin: Prehistory Press.

Wright, H.T. and E. Rupley, in press. Calibrated Radiocarbon Age Determination of Uruk-Related Assemblages. *Uruk Mesopotamia and its Neighbors: Cross-cultural Interactions and their Consequences in the Era of State Formation*. M. Rothman, ed. Santa Fe: SAR Press.

Fig. 4. LC 1 and Late 'Ubaid. (Not to scale.)

a. Değirmentepe. Esin 1983: fig 5, 1; pinkish color, chaff temper, flint scraped. D. 19 cm.

b. Hammam et Turkman IVD. Akkermans 1988: fig. 7, 110, plant and lime temper, scraped surface, orange color, dark core D. 35 cm.

c. Norşuntepe. J/K 17. Hauptmann 1982: pl. 36, 1; bright red-brown, lightly speckled [chaff faced]. D. 16.5 cm.

d. Tepe Gawra XII. Rothman in press a: pl. 11, 254; orange redware, chaff temper. D. 14.8 cm.

e. Tepe Gawra XII. Rothman in press a: pl. 11, 258; no detail. D. 14.2 cm.

f. Tepe Gawra XII. Rothman in press a: pl. 11, 260; buffware, quartz grit and chaff. D. 14.6 cm.

g. Tepe Gawra XII. Rothman in press a: pl. 11, 239; brown ware, chaff temper, bitumen inside. D. 21.5 cm.

h. Hammam et Turkman IVD. Akkermans 1988: fig. 6, 84; plant and lime temper, smoothed surface, buff brown paint. D. 14 cm.

i. Tepe Gawra XIIA. Rothman in press a: pl. 13, 223; light green ware, white grit temper, black paint. D. 13 cm.

j. Norşuntepe. J/K 17. Hauptmann 1982: pl. 36, 3; bright brown, lightly polished. D. 11.25 cm.

k. Tepe Gawra XII. Rothman in press a: pl. 13, 269; buffware, quartz and chaff. D. 10.1 cm.

l. Tepe Gawra XII. Rothman in press a: pl. 13, 233; light green ware, gloss red-brown paint. D. 11.6 cm.

m. Tepe Gawra XII. Rothman in press a: pl.12, 281; no detail. D. 18.3 cm.

n. Shelgiyya. Ball 1997: fig. 4, 18; no other information.

o. Tepe Gawra XII. Rothman in press a: pl. 13, 321; gritty brown ware, red slip, black paint. D. 8.4 cm.

p. Umm Qseir. Late Chalcolithic. Tsuneki and Miyake 1998: fig. 64, 7; chaff-faced ware, black core, black paint on burnished red surface, interior scraped.

q. Tepe Gawra XII. Rothman in press a: pl. 11, 307;

r. Tepe Gawra XII. Rothman in press a: pl. 11, 226; red brown ware, burnished, quartz & chaff. D. 9.7 cm.

s. Norşuntepe. J/K 17. Hauptmann 1982: pl 38, 8; red ocher-colored, coarse ware, black core, chaff, limestone, and coarse sand temper. D. 13.5 cm.

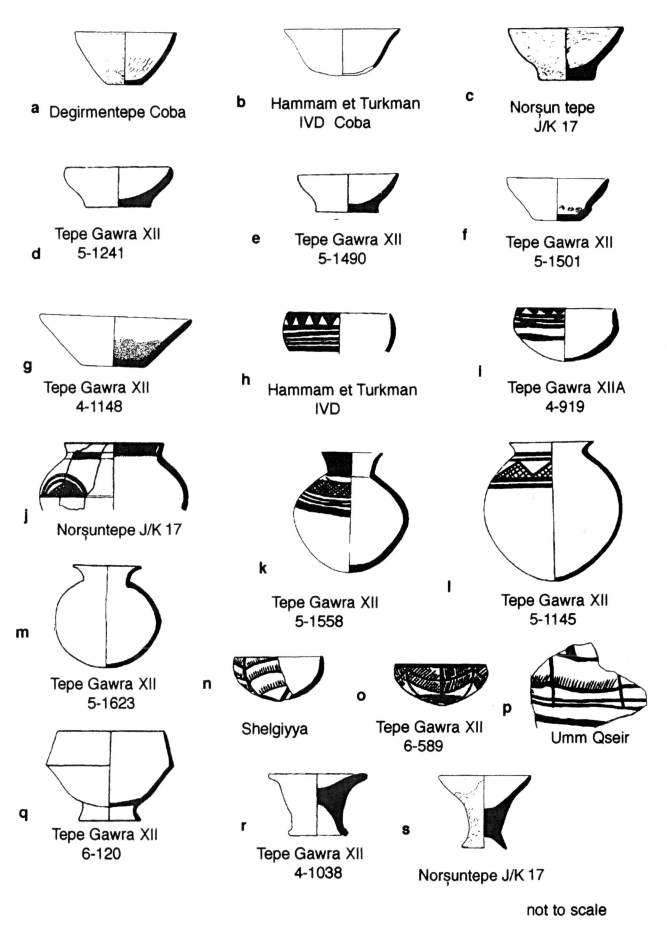

a Degirmentepe Coba

b Hammam et Turkman IVD Coba

c Norşun tepe J/K 17

d Tepe Gawra XII 5-1241

e Tepe Gawra XII 5-1490

f Tepe Gawra XII 5-1501

g Tepe Gawra XII 4-1148

h Hammam et Turkman IVD

I Tepe Gawra XIIA 4-919

j Norşuntepe J/K 17

k Tepe Gawra XII 5-1558

l Tepe Gawra XII 5-1145

m Tepe Gawra XII 5-1623

n Shelgiyya

o Tepe Gawra XII 6-589

p Umm Qseir

q Tepe Gawra XII 6-120

r Tepe Gawra XII 4-1038

s Norşuntepe J/K 17

not to scale

Fig. 5. LC 2 early. (Not to scale.)

a. Tepe Gawra XII. Rothman in press a: pl. 13, 202; green grayware, cream slip, lime temper.

b. Tepe Gawra XI. Rothman in press a: pl. 18, 1378; buffware, sand temper.

c. Tepe Gawra XI. Rothman in press a: pl. 18, 1385; green buffware, sand temper.

d. Tepe Gawra XIAB. Rothman in press a: pl. 15, 724; sand temper.

e. Tell Brak TW 16. Oates and Oates 1991: fig. 7, 4; no detail.

f. Norşuntepe J/K 18-19. Hauptmann 1976: pl. 50, 1 & 3; ocher colored with impressions, sand temper.

g. Norşuntepe J/K 18-19. Hauptmann 1979: pl. 42, 8; reddish gray, chaff, lime, and grit tempering. D. 10 cm.

h. Tepe Gawra XIA. Rothman in press a: pl. 15, 722; buffware, sand temper.

i. Tepe Gawra XA. Rothman in press a: pl. 21, 1814; buffware, sand temper.

j. Tepe Gawra XI. Rothman in press a: pl. 18, 1415; buffware, lime temper. D. 9 cm.

k. Tepe Gawra XI. Rothman in press a: pl. 18, 1416; no detail. D. 13.6 cm.

l. Tell al-Hawa, slopes. Ball *et al.* 1989: fig. 18, 19; no detail.

m. Tepe Gawra XIAB. Rothman in press a: pl. 15, 767; green grayware, quartz grit and chaff. D. 17.0 cm.

n. Norşuntepe J/K 18-19. Hauptmann 1982: pl. 39, 4; bright reddish brown, slightly burnished. D. 21 cm.

o. Tepe Gawra XIB. Rothman in press a: pl. 14, 803; no detail. D. 19.6 cm.

p. Tepe Gawra XIAB. Rothman in press a: pl. 16, 794; no detail. D. 41 cm.

q. Norşuntepe J/K 18-19. Hauptmann 1982: pl. 39, 5; brownish red, dark spotted, gray core, chaff, sand, and lime temper. D. 15 cm.

r. Musharifa, Area A. Oguchi 1987: fig. 14, 25; reddish brown, vegetable and grit temper, creamy brown slip, red-brown paint inside and out.

s. Tepe Gawra XIAB. Rothman in press a: pl. 16, 800; brown ware, white grit, slip. D. 12.8 cm.

t. Tepe Gawra XIB. Rothman in press a: pl. 16, 804; buffware. D. 9.9 cm.

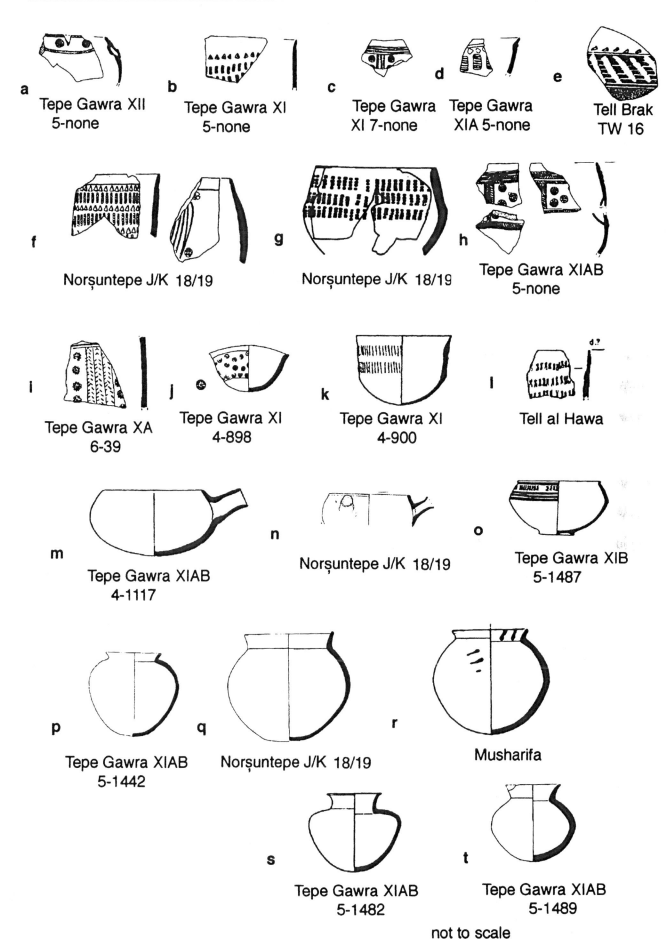

a   Tepe Gawra XII
5-none

b   Tepe Gawra XI
5-none

c   Tepe Gawra
XI 7-none

d   Tepe Gawra
XIA 5-none

e   Tell Brak
TW 16

f   Norşuntepe J/K 18/19

g   Norşuntepe J/K 18/19

h   Tepe Gawra XIAB
5-none

i   Tepe Gawra XA
6-39

j   Tepe Gawra XI
4-898

k   Tepe Gawra XI
4-900

l   Tell al Hawa

m   Tepe Gawra XIAB
4-1117

n   Norşuntepe J/K 18/19

o   Tepe Gawra XIB
5-1487

p   Tepe Gawra XIAB
5-1442

q   Norşuntepe J/K 18/19

r   Musharifa

s   Tepe Gawra XIAB
5-1482

t   Tepe Gawra XIAB
5-1489

not to scale

67

Fig. 6. LC 2 early. (Not to scale.)

a. Tepe Gawra XIAB. Rothman in press a: pl. 14, 775; brown ware, burnished. D. 22 cm.

b. Tepe Gawra XA. Rothman in press a: pl. 21, 1799; buff, brown slip. D. 33.5 cm.

c. Umm Qseir. Tsuneki and Miyake 1998: fig 64, 8; coarse chaff tempered ware, heavy chaff inclusions, dark gray core, dark brown surface, interior scraping, finger impressions on surface. D. 20 cm.

d. Tepe Gawra XI. Rothman in press a: pl. 19, 1475; brown ware. D. 53.5 cm.

e. Tepe Gawra XIA. Rothman in press a: pl. 15, 795; coarse buff ware, wet smoothed. D. 48 cm.

f. Tell al-Hawa, slopes. After Ball *et al.* 1989: fig. 18, 10; no detail.

g. Tepe Gawra XI. Rothman in press a: pl. 19, 1472; brown ware, dark buff slip, brown paint. D. 25 cm.

h. Norşuntepe J/K 18-19. Late Chalcolithic. Hauptmann 1972: pl. 71, 1; buff ware with dark reddish brown paint.

i. Umm Qseir. Tsuneki and Miyake 1998: fig 64, 1; chaff-faced ware, chaff inclusions, buff, greenish yellow surface. D. 32 cm.

j. Arslantepe Late Chalcolithic (VII). Frangipane 1993: fig. 9, 10. Coarse, flint scraped. D. 21 cm.

k. Umm Qseir. Tsuneki and Miyake 1998: fig 64, 10; coarse grit tempered ware, heavy grit, chaff, gray core, dark brown surface, interior scraped and burnished. D. 20 cm.

l. Telul eth Thalathat level VIIa, trenches VIII and IX. Egami 1959: fig. 51, 2; no detail. D. 24.5 cm.

m. Musharifa, Area A. Oguchi 1987: fig. 14, 16; pale brown, straw and sand temper, blade-cut.

n. Tepe Gawra XI. Rothman in press a: pl. 17, 1406. Discarded, no detail. D. 33 cm.

o. Tepe Gawra XI. Rothman in press a: pl. 18, 1396; greenish buff ware. D. 6 cm.

p. Norşuntepe J/K 18-19. Late Chalcolithic. Hauptmann 1976: pl. 50, 7; greenish buff, coffee-colored paint, grit and lime temper. D. 9 cm.

q. Norşuntepe J/K 18-19. Late Chalcolithic. Hauptmann 1976: pl. 50, 11; buff, purplish coffee-colored paint. D. 13.5 cm.

r. Norşuntepe J/K 18-19. Late Chalcolithic. Hauptmann 1976: pl. 50, 9; chalky white, slightly burnished, with black paint. Grit and lime temper. D. 13.5 cm.

s. Tepe Gawra XI. Rothman in press a: pl. 19, 1460; buff ware, brown paint, fine quartz & basalt grit. D. 14.6 cm.

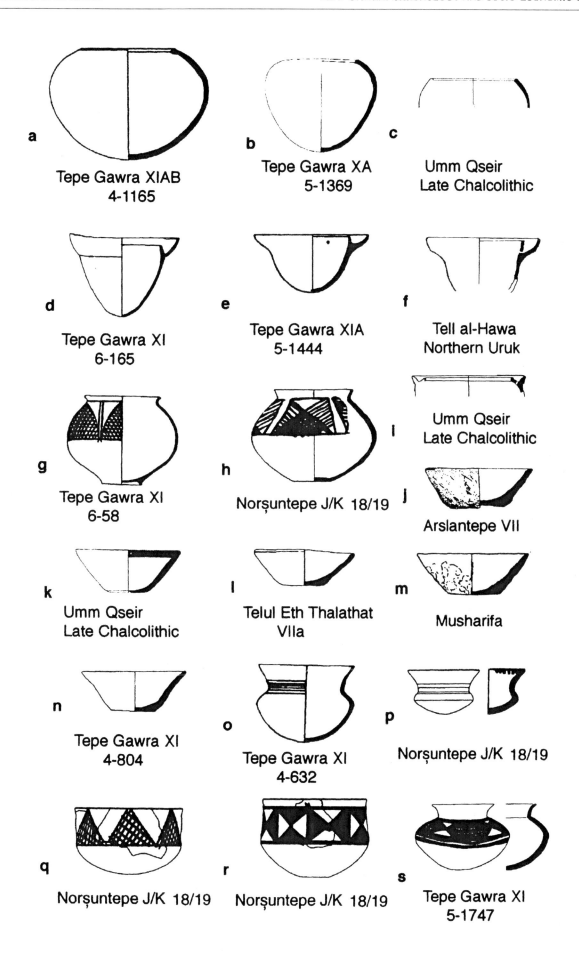

a   Tepe Gawra XIAB 4-1165

b   Tepe Gawra XA 5-1369

c   Umm Qseir Late Chalcolithic

d   Tepe Gawra XI 6-165

e   Tepe Gawra XIA 5-1444

f   Tell al-Hawa Northern Uruk

g   Tepe Gawra XI 6-58

h   Norşuntepe J/K 18/19

i   Umm Qseir Late Chalcolithic

j   Arslantepe VII

k   Umm Qseir Late Chalcolithic

l   Telul Eth Thalathat VIIa

m   Musharifa

n   Tepe Gawra XI 4-804

o   Tepe Gawra XI 4-632

p   Norşuntepe J/K 18/19

q   Norşuntepe J/K 18/19

r   Norşuntepe J/K 18/19

s   Tepe Gawra XI 5-1747

Fig. 7. LC 2 early-late. (Not to scale.)

a. Tepe Gawra XA. Rothman in press a: pl. 21, 1807; grayware, thick brown-red slip, quartz grit. D. unknown.

b. Tell Brak CH 13/14. Oates 1985: XXXI,b, 4; thick, dark red slip over gritty brown paste.

c. Tepe Gawra XI. Rothman in press a: pl. 17, 1450; orange redware, paint on rim, fine basalt and quartz grit. D. 16 cm.

d. Tepe Gawra XI. Rothman in press a: pl. 17, 1402; green grayware. Wheel?. D. 18.4 cm.

e. Tell Brak TW 16. Oates and Oates 1993: fig. 52, 49; orange fabric, chaff and white grit, pale core, red slip, burnished. D. 19.3 cm.

f. Telul eth Thalathat level VIIa, trenches VIII and IX. Egami 1959: fig.50, 5; no detail. D. 23 cm.

g. Tepe Gawra XI. Rothman in press a: pl. 19, 1444; gray brown ware, dark red slip. D. 20 cm. (body), 8.8 cm. (spout).

h. Tepe Gawra XA. Rothman in press a: pl. 22, 1813; reddish-brown ware, buff slip, black paint. D. 17.5 cm.

i. Tepe Gawra XA. Rothman in press a: pl. 22, 1815; buff ware, chaff and sand temper. D. 12 cm.

j. Arslantepe Late Chalcolithic (VII). Frangipane 1993: figure 9, 2.

k. Tepe Gawra XI. Rothman in press a: pl. 20, 1484; coarse brown ware. D. 44 cm.

l. Tepe Gawra XA. Rothman in press a: pl. 21, 1816; light brown ware, reddish brown paint. D. 26.1 cm.

m. Tepe Gawra XA. Rothman in press a: pl. 21, 1819; brown ware, dark brown paint. D. 35.5 cm.

n. Tepe Gawra XA. Rothman in press a: pl. 22, 1821; red ware, light brown slip. D. 25 cm.

o. Tepecik Chalcolithic. Esin 1972 pl. 114, fig 2, t70-759. Ware not specifically described. D. 26cm.

p. Norşuntepe J/K 18-19. Late Chalcolithic. Hauptmann 1972: pl. 71, 71,6; Reddish brown ware with flat dark red paint, dark gray core, a bit of grit and micaceous sand temper. D. unknown.

q. Nineveh mm 55. Gut 1995: pl. 53, 802; red ware, light slip, black paint. D. 31.5 cm.

r. Musharifa Late Chalcolithic. Oguchi 1987: fig 14. 11; reddish brown with vegetable and white grit temper, cream slip, red-brown paint. D. 18 cm.

s. Geoy Tepe. M. Burton-Brown 1951: fig. 5, 634; pinkish clay, polished greenish-white slip, light brown mat paint. D. 27 cm.

t. Telul eth Thalathat level VIIa, trenches VIII and IX. Egami 1959: fig.50, 4; no detail. D. 29 cm.

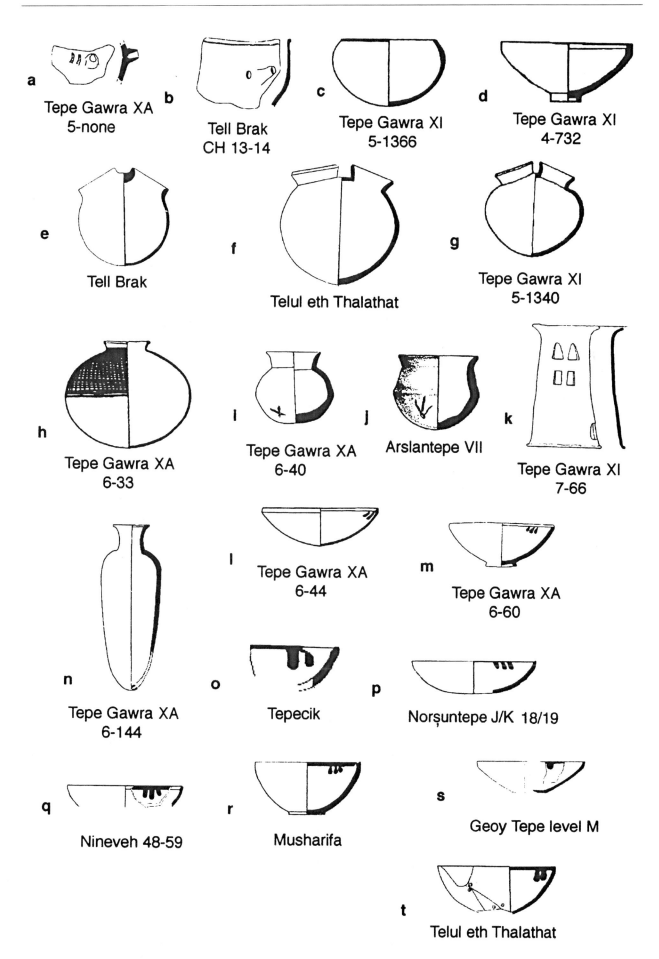

a Tepe Gawra XA
5-none

b Tell Brak
CH 13-14

c Tepe Gawra XI
5-1366

d Tepe Gawra XI
4-732

e Tell Brak

f Telul eth Thalathat

g Tepe Gawra XI
5-1340

h Tepe Gawra XA
6-33

i Tepe Gawra XA
6-40

j Arslantepe VII

k Tepe Gawra XI
7-66

l Tepe Gawra XA
6-44

m Tepe Gawra XA
6-60

n Tepe Gawra XA
6-144

o Tepecik

p Norşuntepe J/K 18/19

q Nineveh 48-59

r Musharifa

s Geoy Tepe level M

t Telul eth Thalathat

Fig. 8. LC 2 late. (Not to scale.)

a. Tepe Gawra X. Rothman in press a: pl. 24, 1949; fine light brown ware. D.20.5 cm.

b. Tepe Gawra IX. Rothman in press a: pl. 25, 2226; buffware, light green buff slip, brown paint. D. 14.3 cm.

c. Tepe Gawra X. Rothman in press a: pl. 24, 1958; light buffware, dark brown paint. D. 27.2 cm.

d. Tepe Gawra X. Rothman in press a: pl. 23, 1942; red ware, cream slip. D. 14 cm.

e. Nineveh mm 60. Gut 1995: pl. 53, 795; pink buff, interior buff, dark gray core, brown paint, wheel made.

f. Tepe Gawra X. Rothman in press a: pl. 23, 1932; green grayware, wheel. D. 10.6 cm.

g. Tepe Gawra X. Rothman in press a: pl. 24, 1924; buffware, cream slip, black paint, wheel. D. 12 cm.

h. Norşuntepe J/K 18-19. Late Chalcolithic. Hauptmann 1972: pl. 71, 2; matt reddish brown on yellowy buff clay. D. unknown.

i. Norşuntepe J/K 18-19. Hauptmann 1982: pl. 38, 5. Matt dark brown paint on reddish background, core burnt sienna with chaff and lime.

j. Tepe Gawra X. Rothman in press a: pl. 24, 1926a; brown ware, chaff temper. D. 29 cm.

k. Tepe Gawra X. Rothman in press a: pl. 29, 1959; light buff ware, dark brown paint. D.25.6 cm.

l. Tepe Gawra X. Rothman in press a: pl. 23, 1944; buffware, fine quartz and chaff temper. D. 22 cm.

m. Tepe Gawra X. Rothman in press a: pl. 23, 1937; brownware, basalt and quartz grit temper. D. 11 cm.

n. Tepe Gawra X. Rothman in press a: pl. 24, 1955; light green grayware, wheel. D. 14 cm.

o. Grai Resh. Lloyd 1940: fig. 7, 5; no detail. D. 9 cm.

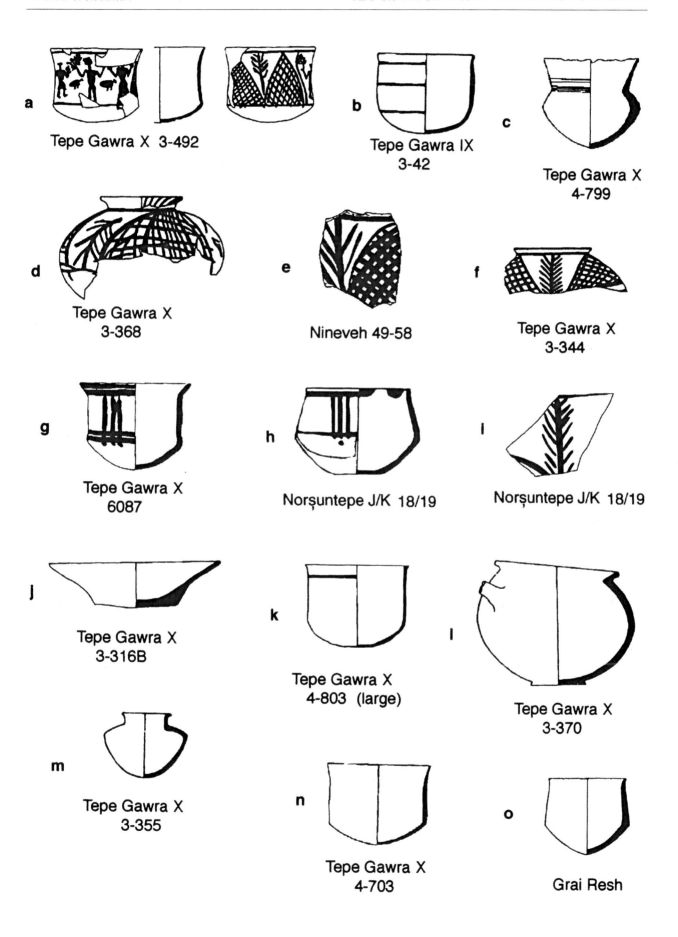

a Tepe Gawra X 3-492

b Tepe Gawra IX 3-42

c Tepe Gawra X 4-799

d Tepe Gawra X 3-368

e Nineveh 49-58

f Tepe Gawra X 3-344

g Tepe Gawra X 6087

h Norşuntepe J/K 18/19

i Norşuntepe J/K 18/19

j Tepe Gawra X 3-316B

k Tepe Gawra X 4-803 (large)

l Tepe Gawra X 3-370

m Tepe Gawra X 3-355

n Tepe Gawra X 4-703

o Grai Resh

Fig. 9. LC 2 late/early 3. (Not to scale.)

a. Tepe Gawra IX. Rothman in press a: pl. 26, 2245; brown ware, chaff and quartz temper. D. 16 cm.

b. Musharifa Late Chalcolithic. Oguchi 1987: fig 14. 12; reddish brown with vegetable and white grit temper. D. 18 cm.

c. Tell Sheikh Hassan Middle Uruk. Boese 1995: page 270, fig. 13, bottom; no detail

d. Tell Brak TW early 14. Oates and Oates 1993: fig 51, 29; fine reddish-brown fabric, no chaff, burnished. D. 8.5 cm.

e. Tepe Gawra IX. Rothman in press a: pl. 25, 2227; gray ware. D. 54 cm.

f. Tepe Gawra IX. Rothman in press a: pl. 25, 2255; green gray ware, sand temper. D. 16 cm.

g. Tell Brak TW 16. Oates and Oates 1993: like fig 54, 67; funnel, orange/brown fabric, gray core, chaff temper.

h. Tepe Gawra IX. Rothman in press a: pl. 25,2239; buff ware. D. 47 cm.

i. Hammam et Turkman VB. Akkermans 1988: fig 9, 149. Plant and lime paste, scraped surface, orange color, dark core D. 23 cm.

j. Grai Resh. Lloyd 1940: fig 7, 6; no detail. D. 11 cm.

k. Tepe Gawra IX. Rothman in press a: pl. 26, 2250; orange red ware, buff slip, quartz grit and chaff temper. D. 19 cm.

l. Tepe Gawra IX. Rothman in press a: pl. 26, 2231; gray ware. D. 12 cm.

m. Hammam et Turkman VB. Akkermans 1988: fig. 10, 153. Sand temper smoothed surface, gray color, dark core. D. 22 cm.

n. Tepe Gawra VIII. Rothman in press a: pl. 28, 2853; buff ware. D. 19 cm.

o. Tepe Gawra IX. Rothman in press a: pl. 25, 2243; buff ware. D. 25 cm.

p. Tepe Gawra VIII. Rothman in press a: pl. 27, 2787; buff ware, orangy tinge, fine quartz and basalt grit. D. 7 cm.

q. Tepe Gawra IX. Rothman in press a: pl. 26, 2233; red brown ware. D. 38 cm.

r. Tepe Gawra IX. Rothman in press a: pl. 25, 2236; green gray ware, basalt and quartz grit. D. 21 cm

s. Tepe Gawra VIIIA/B. Rothman in press a: pl. 29, 2789; buff ware, basalt grit and chaff. D. 9.9 cm.

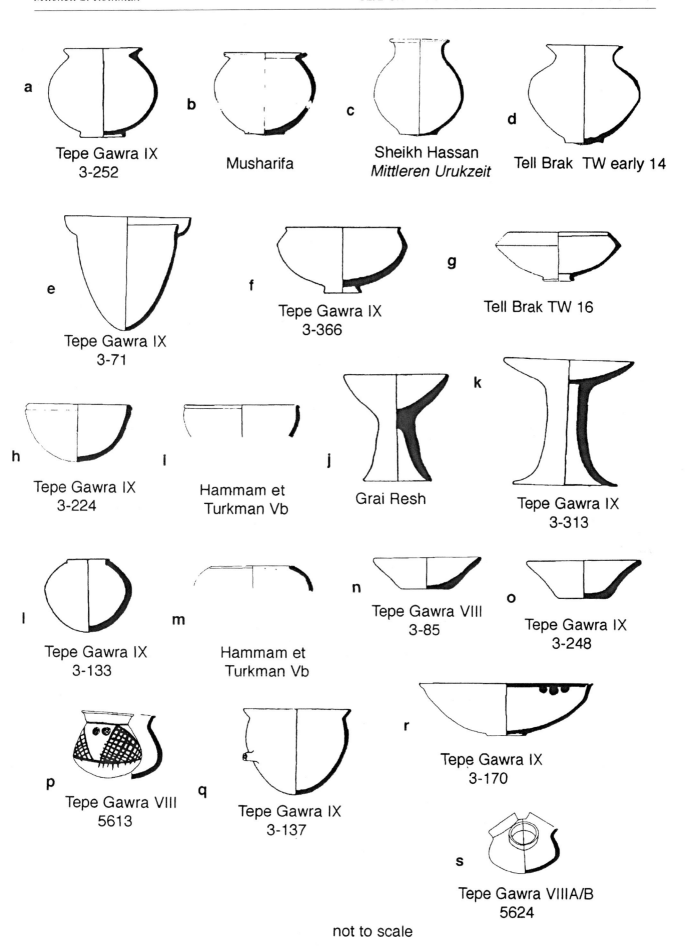

a
Tepe Gawra IX
3-252

b
Musharifa

c
Sheikh Hassan
Mittleren Urukzeit

d
Tell Brak TW early 14

e
Tepe Gawra IX
3-71

f
Tepe Gawra IX
3-366

g
Tell Brak TW 16

h
Tepe Gawra IX
3-224

i
Hammam et
Turkman Vb

j
Grai Resh

k
Tepe Gawra IX
3-313

l
Tepe Gawra IX
3-133

m
Hammam et
Turkman Vb

n
Tepe Gawra VIII
3-85

o
Tepe Gawra IX
3-248

p
Tepe Gawra VIII
5613

q
Tepe Gawra IX
3-137

r
Tepe Gawra IX
3-170

s
Tepe Gawra VIIIA/B
5624

not to scale

Fig. 10. LC 2/3. (Not to scale.)

a. Tepe Gawra VIII. Rothman in press a: pl. 29, 2774; brown ware, wheel, wet smoothed. D. 10.5 cm.

b. Hammam et Turkman VB. Akkermans 1988: fig 9, 139. Plant and lime temper. Burnished surface. Dark core. D. 31 cm.

c. Umm Qseir. Tsuneki and Miyake 1998: fig 63, 6; fine ware, slight chaff inclusions, reddish-brown, light orange surface, lower exterior scraped. D. 11 cm.

d. Tepe Gawra VIII. Rothman in press a: pl. 27, 2791; gray ware, wet smoothed, wheel. D. 6.7 cm.

e. Sheikh Hassan Level 7. Boese 19 : p. 226, pl 12, c. no detail.

f. Nineveh mm 31. Gut 1995: plate 107, s 62; no detail.

g. Tepe Gawra VIIIA. Rothman in press a: pl. 29, 2830; buff ware, wheel. D. 11.8 cm.

h. Tepe Gawra VIIIC. Rothman in press a: pl. 28, 2826; buff ware, wheel, wet smoothed. D. 12 cm.

i. Hammam et Turkman VB. Akkermans 1988: fig 9, 142. Plant temper. Smoothed surface, Cream color, dark core. D. 27 cm.

j. Grai Resh. Lloyd 1940: fig. 7, 8; no detail. D. 16 cm.

k. Nineveh mm 50. Gut 1995: pl. 57, 838; gray ware, polished. D. 14 cm.

l. Tepe Gawra VIIIB. Rothman in press a: pl. 28, 2825; reddish brown ware. D. 19.5 cm.

m. Tepe Gawra VIIIA. Rothman in press a: pl. 28, 2827; green gray ware, wheel, wet smoothed. D. 11.9 cm.

n. Nineveh mm 41. Gut 1995: pl. 54, 811; smoothed sandy surface, light gray. D. 27 cm.

o. Tell Brak TW 16. Oates and Oates 1993: fig. 52, 48; gritty dark salmon fabric, no chaff, pale surface scraped and smoothed. D. 11.1 cm.

p. Tepe Gawra VIII. Rothman in press a: pl. 27, 2779; green gray ware. D. 12.3 cm.

q. Nineveh mm 35. Gut 1995: pl. 107, s67; no detail.

r. Tepe Gawra VIII. Rothman in press a: pl. 27, 2804; buff ware, wheel. D. 12.5 cm. Norşuntepe J/K 18-19. Late Chalcolithic. Hauptmann 1972: pl. 71; 3; outside upper part bright ocher, lower part grayish black, interior bright brown, very hard. D.?

t. Tepe Gawra VIII/VI. Rothman in press a: pl. 29, 2794; green gray ware, wet smoothed, wheel, sand temper. D. 9 cm.

u. Mohammad Arab Period 1. Roaf 1998 : fig 3, 32; buff fabric, grit temper, cream slip. D. unknown.

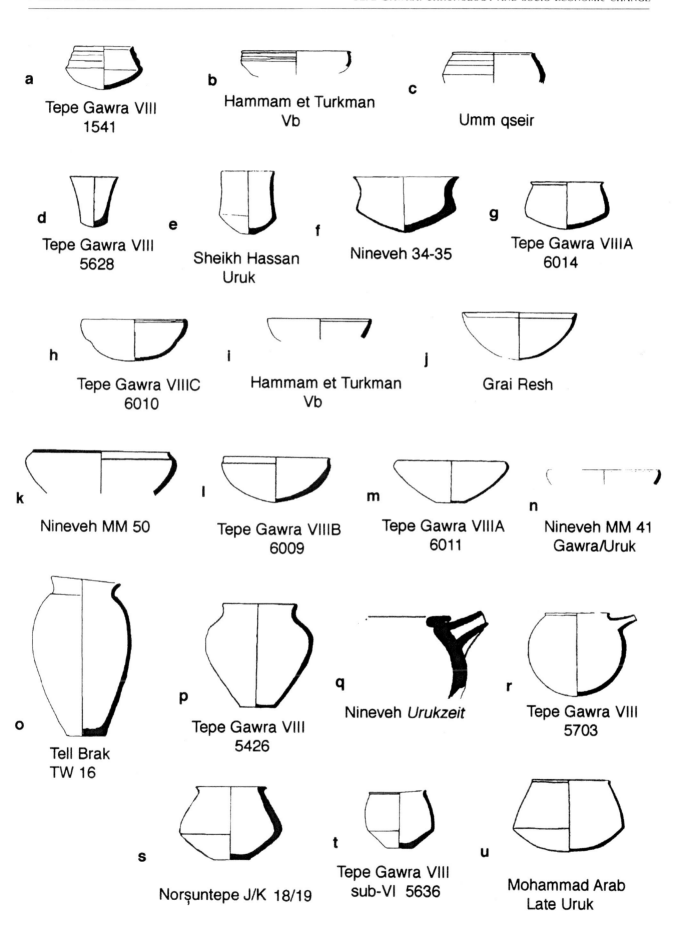

a Tepe Gawra VIII
   1541

b Hammam et Turkman
   Vb

c Umm qseir

d Tepe Gawra VIII
   5628

e Sheikh Hassan
   Uruk

f Nineveh 34-35

g Tepe Gawra VIIIA
   6014

h Tepe Gawra VIIIC
   6010

i Hammam et Turkman
   Vb

j Grai Resh

k Nineveh MM 50

l Tepe Gawra VIIIB
   6009

m Tepe Gawra VIIIA
   6011

n Nineveh MM 41
   Gawra/Uruk

o Tell Brak
   TW 16

p Tepe Gawra VIII
   5426

q Nineveh *Urukzeit*

r Tepe Gawra VIII
   5703

s Norşuntepe J/K 18/19

t Tepe Gawra VIII
   sub-VI 5636

u Mohammad Arab
   Late Uruk

A CHRONOLOGY OF URUK ARTIFACTS FROM GODIN TEPE IN CENTRAL WESTERN IRAN AND IMPLICATIONS FOR THE INTERRELATIONSHIPS BETWEEN THE LOCAL AND FOREIGN CULTURES

Virginia R. Badler

SUMMARY
The history of Uruk type artifacts from Periods VI and V[1] at Godin Tepe[2], an ancient site located near the modern city of Kangavar in central western Iran, is long, varied, and location specific. The site has substantial evidence for continuous occupation from as early as the mid-fifth millennium BC (Young 1986:212). Godin Tepe was probably an important site in the Kangavar valley at the time of the Uruk expansion during the fourth millennium BC due to both its size and location. At 14-15 hectares, it was the largest site in this area during this time period, and was strategically located along a major east-west trade route: the High Road, or Silk Road, that eventually linked the Mediterranean and China. In the later half of the fourth millennium, evidence for contact with Uruk sites to the south is provided by the occurrence of Uruk type artifacts alongside the Godin Tepe local assemblage.

Evidence indicates that Godin Tepe in the preceding (pre-contact) Period VII through early Period VI was a simple rural agricultural village yielding no finds indicative of any degree of social complexity, centralized government, or bureaucracy in the limited areas excavated. Uruk type pottery and small finds first occur (although infrequently) at Godin Tepe in the following middle and late Period VI. The presence of Uruk administrative-linked artifact types of a token and beveled rim bowls, and parallels with the pottery of Middle Uruk Nippur and Tepe Farukhabad in middle and late Period VI could indicate a relationship was already established in the Middle Uruk period as part of the first Uruk expansion. The association with the Uruk culture to the south continued and intensified in the earlier part of Period V, as evidenced by finds from test trenches Operation B, and Operations A and XYZ at the northern edge of the mound. In Operations A and XYZ there is evidence for a building level with additional Uruk pottery types directly underneath the broadly excavated Deep Sounding middle Period V building complex. There is a further increase in quantity and variety of Late Uruk type artifacts in the following middle Period V, particularly in the Deep Sounding buildings. This middle Period V building complex, surrounded by an oval enclosure wall, probably had an administrative function and contained the heaviest concentration and widest variety of Uruk artifacts at Godin Tepe with finds such as four-lugged jars, sealings and tablets. Most Uruk type finds are from the initial floors of these buildings, but finds from later floors (late Period V) also have parallels with sites to the south, as well as small percentages of Transcaucasian type pottery which later dominates the ceramic assemblages of Period IV.[3] Even with the introduction of Uruk type artifacts, the Godin Tepe local material culture continues through middle and late Period VI until the end of Period V.

Analysis of the pottery and architecture of the local and foreign Uruk material cultures suggests a significant degree of interaction between the villagers and foreigners. However, many Late Uruk pottery types present at other sites are absent at Godin Tepe. The incomplete assemblage may be explained by the utilization of local village potters to reproduce selected Uruk pottery types, and the lack of demand for certain Uruk domestic vessels due to the possible absence of foreign Uruk women at Godin Tepe.

LOCATIONS OF EXCAVATED PERIODS VI AND V AT GODIN TEPE
Only a fraction of the mound of Godin Tepe was excavated (Fig. 1). Periods VI and V material comes primarily from two small areas of private dwellings and one broad exposure of a group of administrative buildings. The domestic architecture was from two excavations at opposite ends of the surrounding village, the Brick Kiln Cut (BKC) and Operation B, comprising a total of approximately 190 square meters. The Brick Kiln Cut (Fig. 2, 3) is located to the west near an abandoned brick kiln, and contains material from middle Period VI through late Period V. Approximately 175 meters to the east, Operation B (Fig. 4; dug in 1965 and published in Young 1969), is a step trench along the eroded northern edge of the mound. It contains a more complete sequence from Period VII through early, middle and late Period VI through early, middle and late Period V. The Deep Sounding (D.S.) was a larger exposure ultimately comprising an area of about 550 square meters centered on the summit of the Upper Citadel Mound (dug in 1973; Fig. 5). In this area, a large group of buildings surrounded by an oval enclosure wall with one gateway (Room 4) is now dated to middle and late Period V. Two test trenches dug on the northern edge of the Deep Sounding allow the identification of a pre-oval early Period V.

Operation A (dug in 1965, and published in Young 1969; Fig. 6) is a step trench that includes the full pre- and post-oval sequence of strata. Operation XYZ (dug in 1973; Fig. 6), excavated in 20cm spits, still provides important information about the area of the oval preceding the construction of the middle Period V building complex. Of course, there is a tremendous amount of material from the mound that has not been sampled, and it is entirely possible that some of the conclusions in this report could be changed if new excavation data were available from the site.

THE CHRONOLOGY OF GODIN TEPE
(Chart 1)

EARLY PERIOD VI
Early Period VI at Godin Tepe is characterized by a local culture with a well-developed pottery tradition. Since this phase precedes contact with the Uruk cultures to the south, it will only be briefly described. The material culture of early Period VI, and the preceding Period VII, reflects the stratigraphic continuity at the site. The chronology of these periods is most clear in Operation B (Young 1969:3-10) where there is a continuous sequence of strata (with no major breaks) from Period VII through the end of Period V. Pottery from early Period VI is similar to that of the preceding Period VII, but has a higher percentage of fine painted wares (Young 1969:3). The pottery of late Period VII and early Period VI reflects a continuous ceramic tradition. It is difficult to separate

these two phases on the basis of pottery style.[4] The pottery of early Period VI is characterized by a high proportion of fine painted small bowls and other fine wares.[5] Additionally, there are coarse wares similar to those of Period VII used for large storage jars (similar to Young 1969: fig. 6:3), cooking pots (similar to Young 1969: fig. 6:1, 10) and cooking trays (similar to Levine and Young 1986: fig. 16:2 from the neighboring site of Seh Gabi). Bases are mostly flat (67% in early Period VI Operation B), but there is a significant percentage of pedestal bases (33%), some of which have painted decoration. In general, the pottery was handmade with attention given to finishing: most (including both fine and coarse wares) were slipped and burnished. There are no definite parallels with Uruk pottery. Small finds, as in the preceding Period VII, are limited to flint tools. Godin Tepe at this time was probably a rural agropastorally-based village with no artifacts in the limited area excavated indicative of any degree of social complexity, centralized government, or bureaucracy.

In the other two areas of Godin Tepe, the Brick Kiln Cut and the Deep Sounding, the sequence is less complete. There are no Period VII through early Period VI remains from the Brick Kiln Cut, which was dug to virgin soil (Fig. 2).[6] In the Deep Sounding, there appears to be some late Period VII through early Period VI pottery from the strata under the early Period V remains beneath the Deep Sounding oval. From Operation A, there is some Period VII and early Period VI pottery beneath the early Period V deposit of stratum A35 (Young 1969:6-

Period	Operation B	Brick Kiln Cut	Deep Sounding
VII	B49-B35	(not present)	Operations A strata 36-38 and XYZ spits 13 and lower
VI-Early	B34-B24	(not present)	Operations A strata 36-38 and XYZ spits 5-12
VI-Middle	B23-B22	BKC earliest VI (pre-architectural phase), and phase VI.1.	Absent
VI-Late	B20-19	BKC VI.2 and VI.3	Absent
V-Early (pre-oval)	B17	Phase V early	Operations A strata 34 and 35; Operation XYZ spits 1-4
V-Middle	B14/15	Phase V middle	Operation A stratum 33. Earliest occupation of the buildings within the oval.
V-Late	B12B/C	Phase V late	Operation A strata 32 and 32D

Chart 1. Chronological chart of Godin Tepe Periods VII, VI and V.

8,62; Fig. 6). In Operation XYZ, there is also some Period VII and early Period VI pottery from below spit 3,[7] but the finds are problematic because the operation was dug in arbitrary 20 cm spits (Fig. 6) which do not follow the strata indicated on the drawn section.

MIDDLE AND LATE PERIOD VI

The pottery of middle and late Period VI (Fig. 7, 8, 9, 16; Young 1969: fig. 7:11, 16-28; fig. 8:1, 3, 4, 6, 7, 9-12, 14, 16, 22-24; fig. 9:2, 12, 13) differs from that of early Period VI. There is a marked decrease in labor-intensive painted wares and the coarse wares characteristic of the preceding Period VII, and a corresponding increase in 'common ware' (Young 1969: Table II) which is neither slipped nor painted (Young 1969:5). However, white or cream slipped pottery continues to make up a considerable part of the pottery assemblage (Young 1969:Table II). Pottery of these later phases often exhibits the rilling characteristic of wheel-turned pottery. For the first time there are ring and disk bases, and in Operation B, pedestal bases make up to 50% of the bases, while flat bases decrease to less than 50% of the total number. A number of new shapes are also introduced, some of which show Uruk influence, although local pottery and artifacts predominate in all areas of the mound during Period VI.

The pottery of middle and late Period VI is marked by the first appearance of beveled rim bowls in Operation B,[8] and a number of pottery parallels with the partially published Middle Uruk pottery from levels XX-XVIII of the Inanna precinct at Nippur[9] and with Middle Uruk Tepe Farukhabad. The Middle Uruk finds from both Nippur (Wilson 1986:58) and Tepe Farukhabad (Wright, [ed.] 1981:275) were from domestic contexts similar to Operation B and the Brick Kiln Cut. Both of these sites have unbroken sequences of Middle and Late Uruk and Jemdet Nasr periods (Wilson 1986:57; Wright, [ed.] 1981:71).

The parallels with Middle Uruk Nippur in particular are extensive. Beveled rim bowls at Nippur (Hansen 1965:fig. 4) occur in Inanna Middle Uruk levels (but they are not numerous until Late Uruk level XVI). At Godin Tepe there are only five beveled rim bowl sherds from Operation B middle and late VI strata: two sherds from B23, one sherd from B20, one sherd from B18?-19, and one sherd from B17-19 (all in Tehran, so they could not be drawn). There are similar plain flaring bowls (which can be compared with conical cups in that they have plain flaring rims) in both Middle Uruk Inanna levels (Hansen 1965:fig. 5) and Godin Tepe late Period VI (Fig. 7 [B20 #251, N3 34 #26]). There are short funnel spouted jars from Middle Uruk Nippur (Inanna XX [7N816] and XVII [7NP281] both unpublished) which are similar to a single example from the middle Period VI Brick Kiln Cut (Fig. 8 [N3 28 #1]). The unusual medium grit temper and distinctive manufacturing technique suggest this jar was an import into Godin Tepe. A middle Period VI tall jar (Fig. 8 [Gd 73-301 N3 32]) can be compared to an Inanna

XVIII Uruk type tall jar (7N796, without neck or base, unpublished). Everted rim jars from Middle Uruk Nippur (especially 7N815 from Inanna XX) compare with jars from middle and late Period VI (Fig. 8 [Operation B23 #366, and B20 #239]). There are similar collar necked jars with rope (raised and incised) decoration at the neck base from Middle Uruk Nippur (Inanna XX 7NP317, unpublished) and middle Period VI Operation B (Fig. 8 [B23 #359]). Clusters of applied pellets as exterior jar decoration already occur in middle Period VI Godin (Fig. 8 [B23 #338, with an unusual white shell temper]), but there is a later Late Uruk parallel from Nippur (Inanna XVI, 7NP262, unpublished). Large ledge (expanded) rim bowls from Nippur (Inanna XX, not registered, and XIX 7NP307, both unpublished) compare with Godin Tepe middle and late Period VI examples (Fig. 7 [Operation B23, #387, B20 #223]). There are large inturned rim bowls with an interior bevel both at middle Period VI Godin (Fig. 7 [B23 #385, #388]) and Nippur Inanna level XVI-XVII (7NP 277, unpublished). There are similar trays from Nippur Inanna XIX (Hansen 1965: fig. 8) and Godin late Period VI (Fig. 7 [B20 #252, P4 20 #4]; there are also trays in middle Period VI).

In addition, there are parallels with Tepe Farukhabad Middle Uruk that include coarse handmade grit tempered jars with a thickened or rolled rim (Wright, [ed.] 1981:fig. 42e). Similar bulbous jars (but with a different rim and ware than the Godin Tepe examples) are also found at Middle Uruk Nippur (Inanna XX 7NP319, but in gray ware, unpublished). At Godin Tepe, they are either pink or pink buff before late Period VI (as in early Period VI Operation B26-29, Young 1969:69, fig. 8:5). In late Period VI, most were slipped a distinctive red color (for example, Fig. 9 [Operation B20 #241, B21 #306]).

The pottery parallels with Tepe Farukhabad and Nippur, and the presence of Uruk administrative-linked artifact types of a geometric token[10] (Fig. 8 [Brick Kiln Cut N3 30]) and beveled rim bowls in middle and late Period VI could indicate a relationship was already established in the Middle Uruk period as part of the first Uruk expansion. Significantly, there is also the first occurrence of copper/bronze metal at Godin Tepe (in Operation B, Young 1969:fig. 8:21), which could indicate expanded trade.

There is a noticeable lack of evidence for middle and late Period VI occupation in the area of the Deep Sounding in either Operation XYZ,[11] Operation A, or various test trenches from within the later Period V buildings of the oval. It is not known whether this is due to the terracing or 'bulldozing' (as at Tell Brak [J. Oates and D. Oates 1997:295; this volume, p. 114]) of the remains of the immediately preceding phases. Both these phases of Period VI are present in Operation B and the Brick Kiln Cut. In both locations, strata dating to Period V overlay those dating to the late Period VI phase (Fig. 4, 2). In the northern edge of the Brick Kiln Cut, both late Period VI and Period V phase strata are truncated by an erosion layer topped by Period IV remains (Fig. 2).

EARLY PERIOD V

The beginning of Period V (Operation B17 and B16, early V levels below the Deep Sounding oval [discussed below], and early Period V in the Brick Kiln Cut) is marked by a significant increase in the number and variety of distinctive Uruk ceramics as well as a continuation of some local forms (Fig. 10). For the first time there are string cut bases (Fig. 16 [N3 23]) and Uruk type coarse straw tempered trays (similar to Fig. 11 [A2 1187 #1] and Fig. 13 [B1 479 #212]), and there is a marked increase in the number of beveled rim bowls in Operation B, the Brick Kiln Cut, and the area under the oval building complex in the Deep Sounding. Again, there are parallels with the beginning of the Late Uruk at Nippur. In Inanna XVI, there are increased quantities of beveled rim bowls, and the first appearance of unfinished string cut bases. Additionally, several Godin Tepe local pottery forms show Uruk influence, a phenomenon that will be discussed later.

There is evidence for a Late Uruk building level below that of the main Period V building complex of the Deep Sounding. On the northern edge of the mound, both Operations A strata A34 and A35 and XYZ spits 1-4 (Fig. 6) have considerable Late Uruk remains (Uruk type trays, beveled rim bowls, coarse straw tempered conical cup rims [such as Fig. 10 Operation B17 #159 with pronounced rilling], and string cut bases) well below the walls of the Period V phase buildings. There is not enough excavated evidence to define the nature of the early Late Uruk contact at this time, but an early Period V phase contemporary with the beginning of the Late Uruk Period in the south is proposed in this paper (Chart 1).

MIDDLE PERIOD V

Middle Period V in Operation B (strata B15 and B14) and the Brick Kiln Cut is a continuation of early Period V with no substantial changes in the material remains. Beveled rim bowls, coarse Uruk type trays, coarse conical cup rims and string cut bases continue from early Period V along with local type pottery.

In the Deep Sounding, middle Period V is marked by the major construction of the complex of buildings within the oval (Fig. 5), and the appearance of increased quantities and types of Uruk style pottery (Fig. 11, 12, 9 [B01 58 #1, B01 58 #10]) and small finds on the earliest floors, representing a significant intrusion of foreign material culture. This material is dated by radio-carbon analysis to around 3350 BC (averaging the dates published by Dyson 1987:666-67,677). There were not only selected Late Uruk pot types, but also tablets, cylinder sealings (Weiss and Young 1975:fig. 4, 5), objects of metal (pins, needles, chisels, a spearhead, and a 'standard'), stone (beads, a macehead and spindle whorls), and the occurrence of imported bitumen.

The new pottery introductions again have parallels with Middle and Late Uruk pottery from Nippur. They include wheelmade flaring bowls with a beveled edge rim (Fig. 11 [A2 1185 #30] as Nippur Inanna [XVII 7NP 279]), straight sided carinated bowls (Fig. 11 [A2 1187 #29] as Nippur Inanna XVIII-XVI [XVII-XVIII 7NP 292]), beveled (Fig. 11 [A2 1185 #13]) and folded over (from Room 10, possibly later than middle V:[12] Fig. 13 [B1 517 #6]) varieties of bottle rims (as Nippur Inanna levels XVII-XV), tall jars (Fig. 12 [B01 56 #22] as earlier Middle Uruk Nippur Inanna XIX 7NP 311), and neckless jars (Fig. 13 [B1 479 #181] as Nippur Inanna XVI and XV). Four lugged jars are another middle Period V introduction (Fig. 11 [A2 1187 #41]; Fig. 12 [A01 44 #47/48]) that are the same general type as Nippur Late Uruk four lugged jars (but see discussion below).

There are also trough spouted jars at Godin Tepe (Fig. 11 [A2 1185/1187 #21]; Fig. 13 [painted body only, B1 519 #5]) which do not occur at Nippur, but are present at Susa 17 (LeBrun 1978b fig. 24: 9, 10) and Siyalk IV (Ghirshman 1938 pl. LXXXVIII).

LATE PERIOD V

Architectural and Artifact Changes in the Deep Sounding
The latest floors of the rooms of the Deep Sounding oval are called late Period V, and dated by radio-carbon analysis to 3100-2900 BC (Dyson 1987:666-67,677).[13] There were significant architectural changes within the oval; these are all illustrated on the late Period V plan (Fig. 5), although the order in which they occurred cannot be determined. Both the finds on the latest floors and the architectural modifications suggest a change in function for the oval, a definite lessening of Uruk influence, and the first evidence for contact with Transcaucasian culture evidenced by finds of Transcaucasian pottery and small find types.

There were primarily two types of architectural changes: the blocking of doorways, and the construction of additional walls. The doorways leading from gateway room 4 east to room 3, and from room 3 to room 2a were blocked. All the doorways in the Northern Building Addition (rooms 10-13)[14] were also blocked, and it is likely that this group of rooms went out of use. A group of irregular walls was added to the courtyard, breaking the clear view of the room 18 windows from the north doorway of gateway room 4 and a curtain wall was constructed that shielded the doorways of rooms 19, 20 and 22. A hearth was added to room 20.

The floors of late Period V are sometimes difficult to identify, as they are located immediately beneath the bricky collapse of the Period V buildings. However, in all excavated areas of the Deep Sounding, multiple floors were noted. The finds from the uppermost floor often differed markedly from the earliest floor of the rooms. This is especially true for rooms 2a and 3 of the Southern Complex, room 18 of the Northern Building and room 20.

In room 2a there was a change from an administrative assemblage (finds from the earliest floor include a tablet and a jar sealing) to one indicative of craft and wine production (Badler 1995:51-52). On the late floor were found three large worked stone cores, a metal chisel, an incompletely perforated stone disk (Fig. 18 [Gd 73-281 A2 1179], which may indicate they were made in this room), and a charred wooden disk (Fig. 18 [Gd73-270 A2 1183]) that may have functioned as a spindle whorl.[15] A rectangular bin possibly used for winemaking (Fig. 5) was constructed on this floor. There were also sherds from 'empty' (no visible residue) wine jars (Fig. 14 [A2 1176 #52]) found together with a large funnel (Fig. 14 [A2 1176 #59]) and a heavy lid (Fig. 14 [A2 1176/1179 #63] weighing about a kilogram). Both the funnel and lid were handmade, and of a coarse grit tempered ware similar to Transcaucasian ceramics (the lid type occurs later in Period IV contexts).

Of the 34 artifacts found in room 18, only two were from the Late Period V floor. Although there was one clay jar stopper identified as being from the late floor, there were no other administrative artifacts. Additionally, there was a marked decrease in the number of four-lugged jars found in the room. Room 20, in contrast, contained no small finds in middle Period V, but in late Period V a hearth was added, and the room now contained luxury goods previously found in room 18 (such as stone beads [a complete necklace, Gd 73-69], and rope decorated jars [Fig. 15 Gd73-112, Gd73-113 with bung hole] with wine residue [Badler 1995]; additionally, there was a stone bowl fragment [Fig. 15 Gd73-87]).

Ceramic Changes

The most noticeable change in the late Period V ceramic assemblage is the presence of significant percentages of the Transcaucasian ware that later dominates Godin Tepe in Period IV. If Transcaucasian pottery were not so ubiquitous in late Period V, these sherds could be explained as throw downs from later levels. The late Period V floors of Operation B (strata B12B and C, B12A), the Deep Sounding, and the Brick Kiln Cut all have a mixture of local, Uruk, and Transcaucasian type sherds.

Additionally, there is a small group of pots from late Period V contexts (Fig. 16) which are local Period VI and V in shape, but not in fabric and manufacturing technique. For instance, the shape of sherd A2 1176 #22 can be compared with Period VI and V inturned rim bowls. In contrast to these wheel-made inturned rim bowls, this example is handmade and very irregular with the rim pinched to produce its slight taper. The body is grayish suggesting reduced oxygen firing conditions, and the fabric has a grit temper more similar to the later Transcaucasian wares. Other shapes in handmade Transcaucasian type wares include a flaring plain rim bowl (Gd73-347), a sieve (N3 3 #2), and a shallow dish or tray (N3 3 #1)[16]. An additional tray with a ledge handle (A2 1176 #60, not illustrated) has a similar very

coarse grit temper, and the handle is unique. Since most of these examples occur in late Period V contexts, they were probably not the result of a later Period IV Transcaucasian copying motifs from previously discarded sherds. It is also interesting that all the above shapes are local types originating in Period VI.[17]

In late Period V there are three examples of bowls with interior decoration (Fig. 14 [A2 1183, Gd73-357 A2 1176] and Fig. 17 [B01 78 #30]) made of local Godin fabric. There is no precedent for interior decoration on bowls at Godin Tepe, and one explanation would be Transcaucasian influence on local Godin potters. Interior decoration on flaring bowls was a common Transcaucasian type motif at Godin Tepe (cf. Young 1969:fig. 11:3 [from late V Operation B stratum 13], fig. 11:5 [from a Period IV context]). These vessels may be examples of hybrid ceramics similar to the local/Uruk hybrid vessels discussed below, and indicate that the two cultures were both present and interacting with each other at the end of Godin Tepe Period V.

There are other changes as well. Although jars are much less frequent in late Period V, one exhibits a change in style from the preceding middle phase. Jar A01 67 #1 (Fig. 17) is unique in two respects: the decoration is red on a cream colored slip, and this decoration occurs on the shoulder of the vessel rather than at the carination.

There are a few Uruk types that only occur in this phase such as droop spouts (Fig. 17 [A2 1127]). There is a unique example of a mountain goat in relief on a very large pithos type jar in cream slipped local fabric (Fig. 17 [A01 40, A2 302]). Although the leg of the goat (and other sherds probably belonging to the same jar) was found in a late Period V context in excavation square A01, most of the goat relief was found two to three meters above in a Period III lot in excavation square A2.[18] There are several examples of this type of relief in Late Uruk Pottery, including a jar with two goats and a snake from Choga Mish (Delougaz and Kantor, Alizadeh, ed. 1996 Pt. 2: Pl. 26) and an appliqué design in the shape of a ram's horns from Nippur (unpublished, Inanna XVIII 7NP291).

EVIDENCE FOR THE INTERRELATIONSHIP BETWEEN THE URUK FOREIGNERS AND THE LOCAL GODIN TEPE VILLAGERS

ARCHITECTURE

The middle Period V complex of buildings within the oval wall of Godin Tepe (Fig. 5) has previously been described as functioning as a fort with food rations and weapons (slingballs) being distributed from the windows of room 18 to village recruits queued up in the courtyard (Badler 1989, Badler 2000). There also may have been a trade component as proposed by Weiss and Young (Weiss and Young 1975).[19] There is also considerable evidence for additional interaction between the locals and foreigners: the buildings within the oval wall were most likely built not by foreign Uruk laborers, but by local villagers. The most obvious evidence consists of brick sizes and hearth types.

Although the brick sizes from the buildings within the oval vary (Chart 2), they are similar in dimension to those used in the Brick Kiln Cut in the surrounding village (Fig. 3). The brick sizes are quite different from those of the Uruk sites of Nippur, Uruk, Susa, Tepe Faruhkabad and Siyalk to the south in both absolute length and relative proportions.

The rectangular hearths built against the long wall of the buildings of the Godin Tepe oval complex (Fig. 5) are also quite different from the typical Uruk free standing 'frying pan' hearths (see Oates, this volume, p. 115) located in the center of the room. Although there are few definite hearths in the limited architectural remains of the local village, there is one hearth dating to Period V in the Brick Kiln Cut (Fig. 3 [feature 1, lot P4 7]) which compares closely in its rectangular form and raised platform to the Deep Sounding examples. Drains, however, were probably a foreign Late Uruk introduction and occur exclusively in the Period V buildings of the Deep Sounding Oval (Fig. 18). It is not known whether the original drains were laid horizontally or vertically.

POTTERY

Pottery has a long history at Godin Tepe, with a ceramic repertoire which included shapes such as jars, trays, cooking vessels, spouted vessels, and large and small bowls well established by early Period VI. The high quality of these vessels suggests that specialized craft production was already in place and the pottery was made by skilled artisans.

Beveled Rim Bowls

If a vessel's function is dependent on its shape and size, then the Uruk vessels, when introduced, are functionally redundant shapes. With many local small bowls available, there was no functional need for the beveled rim bowl (Fig. 13 [B1 479 #1, 5, 12, 42]). One explanation for why they were introduced is cost, defined in terms of expenditure and quality of labor. In raw materials, the beveled rim bowl employs similar clay and firing techniques to local vessels, so there is no advantage there. However, these bowls could be hand-made quickly by unskilled workers without additional tools. At Godin Tepe (as at other sites) they are the most irregular of all bowls. Their rims rarely conform to a regular circle (confounding attempts to ascertain rim sherd diameters), and a single vessel may vary considerably in vessel height and wall thickness. While wheel-made coarse straw tempered Uruk conical bowls (Grobe Blumentöpfen [GBT]) could certainly be made quickly, they required both specialized equipment and a skilled artisan. Beveled rim bowls are the least 'expensive' functionally adequate bowl available. They represent the ultimate triumph of function over aesthetics. The bowls and their contents

were no doubt 'distributed' in exchange for labor, as has been suggested most notably by Hans Nissen (recently in Nissen, Damerow, and Englund 1993:14, and Nissen, this volume, p.10).[20] It may be significant, if these cheap bowls were given away to workers employed by the Uruk bureaucracy, that they are usually the first Uruk artifact to appear at a foreign site. Uruk centers to the south could have drawn foreign laborers who later returned to their villages, bringing with them a souvenir of their experience, the beveled rim bowl.

There were no kilns identified at Godin Tepe, but one over-fired beveled rim bowl waster (from the Deep Sounding, lot B01 78, #11) could indicate these crude vessels were made and fired at the site.[21] A ceramic ring scraper (lot B01 69; Fig. 18) with an abraded edge also found in the Deep Sounding was most likely an Uruk introduction (Alden 1988), and could have been used in making large jars.

Although there are some size differences between the Godin beveled rim bowls and those found at other Uruk sites, the technique of making these bowls is remarkably similar at all Late Uruk sites. Because of the pattern of finger impressions on the exteriors of these vessels, it is unlikely that they were made in a mold. All beveled rim bowls I have examined from many Uruk sites (Warka/Uruk, Nippur, Ur, Nineveh, Godin Tepe, Susa, Tepe Farukhabad, Choga Mish, survey material from eastern Turkey [including Kum Ocağı], Samsat, Hacınebi, Habuba Kabira, and Tell Brak) show a pattern of finger impressions consistent with the manufacturing technique illustrated by J. Kalsbeek (Kalsbeek 1980:10). The finger and hand impressions are left from the last phases of manufacture (Kalsbeek 1980:10, number 6-9). There are finger impressions on the exterior and interior immediately below the bevel, and around the exterior body near the base. The bottom of the base often has the impression of the thumb pad adding to its irregularity. The size of the beveled rim bases is also consistent with the size of the human hand used to manufacture them. A fist impression is often seen on the interior (as in Kalsbeek 1980:10, number 9). The consistency of these impressions clearly indicates that whoever made these beveled rim bowls was taught a specific technique of manufacture, and essentially there was a transfer of technology from the heartland to widely separate Uruk sites in the periphery. Another example of a transfer of technology from the Uruk heartland to the site of Godin Tepe is the occurrence of large jars with irregular interior grooves and double strap handles used in brewing beer (similar to Fig. 17 [Gd 73-401 A2 1178], Badler 2000; also see Van Driel, this volume, p. 195).[22]

Four Lugged Jars

The form of the four lugged jar (Fig. 11 [A2 1187 #41]; Fig. 12 [A01 44 #47/48]) is essentially a modification of the earlier, perhaps Uruk influenced, collar necked jar with rope decoration around its neck (Fig. 8 [B23 #359]).

Site	Maximum dimension	Minimum dimensions	Details	Source
GODIN BKC VI	38 cm	15 x 10 cm	Wall J, south face	P4 Godin notes July 14, 1973
GODIN BKC VI	34 cm	? x 10 cm	Wall J doorway, blockage bricks	Godin notes July 14, 1973
GODIN BKC VI	30 cm	16 x 8 cm	Wall K - constructed, breadthwise of 3 bricks, the outer ones on edge, flanking one laid on its wider edge.	P4 Godin notes July 14, 1973
GODIN Op. B17 EV	43 or 42	43 or 42	Wall K	Operation B notes, October 31, 1965
GODIN DS MV B1	40 cm	20 x 6.5 cm	B1 wall BX between rooms 13 and 14 bricks	B1 Godin notes
GODIN DS MV BO1	20 cm	20 x 6 cm	Wall AB between rooms 13 and 12	B1 Godin notes
GODIN DS MV BO1	30 cm	20 x 6 cm	Wall AB between rooms 13 and 12	B1 Godin notes
GODIN DS V	43 cm	18 x 8		Restoration notes; also on restoration photos 1977
GODIN DS V	43 cm	20 x 8		A1 Godin notes, blocking bricks - NE doorway of Wall ES
GODIN DS V	40 cm	? x 7		wall EU, Room 23, A1 Godin notes
GODIN DS V	20 cm	? x 7		wall EU, Room 23, A1 Godin notes
SUSA	20 cm	8 x 8 cm		LeBrun in Finkbeiner and Röllig 1986: 315
URUK-WARKA Uruk and JN	16 (or more) cm	8 x 8 cm	Riemchen (square at end, length more than 2 times square)	Nissen in Finkbeiner and Röllig 1986: 314; for an extensive list see Finkbeiner 1986 Appendix II: 51-52
NIPPUR Middle and Late Uruk	21.5 - 22.5 cm	10.5 - 11.5 x 8.5 - 9.5 cm	Average	Wilson 1986: 58
SIALK IV	30 cm	30 x 10 cm		Ghirshman 1938: 59
TEPE FARUKHABAD Uruk, JN, ED	21-30 cm	10 - 18 cm wide x 6 - 10 cm thick	rectangular or trapezoidal in cross-section	Wright, H.T. (ed.) 1981: 76-77

Chart 2. Uruk period mudbrick sizes

Presumably this plastic rendition of a rope reflects the use of actual rope to secure a lid of a pliable material such as cloth or leather to the mouth of the vessel. The Uruk type nose lugs, carefully pierced to allow a small rope to be threaded through, essentially lower the rope to a position on the body of the vessel as opposed to the neck. The most obvious effect of this change in position is that the rope no longer lies in the concave vessel neck, but instead on a slightly convex, almost flat surface. It would seem that this change in rope position would make the jar easier to seal with a cylinder seal rolled on a wad of clay. In any case, at Godin Tepe this type of jar only occurs in the middle and late Period V Deep Sounding, where cylinder seals were also being used.

From the drawings of Godin Tepe four lugged jars, comparisons can be made with the pottery from the Late Uruk heartland in southern Iraq and Iran. Some of these vessels were no doubt imported from southern or other Late Uruk sites, and close examination of some of the actual jars seems to confirm this conclusion. A Godin Tepe striped jar (Fig. 12 [A1 1152 #68]) in particular is distinct in its color and temper, and compares closely with Nippur jars (7N778 jar with handle, XV-XVI, Royal Ontario Museum 962.143.107 and 7N781 small four lugged jar with rounded base, XVI, Royal Ontario Museum 962.143.108). Other Godin Tepe jars exhibit significant differences from those of the south, in particular, several examples of red slipped jars and one late Period V example of an incised cream slipped four lugged jar.

One explanation for the differences between most Godin Tepe four lugged jars and those from Uruk sites to the south is that the Godin Tepe examples were imitations made by local potters using clay fabric, slips, firing, decoration, and manufacturing and trimming techniques more consistent with the pottery tradition of the preceding Period VI. The fabric of these pots, clay with some grit inclusions but with an added straw temper, is typical of Godin local pottery of both Period VI and Period V, and differs from the grit tempered finer wares of Uruk sites.

Red-slipped pottery was not in itself an Uruk introduction, as there is a long tradition of red-slipped (most likely from iron oxide) pottery from Godin Tepe (Fig. 9).[23] 'Red-Slipped Ware' (Levine and Young 1986:35; Young 1969:3) with a gray unoxidized core is a characteristic coarse ware of Period VII, accounting for up to 17% of the total assemblage (Young 1969:51, Table 1) and continues to occur (although less frequently) in early Period VI (Young 1969:52, Table 2). In late Period VI, red-slipped vessels appear again in the Middle Uruk influenced red-slipped grit tempered coarse jars with a thickened or rolled rim (discussed above). These jars also have gray incompletely oxidized cores. Most red-slipped four lugged jars at Godin Tepe have similar cores, contrasting with the well-made pottery with fully oxidized cores from Uruk sites to the south. Godin Period V four lugged jars can also be cream slipped over a buff pink clay body like the pottery of the preceding Period VI

(Fig. 17 [A1 1151 Gd73-403]). Jars from Uruk sites are usually not slipped, but are made of cream or buff clay. The skill with which most Uruk jars were made is quite high; in general, foreign type pots from Godin Tepe are more poorly made than their southern counterparts.

Decoration
Although many types of incised jar decoration occur in Uruk sites in the south (for instance, at Susa: Level 17B [LeBrun 1978b: fig. 33]; Choga Mish [Delougaz and Kantor, Alizadeh, ed. 1996 Pt. 2:Pl. 24, 25, 120, 121, 122, 123] Habuba Kabira [Sürenhagen 1978: Tab. 6:63, 65; Tab. 35:13, 15-20, 22, 26-29, 34; Tab. 36:40-44, 46-48]), there is only one example of an incised four lugged jar from Godin Tepe (mentioned above, from late Period V, Fig. 13 [A1 1151 Gd73-403]) and no examples of the typical reserved slip prevalent at Uruk sites. There is one Godin example (Fig. 9 [B01 58 #10]) where the decoration is 'wiped away' using a similar technique to reserved slip.

Most Godin Tepe Uruk type jars employ local decorative motifs that were used in the preceding Period VI: horizontal notching (Fig. 17 [A1 1163 #8, Gd73-400 A2 1181]) and rope (incised raised band) decoration (Fig. 19 [A2 1187 #41] and Fig. 12 [A01 71 #16, A01 44 #47/48]). Horizontal notching first appears at Godin Tepe at the end of early Period VI, and continues into late Period VI (Fig. 7 [B19-22 #205, B20 #255]). Rope decoration is the most common decorative motif seen on Godin Tepe four-lugged jars. This type of décor was used at the site from middle Period VI onwards (Fig. 8 [B23 #359]). Additionally, there are some parallels between the painted geometric motifs on Period V four-lugged jars and those on Period VI pottery.

Trimming
The method of trimming vessels at Godin Tepe is also not consistent with typical Late Uruk sites. Period V Uruk type wheelmade jars are trimmed by scraping, sometimes in a diagonal pattern, consistent with the local Period VI tradition. The vessels from the southern Uruk sites are often trimmed by paring down the clay.[24] There are no examples of this method from Godin Tepe.

A case may be made that Godin village potters were imitating the southern Late Uruk jar forms using clay, techniques of manufacture, and decoration that were part of their local ceramic tradition. But there is an interesting dichotomy here: while beveled rim bowls were made like their Uruk counterparts, the Godin potters were evidently not taught how to make the wide variety of four-lugged jars found in the south. A possible explanation is that, as previously suggested, unskilled labor was employed in beveled rim bowl manufacture, while the more challenging Uruk type jars were ordered from skilled village artisans.

String Cut Bases
The string cut bases that are parts of whole vessels from the Brick Kiln Cut and Operation B areas of the village

have an interesting combination of ceramic traditions: the shapes are local, but the method of leaving the base untrimmed is Uruk (Fig. 16 [Gd 73-136 BKC P4 12, Gd 73-34 BKC P4 1, Gd 73-192 BKC N3 23], Fig. 17 [Operation B12B/C #21]). The inturned rim bowl (Fig. 16 [Gd73-302, Gd 73-303, BKC N3 32,Gd 73-136 BKC P4 12]) has a long history at Godin Tepe beginning in Period VII, and the flared plain rim bowl (Fig. 16 [Gd 73-201 BKC P4 34, Gd73-34 BKC P4 1, Gd 73-192 BKC N3 23]) first appears in late Period VI, when both types are commonly wheel-made, trimmed by diagonal scraping below the carination and not slipped. Either the potters adopted this practice of leaving the pots untrimmed to shorten the manufacturing time, or an advance in equipment or technique allowed them to throw pots which did not require trimming off excess clay.

Another example of combining the Uruk and local traditions is the production of small rolled rim bowls on the wheel with a red slip (Fig. 9 [Brick Kiln Cut P4 10 #8]). In the previous Period VI nearly all of these bowls were cream slipped (as Fig. 16 [Brick Kiln Cut N4 20]; these bowls are especially common in the later part of the period). There is also a Period V variant of these bowls (Fig. 16 [Gd73-118 Deep Sounding B01 76, in Iran, described as burnished buff and red]; Fig. 13 [B1 479 #147, not slipped]) which is wheelmade and with a more flaring stance and rather tapered rim. B1 479 #147 was not only wheelmade, but it was also wheel trimmed (there are concentric circles on the base bottom and along the sides of the vessel below the carination which can be seen in the illustration).

Wheel trimming a vessel requires considerable skill and time. The vessel must first be thrown well enough to be quite symmetric. The vessel is then partially dried so it is soft enough to remove the excess clay, but stiff enough to hold its shape when manipulated. The vessel is then centered again on the wheel upside down, and held securely with three pieces of soft clay pressed against the wheel and the vessel. It is perhaps significant that a fired piece of clay with finger impressions such as would be used to hold the vessel to the wheel was found in the same pottery lot. A sharp tool is then used while the wheel is rotating to remove the excess clay. Since the vessel is upside down, it is difficult to gauge just how much clay to remove, and there is always the danger of removing too much and piercing the vessel. Wheel trimming demonstrates an important advance in technique over hand trimming or string cut bases.

THE GENDER FACTOR

The full repertoire of Uruk pottery forms is absent at Godin Tepe. There are no cooking jars with strap or twisted handles,[25] large ovoid storage jars with rounded bases and cylindrical necks, rim spouts or false spouts, or small grit tempered conical cups (Blumentöpfen). The lack of significant numbers of Late Uruk pottery types could be explained both by the absence of Uruk potters

and the utilization of local village potters to reproduce selected Uruk forms, and by the corresponding lack of demand for certain Uruk domestic vessels due to the possible absence of foreign Uruk women at Godin Tepe.

If spinning can be associated with women in this period, then the numbers of local spindle whorls found within the oval, and the corresponding lack of Uruk spindle whorls, could be significant. There are only three typical Uruk spindle whorls found in late Period V (Fig. 18). The lack of evidence for significant numbers of Uruk women would correlate with the interpretation of the primary function of Godin Tepe as a fort, but it also could be true of a trading outpost as well. Textual evidence from the Old Assyrian trading colony at Kültepe in Anatolia (where there is a similar lack of foreign pottery [T. Özgüç 1986:10, 53; Larsen 1976:53]) indicates that at least in the beginning of the period, the Assyrian traders left their wives behind in Assyria (Veenhof 1982:147). In sites such as Habuba Kabira (Sürenhagen 1978) and Jebel Aruda (see this volume) which have been identified as colonies - implying the migration of whole families - the entire material culture has been transplanted and the complete domestic Uruk pottery assemblage is present.[26]

CONCLUSIONS

There is a long history of Uruk artifacts at Godin Tepe suggesting continuous contact from the Middle until the end of the Late Uruk Period during middle and late Period VI, and early, middle, and late Period V. The previously published finds from the Godin Period V oval (Weiss and Young 1975, Young 1986, Badler 1995, Badler et al. 1990, Badler et al. 1996, McGovern et al. 1997, Michel et al. 1992, Michel et al. 1993) date exclusively to middle and late Period V, and represent only the final phases of contact between Godin Tepe and the Late Uruk culture. There is evidence for an extended period of exchange of artifacts and labor between the Uruk people and the Godin Tepe villagers. This suggested use of village labor in both constructing the oval complex and manufacturing Uruk type pottery implies a significant degree of interaction between the two groups. All evidence indicates that the nature of this foreign penetration was a peaceful one, with cooperative mutually beneficial relationships established between these two culturally distinct groups. It is also evident that the Uruk foreigners had considerable political power and resources to build a large fortified complex with limited access on the high point of the mound. However, the evidence available indicates the local Godin Tepe culture was not supplanted by the more complex society to the south. The changes observed in the two areas of the village excavated are not primarily in the small finds, but rather in the pottery. Three types of Uruk coarse vessels (the beveled rim bowl, Uruk type tray, and coarse conical cup) were used in the village. Certain stylistic (the more extensive use of a red slip) and time saving features (such as leaving an unfinished string cut base when making a pot) were also adopted, producing 'hybrid' pots combining local and Uruk ceramic traditions. There is no evidence that the characteristics of Late Uruk society that we find so impressive - the artifacts of a complex society - were adopted by the Godin Tepe villagers. The middle and late Period V tablets, sealings, and seals are found only within the oval complex, and there was nothing found in the surrounding village to suggest that the local people were influenced to develop a higher degree of social complexity than existed previously.[27] It is clear that contact with a more socially advanced culture does not result in emulation or wholesale adoption if there is no perceived practical benefit.

ACKNOWLEDGEMENTS

I wish to thank T. Cuyler Young, Jr. for his generosity and his patience in allowing me to study the material from Godin Tepe, and also to the staff of the Near Eastern and Asian Civilizations of the Royal Ontario Museum for their considerable assistance. I also wish to thank the numerous researchers who allowed me to study their Uruk material: Abbas Alizadeh (Choga Mish), Guillermo Algaze (southeastern Turkey), Rainer Michael Boehmer, Harald Hauptmann, Michael Müller-Karpe, and Felix Blocher (Warka/Uruk), Dominique Collon (Nineveh and Ur), Annie Caubet and Agnes Benoit (Susa and Siyalk), Robert H. Dyson, Jr. (Susa and Ur), Marcella Frangipane (Arslantepe), Donald P. Hansen and Karen L. Wilson (Nippur), C. C. Lamberg-Karlovsky (Siyalk), Joan Oates (Tell Brak), Nimet Özgüç (Samsat), Gil Stein (Hacınebi), Dietrich Sürenhagen (Habuba Kabira), G. van Driel and C. van Driel-Murray (Jebel Aruda), and Henry T. Wright (Tepe Farukhabad). I am deeply grateful to Nicholas Postgate and Stuart Campbell for allowing me to present my paper at the symposium, and for their gracious hospitality. I also wish to thank my husband, Norman Badler, for spending considerable time transforming most of my drawings into plates.

[1] There is a question as to whether 'Period V' at Godin Tepe should be renamed 'Period VI/V' emphasizing the cultural continuity between Periods VI and V. There is substantial cultural continuity between Periods VI and V, and if the periodization of Godin Tepe is on the basis of material culture, then a change from 'V' to 'VI/V' is warranted. However, I prefer to use the periods at Godin Tepe as chronological markers indicating a continuous sequence in time. I am therefore keeping with the original (Young 1969) period names where the strata of Period V directly follow that of Period VI, and precede those of Period IV.

[2] Godin Tepe was excavated in the late 1960's and early 1970's under the direction of T. Cuyler Young, Jr. of the Royal Ontario Museum, Toronto.

[3] In the latest floors associated with Period V buildings, there are significant percentages of Transcaucasian type pottery (in Operation A32, late V floor of oval room 23: 3%; Operation B: B11 8%, B12A 48%, B12B/C 6%, B13 2%).

[4] Young 1969:3: '...the division point has been chosen rather arbitrarily on the basis of a marked increase in painted pottery and a falling off in quantity of Coarse Buff-slipped and Red-slipped Wares in stratum 34, combined with a considerable increase in the amount of Fine White-slipped Ware in stratum 35.'

[5] Young 1969: fig. 7:2, 4-10, 12-14; fig. 8:2, 8, 13, 15, 17.

[6] The pottery from the earliest strata of the Brick Kiln Cut compares with that of Operation B middle Period VI in both shape and decoration. There is a corresponding lack of painted sherds. Although there are only 49 sherds from the earliest seven strata (N3 39, 37, 36, 27, 26, and 22), just four, or 8%, are painted.

[7] E. F. Henrickson assigned spits 12-5 to Period VI, and 4-0 to Period V (E. F. Henrickson 1983:172). This is debatable: there are joins between spits 3 and 5, no doubt due to the fact that the 'burned bits of bricky material, charcoal chunks' stratum on the section extends from spit 1 through the top of spit 5.

[8] Unfortunately the middle and late Period VI Operation B beveled rim bowl sherds are in Tehran and could not be studied in detail. For a further discussion of Middle Uruk beveled rim bowls see Rothman, this volume, p. 56.

[9] These results were first presented in Badler 1988. I am grateful to Donald P. Hansen and Karen L. Wilson for allowing me to study this most important material.

[10] Sifting was rare at Godin Tepe, and in 1973 the importance of tokens was not yet fully recognized. Only six clay tokens in all were recovered from both Periods VI and V. The following tokens were from Period V: clay pellet, round, with thumb-impressed base (Godin 1973 artifact, lot A01 35), conical base, but top expands before break (Godin 1973 artifact, lot A01 72), irregular cone (Gd 73-343, lot A1 1139, room 1, late V), half pierced cone (Gd 73-340, lot A2 1193 room 3-4 doorway, middle V), and irregular flat disk (Godin 1973 artifact, lot B1 506 room 6a).

[11] There is a notable absence of middle and late Period VI forms in the Operation XYZ spits 5-12 assigned by E. F. Henrickson to Period VI. Pedestal bases, one of the hallmarks of Period VI (in Operation B, they make up 33%, 50% and 45% of all bases in early, middle and late Period VI respectively), do not occur in these spits. They are present only in the later spits labeled 'Period V' (two from spit 0, and one from spit 1). There is a noticeable absence of even the most numerous middle and late Period VI small bowl forms. There are no typical middle and late Period VI unslipped straw tempered inturned rim bowls with scraping below the carination, flaring plain rim bowls, or small cream slipped bowls with a rolled or beaded rim. Disk or ring bases, rolled or beaded rim pithos sherds, pithos interiors with knobs or ribs, and sieves are also absent. The presence of 100 cm of bricky wash overlying the spit 7-8 floor could be the stratigraphic evidence for this significant chronological gap.

[12] Sometime after its construction, room 10 was filled with broken pottery (including large quantities of beveled rim bowl sherds) and then sealed. The presence of two pots with Transcaucasian parallels (Fig. 13 B1 479 #169 [with a gray

exterior] and B1 517 #10 [burnished gray and black]) may indicate a date later than middle Period V.

[11] There are three radio-carbon samples from late Period V: SI-2677 (3023-2784 BC) from lot A01 47, room 17, charcoal inside of a large jar on the late floor of the room; SI-2682 (3094-2902 BC) from lot B01 52, room 18, charcoal on the late V floor; and GaK 1072 (3094-2890 BC) from the floor of the hearth of Operation A stratum 32D, the late Period V floor of Deep Sounding room 23 equivalent to lots A1 1162 and A1 1163 (there are sherd joins between them). Two additional samples (SI-2671 and SI-2672) from late Period V lots were from hearths in rooms 17 and 18 that were used in both middle and late Period V, and these gave dates equivalent to middle Period V (3361-3045 BC and 3490-3107 BC).

[14] Rooms 10 and 12 had no hearths, and may have been storerooms. Room 12, with its reinforced walls, could have functioned as a treasury. Room 10 was filled with hundreds of potsherds, some of which are illustrated in Fig. 12.

[15] This wooden disk (Gd73-270) may provide evidence that some spindle whorls were made of wood during this time period. My preliminary studies indicate that wood shrinks an average of 50% after charring. Although this disk is now quite small (1.8 cm in diameter, 0.4 cm thick, and with a perforation 0.4 cm in diameter), its original size would have fallen within the Godin Tepe Periods VI and V stone and 'imitation stone' (blackened terracotta) disk ranges.

[16] R. B. Mason has examined this sherd, and found it has grog in its temper similar to that of Transcaucasian pottery (Mason and Cooper 1999).

[17] The fact that local pottery types, rather than Uruk types, are being imitated could indicate that the Uruk presence has already diminished in late Period V. This supports the contention of T. C. Young, Jr. (personal communication, August 6, 2000) that the Transcaucasians arrived first in Hamadan, effectively blocking the trade route leading to Godin Tepe.

[18] I am grateful to Robert C. Henrickson for bringing this sherd to my attention.

[19] There has been a question as to what sort of trade was taking place. The discovery of wine residues in Godin Tepe large jars (Badler 1995) and in Late Uruk jars and spouted jars from Warka/Uruk, Susa, and Tello (where the climate does not favor grape cultivation) suggests that wine could have been traded during this period (Badler et al. 1996). Other exports from Godin Tepe could have included textiles as there is an increase in spindle whorls in Period V. Although no loom weights were found at Godin Tepe, there is an impression (pseudomorph) of open weave cloth made on a loom (according to Louise Mackay, Royal Ontario Museum Department of Textiles and Costumes, personal communication, September 1996) from within the base of a large jar (Deep Sounding middle Period V, A01 44 #65, and additional large body sherds). Three possibilities are that this cloth was imported from a site which had looms, there are unexcavated loom weights at Godin Tepe, or this cloth was woven on a horizontal (flat) loom which did not require weights (see van Driel, this volume, p. 194).

[20] Nissen reports that these vessels make up to 80% of the total pottery assemblage. However, it must be noted that if the beveled rim bowl functional niche is the 'small bowl' category (open vessels with a rim diameter of less than 25 cm), this type of vessel commonly makes up 50% or more of the total pottery assemblage. At Godin Tepe, small bowls are 58% of early

Period VI Operation B vessels, 55% in middle Period VI, 60% in late Period VI, and 70% in Period V (when 37% of the small bowls are beveled rim bowls). The remainder of the assemblage consists of large bowls (over 25 cm), jars, pots, spouted vessels, and trays.

[21] Only a small area of the site of Godin Tepe was excavated, affecting both the size of our sample and the possible identification of special features such as kilns or other firing installations, which probably would have been located on the outskirts of the village (Wood 1990:33). The site was excavated during the 1960's and 70's, before the widespread use of magnetometry that would have made it possible to locate potential ancient kilns without extensive excavation. There were no kilns or other firing installations identified at the site, although enough clay was locally available to supply a modern brick kiln.

[22] A Choga Mish example of this type (Delougaz and Kantor, Alizadeh, ed. 1996 Pt. 1:414,Pt. 2 Plate 99C [IV-142a]) was found alongside a spouted jar (IV-139), a large spouted jar (IV-141) and a stick-ladle (IV-140) with a beveled rim bowl set in its mouth like a lid. If beer was made in this jar, perhaps this group of pottery is not fortuitous. The ladle could have been used to help fill the spouted jars. And, the beveled rim bowl functioning as a lid is just one of the many examples of the range of functions for this bowl.

[23] Munsell readings of Godin Tepe red ware, surface (core): VII type 'red-slipped ware' (Levine and Young 1986:35) from early Period VI Operation B: B33 #504 2.5YR 6-5/6, 2.5 YR N4/); B33 #497 2.5YR 6/6 (2.5 YR 6/8); B30-32 #450 5YR 6-5/6, rim 5YR 7-6/6 (2.5 YR N4/-N3/); B30-32 #457 10R 4/8 (5YR 5/4); late Period VI rolled rim jars: B21 #306 10R 5/6 (7.5YR N4/-N3/); B20 #241 10R 5/6, (7.5 YR N4/); Brick Kiln Cut Period V: P4 10 #8 5YR 6/6 (pink buff edges, gray center); Deep Sounding middle Period V: B01 58 #1 10R 6/8, 2/5 YR 6/6 (2/5 YR 6/6); B01 58 #10 10R 5/8 red slip, 5YR 6/4 interior, white paint 5YR 7/4 (2.5YR N4/).

[24] For example, at Nippur (Nippur vessel divided bowl 7N820 ROM 962.143.110) and at Choga Mish in southern Iran (small base Ch.M. III R19/3).

[25] Smoke blackened cooking pots from the Godin Tepe middle and late Period V oval consist of a large handmade grit tempered bowl (similar in shape and size to a modern wok): Fig. 11 (A2 1187 #36) and Fig. 14 (B01 53/51/49 #26).

[26] There is a similar phenomenon at Godin Tepe when Period IV is dominated by all aspects of Transcaucasian material culture - architecture, pottery, small finds such as beads and tools, and even dietary habits - suggesting a migration had taken place. In some areas of Godin Tepe, this culture appears overlying eroded areas of the mound, while in other parts a chronological gap in settlement is not evident. Contemporary villages in the Near East commonly have some areas that are currently unused. It seems logical that newcomers would settle in these particular areas in an already inhabited village, and the stratigraphy of site as a whole must be carefully examined before coming to any general conclusions about its chronology.

[27] I observed a similar event in the village next to Titriş Höyük in southeastern Turkey. The villagers readily reused our vessels (for instance, discarded bottles gathered from the trash pit each morning by the village children, or metal pails used for artifact collection which somehow made it to the village to be reused as water containers), but had no interest in our bureaucracy.

REFERENCES

Alden, J. R., 1988. 'Ceramic Ring Scrapers: An Uruk Period Pottery Production Tool,' *Paléorient* 14(1), 143-150.

Badler, V. R., 1988. 'The Uruk Period Pottery Development of Godin VI-V and Nippur Inanna XXI-XV,' XXXVe Rencontre Assyriologique Internationale, Abstracts.

Badler, V. R., 1989. 'Social Structure Changes Suggested by Artifact Assemblages of Godin V and VI,' in Out of the Heartland: The Evolution of Complexity in Peripheral Mesopotamia During the Uruk Period, workshop organized by M. S. Rothman, abstract published in *Paléorient* 15(1), 277-278.

Badler, V. R., 1995. 'The Archaeological Evidence for Winemaking, Distribution and Consumption at Proto-Historic Godin Tepe, Iran,' in P. E. McGovern, S. J. Fleming, and S. Katz (eds.), *The Origins and Ancient History of Wine*, Gordon and Breach, New York, 45-56.

Badler, V. R., 2000. 'The Dregs of Civilization: 5000 Year-Old Wine and Beer Residues from Godin Tepe, Iran,' *Bulletin of the Canadian Society for Mesopotamian Studies*, Volume 35, 48-56.

Badler, V. R., P. E. McGovern, and R. Michel, 1990. 'Drink and Be Merry! Infrared Spectroscopy and Ancient Near Eastern Wine,' in W. R. Biers and P. E. McGovern (eds.), *Organic Contents of Ancient Vessels: Materials Analysis and Archaeological Investigation*, MASCA, The University Museum of Archaeology and Anthropology, University of Pennsylvania, 25-36.

Badler, V. R., P. E. McGovern, and D. L. Glusker, 1996. 'Chemical Evidence for a Wine Residue from Warka (Uruk) Inside a Late Uruk Period Spouted Jar,' *Baghdader Mitteilungen* 27, 39-43.

Delougaz, P. and H. J. Kantor, Abbas Alizadeh (ed.), 1996. *Chogha Mish, Volume 1: The First Five Seasons of Excavations 1961-1971*. The Oriental Institute, University of Chicago.

Dyson, R. H., Jr., 1987. 'The Relative and Absolute Chronology of Hissar II and the Proto-Elamite Horizon of Northern Iran,' in O. Aurenche, J. Evin, and F. Hours (eds.) *Chronologies in the Near East*, BAR International Series 379, Oxford, 647-678.

Finkbeiner, U. and W. Röllig (ed.), 1986. *Ǧamdat Naṣr — Period or Regional Style?*, Reichert, Wiesbaden.

Ghirshman, R., 1938. *Fouilles de Sialk près de Kashan*, Volume 1, Librairie Orientaliste, Paul Geuthner.

Hansen, D.P., 1965. 'The Relative Chronology of Mesopotamia. Part II. The Pottery Sequence at Nippur from the Middle Uruk to the End of the Old Babylonian Period (3400-1600 BC),' in R.W. Ehrich (ed.), *Chronologies in the Old World*, 201-214.

Henrickson, E. F., 1983. *Ceramic Styles and Cultural Interaction in the Early and Middle Chalcolithic of the Central Zagros, Iran*, Doctoral dissertation, Department of Anthropology, University of Toronto, University Microfilms, Ann Arbor.

Kalsbeek, J. 1980. 'La Céramique de Série du Djebel 'Aruda (à l'époque d'Uruk),' *Akkadica* 20, November-December 1980, 1-11.

Larsen, M. T., 1976. *The Old Assyrian City-State and its Colonies*, Akademisk Forlag, Copenhagen.

LeBrun, A., 1978a. 'Suse chantier "Acropole 1",' *Paléorient* 4, 177-192.

LeBrun, A., 1978b. 'Le niveau 17B de l'Acropole de Suse,' *Cahiers de la Délégation Archéologique Française en Iran* 8, 57-154.

Levine, L. D., and T. C. Young, Jr., 1987. 'A Summary of the Ceramic Assemblages of the Central Western Zagros from the Middle Neolithic to the Late Third Millennium B.C.,' in J-L. Huot (ed.), *Préhistoire de la Mésopotamie*, CNRS, Paris, 15-53.

Mason, R. B. and L. Cooper, 1999. 'Grog, petrology and Early Transcaucasians at Godin Tepe', *Iran* 37, 25-31.

McGovern, P. E., U. Hartung, V. R. Badler, D. L. Glusker, and L. J. Exner, 1997. 'The Beginnings of Winemaking and Viniculture in the Ancient Near East and Egypt,' *Expedition* 39(1), 3-21.

Michel, R. H., P. E. McGovern, and V. R. Badler, 1992. 'Chemical Evidence for Ancient Beer,' *Nature* 360, 5, November 1992, 24.

Michel, R. H., P. E. McGovern, and V. R. Badler, 1993. 'The First Wine and Beer: Chemical Detection of Ancient Fermented Beverages,' *Analytical Chemistry* 65(8), 408 A-413 A.

Nissen, H. J., P. Damerow, and R. K. Englund, 1993. *Archaic Bookkeeping: Early Writing and Techniques of Economic Administration in the Ancient Near East*, University of Chicago Press.

Oates, J. and D. Oates, 1997. 'An Open Gate: Cities of the Fourth Millennium BC (Tell Brak 1997),' *Cambridge Archaeological Journal* 7(2), 287-307.

Özgüç, T., 1986. *Kültepe-Kanis II*, Türk Tarih Kurumu Basımevi, Ankara.

Sürenhagen, D., 1978. Keramik-produktion in Habuba Kabira-Süd, Untersuchungen zur Keramikproduction innerhalb der Spät-Uruklichen Siedlung Habuba Kabira-Süd in Nordsyrien, (*Acta Praehistorica et Archaeologica* 5/6, 1974/75), Verlag Bruno Hessling, Berlin, 43-164.

Veenhof, K. R., 1982. 'The Old Assyrian Merchants and their Relations with the Native Population of Anatolia,' in H. J. Nissen and J. Renger (eds.), *Mesopotamien und seine Nachbarn*, RAI 25, Dietrich Reimer, Berlin, 147-160.

Weiss, H. and T. C. Young, Jr., 1975. 'The Merchants of Susa: Godin V and Plateau-Lowland Relations in the Late Fourth Millenium B.C.,' *Iran* XIII, 1-17.

Wilson, K.L., 1986. 'Nippur: The Definition of a Mesopotamian Ǧamdat Naṣr Assemblage,' in U. Finkbeiner and W. Röllig (eds.), *Ǧamdat Naṣr -- Period or Regional Style?*, 57-90.

Wood, B. G., 1990. *The Society of Pottery in Ancient Palestine: The Ceramic Industry and the Diffusion of Ceramic Style in the Bronze and Iron Ages*, JSOT/ASOR Monographs 4, Sheffield Academic Press.

Wright, H.T. (ed.), 1981. *An Early Town on the Deh Luran Plain. Excavations at Tepe Farukhabad*, Museum of Anthropology, University of Michigan, Ann Arbor.

Young, T. C. Jr., 1969. *Excavations at Godin Tepe: First Progress Report*, Royal Ontario Museum, Toronto.

Young, T. C. Jr., 1986. 'Godin Tepe Period VI/V and Central Western Iran at the End of the Fourth Millennium,' in U. Finkbeiner and W. Röllig (eds.), *Ǧamdat Naṣr -- Period or Regional Style?*, Reichert, Wiesbaden, 212-228.

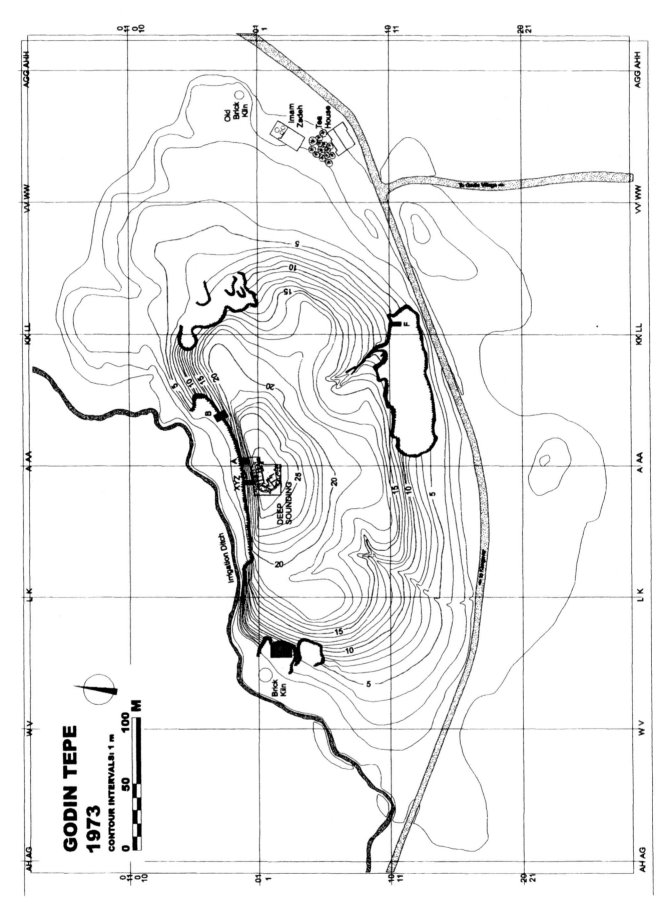

Figure 1. Contour map of Godin Tepe 1973.

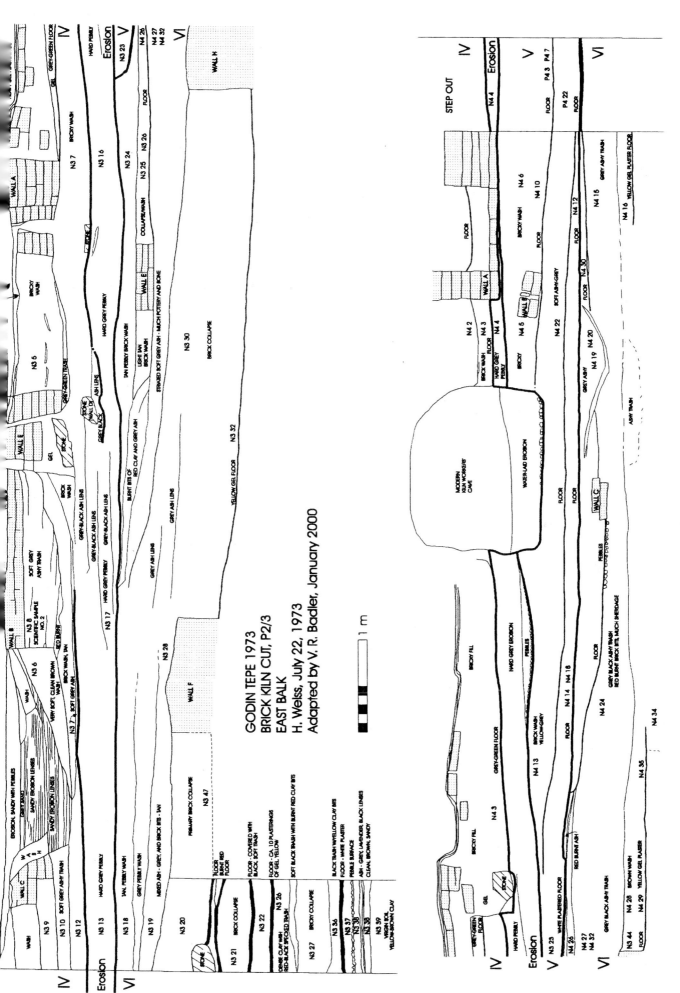

Figure 2. Brick Kiln Cut section

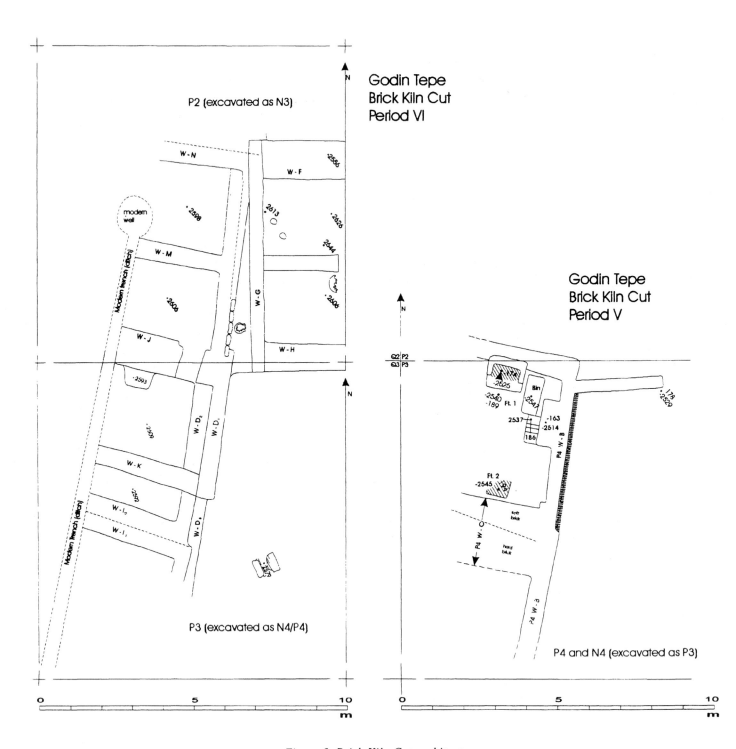

Figure 3. Brick Kiln Cut architecture

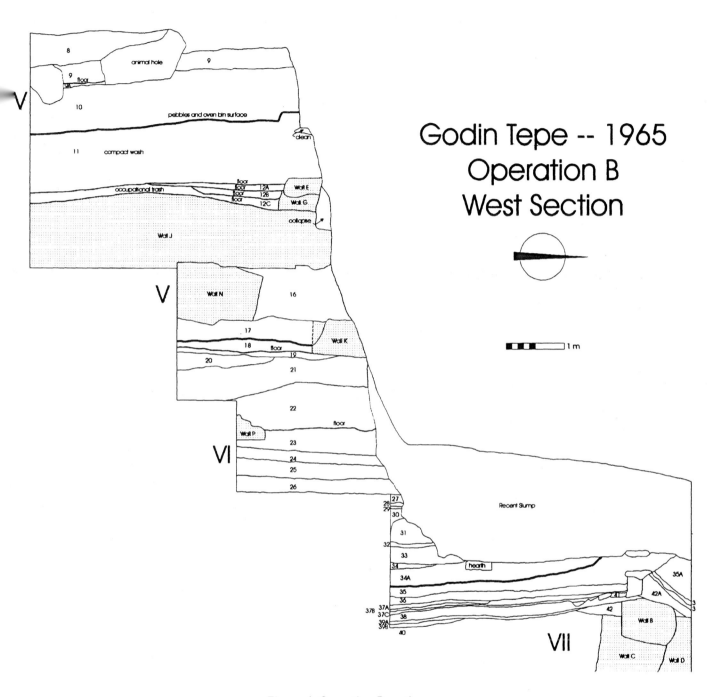

Figure 4. Operation B section

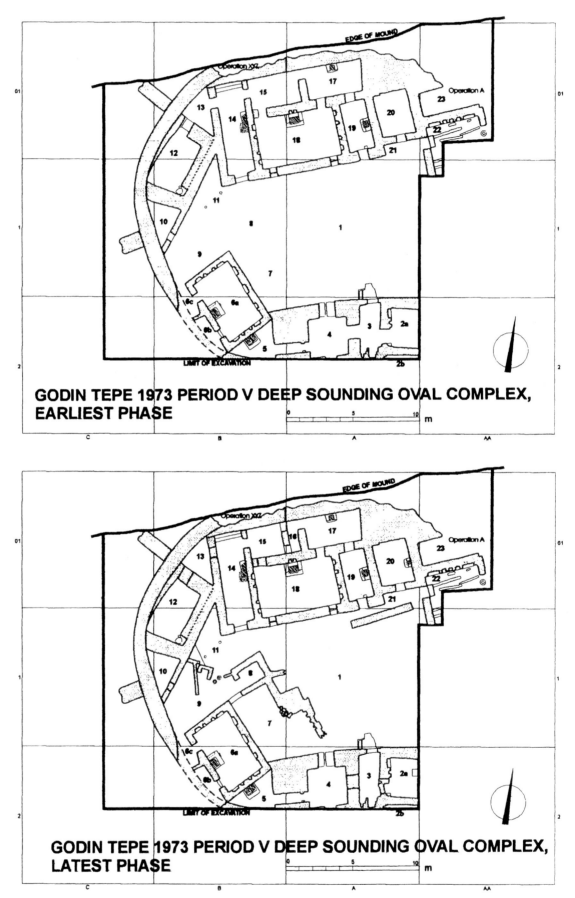

Figure 5. Godin Tepe Deep Sounding Period V architecture.

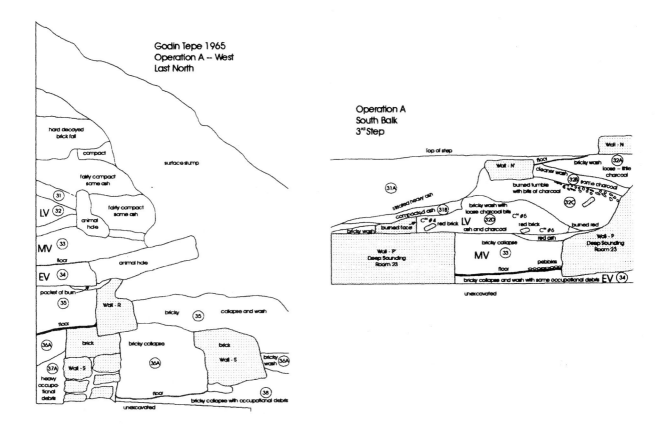

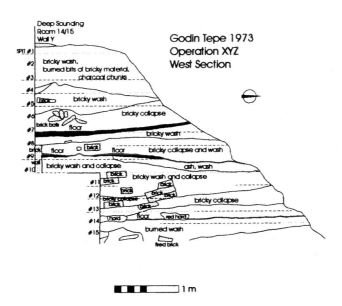

Figure 6. Godin Tepe Operation A and XYZ.

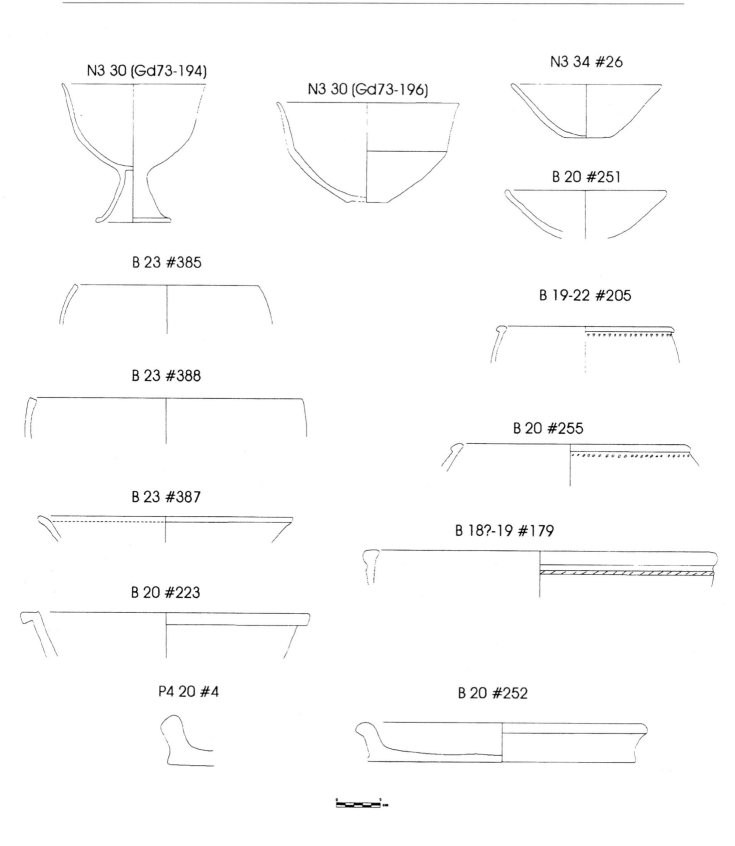

Figure 7. Godin Tepe Middle and Late Period VI.

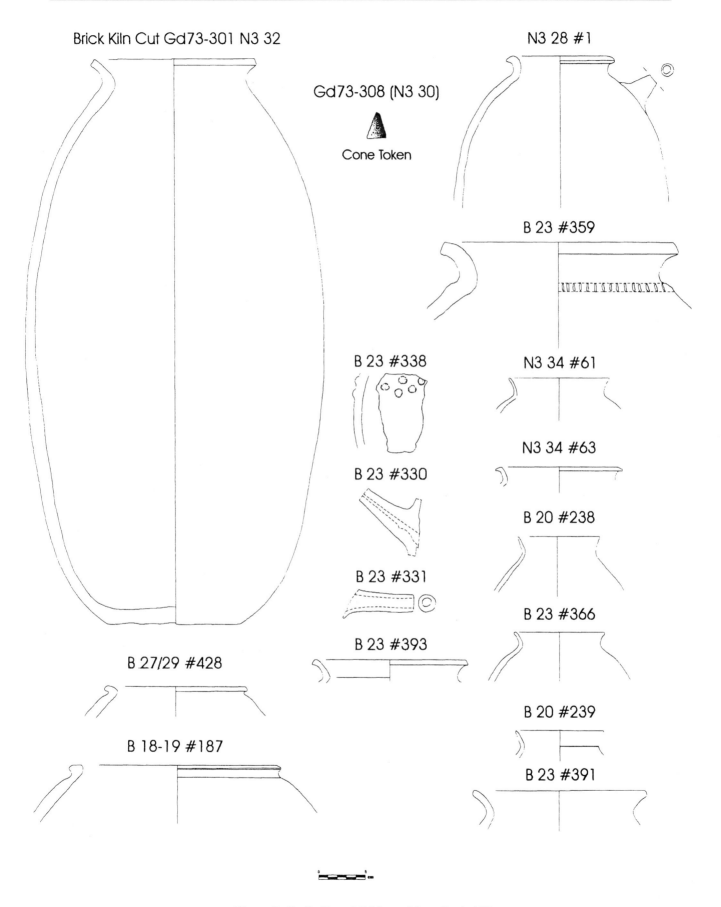

Brick Kiln Cut Gd73-301 N3 32

Gd73-308 (N3 30)

Cone Token

N3 28 #1

B 23 #359

B 23 #338

N3 34 #61

B 23 #330

N3 34 #63

B 23 #331

B 20 #238

B 23 #393

B 23 #366

B 27/29 #428

B 20 #239

B 23 #391

B 18-19 #187

Figure 8. Godin Tepe Middle and Late Period VI.

Period VII Type Red Slipped Coarse Ware from Early Period VI Strata

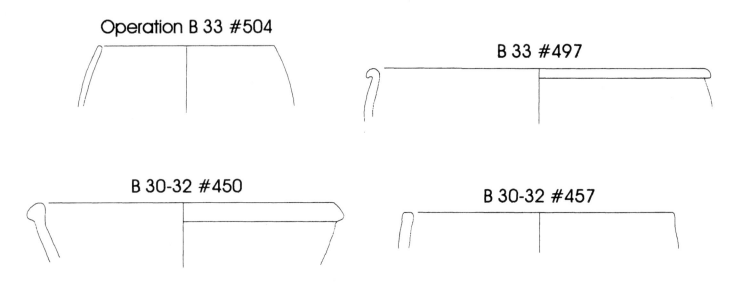

Operation B 33 #504

B 33 #497

B 30-32 #450

B 30-32 #457

Late Period VI Red Slipped Jars   Middle Period V Red Slipped Jars

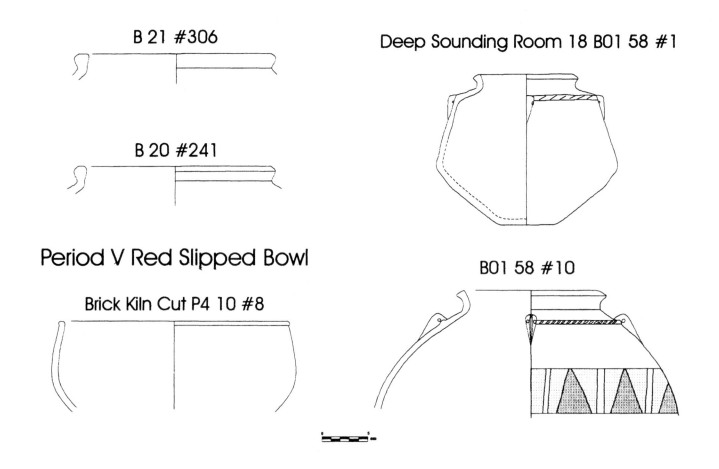

B 21 #306

B 20 #241

Deep Sounding Room 18 B01 58 #1

Period V Red Slipped Bowl

Brick Kiln Cut P4 10 #8

B01 58 #10

Figure 9. Godin Tepe red slipped pottery.

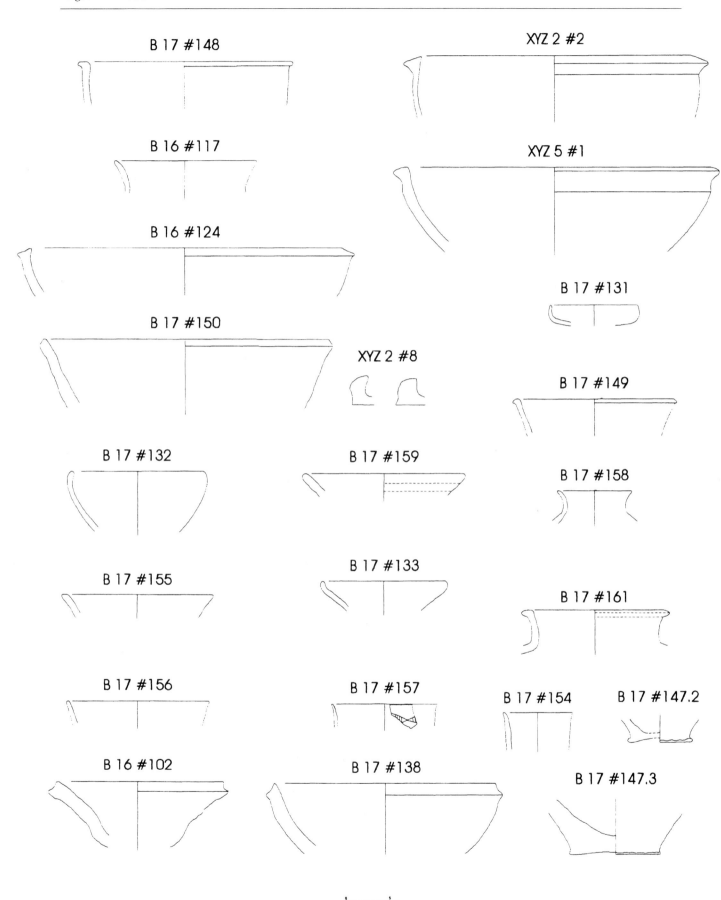

Figure 10. Early Period V pottery.

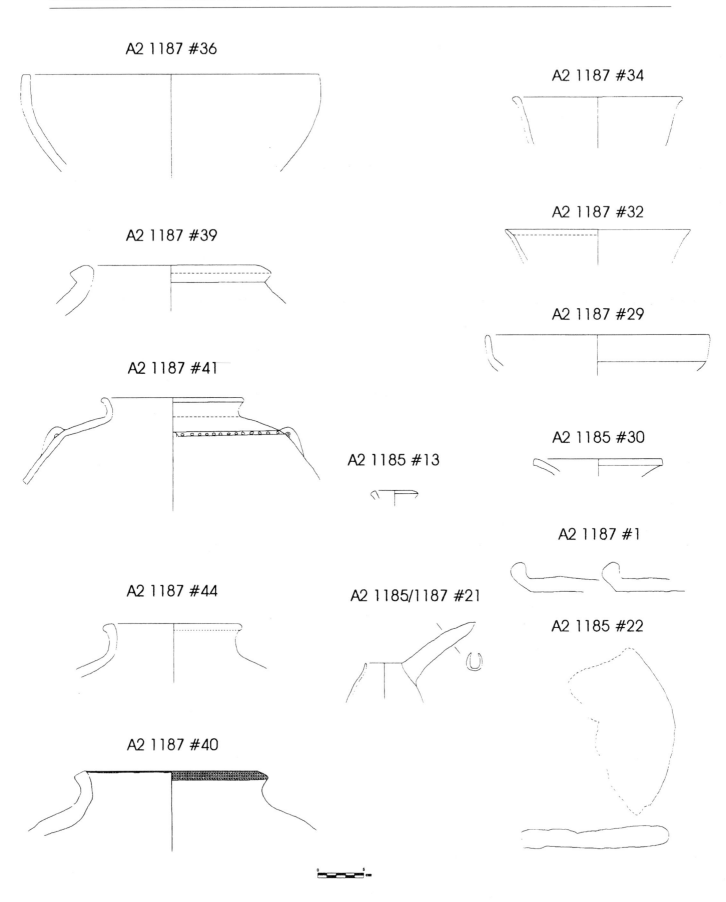

A2 1187 #36

A2 1187 #34

A2 1187 #39

A2 1187 #32

A2 1187 #29

A2 1187 #41

A2 1185 #13

A2 1185 #30

A2 1187 #1

A2 1187 #44

A2 1185/1187 #21

A2 1185 #22

A2 1187 #40

Figure 11. Room 2a earliest phase pottery (Middle Period V).

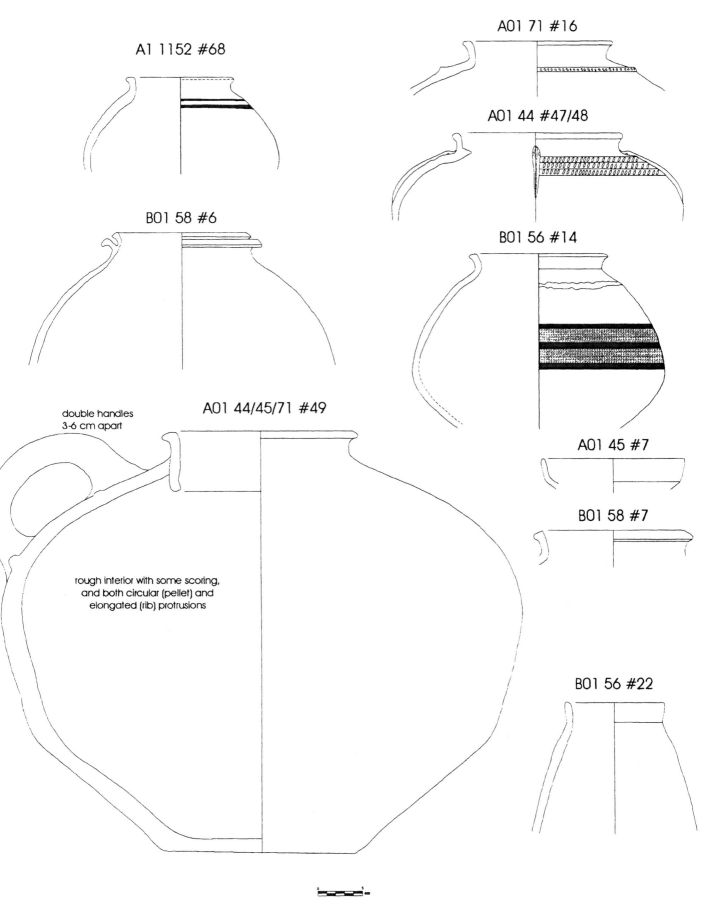

Figure 12. Room 18 earliest phase pottery (Middle Period V).

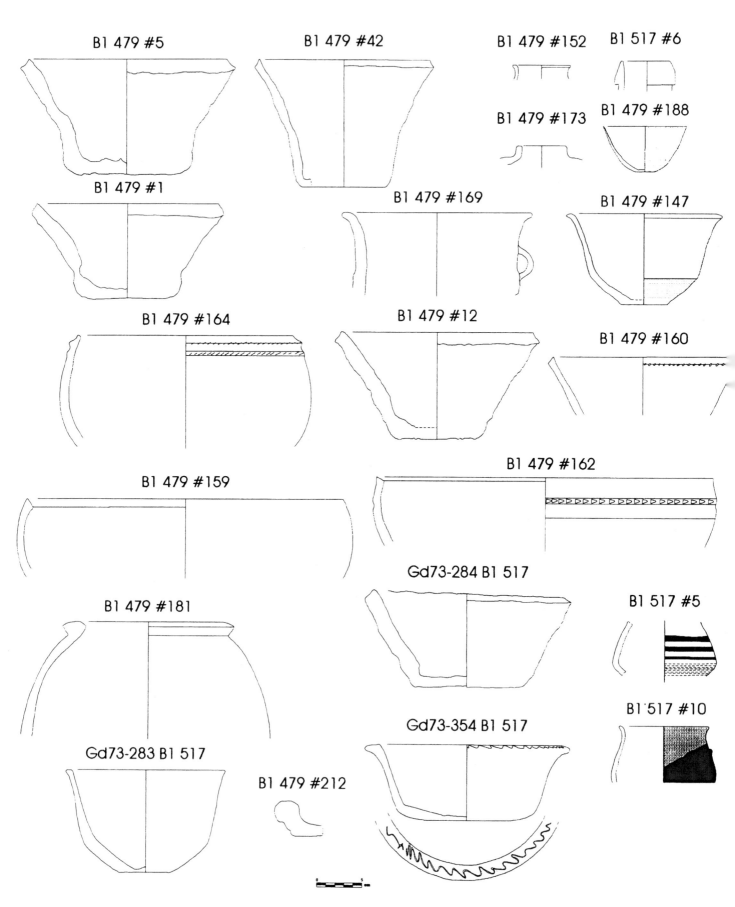

Figure 13. Room 10 Period V pottery.

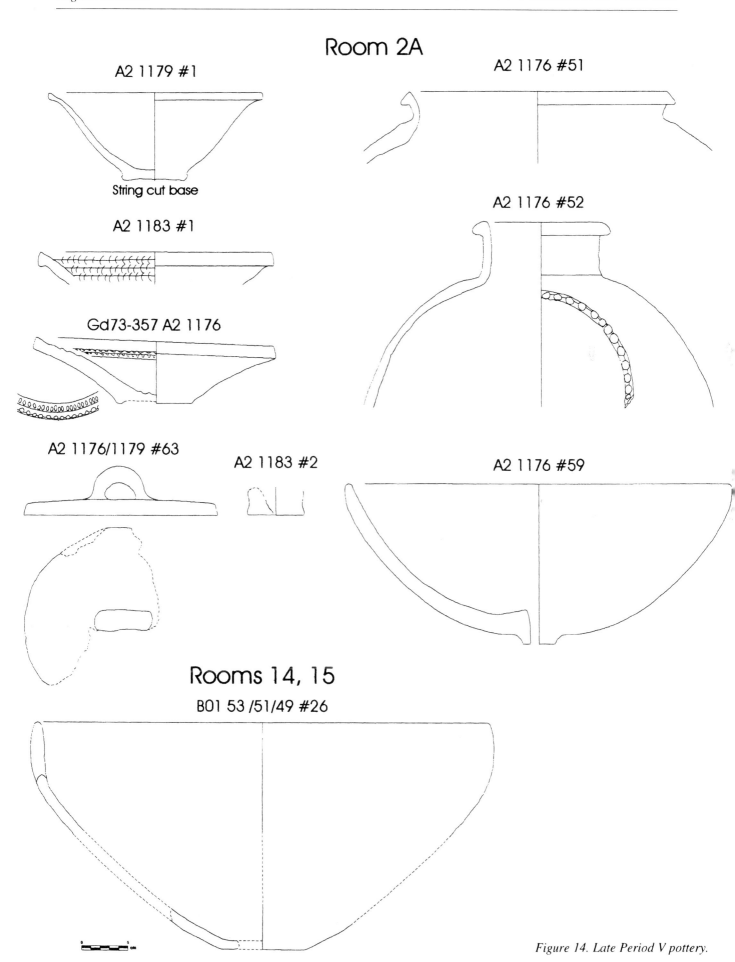

Room 2A

A2 1179 #1

String cut base

A2 1183 #1

Gd73-357 A2 1176

A2 1176/1179 #63

A2 1183 #2

A2 1176 #51

A2 1176 #52

A2 1176 #59

Rooms 14, 15

B01 53 /51/49 #26

Figure 14. Late Period V pottery.

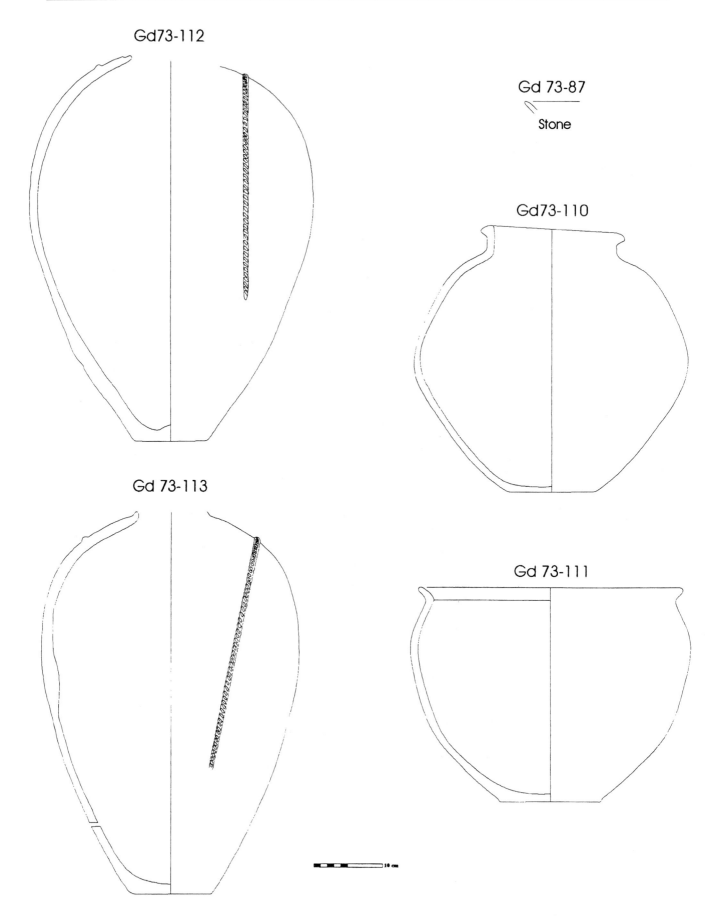

Figure 15. Room 20 (A01 56) Late Phase (Late Period V).

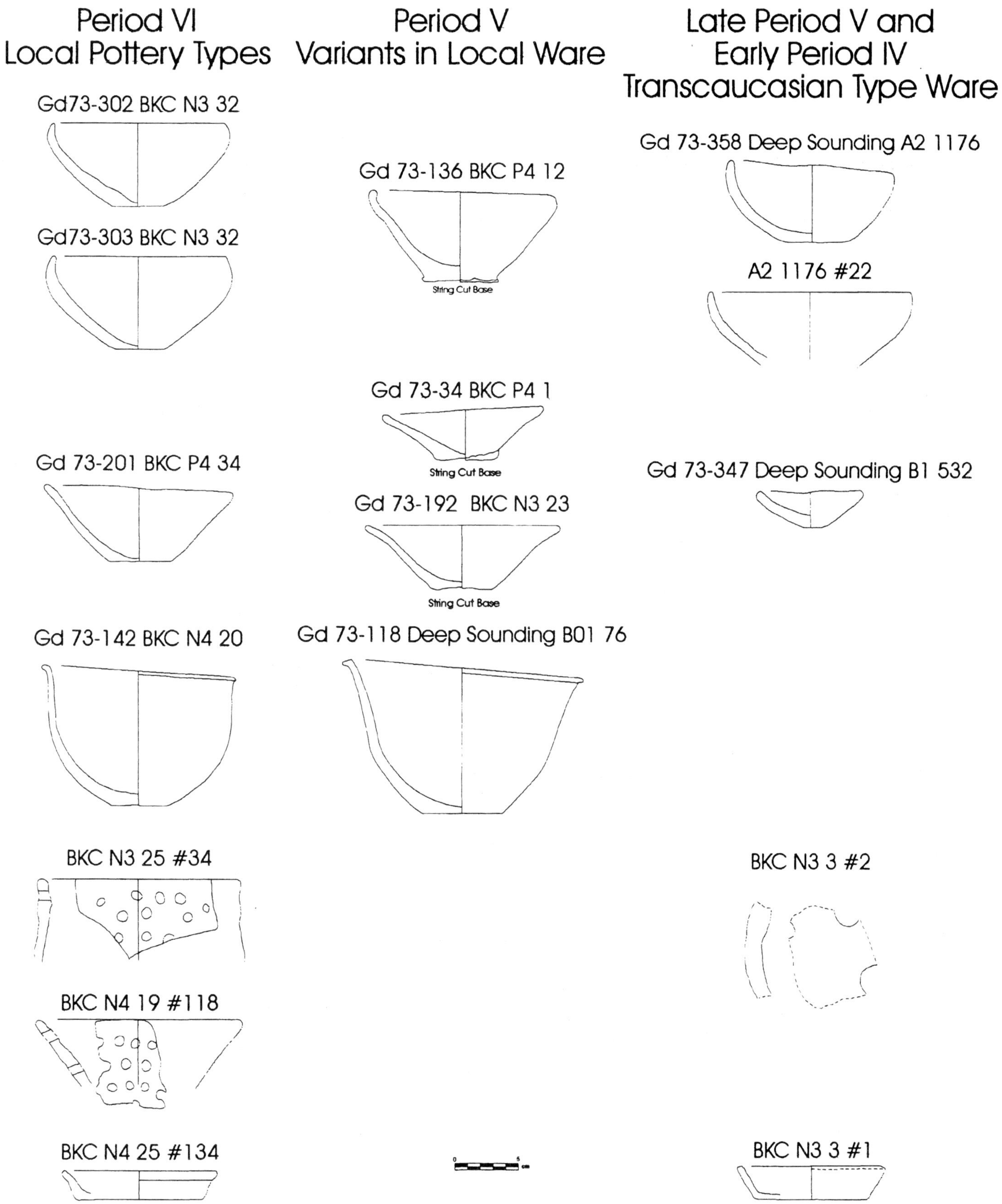

Period VI
Local Pottery Types

Gd73-302 BKC N3 32

Gd73-303 BKC N3 32

Gd 73-201 BKC P4 34

Gd 73-142 BKC N4 20

BKC N3 25 #34

BKC N4 19 #118

BKC N4 25 #134

Period V
Variants in Local Ware

Gd 73-136 BKC P4 12

String Cut Base

Gd 73-34 BKC P4 1

String Cut Base

Gd 73-192 BKC N3 23

String Cut Base

Gd 73-118 Deep Sounding B01 76

Late Period V and
Early Period IV
Transcaucasian Type Ware

Gd 73-358 Deep Sounding A2 1176

A2 1176 #22

Gd 73-347 Deep Sounding B1 532

BKC N3 3 #2

BKC N3 3 #1

Figure 16. Godin Tepe pottery: local, Uruk influenced, and Transcaucasian type ware in Periods VI and V.

107

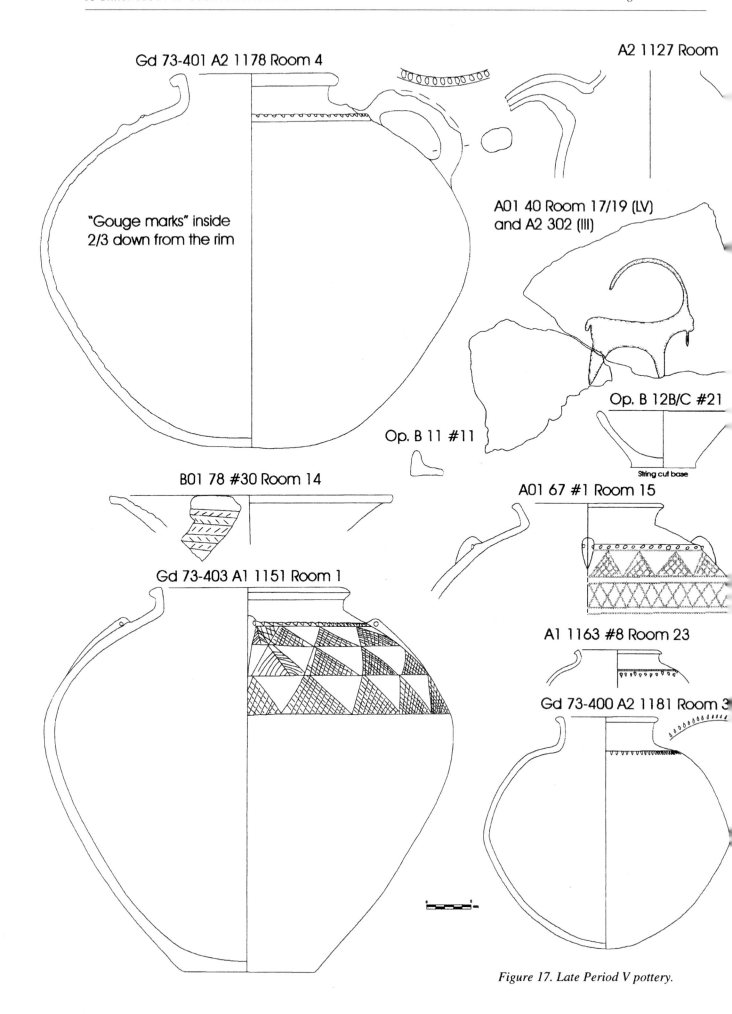

Gd 73-401 A2 1178 Room 4

A2 1127 Room

"Gouge marks" inside
2/3 down from the rim

A01 40 Room 17/19 (LV)
and A2 302 (III)

Op. B 11 #11

Op. B 12B/C #21

String cut base

B01 78 #30 Room 14

A01 67 #1 Room 15

Gd 73-403 A1 1151 Room 1

A1 1163 #8 Room 23

Gd 73-400 A2 1181 Room 3

Figure 17. Late Period V pottery.

Drainpipes

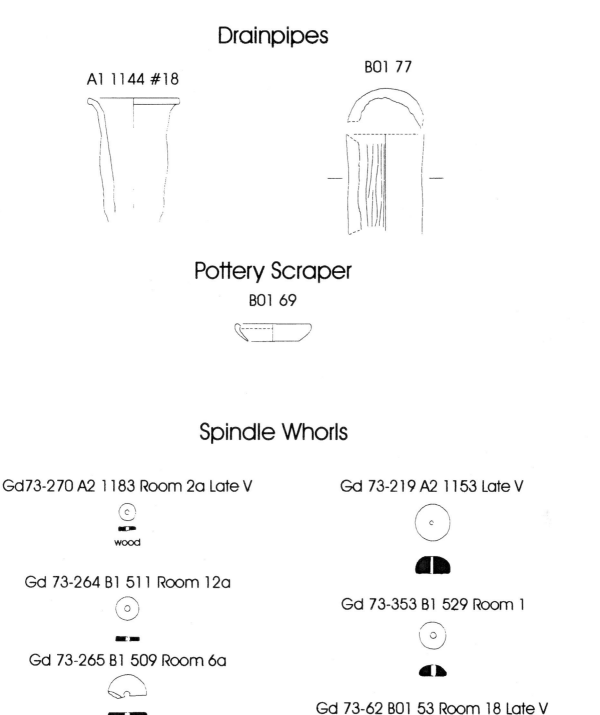

Pottery Scraper

Spindle Whorls

Figure 18. Godin Tepe Deep Sounding miscellaneous objects.

TELL BRAK: THE 4TH MILLENNIUM SEQUENCE AND ITS IMPLICATIONS

Joan Oates

SUMMARY

Brak has made 3 major contributions to our understanding of the 4th millennium:

1) a long stratigraphic sequence
2) evidence for urban complexity *early* in the 4th millennium, and
3) stratified evidence for a developed recording system in the Northern Middle Uruk phase.

Up to now 9-10 m of well-stratified 4th millennium deposits have been excavated in Area TW. These results are complemented by deep soundings in Area CH. This paper summarises the dating evidence and attempts briefly to address more general topics such as economy and southern contact. The phasing terminology deliberately retains the term 'Uruk' as more chronologically informative than the much vaguer and often inconsistent 'chalcolithic'.

ROUGH STRATIGRAPHIC SUMMARY

early Nin 5	TW Level 1		painted and plain Ninevite 5	c. 2800 BC
pre-Nin 5/post-Uruk	TW	2-8	local + southern ED I pottery includes pottery = Karrana 3, Hassek etc.	c. 2900 BC
Jamdat Nasr	TW	9-10	includes southern JN types	c. 3100 BC
Late Uruk	TW	11-12	= Habuba material (Uruk VI/V)	34-3200 BC
Middle Uruk	TW	13	local 'chalcolithic' + southern pottery similar Sh. Hassan, Qraya etc.	
Northern Middle Uruk	TW	14-18	local chalcolithic, fine and chaff wares	c. 3500 BC
Northern Early Uruk	TW	19-	= Gawra XI-A to IX; pottery found in large quantity in levelling fills in Area CH	
Post or Terminal 'Ubaid	Area CH and Eye Temple Platform; = Gawra XII, sprig ware and 'sealing wax ware'			c. 4000 BC
Late 'Ubaid	CH Levels 18/19-22 (-14 m B.S.)			c. 4200 BC
[*Hajji Muhammad* *Halaf* *PPNB*	sherds found in bricks sherds found largely in Eye Temple area obsidian lunates and Çayönü rods, also probably from mud-bricks]			

Preliminary reports: *Iraq* 53 (1991), 55 (1993), 56 (1994), 60 (1998); *Cambridge Archaeological Journal* 7 (1997).
Final report: Joan Oates, David Oates, Geoff Emberling and Helen McDonald, *Excavations at Tell Brak*. Vol. 3: *The Uruk and 'Ubaid Periods*, in preparation for publication in 2002.

The term 'Uruk' is used in this paper in a broad chronological sense, covering the whole of the 4th millennium and with specific reference to the sequence at Tell Brak. The often-preferred term 'chalcolithic' is rejected as being less chronologically informative, since it can be applied to both 5th and 4th millennium materials in Mesopotamia and, despite the admirable efforts of the Sante Fe conference, there remains elsewhere a lack of agreement with respect to its subdivisions. The paper will focus first on the 4th millennium sequence as attested at Brak, to establish the fact of 'time', since this provides the framework within which to attempt to understand the development of society at this time. This evidence for extensive 'time' is, moreover, lacking from the Uruk

sequences up to now excavated in southern Mesopotamia, though it can also be seen at sites like Farukhabad (Wright 1981).

At Brak 4th millennium materials have been excavated in two areas, TW at the northern and CH at the southern limits of the site (Fig. 1). A series of small off-site soundings (Fig. 2) carried out in 1998, under the direction of Geoff Emberling, has revealed an extensive distribution of early to middle 4th millennium pottery to the east, while occupation of Northern Middle Uruk date is well-attested on a corona of small tells surrounding the main mound (*Iraq* 55, 1993, fig. 39; Emberling 1999). Pottery closely comparable with Gawra XI-A to X (our Northern Early Uruk) has been excavated in Areas CH

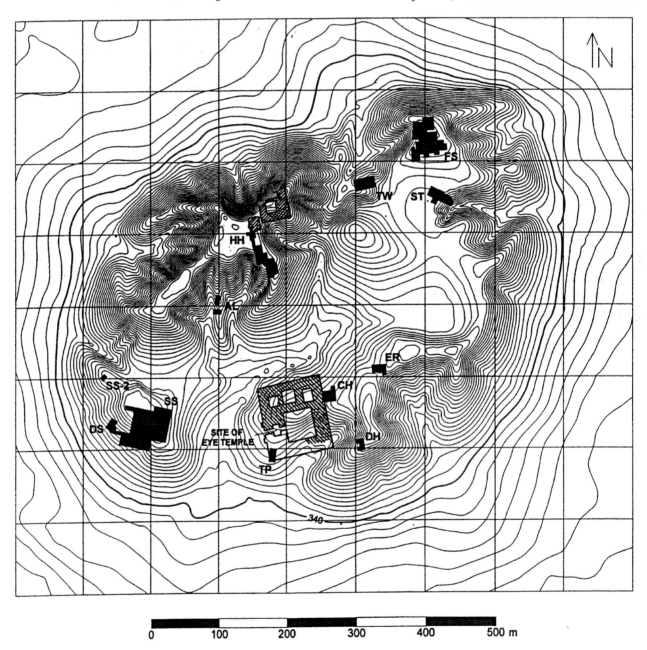

Fig. 1. EDM contour plan of Tell Brak, courtesy of G. Emberling, T. Skuldbøl, and T. Larsen.

and low on the northwest ridge of the tell (HS spur); it has also been recovered from test soundings 14, 15, 16 on the south slopes of the tell, below Area CH, and 11, 27, and 28, to the northeast (Fig. 2). Northern Middle Uruk types, as defined in *Iraq* 55, 1993, have been excavated in Areas CH, TW and HS; NMU sherds have been recovered from Tell Majnuna and T2, as well as the tells on which the villages of Majnuna and Temmi are situated, and from soundings 3 below Area TW, 13-17 on the south and southeast slopes below Areas CH and ST and, to the east, in soundings 11, 27, 29, 30 (see also Emberling *et al.* 1999).

Where one defines the edge of the main mound is complicated by the fact that its lower slopes are now under cultivation; its area can be calculated at 40 hectares at the 340 m contour, but is more likely to be of the order

of 65 hectares, certainly small by Warka standards but a large mound nonetheless. The largest total area of settlement would appear to date to the Northern Middle Uruk period (over 100 ha), while the post-'Ubaid, Gawra XIA-to-X-type occupation now defined by the 1998 survey appears also, rather to our surprise, to occupy at least some 45 ha, with possibly continuous settlement along the southern reaches of the tell and to the east in the direction of Temmi village, itself an Uruk tell. A similar situation obtains at Hamoukar where large quantities of early Gawra pottery are present on small tells outside the visible limits of the main site and in the adjacent ploughed fields.

At Brak our deepest soundings have been carried out in Area CH, an area of complex monumental buildings including the Eye Temple and the Naram-Sin Palace.

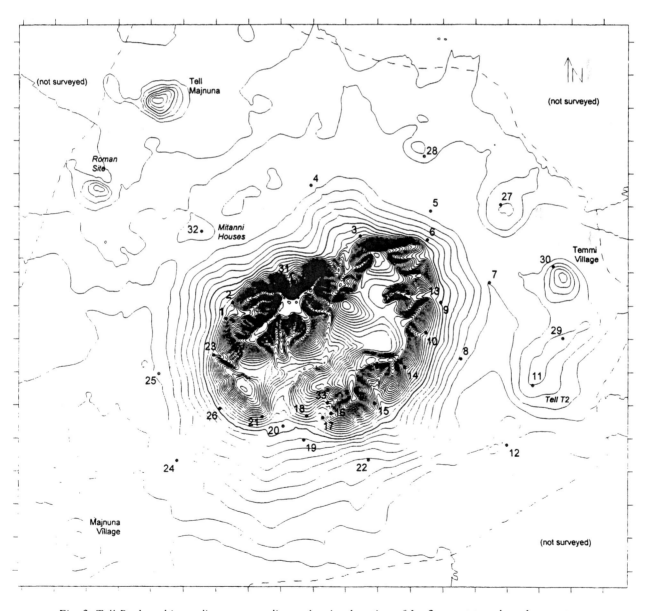

Fig. 2. Tell Brak and immediate surroundings, showing location of 1 x 2 m test trenches; 1 m contours, 100 m intervals indicated (after Emberling et al. 1999, Fig. 26).

The ancient bull-dozing undertaken for these building operations has, unfortunately, rendered stratigraphic interpretation exceedingly difficult. It is here, however, that we have recovered evidence for 5th and 4th millennium occupation as yet not reached in the better-preserved levels of Area TW. In Area CH we have identified several levels of 'Ubaid occupation, above which are massive deposits of Gawra XI-A to X pottery, indistinguishable from the pottery at Gawra itself, even, on some of the fine wares, to the very distinctive bubble effect produced in the firing. Between this material and the 'Ubaid levels are found the sprig ware of Gawra XII and Mallowan's 'sealing wax ware', which is demonstrably not Halaf, despite some claims to the contrary. It is this Area CH pottery that is published in J. Oates 1986, where what we now know to be Northern Middle Uruk material is, regrettably, seriously mis-dated (the earlier Gawra type sherds are illustrated on pl. 7 and in J. Oates, *Iraq* 49, 1987, Fig. 3, where sherds 4 and 5 illustrate sprig ware). Large quantities of obsidian were found in these late 5th and early 4th millennium levels.

Area TW, by contrast, has provided a secure sequence of apparently largely domestic structures, sealed by a massive Old Babylonian complex. The latest level in the stratified sequence (Level 1) contains a few sherds of plain and painted Ninevite 5, with what we have referred to as 'proto-Ninevite 5' in the immediately preceding levels (see *Iraq* 53, 1991). No incised Ninevite 5 has been recovered from any of the sealed levels, but it is common in the poorly stratified deposits that lie above Level 1, beneath and further disturbed by the Old Babylonian building. Since large quantities of Ninevite 5 pottery have been found over the whole of the main tell

at Brak, the fact that not a single sherd has been recovered from the earlier levels in TW suggests that these levels, that is, TW Level 2 and below, do actually date from before its introduction at the site. Levels 2-6 also contain some southern ED I material (*Iraq* 53, Fig. 7), while Levels 2-8 lie above a Jamdat Nasr-related horizon, suggesting a substantial passage of time between true Late Uruk and Ninevite 5, in contrast with the common assumption of overlap. Only the proto-Ninevite 5 is represented in the upper TW levels, though not in large quantity. Typical of Levels 2-6 are the footed vessels, pierced tab-lugged jars and ribbed cups with ring bases published in *Iraq* 53, Figs. 7, 8; as noted above, these are found without Ninevite 5 but together with ED I pottery indistinguishable from south Mesopotamian types.

Bevelled rim bowls are found as late as Level 5, clearly *in situ*. Only the bases differ from the classic form (see *Iraq* 55, 1993, fig. 38). Associated with a few sherds of Jamdat Nasr polychrome, and indeed confined to this horizon, are wheel-made, cut-rim and bevelled rim conical bowls indistinguishable from those known from sites like Nippur and Jamdat Nasr itself. Tall 'flower pots', known also at sites like Warka and Susa, come from a deep pit dug into a Late Uruk building from Level 10 ('Jamdat Nasr'). At Brak this type is not found in Late Uruk contexts. (The mass-produced types are illustrated in *Iraq* 55, fig. 54.) Also present in the 'Jamdat Nasr' levels was an unusual type of very large, painted chalice with fugitive scarlet paint, for which we know no parallels (*Iraq* 55, fig. 22).

It is only in Level 11 that we reach the distinctive southern Uruk repertoire known also at Habuba South, Jebel Aruda and Sheikh Hassan. In Area TW no *in situ*

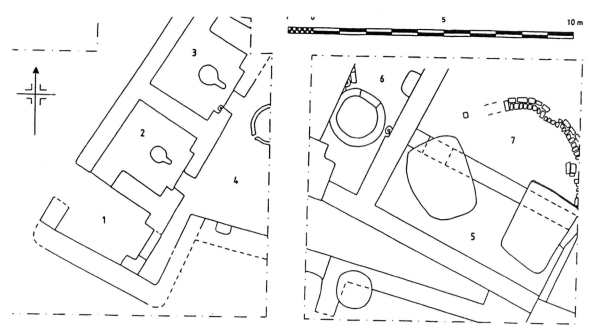

Fig. 3. Area TW, Level 11 plan (Late Uruk).

Fig. 4. Seal impressions from the Area TW
Level 12 Late Uruk pits, scale 1:1.

Fig. 5. Impression of Middle Uruk seal
from Area TW Level 13, 1:1.

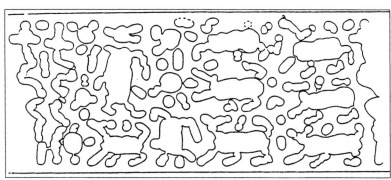

local chalcolithic pottery has as yet been found in associ-ation with the well-stratified and well-preserved Late Uruk material. Unfortunately we do not yet know whether this pattern is repeated over the whole of Brak. The material from Area CH consists of a mixture of local chalcolithic and southern Uruk types, but unfortunately none of the southern material is *in situ.*

The Late Uruk buildings in Area TW consist of a very large house of which only a part was excavated in the original trench, together with a series of small rooms with 'frying pan' hearths across an open courtyard to the west (Fig. 3). Of particular interest in the Late Uruk lev-els (11-12) is evidence both for the manufacture of Canaanean blades and the casting of copper axes. Large flint cores, a number of blades and a large piece of obsid-ian weighing over 2 kg were found in association with a small circular structure in the western courtyard of the original trench (J. Oates 1993, pl. 5; *Iraq* 55, figs. 35, 23, and note that the Late Uruk building illustrated in fig. 23 is now attributed to Level 11). Unusual evidence for cast-ing was found in a surviving impression of a 'form' for the mould of a metal axe (illustrated in Oates and Oates 1997, fig. 16).

The earliest Late Uruk buildings (Level 12), below those shown on the plan (Fig. 3), had been heavily destroyed (perhaps deliberately), creating a large open space over which were later built the *suq*-like small

rooms at the western side of the plan (Fig. 3; photographs in Oates and Oates 1997, figs. 9, 13). In this open space a large number of pits had been dug (Level 12), which contained pottery and very large quantities of seal impressions. The sealings themselves are very like those from Habuba and Jebel Aruda (Fig. 4; see also Emberling *et al.* 1999, fig. 30). Interestingly, many from the two largest pits had been scrunched up while still moist, implying transactions involving a relatively short time span. Complex, pierced tokens are found in these pits, which represent an early phase of Late Uruk activity at Brak (Oates and Oates 1997, fig. 15).

Relatively little survived of Level 13, but a sherd pavement in the main trench yielded an interesting col-lection of Middle Uruk pottery identical with vessels from sites like Sheikh Hassan and Qraya, together with many vessels of local chalcolithic types, in particular the very distinctive 'casseroles', trays and cooking pots (see *Iraq* 55, fig. 24). Exclusive to Level 13 are the 'type fos-sil' Middle Uruk conical bowls with small pouring lip (*Iraq* 55, Fig. 51:35). Perhaps the most interesting single find was the very large and splendid cylinder seal of which an impression is illustrated in Fig. 5 (photograph in *Iraq* 55, fig. 44). Large numbers of spindle whorls were found in this level.

Below Level 13, in which there was a clear mix of northern and southern materials, lay four further building levels in which almost all the pottery consisted of local chalcolithic types. Indeed throughout Levels 14-18 we are dealing with an entirely indigenous material culture, which we have designated 'Northern Middle Uruk' since the earlier materials of Gawra XI-A to X lie still below. The NMU pottery consists of the chaff-tempered kitchen fabric found already in Level 13, together with a large quantity of very beautiful, often highly burnished, mineral-tempered fine ware vessels. The single southern vessel that we could identify is illustrated in *Iraq* 55, fig. 51:31. These NMU levels are characterised by well-built houses, some with high status goods. This is particularly true of the Level 16 house (*Iraq* 55, 175-76), in which were found a bead of heavy, rolled gold sheet, objects of ivory and here and in an associated pit the only Eye Idols to have been found *in situ* at Brak. At least one wall of the Level 16 house was ornamented with a row of semi-

columns just visible on the left hand central wall in *Iraq* 55, fig. 27. This wall ornament suggests that the Level 16 structure may not have been an ordinary house, but the plan and the niched walls are anticipated in Level 17, while the Level 14 house has a doorway with well-defined reveals (*Iraq* 55, fig. 25), suggesting an elaboration of architecture associated with the ordinary residential plan. An elaborately niched building found in the western trench in 1997, unfortunately badly damaged by the overlying Late Uruk pits, can be identified as a formal, public building with more certainty; its excavation remains to be completed (Oates and Oates 1997, fig. 17; Emberling *et al.* 1999, fig. 7).

Notable in the NMU levels is evidence for the development of increasingly elaborate recording systems. A large numerical tablet, which closely resembles a *juss* specimen from Warka recently published by Julian

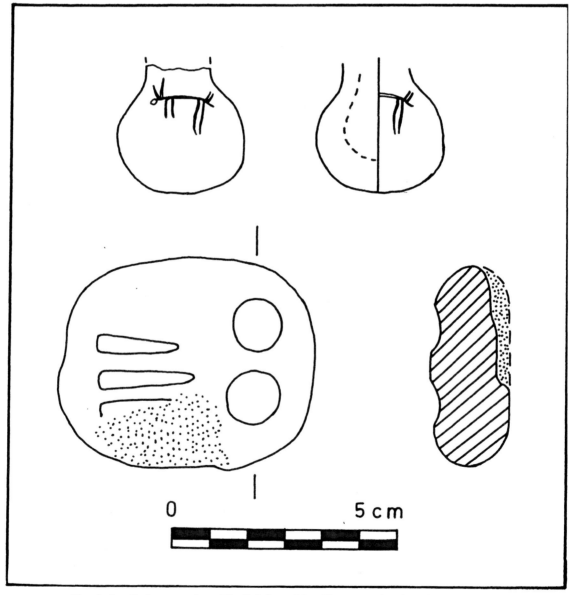

*Fig. 6. Small clay container (?bulla) from 4th millennium sherd packing in Area FS;
numerical tablet from well-stratified Northern Middle Uruk context in Area CH.*

Fig. 7. 'Notational' marks, incised before firing on shoulders of Northern Middle Uruk jars, Area TW Levels 15-16, scale 1:2.

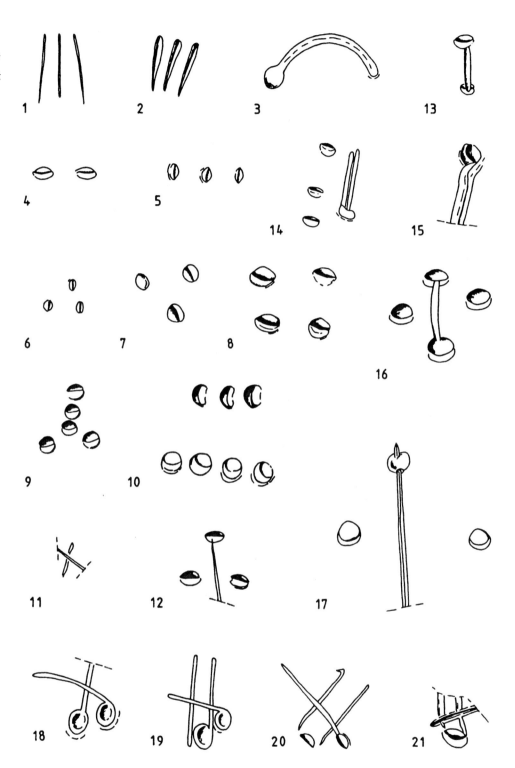

Reade and said to resemble tablets from the Anu Ziggurrat deposits (Fig. 6; Reade 1992), was clearly stratified in Area CH *below* a hearth with a radiocarbon determination (BM-2915) virtually identical with BM-2900 from the Level 16 house, that is c. 3500 cal BC, dates which correspond closely with the sequence at Sheikh Hassan (*Iraq* 56, 1994, 175; Boese 1995, fig. 15) and recently published determinations from Warka (Boehmer 1991). At Brak, tokens of this date were solely of simple geometric shapes in both clay and stone. Some 80 Level

16 vessels bore distinctive marks incised before firing, in the case of the jars, on the shoulder (Fig. 7). Interestingly, the same type of mark was associated with the same type of jar, while a different series had been applied to platters and casseroles (Fig. 8), suggesting the probability of very specific meanings, perhaps relating to the contents of the vessels or to the identification of specific households, or both. Two pictographic dockets – (?) '10 sheep', '10 goats' – found in fill in 1984 (Jasim and Oates 1986, pl. 2a) can now be dated by their associated pottery to this

same Northern Middle Uruk horizon, an attribution supported by the presence of other objects of similar style, including the small, hollow container (Fig. 6).

Possibly the most interesting feature of the NMU settlement at Brak, however, is its size. As we have already indicated, the settlement exceeds 100 ha at this time including, as far as we can tell, the whole of the main mound and a number of the small sites that encircle Brak, including the villages of Temmi and Majnuna, to the east and west of Brak respectively, together with Tell Majnuna (Mallowan's Site EH) to the north and T2 to the southeast (Fig. 2; see also *Iraq* 55, fig. 39). Estimates for the total occupied area at this time vary from c. 110 to something of the order of 160 ha, depending on how the

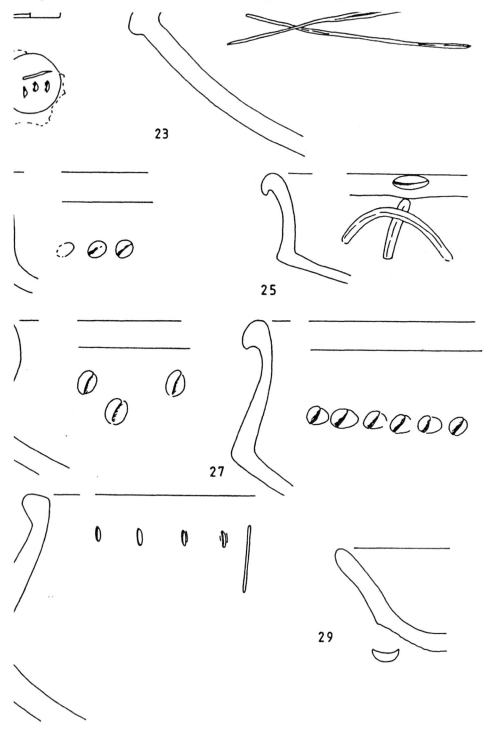

Fig. 8. Incised marks on casseroles and open bowls, largely from Area TW Level 16, scale 1:2.

size of the smaller tells is calculated. It was a considerable surprise to us to realise that this Northern Middle Uruk phase constitutes the largest settlement attested at Brak at any period. Some of the most elegant fine ware comes from the outer, smaller mounds, especially Tell Majnuna and T2, suggesting the possibility of stratified neighbourhoods.[1]

Below Level 18 the character of the settlement changes completely. This marks in fact the only visibly abrupt interruption in the 4th millennium sequence in Area TW. The earlier settlement had been very carefully levelled and a fine red surface prepared for the construction of the Level 17 houses (Oates and Oates 1997, fig. 3). This seemingly radical change in settlement pattern was accompanied by an unusual number of burials, largely infant, dug into the walls of the previous settlement (Oates and Oates 1997, figs. 6, 7), and reinforcing our interpretation of ritual preparation of the construction level of the new settlement since such burials were not found in the later NMU levels. As noted earlier, in Area TW we have yet to reach levels contemporary with Gawra XI-A to X from which come, *inter alia*, the very fine and well-known stamped and appliqué vessels. (That these are well-represented at Brak can be seen in J. Oates 1986, pl. 7, and *Iraq* 49, 1987, fig. 3:6, 7.) However, two complete vessels from the Level 17 (NMU) house were made in the very distinctive 'bubbly' fashion of the impressed and appliqué fabric of Gawra (Fig. 9), suggesting that Level 17, in Area TW the earliest up to now from which we have pottery in a secure context, is not far distant in time from levels which we expect to find below, with Early Northern Uruk pottery of Gawra type.

In 1997, the lowest levels excavated in the eastern trench (19 and 20) revealed, much to our surprise, monumental walls some 2 m in width and built of very large bricks (55 x 30 x 8 cm) (Fig. 10). These are possibly part of a massive perimeter wall which has been identified across the wadi in Area TW itself and further along the north side of the tell, some 300 m to the west (Matthews 1996, fig. 5). In Area TW we have as yet no reliably stratified pottery associated with these walls, but that apparently associated with the wall on the northwest spur is of early Uruk attribution (Matthews 1996, fig. 6), as are sherds found in deposits in the northwest corner of TW east, into which the monumental walls had been trenched. The plan of these levels shows also a monumental gateway, found unfortunately in the deepest and least accessible part of the trench, some 11 m below the surface. The gate itself contains a massive threshold, a single piece of basalt some 2 x 1.5 m in area and 29 cm thick. It is not clear at present whether this is a city gate (though there seems to be an open space to the north) or the entrance to some monumental enclosure. One of the goals of our current excavations is to open up a larger area here in order further to investigate this unique and impressive structure.

Thus, to summarise, the investigation of the 4th millennium at Brak suggests an urban settlement with

fortification walls, monumental architecture and elite goods, occupying some 45 ha already early in the 4th millennium, a degree of indigenous urbanism not previously suspected at this time, even in the south. This observation is reinforced by the remarkable growth of the NMU settlement, with what may have been elite residences or even public institutions on the outlying tells. Certainly it is incontrovertible that a considerable degree of stratification and organisation is present well before the period of Uruk contact. This is not to say that there was no contact with the south – at Brak we know that this was likely at least by the early 5th millennium (see the Hajji Muhammad pottery from Brak, *Iraq* 49, 193-4) – only that this urban complexity would seem to be a genuinely indigenous feature. At the same time complex administrative and recording procedures are attested, themselves the product of a remarkable history of such development in the north, most recently and emphatically illustrated at Samarran Sabi Abyad (Akkermans and Duistermaat 1997). That Brak's 4th millennium urbanism is not a unique phenomenon can be seen in the size of contemporary Hamoukar and even at the smaller site of Hacinebi with its fortified wall, monumental stone platforms and other public architecture (Stein 1998, 233).

We must now turn to the type or types of economy that lay behind these developments. Environmentally, both Brak's access to the rich, rainfed agricultural lands of the Khabur basin and its position as a Gateway City, at the southern limits of these rainfed lands and dominating

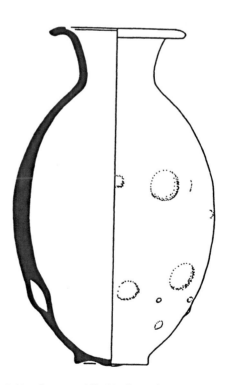

Fig. 9. A Northern Middle Uruk jar from Area TW Level 17, made of the fine cream 'bubbly' fabric well-attested at Gawra in Levels XI-A to X and in comparable Northern Early Uruk vessels from Brak (ht. 17.8 cm).

one of the major routes from the Tigris valley leading not only to the rich produce of the basin itself but to the metals of Anatolia, must have been significant factors in the continuing importance of the site. Not surprisingly, the 4th millennium crops seem much the same as those common in the third millennium and even more recent times – wheat, barley, pulses and linseed; important to our arguments is the fact that there is no visible change in food preference or agricultural practice from the indigenous NMU levels to those of the Late Uruk settlement (Green 1999). At the same time the archaeological evidence emphasises the role of wool and textiles throughout the 4th millennium: very large numbers of spindle whorls were found, especially in the Middle Uruk levels, while clay objects that were possibly loom supports or, a more recent suggestion, twining devices for plaiting thread or yarn (Fortin 1999, 29, 183) are one of the most characteristic features of the ENU phase [the latter are the large clay objects sometimes erroneously confused with the smaller stone 'spectacle idols']. Relevant to this is the high percentage of sheep/goat not only in the Late Uruk levels (over 80%) but also in those earlier levels that could equally be categorised as local chalcolithic, where the percentage was an unusually high 75%, with 10% cat-

tle and 5% pig. This is in marked contrast with the more usual high percentage of cattle and pig at contemporary late chalcolithic sites (compare, for example, Hacinebi, Stein 1998, 234-36), and even greater than the Akkadian figures at Brak (50-60% sheep/goat). Brak's access to the grazing lands of the Jazira may well be an important factor in this apparently local specialisation, further support for Adams' view that one aspect of the growth of early cities lay in their coordination of disparate ecological zones, a situation well-exemplified by Brak.

The archaeological evidence attests both metalworking and the making of Canaanean blades at Late Uruk Brak, perhaps here a hint of products desired in the south. Certainly metal was important at Warka at this time, witnessed both in the archaeological evidence and the archaic texts (Nissen 1995, 475 and n. 11). Another possible product was salt, perhaps involving the tens of thousands of bevelled rim bowls found at the site (see Buccellati 1990); indeed at Brak, Sheikh Hassan and Qraya an association of bevelled-rim bowls with hearths or ovens has been observed. We have no direct evidence of salt production at Brak but two Late Uruk ovens were literally stacked with bevelled-rim bowls while the possibility of salt flats in the neighbourhood of Khatuniya or

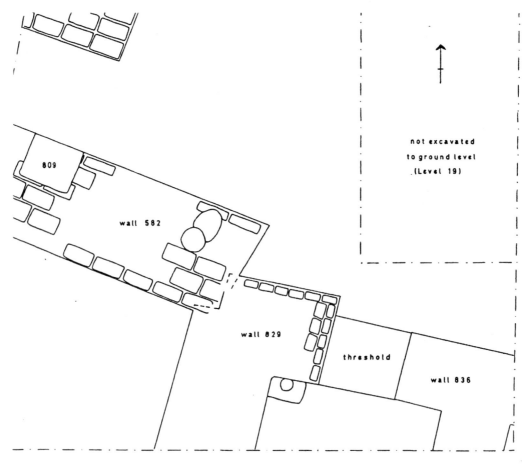

Fig. 10. Plan of the eastern trench of Area TW, Levels 18, 19.

elsewhere in the drier steppe south of Brak is not implausible. Certainly they now exist north of Deir ez-Zor, and the low ground around Khatuniya is today very saline.

What can Brak tell us of the nature of the phenomenon of 'Uruk contact'? Unfortunately we remain uncertain whether the structures excavated in Area TW represent a limited area of southern occupation within a larger indigenous settlement, or whether the whole site was not only dominated but actually occupied by an immigrant, southern population. Certainly there is a mixture of northern and southern pottery types in Area CH, but there the bull-dozing operations that accompanied its monumental constructions have left us virtually no *in situ* material, only enormous deposits of pottery in massive levelling fills. As far as TW is concerned, however, we can assert with confidence that there is no possibility that the southern material represents emulation by a local elite. The *in situ* material found within Levels 11-12 comprises a full range not only of exclusively southern ceramics, but of architecture and administrative paraphernalia as well. At least some of the 'southern' pottery seems to have been made at Brak, but both the persistence and the dominance of southern material culture suggests not acculturation but a population distinct from the producers and consumers of the local NMU chalcolithic. Logically, it seems to us unlikely that the local population, which was of considerable size, simply disappeared, but we have as yet no direct evidence to support this view. Interestingly, although the Late Uruk architecture at Brak has distinctly southern characteristics unlike that of the NMU levels, and one can certainly make a strong case for southern influence in the design and fittings of the contemporary Eye Temple, even the NMU house plan has more in common with southern architecture than that of Anatolia or western Syria. As at contemporary Gawra, this may owe much to a northern 'Ubaid tradition.

It has become unfashionable to suggest that the

Uruk phenomena in northern Syria and southern Anatolia represented attempts by the cities of the south to gain access to important resources (despite the 'Ubaid evidence from Değirmentepe), but this remains perhaps the most plausible explanation, supported by the evidence for metal- and/or flint-working at sites like Sheikh Hassan, Hacinebi Tepe, Hassek Höyük and Brak. Such southern activity does not necessarily involve 'control' in any political sense, though sites like heavily walled Habuba South and its Uruk neighbours present some problems of interpretation in this respect. Recent emphasis has been on 'trade diaspora', more in the nature of the Old Assyrian 'colonies', and such an interpretation certainly better fits sites like Hacinebi (see, most recently, Stein 1998). But until we have more lateral exposure of Late Uruk Brak – a problem which will not easily be resolved given the depths of overlying second and third millennium deposits at the site – we remain unable to determine the precise nature of the Uruk incursion into the Khabur. What is clear at Brak, however, is the indigenous growth of urban complexity, attested both in terms of site size and formal architecture not only in Area TW but also in CH where there is an impressive sequence of monumental buildings and where we can now date the earliest phase of the Eye Temple to the middle of the 4th millennium. Although what we have excavated of the Late Uruk settlement stands out as 'other', there is, as we have seen, no evidence that its presence had any great impact on the local economy. Nor is there an abrupt change in either social or political complexity. Unusually at Brak, with the disappearance of the Late Uruk settlement contact with the south continues, but further excavation is necessary before we can begin to understand the nature of the early 3rd millennium city, at which time the outlying tells are no longer occupied.

Note: Observant readers will have noticed a slight change in level attributions from the preliminary reports. There are now two major Late Uruk building phases (11-12) and, in the 2000 season, it was demonstrated that the 'niched building', published in *CAJ* 1997, abuts against the monumental walls of what was published then as Level 18; it is also earlier than the Level 17 house. For

these reasons, the 'niched building' has now been designated Level 18, and the monumental walls published in the *CAJ* article, with which we have as yet no associated material culture, become Levels 19 and 20. These minor level changes in no way alter the wider interpretation of the 4th millennium sequence.

[1] In the 2000 season several NMU pottery kilns were discovered on T2.

REFERENCES

Akkermans, P. and K. Duistermaat, 1997. Of storage and nomads: the sealings from Late Neolithic Sabi Abyad, Syria, *Paléorient* 22, 17-44.

Boehmer, R.M., 1991. 14C-Daten aus Uruk und Abydos – Ägyptisches (?) im frühen Nordsyrien, Sumer und Elam, *Bagh. Mitt.* 22, 223-30.

Boese, J., 1995. *Ausgrabungen in Tell Sheikh Hassan I.* Saarbrücker Druckerei u. Verlag.

Buccellati, G., 1990. Salt at the Dawn of History, in P. Matthiae, M. van Loon and H. Weiss, *Resurrecting the Past* (Adnan Bounni Festschrift), 17-40. Istanbul: Nederlands Hist-Arch. Inst.

Emberling, G., 1999. When There's a There, There: On the Origin of Cities in Mesopotamia, paper presented at Society for American Archaeology Annual Meeting, 27.iii.99.

Emberling, G. et al, 1999. Excavations at Tell Brak 1998: preliminary report, *Iraq* 61, 1-41.

Fortin, M., 1999. *Syria. Land of Civilizations.* Québec: Les éditions de l'homme.

Green, W.A., 1999. *Agriculture and Colonialism: Tell Brak in the Uruk Period.* M.Phil. dissertation, Dept. of Archaeology, University of Cambridge.

Jasim, S.A. and J. Oates, 1986. Early tokens and tablets in Mesopotamia: new information from Tell Abada and Tell Brak, *World Archaeology* 17, 348-62.

Matthews, R. J., 1996. Excavations at Tell Brak, 1996, *Iraq* 58, 65-77.

Matthews, R.J., W. Matthews and H. McDonald, 1994. Excavations at Tell Brak, 1994, *Iraq* 56, 177-94.

Nissen, H.J., 1995. Kulturelle und politische Vernetzungen in Vorderen Orient des 4. und 3. vorchristlichen Jahrtausends, in U. Finkbeiner, R. Dittmann and H. Hauptmann (eds.), *Beiträge zur Kulturgeschichte Vorderasiens* (Boehmer Festschrift), 473-90.

Oates, J., 1986. Tell Brak: the Uruk/Early Dynastic sequence, in U. Finkbeiner and W. Röllig (eds.), *Ğamdat Naṣr, Period or Regional Style?*, 245-71. Wiesbaden: Dr Ludwig Reichert Verlag.

Oates, J., 1993. Trade and power in the fifth and fourth millennia BC: new evidence from northern Mesopotamia, *World Archaeology* 24, 403-22.

Oates, J. and D. Oates, 1997. An open gate: cities of the fourth millennium BC (Tell Brak 1997), *Cambridge Archaeological Journal* 7, 287-96.

Reade, J., 1992. An early Warka tablet, in B. Hrouda, S. Kroll and P. Spanos (eds.), *Von Uruk nach Tuttul* (Eva Strommenger Festschrift), 177-79. Munich: Profil Verlag.

Stein, G., 1998. World System Theory and Alternative Modes of Interaction in the Archaeology of Culture Contact, in J. G. Cusick (ed.), Occasional Paper 25, Southern Illinois University, 220-55.

Weber, J., in preparation. Animal remains from Tell Brak *(Brak,* vol. 3).

Wright, Henry T., (ed.) 1981. *An early town on the Deh Luran Plain, Excavations at Tepe Farukhabad.* Ann Arbor.

'NON-URUK' DEVELOPMENTS AND URUK-LINKED FEATURES ON THE NORTHERN BORDERS OF GREATER MESOPOTAMIA

Marcella Frangipane

The presence of features linked to or even identifiable with Uruk culture in a vast geographic area covering the whole of the Tigris and Euphrates basins and the surrounding regions, while not exactly a novelty in the region (the Ubaid culture had already manifested similar widespread links over the same vast geographic area), has particularly excited the interest of scholars of Near Eastern prehistory because of the correlation with a substantial increase in the organisational complexity of the societies involved, leading to a radical change in their structures. The vast scale of the urban phenomenon in southern Mesopotamia and the magnitude of the economic, administrative and probably also political centralisation that occurred in the city of Uruk itself, and the presence in the Middle Euphrates of what were undoubtedly colonial type sites, encouraged the formation of a monocentric perspective, in which the 'urban' or 'state' model, together with elements of the Uruk culture, spread from the alluvial plain to the northern regions of Mesopotamia. These regions are considered to have been receptive to these influences, albeit participating to different degrees and in different ways depending on the findings unearthed on individual sites and, to an even greater extent, on the point of view of the scholars dealing with the subject.

Research carried out in recent years, however, has revealed both the complexity and the variety of the situations existing in the northern areas, and has identified features peculiar to the north. But it has also revealed the local roots in the north of certain phenomena that are characteristic of what is known as Mesopotamian urbanisation, such as the administrative use of seals which, in the Syro-Anatolian regions, dates back to the Neolithic period (as clearly evidenced from the discoveries at Sabi Abyad (Akkermans, Duistermaat 1996)), or the mass production of bowls, which has been very well documented in the same areas since at least the end of the 5th millennium. At the same time, recent discoveries at Tell Brak, Sheikh Hassan and Hacinebi, which have pushed back in time the emergence in the north of Uruk elements belonging to the southern tradition, have broadened the timeframe of the whole phenomenon indicating not only its gradualness, but also its nature of interaction between correlated parallel developments.

Arslantepe is both an extreme case and an emblematic example of this process. When we first discovered the extensive period VI A public area we stressed the essentially local character of the culture it expressed, even though we did not underestimate the powerful influence of southern Late Uruk culture (Frangipane, Palmieri 1988-89; Palmieri 1981). This not only emerged in a number of aspects of material production but also seems to have conditioned the modes and the forms of economic and administrative centralisation. The findings brought to light in recent years have pushed even further back in time the fundamental stages of this development, thereby emphasising the local roots to such an extent that new prospects are now opening up.

THE DEVELOPMENT OF LOCAL HIERARCHICAL SYSTEMS IN THE NORTH IN THE FIRST HALF OF THE 4TH MILLENNIUM. NEW DATA FROM ARSLANTEPE

The stratigraphic sequence of Arslantepe is now very clear from the beginning of the 4th millennium onwards (using calibrated C14 dating), when a long succession of levels with a homogeneous and rather conservative culture starts characterising the development of the so-called period VII. Various C14 calibrated dates place period VII around 3700 - 3500 BC (Di Nocera 2000), but, since these dates do not apply to either the last levels belonging to this period or the earliest part of its sequence, the whole period can be seen as covering most of the first half of the 4th millennium and the beginning of the second half up to about 3400 BC. This long time span is confirmed by the discovery in recent years of its direct stratigraphic superimposition above levels that can be dated to the end of the 5th millennium (period VIII) and are characterised by a cultural aspect which for the time being we might define as post-Ubaid[1] (Frangipane 1993b), and by the fact that it lies directly below period VI A buildings, which have been dated to the last centuries of the 4th millennium (3300/3350 - 3000 BC) (Di Nocera 2000).

In period VII Arslantepe reached its maximum expansion, densely occupying the whole area of the mound, and it was probably in this period that the areas within it to be used for the functions of the elites were defined. While in the NE zone common dwellings have been found built directly on virgin soil, made up of small buildings of one or two rooms, with external working areas and graves with poor funerary gifts under the floors of the dwellings (Palmieri 1978), the W/SW zone of the mound has revealed monumental buildings at a much higher level on what must have been the top of the mound in those days, created by the stratification of older levels in that zone. It is here that period VII has a substantial sequence comprising a deposit some three metres deep, on which a complex of period VI A buildings were built in stratigraphic continuity. The totally continuous development is evidenced from two elements, one functional, and one stratigraphic. As far as the first element is concerned, the main period VII building brought to light in this area so far is a huge monumental building with walls some 1.20 metres thick, decorated with wall paintings on white plaster and with plastered mud-brick columns, probably for decorative purposes, lined up along the walls (Fig. 1). This structure has not yet been fully unearthed, but it does not appear to be either a religious or an administrative public building judging from the architectural features or the materials found inside it (Frangipane 1993a). The same characteristics can be seen in the next complex of rooms superimposed upon it, belonging to period VI A (Frangipane 1993b) (Fig.2). Both might have been the elite's buildings, but they were residential in character.

The second important indicator of continuity has to do with the direct juxtaposition of the construction levels of period VI A on those of period VII without any stratigraphic interruption, and sometimes following the same layout.

The floor plan of some of the most important buildings found in the W area of the mound seem to indicate, among other things, that in periods VII and VI A there was a bipartite module, with a large rectangular room with only one extended side, leading to two smaller rooms (Fig.2: A562-A747-A727). The fact that this kind of architectural layout possibly existed at Arslantepe in the dwellings of the elites in the 4th millennium establishes a major linkage with the public architecture. This link is particularly strong with the ceremonial/religious architecture which, in period VI A, seems to have had the same original bipartite floor plan which is clearly recognizable in both temple buildings in the monumental complex in the SW area (Fig.3). The identification of a possible architectural tradition for private buildings from at least period VII also suggests that the public architecture of Arslantepe was local in origin, and the shape of the temple seems to have been based on the 'house', as the tripartite buildings were in the Mesopotamian world.

Confirmation of the strictly local origin of the bipartite pattern of Arslantepe's temples comes from the discovery, during recent excavation campaigns, of a huge period VII ceremonial building (Building XXIX) situated in what was later to become the VI A large public area,

even though it was moved slightly towards its north-west outer edge (Fig. 4). This building was of an extraordinary monumental nature, standing on an impressive base of stone slabs and bricks which raise it up over the surrounding surface area, and whose dimensions and architectural features leave no doubt whatsoever about its public ceremonial function (Figs. 5a and 5b). This building, despite serious damage caused to it by modern quarrying and by trenches dug during the old French excavations in the Thirties and Fifties, had a ground plan comprising a huge internal central room 17.50 metres long and 7 metres wide, with niches in the walls which, being near the corners, combined with the movement of the wall in the proximity of doors to create the impression of niches with multiple entries. The doors, situated at the ends of the long sides, may well have been present on all four corners, even though we can only recognise two with any certainty, due to the seriously damaged structure. In the centre of the room was a large platform measuring 5 x 2.50 metres, with a hearth place, and scattered around the platform on the floor were dozens and dozens of mass produced bowls typical of period VII (Fig. 6), some of them with flint-scraped bottoms, others with flat or string-cut bases (Fig. 7). These bowls, which in the central room were almost the only *in situ* materials present, were also plentiful in a smaller side room, which is only partly preserved. Unlike the large central room, here they were mostly upside-down and piled in rows, as they were ready to be used (Fig. 8). In this room, numerous clay sealings were also found, concentrated in the southern zone, some of them on the floor together with the bowls, and others in a superimposed dump, which also contained other bowls, as they had been re-deposited or had fallen down from somewhere else (perhaps from the roof) where they may have been discarded.

For the first time at Arslantepe, we therefore have documentation of a huge public building from the first half of the 4th millennium, in which the main activity performed was redistribution, probably in a ritualised or ceremonial form, and in which administrative control was exercised over goods. This structure, which is the largest so far known from the whole of the region, and appears to be also larger and more impressive than the period VI A 'temples' considered individually (Fig. 4), belongs to a period marked by a local culture without any sign of Uruk influence. Economic and administrative centralisation which was a particularly pronounced function in the later period VI A, and which we had attributed to southern influence over the local socio-economic system and in particular on the organisation the local elites laid down, was already one of the main functions of the hierarchies at Arslantepe before the so-called Uruk expansion towards the northern regions.

The ceremonial building at Arslantepe marks the final phase of period VII in stratigraphic terms, because it was underneath what was probably a residential structure belonging to period VI A. This final moment was identifiable mainly by the appearance of certain novelties in a context of traditional products, which was the evident outcome of an internal development in the mass production of pottery. It reveals heightened experimentation with production techniques perhaps to meet the need to raise output, judging from the emergence, alongside the traditional flint-scraped or handmade bowls, of conical bowls and slightly carinated beakers with string-cut bases made on the fast wheel (Figs. 9a and b, 10b). It is interesting to note that the string-cut marks also appear on a number of flint-scraped bowls with an unscraped base which indicates the combined use of various different techniques and solutions, which is typical of experimental and innovative phases (Figs. 7 and 10b:2).

This gradual process of change, which is rarely documented by archaeological records, is recognisable in a complex of long adjacent rooms (Fig. 4) lying stratigraphically above the period VII building with columns (Fig. 1) and directly below the period VI A residential complex (Fig. 2). These rooms, which have very stout walls in proportion to their size, do not seem to have been used as dwellings as such, and seem to have been connected with occupational activities or used as stores for handicraft products and materials (several dozen obsidian arrow heads and large quantities of ochre have been found there).

On the floors, in addition to a ceramics inventory typical of the final moment of period VII, characterised by a wheel-made mass production of bowls and beakers with string-cut bases, for the first time a new fabric appears, though in very low quantity, that was subsequently to be typical of period VI A: hand-made red-black burnished ware. This heralded on this site, and elsewhere, a ceramic tradition that was subsequently to characterise the whole Anatolian Early Bronze Age. It is the first indication of the existence of a network of relations between the Central and Eastern Anatolian regions, in which the area of Malatya must have been a meeting point between the different component parts. For the Late Chalcolithic red-black pottery of Arslantepe shares some profiles with Central Anatolian Late Chalcolithic/EB I sites, such as Alişar and Alaca Höyük (Orthman 1963); on the other hand, as far as fabrics and manufacturing techniques are concerned, it closely resembles the later VI B1 (EBI) wares which in turn are related to the Transcaucasian environment. It is possible that the appearance of red-black pottery at Arslantepe was linked to the emergence in the region of groups from the northeast, from the Kura-Arax regions. Whatever the origin of this new fabric, the fact remains that in the final level of period VII its appearance, together with that of a few sherds of very fine light-coloured ware, broke the traditional homogeneity of the Chalcolithic ceramics, suggesting that there was an enlargement of external contacts and probably also a change in the organisation of production and the people involved in it.

All the period VII ceramics in fact used the same type of paste, mainly chaff-tempered, in which the different degrees of coarseness were due exclusively to the size of the vessels, and they were hastily fired, leaving a grey core inside the section, which provides technological justification for the widespread use of straw in the paste. The use of this homogeneous technology to manufacture all types of vessels suggests that the potters organised their work on a communal, or at least co-operative basis, in response to new needs for mass production. A further element in support of this hypothesis is the frequent, but not general, use of very simple and repetitive potter's marks on various types of vessels (Trufelli 1994), more for the practical need of potters to identify their own products which were perhaps taken to common areas for drying and firing, rather than to distinguish them for their customers. This would also account for the fact that only some of the vessels bore potter's marks (perhaps one for each group of items taken for firing) rather than all of them, while the use of one and the same mark for different types of vessels ties in with the homogeneity of production and the absence of internal specialisation (each potter producing a range of different vessels) (Frangipane in press a).

The highly standardized Arslantepe period VII pottery production therefore derives from the production methods and technologies that had become established in the 4th millennium. This explains the widespread occurrence of certain more specifically technical features shared by all the Late Chalcolithic production in the northern regions of Greater Mesopotamia: chaff-tempered paste, quick firing, rough surfaces, the use of a rotating device in their manufacture which affected the profiles of the vases, particularly the necks, which have the characteristic inner corrugations.

If the technological features and production procedures link Arslantepe period VII pottery to other Late Chalcolithic assemblages of the Syro-Anatolian and Upper Mesopotamian regions, the more specifically cultural aspects, and hence the typological traits, show both general characteristics shared by all these areas - such as the very pronounced complex shapes of the thickened rims, particularly on the bowls, or the internal undulations of the necks, obtained as a result of the wheel-turning (Frangipane 2000, fig. 2:1-10) - and many features peculiar to Malatya. These are the predominance of red slip on the majority of shapes, the presence of typical forms such as small standardised carinated beakers (Fig. 11), and the absence of many characteristic profiles of Upper Mesopotamia proper such as the casseroles.

The absolute dating of period VII, stated on the basis of C14 dates and stratigraphic ante quem and post-quem limits, establishes a chronological parallelism with Early and Middle Uruk in Lower Mesopotamia and reflects the continuity of 4th millennium local cultural developments in the north, in those regions where the impact of new Uruk features came much later, and in a form that had already been subject to other influences and transformed. Amuq phase F might also be an example of a similar development, as perhaps most of the region west of the Euphrates Valley and north of the Taurus might be, suggesting a variety of cultural cores in the north of Greater Mesopotamia (Frangipane 1993; Lupton 1996, fig. 2.4; Butterlin 1998), which, in my opinion, account for the variety of different outcomes, in terms of both forms and timing, of the establishment of an Uruk culture in the North.

THE FORMATION OF A 'NORTHERN LATE URUK CULTURE' AT THE END OF THE 4TH MILLENNIUM: A REITERATED ACCULTURATION PROCESS IN GREATER MESOPOTAMIA

The appearance on the scene of groups of southern origin around the middle of the 4th millennium took different forms and produced different effects in the geographical areas which already had diversified cultural features in the first half of the millennium. The impact seems to have been strong and early in the Middle/Upper Euphrates Valley as far as the Taurus and on the Khabour, with presences like Sheikh Hassan and Hacinebi early on (Boese 1995; Stein *et al.* 1996) and Habuba Kabira, Jebel Aruda, and Hassek Höyük later on (Sürenhagen 1974-75; Van Driel, van Driel-Murray 1983; Behm-Blancke (ed.)1981; 1984), in addition to the numerous sites with clear remains of Uruk culture that have been identified in the surveys (Algaze *et al.* 1994). The most interesting case, lastly, is Tell Brak (even though the excavations, which are still far too limited in extent in terms of the dimensions of the site, leave many points to be clarified) because the sequence is complete and it is possible to identify the gradual way in which Uruk elements penetrated the local contexts (TW 16-13) until total cultural assimilation was achieved at the end of the 4th millennium (TW 12) (Oates and Oates 1993).

Much less pronounced, and at all events completely absent in the phases corresponding to Middle Uruk, is any visible Uruk component in the areas west of the Euphrates and north of the Taurus where, as we have already said, the local Late Chalcolithic features appeared to be distinct.

Finally, it is difficult to appraise exactly what happened along the Tigris Valley and the bordering regions because of a lack of sufficient data: Tepe Gawra, where there were no elements of Uruk culture whatsoever, indeed had a sequence that related only to the phases prior to the middle of the 4th millennium (Rothman, Peasnall 1999), while Nineveh, which seems to have had a fully Uruk culture in the late 4th millennium (Nin. 4), has not any reliable stratigraphy that could account for the transformation process in phase 3 (Campbell Thompson, Mallowan 1933; Gut 1995).

The new waves of migrations of southern people, probably different in terms of scale and provenance, followed specific routes which essentially revolved around the Euphrates, reaching as far as the Khabour, and only established privileged relations with a few of the local cultures which were not those of the geographical areas that were better endowed with raw materials. This differs from a settlement pattern designed for commercial purposes (Algaze 1992). This is also contradicted by the gradual and pervading nature of the change which seems to have been set in motion in the Jezira and the corresponding stretch of the Euphrates by prolonged interaction which took different forms across time. Once again Tell Brak provides important clues to understand the nature of this phenomenon. The scale of magnitude of the site, also in functional terms, and the increasingly more significant findings suggesting a hierarchical organisation (imposing architecture which was perhaps public) in the phase preceding any Uruk interference (Oates and Oates 1997), make it hardly credible that a colonisation of such a magnitude to produce the far-reaching transformation of local society which is observable at the end of the 4th millennium took place in this centre. A similar transformation, on the other hand, can be seen in all the other investigated sites of a certain Late Uruk date in Upper Mesopotamia, and this phenomenon, though it certainly must be related with the interaction with southern components, cannot be seen as simply a consequence of the interference by small groups of colonists.

At Arslantepe as in other regions not primarily affected by the impact of the relations established with the groups of southern origin, participation in the new culture, albeit to a more marginal degree, only occurred at the end of the period when all the regions of Greater Mesopotamia already belonged to a new Late Uruk world. This change occurred quite suddenly as far as the features of handicraft production were concerned, particularly pottery, which was strongly influenced by Late Uruk taste and technology. It on the contrary appeared as a development and an expansion of phenomena that were already evident in the previous period as regards the overall organisation of society with the upgrading of the centralised redistribution system. Even sectors of pottery-making more closely linked to the new needs and functions of the centralised society, such as the mass production of bowls for the distribution of meals, show gradual growth in a process with obvious local roots.

Mass-produced bowls are one of the most significant features of Late Chalcolithic production in the northern Mesopotamian environment, and each of the main cultural regions there had their own way of making these products. Arslantepe, like many other northern sites, did not used bevelled rim bowls, and adopted a production process, which probably started with the Coba bowls tradition, perhaps using some rotating device, although combined with hand manufacturing techniques. What is interesting here is that in Arslantepe, thanks to the detail of the sequence and the large sample of excavated areas, which made it possible to bring to light large homogeneous assemblages of materials *in situ*, we can recognise all the steps in the development of this particular type of production. One can therefore see that for a long time different techniques co-existed: firstly flint-scraped bowls and large flat-bottomed conical bowls (Fig. 9a), subsequently joined by string-cut conical bowls, which prevail at the end of the period and were later to lead to the flower pot types of period VI A (Fig. 13b).

The widespread presence of mass-produced bowls - if we consider these bowls to have been utensils for the distribution of food to large sections of the population, which I feel is the most likely explanation at the present stage of knowledge - was an indirect indicator of the existence of a class of people who were able to centralise resources and redistribute food and consequently influence the organisation of bowl production.

As we have already seen, centralisation as a distinctive feature of at least part of the economy and the early management of power by the religious elites, or those with strong ideological legitimation, was already evident in period VII and was therefore not the result of imitating southern society. Public architecture, too, which was the highest expression of these elites and the way they operated, possesses original features in terms of shapes, forms and the arrangement of spaces in relation to functions.

The large period VII ceremonial building (XXIX) accounts for the architectural features of the period VI A public complex and all those elements which in that period still seem to be alien to the Mesopotamian tradition in the strict sense of the term. The extraordinary complex of monumental public buildings occupying a large part of the southwestern area of the mound at the end of the 4th millennium BC (Fig. 4), was arranged in such a way that buildings with different public functions were located at different altitudes by terracing what was then the slope of the tell, which had grown probably due to the existence in that area of a monumental architecture in earlier periods. The functional diversification of the areas and the architectural unity of the buildings make them appear as parts of a large palace-like complex, in which religious and important structures are found on the higher terraces, while the service areas (stores, a courtyard, an access road or corridor) are in the lower parts (Frangipane 1997). More than two thousand clay sealings bearing the impressions of about 200 different seals have been found *in situ*, some in the stores, where they were sealing the containers or had only just been removed from them, but the majority in dumping places where they had been discarded after use, probably after a series of checking and accounting operations (Frangipane, Palmieri 1983; Ferioli, Fiandra 1983; 1994; Frangipane 1994).

The very intense economic activities had their own areas in which to be carried out, but they were also performed in association with ceremonial or religious func-

tions, since concentrations of foodstuffs and administrative materials (sealings) were both also found inside the two structures we interpreted as temples (Temple A and B) (Fig. 4). These structures were built according to a highly standardised bipartite floor plan and had internal items which were probably used for religious purposes, such as a double central podium and an altar set against the end wall with niches on the short sides.

Wall paintings decorated the entrances and all the passageways with figurative representations showing human or anthropomorphic figures with standardised repetitive features, and narrative scenes, using images which may all have been linked to a clearly defined ideology.

Even though certain elements, such as the emphasis on the large central room or the niches in the walls, may be part of some generic Mesopotamian tradition, probably shared by all the regions that gravitated around the Tigris and the Euphrates from the Ubaid period onwards, the Arslantepe architecture is dominated by original elements which can now be ascribed to a local Chalcolithic tradition. Even the strange shape and position of a niche with multiple entries on one of the long sides of Temple B near the corner with the end wall might be interpreted as reminiscent of the shape of a similar multiple niche found in the corner wall of the central room in period VII Building XXIX, where it was moulded in conjunction with a door. There is even more evident linkage between the wall paintings of period VI A and the Chalcolithic tradition of painting walls which was common not only at Arslantepe but throughout the Anatolian Upper Euphrates valley, as evidenced at Değirmentepe (Esin 1983) and Norşuntepe (Hauptmann 1976).

The most significant differences between the public building of period VII (Building XXIX) and the later Late Uruk period buildings are the isolated and dominant position of the former, which is actually raised up on a platform, and the different functions suggested by some of the architectural features and above all by the materials found on the floors. For, whereas the central room of the period VI A temples was protected and only had one entry through one of the small side rooms, the large room of the period VII building must have had several entries, perhaps four, one at each corner (even though only two of them are clearly preserved today). Furthermore, different use and activities performed in the latter are suggested by the absence of *podia*, the presence of a central large platform with a hearth, and the correlation between this and the large quantity of mass-produced bowls scattered everywhere in the southern half of the room. These bowls are actually the only material found *in situ* in Building XXIX, unlike the later temples (A and B) where the presence of different classes of vessels, whether concentrated in the side rooms, as in Temple A (Frangipane, Palmieri 1983), or in the main large room, as in Temple B (Frangipane 1997), indicated a variety of different activities, both religious and related to storage and redistribution. Wall paintings also had a different function: in the period VII building they decorated the interior of the main room on the end wall and the whole of the northeast corner, in contrast to the lack of decorations in the corresponding rooms from period VI A temples, which on the contrary have decorations only on the outer walls. These differences are functional (they point to a different social use of the public buildings) but they may also suggest an evolution in time in the function and characterisation of the public sphere.

Despite the continuity of tradition and the structural and organisational similarities, changes in fact occurred in period VI A, and they were substantial. They can be seen in the craft products and indicate changes in the relationships between producers, customers, and consumers, as well as a more marked influence than in the past of external relationships. These relations were mainly with Late Uruk groups, but also other populations who probably arrived in the Malatya plain from the north-east. The pottery therefore shows the assimilation of new techniques and fashions from outside, but it also certainly reflects a re-organisation of production. Pottery of period VI A now clearly consists of four classes of products, made in different ways and probably also by different craftsmen: a) a new *wheel-made fine or semi-fine light-coloured ware* with standardised profiles and dimensions, and specialised in terms of the shapes and functional classes (necked jars, often with reserved slip decoration, small fine jars, high-stemmed bowls, beaked bowls and very rare examples of fine bowls with a bead rim) (Figs. 12, 13a); b) *coarse wheel-made conical mass-produced bowls* (Figs. 12:5 and 13b); c) *hand-made red-black burnished ware,* also specialised in terms of the shapes, consisting only of small fine jars or jugs, handled cups and high-stemmed bowls (Fig. 17); d) *kitchen ware,* comprising cooking pots and pithoi.

The wheel-made light-coloured ware reveals a late Uruk influence in the general look of the pottery, in jar profiles with high shoulders and cylindrical necks, and in the frequent use of reserved slip decoration (Fig. 12: 6-8). However this production is characterized by its marked originality, both in the repertoire of the forms and shapes, and in the paste and manufacturing techniques. Despite the fact that in this period the wares were very different from those belonging to period VII, and reflected a new Uruk-like taste, the paste used was still straw-tempered even though the straw is very fine and almost invisible on the surface, the surfaces are often slipped, even though clay of the same colour as the paste is used, and they are at any rate always very smoothly finished. These are all features of the traditional manufacturing techniques and reflect the fact that the taste for slipped surfaces typical of period VII pottery still persisted.

A similar continuation of local traditions has been found in the manufacture of pottery at Hassek Höyük (Helwing 1999), which is the closest in similarity to the Arslantepe pottery, especially as far as the shape of the

necked jars is concerned, but also in some details and specific aspects, such as the use of a characteristic incised herring-bone motif delimited by one or two small knobs on the jar shoulders (Fig. 12:7). There are apparently similar features in the Late Uruk pottery from Tepecik (Esin 1982)[2] so that one can recognize a 'northern area' of the Late Uruk world in which the craftsmen interpreted the Mesopotamian models in terms of the local taste and traditions.

Arslantepe VI A pottery also shows its marked autonomy in the repertoire of its shapes, which is much more restricted in terms of variety and less Uruk-like than the pottery of Hassek Höyük. It comprises few shapes, each one highly standardized in terms of profiles and dimensions, and therefore very clearly defined presumably for one particular use: large and medium-sized jars, small-necked jars, high-stemmed bowls with cut-out decoration on the stems, a few spouted bowls with a typical Arslantepe profile (Fig. 12). This marked specialisation is wholly new feature of period VI A, which, coupled with the disappearance of potters' marks, suggested the work of the craftsmen had been completely re-organised to meet the needs of a more specialized clientele, and may even have been, at least partially, controlled from the centre.

The influence of Late Uruk production was probably also exercised through direct familiarity with products that were perhaps imported and/or with foreign craftsmen. A few proper Late Uruk vessels have been found *in situ* side by side with the local assemblage in the main buildings in the public complex (Fig. 14): four bent-spouted bottles found in one of the storerooms (Fig. 15a) and in Temple A (Fig. 14:1), of which only two really seem to be alien to local production in shape, grit-tempered paste, and rough surface; two typical elongated jars (Figs. 14:4-5;15b) and a small red slipped jar with a sharp shoulder (Figs. 14:2; 16) in Temple B; a small four-lugged jar very similar to Tepecik and Hassek examples (Behm-Blancke (ed.) 1981, fig.23:2; Esin 1982, fig. 72:15-16) in Temple A (Fig. 14:3). A few bevelled rim bowl fragments have been also found in the filling layers, but their interpretation is rather difficult: their number is in fact so low they cannot be considered part of the mass production, which, at Arslantepe, exclusively consist of conical bowls made on the fast wheel, extremely standardized as for the forms and sizes and very similar to the Mesopotamian flower pots.

The other two classes which, together with the wheel-made categories, make up the inventory of period VI A pottery are both hand-made and probably refer to different ambits of production. The kitchen ware, which includes both cooking pots and large storage jars or pithoi, unlike the previous period VII cooking pots is completely hand-made and may have been domestically produced. The red-black burnished ware seems to reflect a different pottery manufacturing tradition in both technology and taste and probably originated in a different environment. Its production may have required specialised craftsmen who might have been of foreign origin, or may have been made elsewhere.

It is in this period, at the end of the 4th millennium, that black or red-black burnished pottery spread throughout Anatolia, showing that there was a sort of cultural substrate shared by many different communities running from central to eastern Anatolia and to the Caucasus. Red-black pottery did not, however, move beyond the barrier of the Taurus except for a few examples of imported items, constituting yet another element which distinguishes the northern part of the Late Uruk world, of which Arslantepe and Tepecik were fully part, while Hassek Höyük was incorporated into it to a marginal degree, being more closely linked to the Late Uruk cultures of the Middle/Upper Euphrates. The Arslantepe VI A red-black burnished pottery (Fig. 17) shows similarities in its shapes with central Anatolian examples from Alişar and Alaca Höyük (Orthman 1963), but the paste and the technical and aesthetic features are identical to those found in the later period VI B1 pottery, with evident Transcaucasian links (Frangipane 2000).

The variety and diversity of the pottery productions in this period indicate a considerable opening up of new contacts and relations in different directions, which is the second aspect of novelty in period VI A.

This may have had to do with the major development of metallurgy in this period as a result of which the range of objects produced grew considerably, even though this occurred in what seems to have been above all an elite environment, with a refined technology and the production and testing of various different alloys.

Metallurgy is an activity with a strong local tradition because of the abundance of raw materials in that region: but at the end of the fourth millennium there was a sharp increase in both quality and quantity which may have been due not only to an increased demand for different products from the elites, but also an enhanced capacity to organise production and control the collection of raw materials by broader and more regular contacts with other environments. In this regard it is interesting to see the extraordinary similarity in the different types of objects and manufacturing techniques between the metals used in period VI A and those found in the so-called 'royal tomb' dating from the beginning of the third millennium (period VI B), where Transcaucasian elements are evident. Identical spearheads, an identical composition of copper and arsenic, antimony and nickel, identical silver inlay decoration, the presence of gold and the abundant use of silver. It is therefore possible that the whole of eastern Anatolia and the Transcaucasus had major links in the metallurgy industry and that this also grew as a result of heightened demand from the early urban centres of the Euphrates valley and perhaps even from Mesopotamian groups further south.

The broadening of the area of interaction between different peoples and perhaps the establishment of new forms of interaction can be seen from the physical circu-

lation of craftsmen's models, and also in part of products, which is certainly typical of the latter half of the fourth millennium throughout the whole of Greater Mesopotamia, perhaps accompanied by actual population shifts. The importance of trade to these societies does not, however, seem sufficient to justify the assumption that trade was the primary cause of these shifts and this interaction. The forms and the stages of the penetration of southern Uruk features into the northern Syro-Mesopotamian area seem to be more the results of the intensification of contacts, for reasons we do not know, that groups of southern origin, moving northwards according to a pattern already working in earlier periods, maintained with the local populations. It is sufficient to mention the example of Susa and Susiana, where a complete cultural assimilation with Mesopotamia took place in the Late Uruk period, whereas this homogeneity was broken in the Protoelamite period in connection with the expansion of trade roots towards the east passing through the Elam.

What makes the forms of these contacts, and hence their archaeological visibility, so different in the latter half of the fourth millennium is not only an intensification and increase in the scale of the physical population shifts, in my opinion, but the changed organisation of society in both the south and the north. The presence of powerful hierarchies governing the communities was a discriminating factor which must have changed the forms and also the nature of traditional relationships, directing them towards the needs of the dominant groups. The interaction that one finds, for example, in Upper Mesopotamia and in the Middle Euphrates, even though it is still not clear, seems to have been very broadly based and to have had the effect of transforming lifestyles and cultural models, partly along the lines of what had happened at the beginning of the Ubaid period in the transition from Halaf. The highly centralised management of relations, however, magnified the effects of the phenomenon in the fourth millennium.

The regions north of the Taurus, on the other hand, were only marginally affected and only much later by this phenomenon, strengthening the idea that it was not so much for reasons of trade or for finding raw materials that southern groups settled in the north. It is precisely here, where contacts were less intense, that these contacts were probably caused mostly by trade needs, as evidenced from the development of metallurgy and the broadening external relations at Arslantepe. Trade, however, while growing in importance, does not seem to have become the key issue in the economy of Arslantepe which, in the period of the full development of centralisation in period VI A, appears to have been based on staple products and the exploitation of the labour force, indicated by the clay sealings/bowls linkage and the use of central stores for food products.

The action and perhaps even the pressure that was brought to bear by the foreign component on the functions of the central hierarchies and more generally perhaps the difficulties the latter found in managing multiple relations with different groups, may have been not so much a source of development but one of the causes of the abrupt and definitive collapse of the centralised system of Arslantepe around 3000 BC.

The most significant factor of the Late Uruk phenomenon was, therefore, not so much the stimulation of secondary states under the southern influence as the maximum establishment of that capillary and intense system of mutual relationships between different components based on the capacity of the Mesopotamian populations to shift around the vast territory lying between the Tigris and the Euphrates. This created again one of the forms of cultural homogenisation that were the basis and the reason of the existence of Greater Mesopotamia (Frangipane, in press b). I feel that it is becoming increasingly more difficult to talk in terms of colonies and local groups once we are dealing chronologically with the full Late Uruk period. The whole of northern Mesopotamia was, in a certain sense, 'Urukized', and confirmation of this far-reaching transformation of the northern cultures can be seen from the continuity of the Uruk craft tradi-

tions and pottery production that one finds at the beginning of the third millennium throughout the whole area of the Middle and Upper Euphrates, but also, to a different extent, in the more eastern territories. Here the emergence of phases that are quite rightly considered to be the transition between Uruk and Ninevite 5 or Proto-Ninevite 5 (Oates 1993; Killick 1986) emphasizes this continuity after the so-called collapse of Late Uruk power systems.

It was perhaps the political structures that changed. The possible clearer definition of political territories, which was the effect of centralization and the increasing gradual interference in the population economy by the central institutions in the fourth millennium (imposing taxes and the demand for manpower makes it necessary to define the territory which belongs to the authorities), produced what has been called the 'regionalization' of the third millennium. It was in this context that the area of Malatya and other regions that had previously formed part of the Late Uruk relation system embark upon a new phase in history separate from that of the rest of the Mesopotamian world, and linked to that Transcaucasian environment which was to become increasingly more expansive throughout the course of the third millennium.

---

[1] These levels, found on a low terrace on the western flanks of the mound, consisted of domestic structures and showed a pottery assemblage, which is new for the site and poorly known for the region as a whole, though it now find comparisons in the sequence of Oylum Höyük (Özgen et al. 1999). This pottery is distinguished by the use of mixed tempered pastes, rough sur-

faces often treated with a kind of light scraping, simple jar shapes typical of Ubaid and earlier repertoires, and a characteristic incised decoration.

[2] I would like to thank Prof. Ufuk Esin for having shown me some of the material kept at Istanbul University.

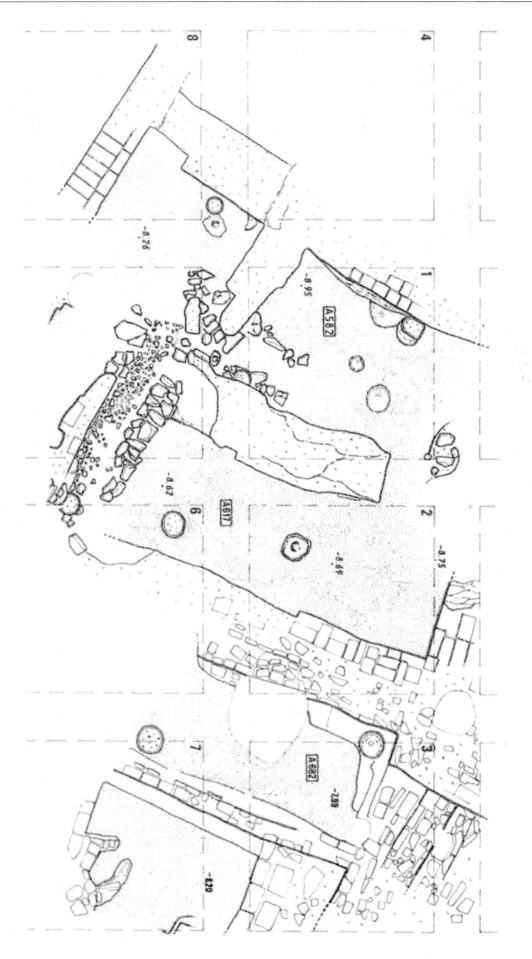

Fig.1. Arslantepe. Plan of period VII private monumental building with columns (western excavation area).

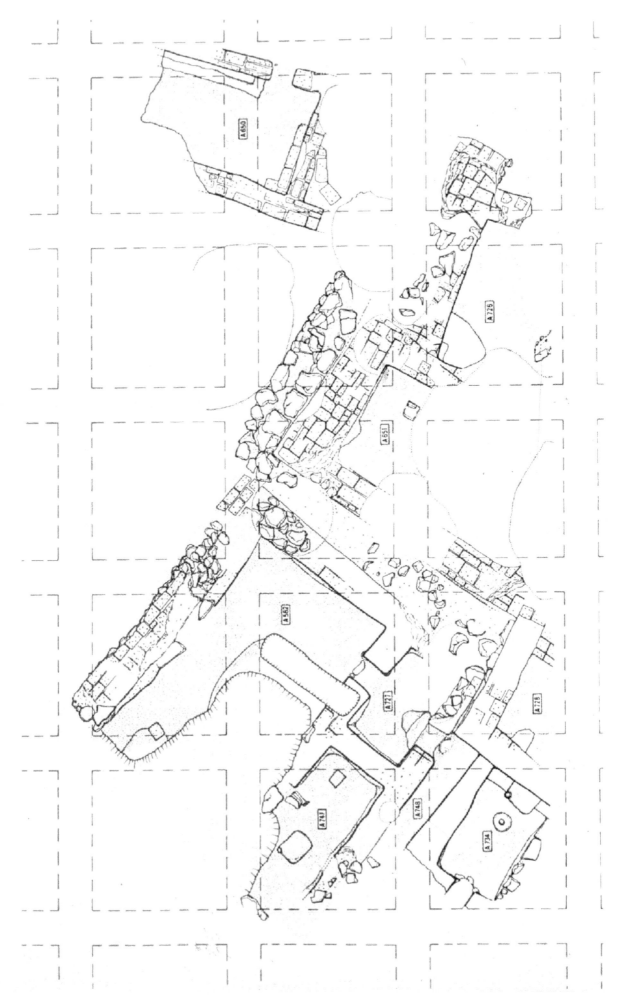

Fig. 2. Arslantepe. Plan of the private building complex from period VI A (western excavation area).

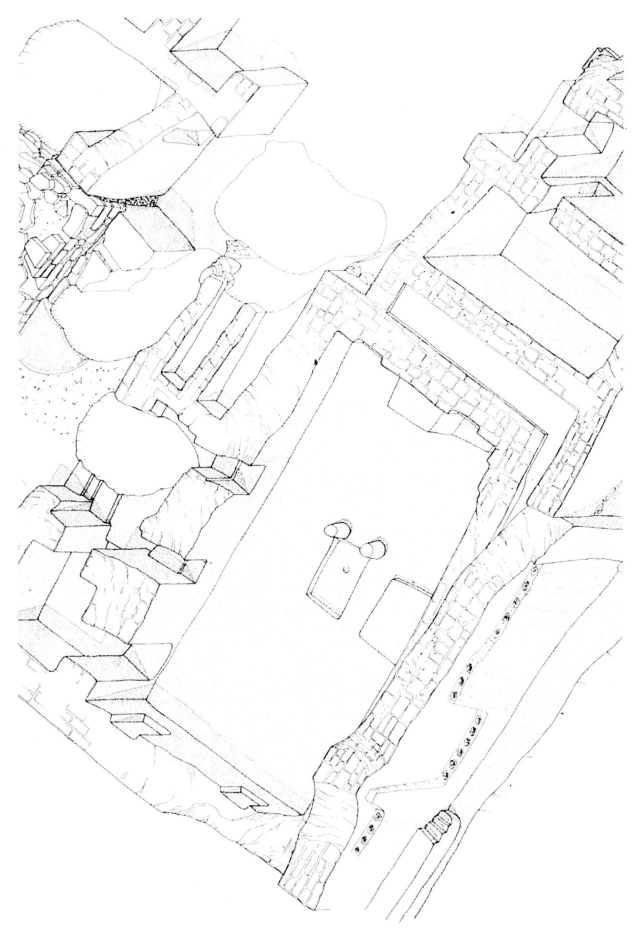

Fig. 3. Arslantepe. Isometric view of Temple B in the monumental public area from period VI A (south-western excavation area).

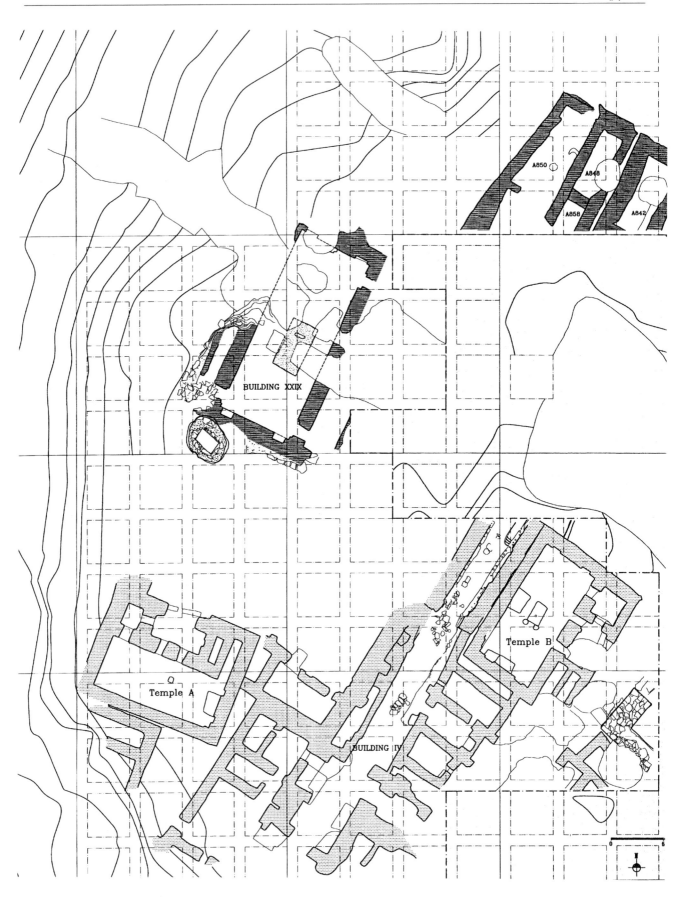

Fig. 4. Arslantepe. Monumental buildings from the final phase of period VII (dark grey) and period VI A (light grey).

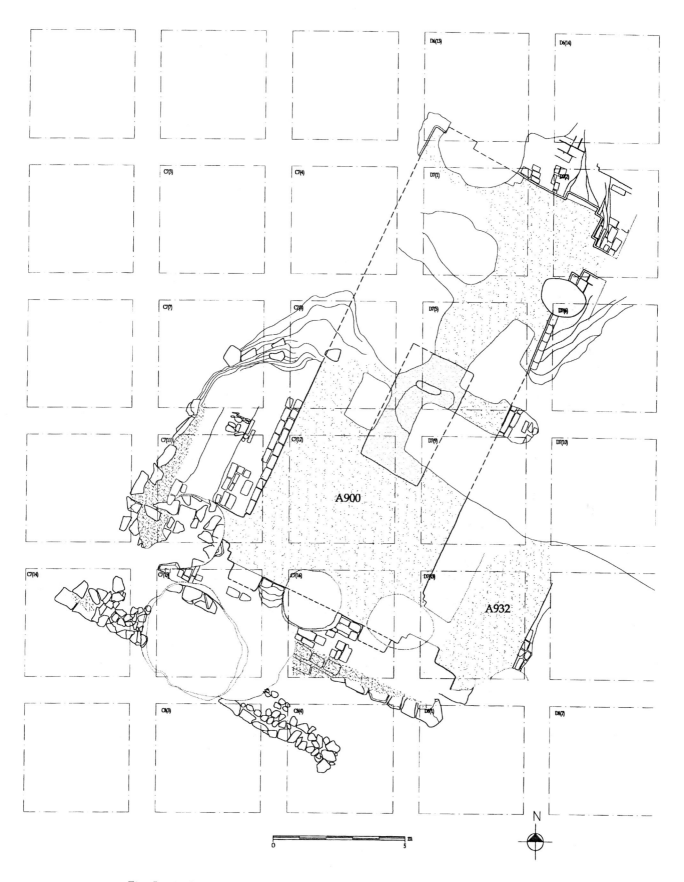

Fig. 5a. Arslantepe. Plan of period VII ceremonial building (Building XXIX).

Fig. 5b. Arslantepe. View from the south of Building XXIX.

Fig. 6. Arslantepe. The southern half of the large room (A 900) in Building XXIX with bowls in situ *spread on the floor.*

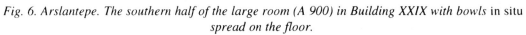

Fig. 7. Arslantepe. Some of the mass-produced bowls from Building XXIX.

Fig. 8. Arslantepe. Mass-produced bowls in situ *on the floor of the side-room (A932) in Building XXIX.*

Fig. 9a. Flint-scraped and conical bowls from period VII at Arslantepe.

Fig. 9b. Arslantepe. Small wheel-made beakers with string-cut bases from the final phase of period VII.

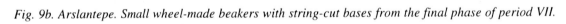

(left and below) Fig. 10a. Arslantepe. Chaff-faced red-slip jars from period VII. The example below is a late type developed at the end of the period.

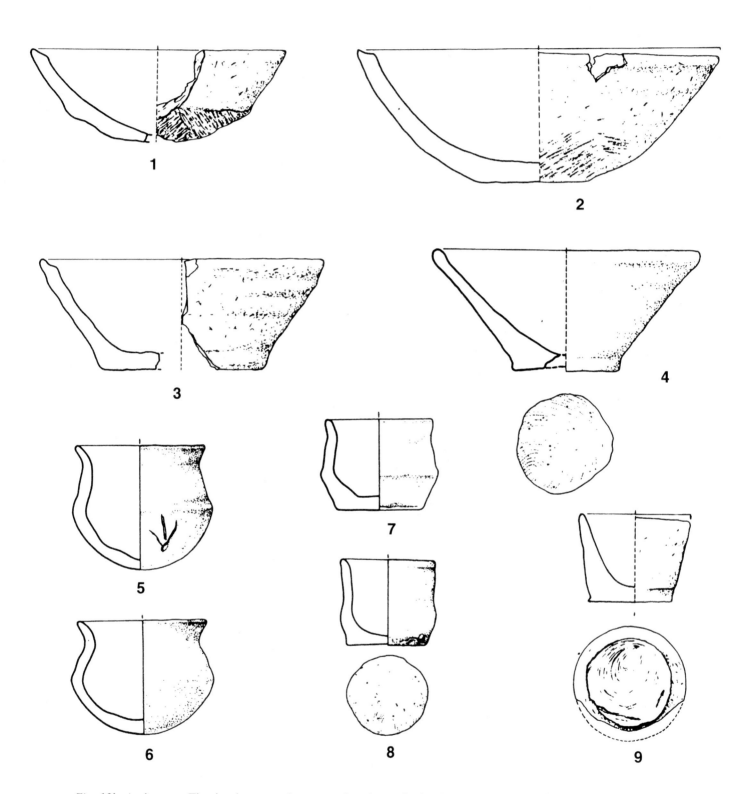

Fig. 10b. Arslantepe. The development of mass-produced vessels (bowls and beakers) from period VII to VI A.

Fig. 11. Arslantepe. Typical carinated chaff-faced beakers from period VII.

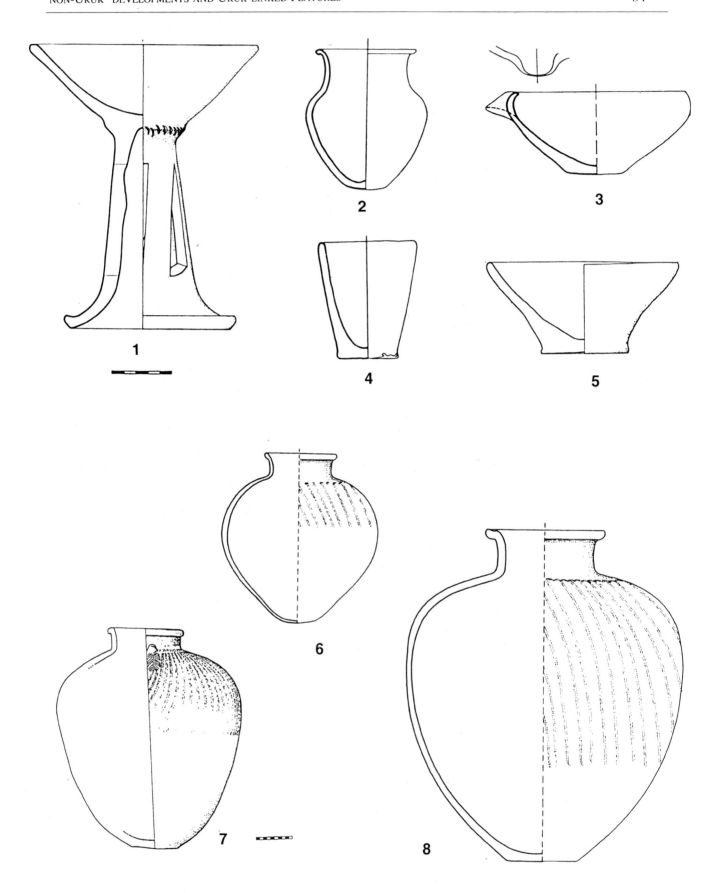

Fig. 12. Arslantepe. Profiles of period VI A wheel-made pottery.

Fig. 13a. Arslantepe. Period VI A necked jars.

Fig. 13b. Wheel-made mass-produced bowls from period VI A.

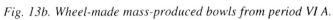

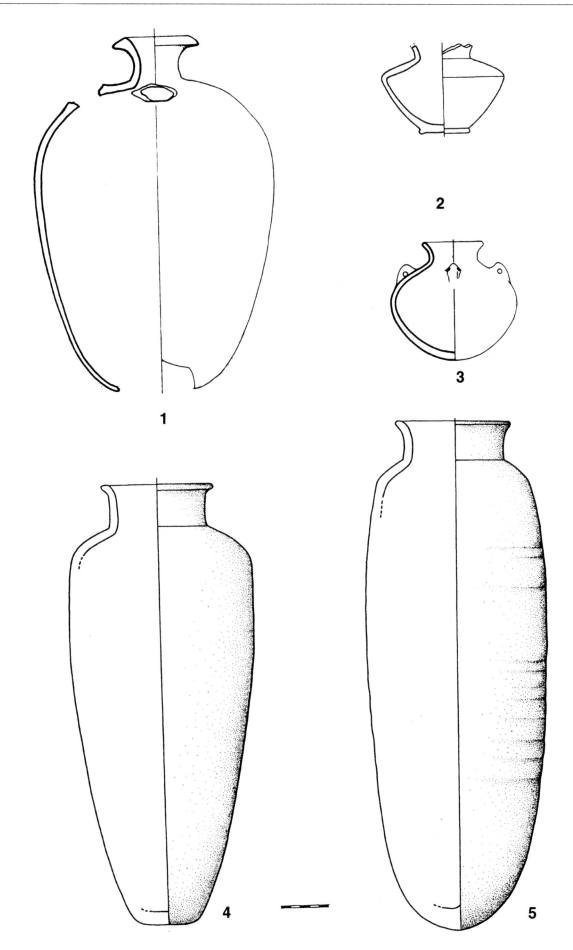

Fig. 15a (left). Spouted bottle found in one of the
store-rooms in the palatial complex of period VI A at
Arslantepe.

Fig. 15b (below). Arslantepe. The two characteristic
Late Uruk elongated jars found in Temple B.

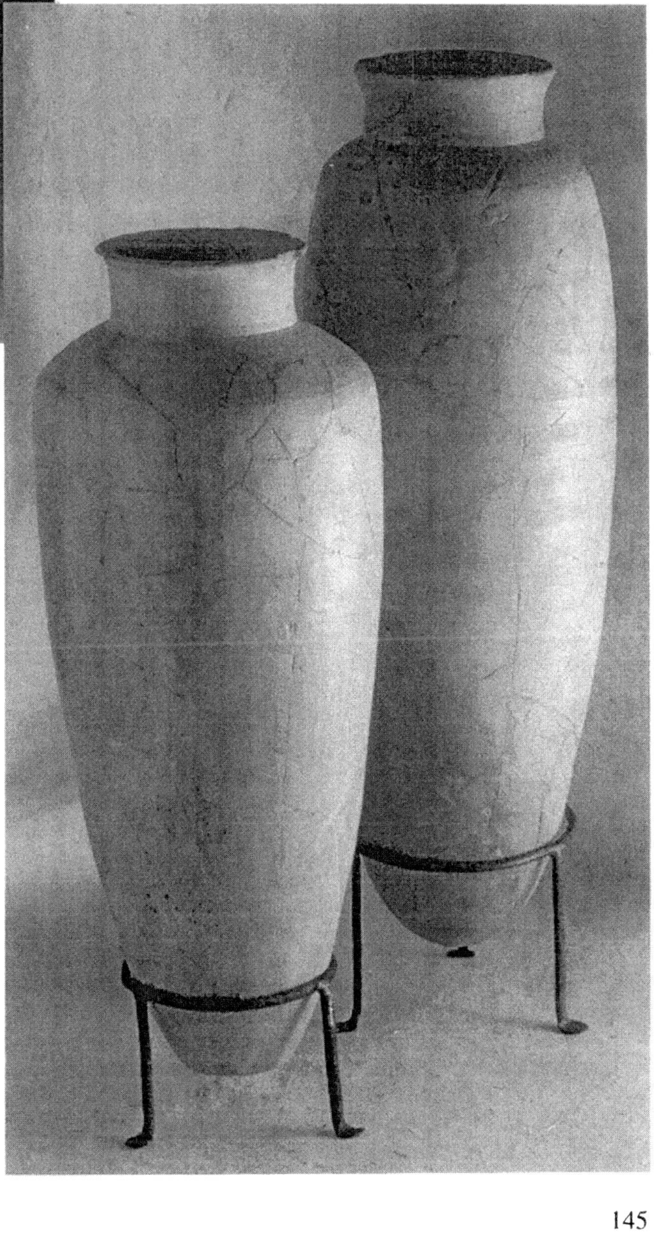

Fig. 14 (opposite). Late Uruk vessels found at
Arslantepe in the monumental public area.

Fig. 16. Small vessels from Arslantepe VI A. local wheel-made small jar, red-black jug, and the unique find of a Late Uruk red-slipped jar.

Fig. 17. Red-black burnished shapes from Arslantepe VI A.

BIBLIOGRAPHY

Algaze, G., 1993. *The Uruk World System*, Chicago.

Algaze, G., Breuninger R., Knudstad J., 1994. 'The Tigris-Euphrates Archaeological Reconnaissance Project: Final report of the Birecik and Carchemish Dam survey areas', *Anatolica* 20, 1-96.

Akkermans, P.M.M.G., Duistermaat K., 1996. 'Of storage and nomads. The sealings from Late Neolithic Sabi Abyad, Syria', *Paléorient* 22/2: 17-32.

Behm-Blancke, M.R. (ed.), 1981. 'Hassek Höyük', *Istanbuler Mitteilungen*, 31, 5-82.

Behm-Blancke, M.R. (ed.), 1984. 'Hassek Höyük', *Istanbuler Mitteilungen*, 34, 31-149.

Boese, J., 1995. *Ausgrabungen in Tell Sheikh Hassan I.* Saarbrücker Druckerei und Verlag, Saarbrüchen.

Butterlin, P., 1998. 'Espaces Urukéens en Syrie: Problèmes de cartographie et de méthodologie', in M. Fortin, O. Aurenche (eds.), *Espace Naturel, Espace Habité en Syrie du Nord (10e - 2e Millénaires av. J-C.)*, Maison de l'orient Méditeranéen, Lyon, 149-166.

Campbell Thompson, R., Mallowan, M.E.L., 1933. 'The British Museum Excavations at Nineveh 1931-32', *Annals of Archaeology and Anthropology* 20.

Di Nocera, G.M., 2000. 'Radiocarbon datings from Arslantepe and Norsuntepe: The fourth-third millennium absolute chronology in the Upper Euphrates and Transcaucasian region', in C. Marro (ed.), *From the Euphrates to the Caucasus: Chronologies for the 4th-3rd millennium B.C.*, Istanbul.

Esin, U., 1982. 'Tepecik excavations, 1974', *Keban Project 1974 Activities*, Ankara, 71-118.

Esin, U., 1983. 'Zur Datierung der vorgeschichtlichen Schichten von Değirmentepe bei Malatya in der östlichen Türkei', in R.M. Boehmer, H. Hauptmann (eds.), *Beiträge zur Altertumskunde Kleinasiens*, Mainz, 175-190.

Ferioli, P., and Fiandra, E., 1983, Clay-sealings from Arslantepe VI A: Administration and Bureaucracy. *Origini* 12 (2): 455-509.

Ferioli, P., Fiandra, E., 1994. 'Archival techniques and methods at Arslantepe', in P. Ferioli, E. Fiandra, G.G. Fissore, M. Frangipane (eds.), *Archives before Writing*, Roma, 149-161.

Frangipane, M., 1993. 'Local components in the development of centralized societies in Syro-Anatolian region', in Frangipane M., Hauptmann H., Liverani M., Matthiae P., Mellink M. (eds.), *Between the Rivers and over the Mountains. Archaeologica Anatolica et Mesopotamica Alba Palmieri Dedicata*, Roma, Università 'La Sapienza', 133-161.

Frangipane, M., 1994a. 'The record function of clay sealings in early administrative systems as seen from Arslantepe-Malatya', in P. Ferioli, E. Fiandra, G.G. Fissore and M. Frangipane (eds.), *Archives before Writing*, Torino-Roma, 125-136.

Frangipane, M., 1994b. 'Excavations at Arslantepe-Malatya, 1992', *XV Kazı Sonuçları Toplantısı*, Ankara 1993, 165-176.

Frangipane, M., 1997. 'A 4th millennium temple/palace complex at Arslantepe-Malatya. North-south relations and the formation of early state societies in the northern regions of Greater Mesopotamia', *Paléorient*, 23/1, 45-73.

Frangipane, M., 1998. 'Arslantepe 1996: the finding of an E.B.I 'royal tomb'', *XIX Kazi Sonuçlari Toplantisi*, Ankara 1997, 291-309.

Frangipane, M., in press a. 'Specialised craft activities and centralisation in the 4th millennium society at Arslantepe-Malatya', in, Coqueugniot E. (ed.), *Artisanat et notion d'artisanat au Proche-Orient depuis l'époque pré-urbaine*, Séminaire de recherche, Maison de l'Orient Méditérranéen, Lyon.

Frangipane, M., 2000. 'The Late Chalcolithic/E.B.I sequence at Arslantepe. Chronological and cultural remarks from a frontier site', in C. Marro (ed.), *From the Euphrates to the Caucasus: Chronologies for the 4th-3rd millennium B.C.*, Istanbul.

Frangipane, M., in press b. 'Centralization processes in Greater Mesopotamia. Uruk 'expansion' as the culmination of an early system of interregional relations', in M.Rothman (ed.), *Uruk Mesopotamia and its Neighbors: Cross-cultural Interactions and their Consequences in the Era of State Formation*, SAR, Santa Fe.

Frangipane M., Palmieri, A., 1983. 'A protourban centre of the Late Uruk period', *Origini*, 12/2, 287-454.

Frangipane M., Palmieri A., 1988-89. 'Aspects of Centralization in the Late Uruk Period in Mesopotamian Periphery'. *Origini*, 14/2, 539-560.

Gut, R.V., 1995. *Das Prähistorische Ninive*. Mainz.

Hauptmann, H., 1976. 'Die Grabungen auf dem Norşuntepe, 1972', *Keban Project 1972 Activities*, Ankara, 41-100.

Helwing, B., 1999. 'Cultural interactions at Hassek Höyük, Turkey. New evidence from pottery analysis', *Paléorient* 25/1, 91-99.

Killick, R., 1986. 'The Eski Mosul region', in U. Finkbeiner, W. Röllig (eds.), *Ǧamdat Naṣr. Period or Regional Style*, Wiesbaden, 229-244.

Lupton, A., 1996. *Stability and Change*, BAR International Series 627, Oxford.

Oates, D., Oates, J., 1993. 'Excavations at Tell Brak 1992-93', *Iraq*, 55, 155-199.

Oates, D., Oates, J., 1997. 'An open gate: cities of the fourth millennium B.C. (Tell Brak 1997)', *Cambridge Archaeological Journal*, 7/2, 287-297.

Orthmann, W., 1963. *Die Keramik der Frühen Bronzezeit aus Inneranatolien*, Berlin.

Özgen, E., et al., 1999. 'Oylum Höyük 1997-98. Die spätchalkolitische Siedlung auf der Westterrasse', *Anatolia Antiqua*, 7, 19-67.

Palmieri, A., 1978. 'Scavi ad Arslantepe (Malatya)', *Quaderni de 'La Ricerca Scientifica'*, 100, CNR, Roma, 311-373.

Palmieri, A. 1981. 'Excavations at Arslantepe (Malatya)', *Anatolian Studies* 31, 101-119.

Rothman, M.S., Peasnall, B., 1999. 'Societal evolution of small pre-state centers and polities: the example of Tepe Gawra in northern Mesopotamia', *Paléorient* 25/1, 101-126.

Stein, G. and Misir, A., 1994. 'Mesopotamian-Anatolian interaction at Hacinebi, Turkey', *Anatolica*, 20, 145-189.

Stein, G. et al., 1996. 'Uruk colonial expansion and Mesopotamian communities: an interim report on the 1992-93 excavations at Hacinebi, Turkey', *American Journal of Archaeology*, 100/2, 205-260.

Sürenhagen, D., 1974-75. 'Untersuchungen zur Keramikproduktion innerhalb der späturukzeitlichen Siedlung Habuba Kabira-Süd in Nordsyrien', *Acta praehistorica et archaeologica*, 5/6, 43-164.

Trufelli, F., 1994. 'Standardisation, mass production and potter's marks in the Late Chalcolithic pottery of Arslantepe (Malatya)', *Origini*, 18, 245-288.

Van Driel G., van Driel Murray C. 1983. 'Jebel Aruda, the 1982 season of excavations: Interim report'. *Akkadica* 33: 1-26.

THE URUK EXPANSION IN ANATOLIA:
A MESOPOTAMIAN COLONY AND ITS INDIGENOUS HOST
COMMUNITY AT HACINEBI, TURKEY

Gil J. Stein

INTRODUCTION

One of the main research problems in the archaeology of early civilizations concerns the ways in which the rise of the first urbanized state societies affected the political and economic development of neighboring regions. We have seen that state societies developed in Mesopotamia during the Uruk period (Nissen 1988; Pollock 1992; Wright and Johnson 1975). Almost immediately, these urbanized polities seem to have begun a process of commercial and colonial expansion into neighboring areas of Iran, Syria, and Anatolia in what is, as far as we know, the world's earliest colonial network (Algaze 1993; Stein 1999b; Sürenhagen 1986). These colonies appear to have been intended to get access to raw materials such as copper, lumber, and semiprecious stones from the neighboring highland zones of the Taurus and Zagros mountains. Although a number of the Uruk colonies have been excavated, until recently we knew almost nothing about how these implanted settlements actually worked, or what their effect was on the development of civilizations in neighboring regions such as Anatolia, Syria, and highland Iran.

Excavations at the site of Hacınebi tepe in the Euphrates valley of southeast Turkey have begun to give us a new and different perspective on the organization of the Uruk expansion (Fig. 1), and more generally on the ways that ancient colonies functioned. Hacınebi is an ideal site for this research because it was a local Anatolian town where, in 3700 BC, the Mesopotamians established a small trading colony. The site has two main occupations in the fourth millennium BC: a series of earlier phases, when only the indigenous southeast Anatolian culture was present at the site, and above that an occupation phase where a small enclave of Uruk traders lived in the midst of its local Anatolian host community.

As a result, the Hacınebi excavations allow for two complementary forms of archaeological analyses. First, by comparing the earlier phases with the later occupation, we can determine the degree of Anatolian social complexity before the Uruk expansion, while also measuring the extent to which Uruk trade and colonization affected local socio-political development. In addition, by comparing the Mesopotamian and local Anatolian parts of the site during the later occupation, we can for the first time reconstruct the economic and political relations between the colonies and their host communities. In other words, we can test models about how the Uruk expansion actually worked on the ground at the point of contact between these two very different complex societies.

From 1992-1997, Northwestern University conducted six seasons of excavation at the site of Hacınebi, in the Euphrates river valley of southeast Turkey (Stein et al. 1996, 1997, 1998). The 3.3 ha roughly triangular-shaped mound of Hacınebi is situated on an easily defensible east-west oriented spur that drops down steeply to the Euphrates river on the west, and into deep canyons to the north and south. Cultural deposits are approximately nine meters deep at the east end of the mound, becoming gradually shallower toward the west, as the natural surface of the spur slopes down toward the bluffs overlooking the Euphrates. Eighteen trenches were excavated at the site, exposing a total area of ca. 1400 m^2 and reaching sterile soil in three main parts of the site (Fig. 2): Area A in the northeast, Area B in the southeast, and Area C along the west spur. This work has defined two main fourth millennium BC occupations at Hacınebi, based on stratigraphy, architecture, and associated ceramics (Fig. 3a and 3b): Phases A and B1 with almost exclusively local southeast Anatolian Late Chalcolithic ceramics, and an overlying Phase B2 which had both local and south Mesopotamian Uruk types. The Late Chalcolithic occupations have been radiocarbon dated to the fourth millennium BC, i.e. both before and during the period of the Uruk Expansion. The only post-Chalcolithic deposits at Hacınebi are an Early Bronze Age I cemetery (ca. 3100-2800 BC) at the east edge of the site, an Achaemenid/Hellenistic occupation (ca. 500-100 BC) over the entire area of the mound, and a small Roman period farmstead at the west end of the site. The limited amount of later occupation at Hacınebi provides a rare chance to make the broad horizontal exposures necessary to recover a representative sample from a fourth millennium BC settlement.

HACINEBI PHASES A AND B1

Phases A and B1 are the earliest occupation of the site, ranging in date from 4100-3700 BC. We have exposed over 800 square meters of this occupation, in three different parts of the site, making this the largest available sample of material from this time period in the Taurus piedmont zone. The ceramics are mostly chaff-tempered, hand-made, flint-scraped "hammerhead" bowls and "casseroles" that are purely local Anatolian in character (Fig. 4); these form part of a local ceramic assemblage that is widely distributed from the Euphrates valley (e.g. at Kurban Höyük -- see Algaze 1990) in the west across to Leilan (Schwartz 1988) and Brak (Oates 1986) in northeast Syria and Tell al-Hawa in the north Iraqi Jezira (Wilkinson and Tucker 1995). In chronological and technological terms, these ceramics are broadly similar to the Amuq F assemblage (Braidwood and Braidwood 1960). A small percentage of this assemblage consists of wheel-made grit (or fine chaff-) tempered fine wares in a distinctly indigenous tradition (Pearce Edens 1998). There is no evidence for commercial contact with Mesopotamia during Hacınebi phase A and early phase B1. It is not until late in the B1 sequence that Uruk style bevel rim bowls begin to appear in the stratigraphic sequence alongside the local Late Chalcolithic assemblage, foreshadowing the widespread appearance of a full range of Uruk material culture in the overlying phase B2.

Several lines of architectural and artifactual evidence indicate that indigenous complex societies had developed in this part of southeast Anatolia during the early fourth millennium phases A and B1 at Hacınebi. This development offers a striking parallel to the evidence for indigenous complexity at the site of Arslantepe (Frangipane 1993).

At the northeast corner of the Hacınebi mound, a monumental terrace and platform complex was constructed at this time (Fig. 5). The platform may have been the foundation for either elite residences or some kind of public building. At the south end of the site, a massive 3 meter thick niched and buttressed enclosure wall was preserved to a height of more than 3 meters (Fig. 6). In the west part of the site, a group of two adjacent buildings with long, narrow stone rooms were constructed in phase A; these may represent storage magazines of some sort (Fig. 7). Both metallurgical artifacts such as open faced moulds for casting copper (Özbal et al. 1998) and administrative artifacts (Pittman 1998) were found associated with these structures. Complete house plans have also been exposed, showing us the domestic architecture that existed alongside of these larger, special purpose structures in the early fourth millennium (Fig. 8).

Phases A and B1 have also yielded evidence for long distance exchange networks trading prestige goods such as chlorite pendants from the east, and marine shell ornaments from the Mediterranean to the west of the site. Most importantly, the pre-contact phases at Hacınebi show the presence of a highly evolved copper production (Özbal 1997; Özbal et al. 1998). It is important to emphasize that copper smelting and casting was the most advanced technology of the 4th millennium BC. Every stage of this process, from raw materials to finished products is present at Hacınebi. At the south end of the site, in an open air industrial area, four contemporaneous smelting pit furnaces were found. Excavations in Area C at the

west end of the site have recovered a tuyere or blowpipe used to heat the ore for smelting in an open pit furnace. Tuyere technology is also known from the slightly earlier site of Değirmentepe in the Euphrates valley ca. 150 km to the north of Hacınebi. The pre-contact occupation also yielded crucible fragments still containing copper and slag. We also have several examples of open-faced casting moulds, one of which has a tiny prill of copper still embedded in it. Finally, we have several complete examples of the finished products such as copper chisels and pins. The nearest copper sources are the famous Ergani copper mines, some 200 km upstream from Hacınebi. Taken together these materials provide clear evidence for long distance ore trade and metallurgy BEFORE the period of intensive trade contact with Uruk Mesopotamia. The scale and sophistication of the technology strongly suggest that this was the province of craft specialists.

In addition to the evidence for prestige goods, long distance exchange, and craft specialization, the pre-contact period at Hacınebi was characterized by the use of complex administrative or record keeping technology in the form of an indigenous tradition of stamp seal use. Interestingly, both simple and complex seal designs were in use - this might possibly reflect differences in either the functions of the seals or the relative status of the seal users. The Hacınebi glyptic material is currently being analyzed by Holly Pittman (Pittman 1998, 1999).

Finally, mortuary evidence from Hacınebi suggests that hereditary elites and social stratification had developed at the site in the pre-contact period. The standard funerary practice in this area was to bury children in jars beneath the floors of houses. Virtually all of these contained the skeleton and nothing else. However, one of these pre-contact child burials was exceptional in that it had one copper and two silver rings as grave goods. This is some of the earliest silver in Anatolia, and clearly was a highly valued prestige good. Preliminary chemical tests by Hacınebi project conservator Tania Collas and by archaeometallurgist Hadi Özbal from Boğaziçi University in Istanbul indicated that the earrings are silver and NOT lead. The presence of these prestige goods in this child burial, and its clear difference from 95% of the other child burials strongly suggests that social ranking and hereditary elite status had developed at Hacınebi in the pre-contact period at the beginning of the 4th millennium BC.

Phases A and B1 at Hacınebi are important because they give us a baseline for comparison to see how the local Anatolian culture did or did not change during the later phase of culture contact and colonization by Uruk Mesopotamia. What we see is a settlement with an advanced level of craft specialization; long-distance trade; monumental public architecture and possible elite residences, burial evidence for hereditary elites, and the existence of a complex administrative system based on stamp seals, used to monitor the movement, storage, exchange, and disbursement of economic goods. In other words, when the Mesopotamian traders settled at

Hacınebi, they were encountering NOT a simple egalitarian village, but rather a wealthy and complex polity, perhaps a small scale chiefdom, that controlled access to and production of copper.

PHASE B2

Over 1300m² of the phase B2 settlement have been exposed in three separate parts of Hacınebi. In this phase, the local Anatolian Late Chalcolithic tradition continues, but alongside it we see the sudden appearance of Uruk material culture from southern Mesopotamia as a second, separate component in the assemblage. In many cases, the two ceramic traditions are mixed together in the same deposits. But there are also some clear differences between the north and south parts of the phase B2 settlement in the distribution of Uruk and Local Late Chalcolithic material. In the south area - local Late Chalcolithic ceramics, architectural traditions and religious figurines predominate, continuing smoothly from phase B1. The local administrative technology of stamp seals continues – as in the earlier phase, we have found both elaborate and simpler stamp seals and even the uncarved seal blanks used as part of their administrative system.

However, in contemporaneous deposits that are distinct from this local Anatolian material, the north part of the site has also yielded high concentrations of Uruk Mesopotamian artifacts; the evidence suggests that a Mesopotamian trading colony was present at the site. Mesopotamian artifacts are not just limited to ceramics, but rather represent the full range of Uruk material culture used in both public and domestic contexts. These different forms of Uruk material culture are found together and are spatially distinct from contemporaneous local Anatolian deposits. The South and West areas of the phase B2 settlement have predominantly Local Late Chalcolithic material culture. In stark contrast, Uruk material is highly localized within the North area. In a few exceptional deposits, we have even been able to recover *in situ* Uruk deposits, such as a domestic assemblage found on the floor in the corner of a kitchen area, and another small room with ceramics on the floor.

We have large amounts of typical wheel-made mineral-tempered Uruk ceramics in the full range of typical Mesopotamian forms, functional categories, and decorative techniques (Figs. 9, 10, 11 - see also Pollock and Coursey 1996). These include serving vessels such as conical cups and the ubiquitous bevel rim bowl, which form up to 50% of those deposits that contain only Uruk material. Phase B2 has also yielded a wide range of standard Uruk storage jars with round and low expanded band rims. Typical Uruk spouted jars and domestic pottery such as cooking pots with strap handles and comb incised bands are also present in these contexts, along with the very common hand-made chaff-tempered Uruk trays. In addition, ceramic ladles and a small number of jars with nose lugs and incised decoration occur in these phase B2

deposits. The pottery is decorated with the full repertoire of Uruk techniques, including red slip or wash, cross-hatched incised bands and triangles, fingernail impressions, and finger-impressed appliqué bands. In short, the Uruk assemblage at Hacınebi is not just a few beveled rim bowls, but rather it represents a full range of forms and functions such as food preparation, food serving, storage, and transportation.

But Uruk material culture at Hacınebi is not limited to ceramics. We have at Hacınebi Mesopotamian style architectural decorations such as the typical baked clay wall cones (Fig. 12: A-D), used to mark off Uruk temples and other public buildings in both southern Mesopotamia and in Uruk colonies such as Jebel Aruda (Rouault and Masetti-Rouault 1993: plate 124) and Hassek (Behm-Blancke 1989). Hacınebi also provides evidence for the use of the Mesopotamian system of metrology or measurements, such as cruciform grooved stone weights (Fig. 12: F). These weights (sometimes also interpreted as maceheads), are known from sites such as Susa Acropole I:18 (Henry Wright, personal communication) in the Uruk heartland of southern Mesopotamia, and from well documented Uruk colonies in Syria such as Habuba Kabira (Rouault and Masetti-Rouault 1993: plate 148) and Sheikh Hassan (Boese 1995: 175, plate 13b). Mesopotamian style ornaments are also present at Hacınebi; a conical headed copper pin found in phase B2 Uruk deposits has exact parallels in the Uruk colony at Tell Sheikh Hassan (Boese 1995: 224, plate 10-d) and at southern sites such as Tello and Susa, where these pins are found in abundance (Tallon 1987: numbers 934, 936, 937; I am grateful to Dr. Barbara Helwing for bringing the parallels at Tello and Susa to my attention). The Uruk deposits have even yielded sickles made out of baked clay - a uniquely Mesopotamian solution developed in an environment where flint was a rare imported commodity (Fig. 12: E). Baked clay sickles are very common in south Mesopotamian cities (Benco 1992), but almost never found in Anatolia, where flint is extremely common. There is no rational reason why any Anatolian person would ever make or use a baked clay sickle.

Some of the best evidence for the existence of a colony is the fact that the North part of the site has evidence for the complete range of Mesopotamian style administrative or record keeping technology: the two communities at Hacınebi used very different record keeping technologies (Pittman 1999). The Anatolians used stamp seals, which are pressed once into the clay (Fig. 13), while the Mesopotamians used cylinder seals, which are rolled over the clay, creating a long band with a repeating design. We have a hollow clay ball/bulla found with clay tokens still inside it, while bearing the impressions of 2 separate Uruk cylinder seals on the outside (Fig. 14). We have also recovered mushroom shaped clay jar stoppers with Mesopotamian cylinder seal impressions and a clay tablet, also with an Uruk cylinder seal impression. This is the first such tablet ever found in Turkey.

Except for the clay ball, which was a surface find, all the Mesopotamian cylinder seal impressed artifacts always occurred in deposits with only Uruk pottery, while the local style stamp seals have always been found in deposits with only Local pottery.

Most remarkably, we can now prove that at least some of these seal impressed artifacts were made in the Uruk heartland and brought to Hacınebi. Instrumental Neutron activation analyses by M. James Blackman of the Smithsonian Institution have shown that the tablet and many of the jar sealings are made from clays native to the Susa area and the Deh Luran plain in southwestern Iran (Blackman 1999). Other administrative artifacts use Uruk cylinder seals on local clay. The Neutron activation results are completely consistent with what one would expect to see if a small enclave of Uruk traders was both receiving goods from its homeland while also sealing and storing goods on site.

Other chemical analyses demonstrate the existence of trade links and the movement of goods from southern Mesopotamia to Hacınebi. An additional form of distinctively Mesopotamian material culture at the site is bitumen. Bitumen sources are common in Southern Mesopotamia, where in the Uruk period this material was ubiquitous as a construction material, sealant and raw material for a variety of functional or decorative objects. Mark Schwartz's chemical analysis of the bitumen from Hacınebi show that at least some of the bitumen at Hacınebi matches the chemical composition of southern Mesopotamian sources such as Hit and the Deh Luran area (Schwartz, *et al.* 1999); this suggests that in phase B2 at least some of the Hacınebi bitumen was either a trade good exported from Mesopotamia to southeast Anatolia, or else the packaging within which some other trade good was transported.

Finally, animal bone remains can provide particularly strong evidence for the presence of a Mesopotamian enclave at Hacınebi, since food preferences and food preparation procedures are often very culture-specific. Analyses by Gil Stein, Jeffrey Nicola (Stein and Nicola 1996), and Lauren Bigelow (Bigelow 1999) show that the faunal remains associated with Uruk artifacts at Hacınebi match closely with known Mesopotamian food preferences while differing markedly from the animal bones associated with Anatolian contexts. The Uruk enclave at Hacınebi, and virtually all Uruk sites in the south, show a very strong preference for sheep and goat meat, while the Anatolians preferred a more mixed diet with significant amounts of cattle and pig in addition to sheep/goats (Fig. 15).

Taken together, the distinctively Mesopotamian ceramic, architectural, administrative, and other forms of material culture used in both public and domestic contexts at Hacınebi are completely consistent with both general criteria for the identification of colonies in the archaeological record, and with the specific complex of material characteristic of Uruk colonies and settlements in the southern Mesopotamian homeland (Stein 1999a). The Hacınebi data are consistent with the evidence from sites such as Sheikh Hassan and Tell Brak in showing that the Uruk expansion started much earlier, and lasted much longer than researchers had previously thought. The period of Uruk contact at Hacınebi seems to have begun towards the end of the Middle Uruk period, and extended into the first part of the Late Uruk period (Fig. 3b). Our ceramics also show that the Uruk presence at Hacınebi predated the settlement of Late Uruk colonies such as Habuba Kabira and Jebel Aruda. Hacınebi has almost none of the tall spouted bottles or sharp shouldered storage jars of these sites. In short, the evidence from Hacınebi, Sheikh Hassan and Brak tells us that we can no longer view the Uruk expansion as a short-lived phenomenon. Instead the Uruk Expansion must be seen as an interregional trading relationship that lasted from the Middle Uruk almost to the end of the Late Uruk period - a time span possibly as long as 500 years.

THE ORGANIZATION OF URUK-ANATOLIAN INTERACTION

What was the organization of social and economic relations between the colony and its host community at Hacınebi? Did the Uruk colonial enclave dominate its Anatolian neighbors, or did it trade with them as equals? First of all, we see no signs of violence or conflict at Hacınebi. The two groups seem to have coexisted peacefully for an extended period at the site. But how did they co-exist? If the Mesopotamians had controlled the local Anatolian inhabitants, then we would expect to see unequal patterns of exchange, where the local people supplied the colonists with foodstuffs and craft items, while receiving little if anything in return. It is highly significant that we do NOT see a pattern like that. Several lines of evidence suggest that the Mesopotamian and Anatolian parts of the site were essentially autonomous economic entities, with little evidence for asymmetric exchange.

In examining the chipped stone from Hacınebi, Christopher Edens found manufacturing debris such as core fragments and cortical flakes from the production of blades and bladelets on both the Uruk and the Local areas (Edens 1999).

Stone tool forms in the Uruk and Anatolian midden deposits suggest that both parts of the site were engaged in agricultural production. However, traces of bitumen hafting in the typical locations for sickle blades and silica gloss or 'sickle sheen' are present in about the same proportions on lithics from both Local and Uruk contexts. This is extremely important because it suggests that the people who generated the midden in the Uruk part of the site were harvesting their own cereals, rather than being provided with food by other people at the site.

Overfired kiln wasters show that the colonists were making their own pottery. The small finds show several activities that were practiced on both the Uruk and Local parts of the site. The distribution of loom weights, pierced sherds, and hemispheric spindle whorls is strong evidence for textile production by both Mesopotamians and Anatolians.

Were the people in the Uruk part of the site being provided with meat, or were they raising and processing their own animals? We can examine this question by seeing what body parts are present. Generally, when a sheep or goat is butchered, the head and foot bones are removed and discarded. The body parts with the most meat on them are the forelimb and hindlimb. If the Mesopotamians were being supplied with meat by the local people, then we would expect to see many limb bones, but very few head or foot bones in Uruk contexts. However, since all of the main bodyparts are present, and there is no clear predominance of the meat rich limb bones, this shows that the people on both the Uruk and local contexts were processing their own animals, and were NOT being provided with meat from any other part of the site.

Perhaps the most telling evidence for the economic autonomy of the two communities at Hacınebi comes from the administrative or record keeping artifacts. The Mesopotamians and Anatolians each had their own, culturally specific record keeping systems. The seals and sealings were used to monitor the delivery, storage and disbursement of goods. If the Mesopotamians were being supplied with food, craft goods or other commodities by the local people in a system of asymmetric exchange, then we would expect to find large amounts of Anatolian seals in the Mesopotamian part of the site - reflecting the receipt of these goods. However, this is NOT the case. All the Mesopotamian style cylinder sealings occur exclusively with Mesopotamian pottery, while virtually all of the Anatolian sealings occur with the local pottery. Out of more than 450 Local Anatolian seal impressions dating to phase B2, only 2 were found in association with Uruk Mesopotamian material cultures. This means that the two record keeping systems were monitoring parallel but completely separate spheres of exchange. The Anatolians were not delivering valuable sealed commodities to the Mesopotamians.

CONCLUSIONS

The available evidence indicates that a small trading enclave of southern Mesopotamians was present at Hacınebi during the latter part of the Middle Uruk period (equivalent to Hacınebi phase B2). Both Anatolians and Mesopotamians raised their own crops, slaughtered their own animals, made their own pottery, wove their own clothes, and stored their own goods. There is absolutely no evidence to suggest that the Mesopotamians were politically, socially, or economically dominant at Hacınebi. There is no evidence for fortifications, warfare, or violent destruction at the site. The two groups seem to have lived together peacefully for an extended period of two to three centuries. The Mesopotamians traded with their local host community as equals rather than as colonial masters.

A diachronic comparison of the earlier (phases A and B1) and later (B2) occupations at Hacınebi can help us understand the organization of the Uruk colonial network and its impact on the indigenous societies of southeast Anatolia in the fourth millennium BC. Several conclusions are clear. First, the data from both Hacınebi and Arslantepe show us that Mesopotamians came into contact with Anatolian polities that had already developed a high degree of social, economic, and technological complexity. The indigenous polities cannot be dismissed as primitive societies, ripe for domination by a more advanced civilization. Second, the Uruk expansion began in the Middle Uruk period, and lasted well into the Late Uruk period - a period of at least 300 and possibly as long as 500 years. Third, the interaction between the Uruk colonists and the local population at Hacınebi was both peaceful and symmetric, with each group retaining considerable economic autonomy. The differences between the symmetric, peaceful social relations at Hacınebi, and the evidence for competition or conflict at sites like Habuba suggest that there was considerable variation in the organization of the Uruk colonial network. Where local population was sparse and poorly organized, the Mesopotamians may well have been able to dominate them for a short time. However in the more distant regions where indigenous populations were larger and more socially complex, as at sites like Godin or Hacınebi, then the Uruk merchants were forced to adapt to local conditions, trading with their local hosts on an equal basis. This was a complex, highly variable, and long-lived trading system whose workings we are only now beginning to understand.

ACKNOWLEDGEMENTS:

I wish to express my appreciation to the Turkish Ministry of Culture, General Directorate of Monuments and Museums for permission to conduct the field research at Hacınebi. Thanks are also due to the staff of the Şanlıurfa Museum and its directors - the late Adnan Mısır and his successor Eyüp Bucak - for their administrative assistance. The project was funded with support from the National Science Foundation (grant number SBR-9511329), the National Endowment for the Humanities (grant numbers RO-22448, RK-20133-94 and RZ-20120), The National Geographic Society (grant numbers 4853-92, 5057-93, 5295-94, and 5892-97), the Wenner-Gren Foundation for Anthropological Research (grant number 6309) the Kress Foundation, the American Research Institute in Turkey (ARIT), the de Groot Fund of the Metropolitan Museum of Art, Faculty Research Grants from Northwestern University, and the generosity of private donors, most notably Joseph and Laura Kiser, Bill and Sally Anderson, and Paul and Mary Webster. Finally, I thank all the staff members of the Hacınebi project for their dedication and skill in the excavation of the site and the analysis of the artifacts.

REFERENCES

Algaze, G., ed., 1990. *Town and Country in Southeastern Anatolia, Volume 2: The Stratigraphic Sequence at Kurban Höyük.* Chicago: University of Chicago, Oriental Institute Publication 110.

Algaze, G., 1993. *The Uruk World System.* Chicago: University of Chicago Press.

Behm-Blancke, M. R., 1989. Mosaikstifte aus der Uruk-Zeit am Oberen Euphrat. *Istanbuler Mitteilungen* 39:73-83.

Benco, N. L., 1992. Manufacture and Use of Clay Sickles from the Uruk Mound, Abu Salabikh, Iraq. *Paléorient* 18(1):119-133.

Bigelow, L., 1999. Zooarchaeological Investigations of Economic Organization and Ethnicity at Late Chalcolithic Hacınebi: A Preliminary Report. *Paléorient* 25:83-89.

Blackman, M. James, 1999. Chemical Characterization of Local Anatolian and Uruk Style Sealing Clays from Hacınebi. *Paléorient* 25:51-56.

Boese, J., 1995. *Ausgrabungen in Tell Sheikh Hassan I. Vorläufige Berichte über die Ausgrabungskampagnen 1984-1990 und 1992-1994.* Saarbrücken: Saarbrücker Druckerei und Verlag.

Braidwood, R., and L. Braidwood, 1960. *Excavations in the Plain of Antioch.* Chicago: University of Chicago Oriental Institute.

Edens, C., 1999. The Chipped Stone Industry at Hacınebi: Technological Styles and Social Identity. *Paléorient* 25:23-33.

Frangipane, M., 1993. Local Components in the Development of Centralized Societies in Syro-Anatolian Regions. In *Between the Rivers and Over the Mountains.* M. Frangipane, H. Hauptmann, M. Liverani, P. Matthiae, and M. Mellink (eds.) Pp. 133-161. Rome: Universita di Roma 'La Sapienza'.

Nissen, H., 1988. *The Early History of the Ancient Near East 9000-2000 BC.* Chicago: University of Chicago Press.

Oates, J., 1986. Tell Brak: The Uruk/Early Dynastic Sequence. In *Ǧamdat Naṣr. Period or Regional Style?* U. Finkbeiner and W. Röllig (eds.) Pp. 245-273. Wiesbaden: Dr. Ludwig Reichert Verlag.

Özbal, H., 1997. Early Metal Technology at Hacınebi Tepe. In G. Stein, K. Boden, C. Edens, J. Edens, K. Keith, A. McMahon, and H. Özbal, Excavations at Hacınebi Turkey - 1996: Preliminary Report. *Anatolica* 23:139-143.

Özbal, H., B. Earl, and M. Adriaens, 1998. Early Fourth Millennium Copper Metallurgy at Hacınebi. In G. Stein, C. Edens, J. Edens, K. Boden, H. Özbal, B. Earl, M. Adriaens, and H. Pittman, Southeast Anatolia Before the Uruk Expansion: Preliminary Report on the 1997 Excavations at Hacınebi, Turkey. *Anatolica* 24:167-170.

Pearce Edens, J., 1998. 1997 Pottery, pp 160-164. In Stein, Gil, C. Edens, J. Pearce Edens, K. Boden, N. Laneri, H. Özbal, B. Earl, M. Adriaens, and H. Pittman. Southeast Anatolia Before the Uruk Expansion: Preliminary Report on the 1997 Excavations at Hacınebi, Turkey. *Anatolica* 24:143-193.

Pittman, H., 1998. Preliminary Comments on the Glyptic found in the 1997 Season at Hacınebi Tepe. In G. Stein, C. Edens, J. Edens, K. Boden, H. Özbal, B. Earl, M. Adriaens, and H. Pittman, Southeast Anatolia Before the Uruk Expansion: Preliminary Report on the 1997 Excavations at Hacınebi, Turkey. *Anatolica* 24:170-173.

- 1999. Administrative Evidence From Hacınebi Tepe: An Essay on the Global and the Local. *Paléorient* 25:43-50.

Pollock, S., 1992. Bureaucrats and Managers, Peasants and Pastoralists, Imperialists and Traders: Research on the Uruk and Jemdet Nasr Periods in Mesopotamia. *Journal of World Prehistory* 6(3):297-336.

Pollock, S., and C. Coursey, 1996. Hacinebi Uruk Pottery: Preliminary Report, in G. Stein *et al.*, 1996, pp 233-239.

Rouault, O., and M. G. Masetti-Rouault (eds.), 1993. *L'Eufrate e il Tempo: La Civilta del Medio Eufrate e della Gezira Siriana.* Milan: Electa.

Schwartz, G., 1988. *A Ceramic Chronology from Tell Leilan.* New Haven: Yale University Press.

Schwartz, M., D. Hollander, and G. Stein, 1999. Reconstructing Mesopotamian Exchange Networks in the Fourth Millennium BC: Geochemical and Archaeological Analyses of Bitumen Artifacts from Hacınebi, Turkey. *Paléorient* 25:67-82.

Stein, G., 1999a. Material Culture and Social Identity:

The Evidence for a 4th Millennium BC Uruk Mesopotamian Colony at Hacınebi, Turkey. *Paléorient* 25:11-22.

- 1999b. *Rethinking World Systems: Diasporas, Colonies, and Interaction in Uruk Mesopotamia.* Tucson: University of Arizona Press.

Stein, G., Bernbeck, R., Coursey, C., McMahon, A., Miller, N., Misir, A., Nicola, J., Pittman, H., Pollock, S., and Wright, H., 1996. Uruk Colonies and Mesopotamian Communities: An Interim Report on the 1992-3 Excavations at Hacınebi, Turkey. *American Journal of Archaeology* 100:205-260.

Stein, G., Boden, K., Edens, C., Edens, J. P., Keith, K., McMahon, A., and Özbal, H., 1997. Excavations at Hacınebi, Turkey - 1996: Preliminary Report. *Anatolica* 23:111-171.

Stein, G., Edens, C., Edens, J. P., Boden, K., Laneri, N., Özbal, H., Earl, B., Adriaens, M., and Pittman, H., 1998. Southeast Anatolia Before the Uruk Expansion: Preliminary Report on the 1997 Excavations at Hacınebi, Turkey. *Anatolica* 24:143-193.

Stein, G., Edens, C., Miller, N., Özbal, H., Pearce, J., and Pittman, H., 1996. Hacınebi, Turkey: Preliminary Report on the 1995 Excavations. *Anatolica* 22:85-128.

Stein, G., and Nicola, J., 1996. Late Chalcolithic Faunal Remains from Hacınebi. pp 257-260 in G.J. Stein et al. "Uruk Colonies and Mesopotamian Communities: An Interim Report on the 1992-3 Excavations at Hacınebi, Turkey". *American Journal of Archaeology* 100:205-260.

Sürenhagen, D., 1986. The Dry-Farming Belt: The Uruk Period and Subsequent Developments. In *The Origins of Cities in Dry Farming Syria and Mesopotamia in the Third Millennium BC*. H. Weiss, ed. Pp. 7-43. Guilford (CT): Four Quarters Publishing Co.

Tallon, F., 1987. *Métallurgie Susienne I: de la Fondation de Suse au XVIIIe avant J.-C.* Paris: Ministère de la culture et de la communication : Editions de la Réunion des musées nationaux.

Wilkinson, T.J., and D.J. Tucker, 1995. *Settlement Development in the North Jazira, Iraq.* Iraq Archaeological Reports 3, British School of Archaeology in Iraq. Warminster (UK): Aris and Phillips.

Wright, H., and G. Johnson, 1975. Population, Exchange, and Early State Formation in Southwestern Iran. *American Anthropologist* 77:267-289.

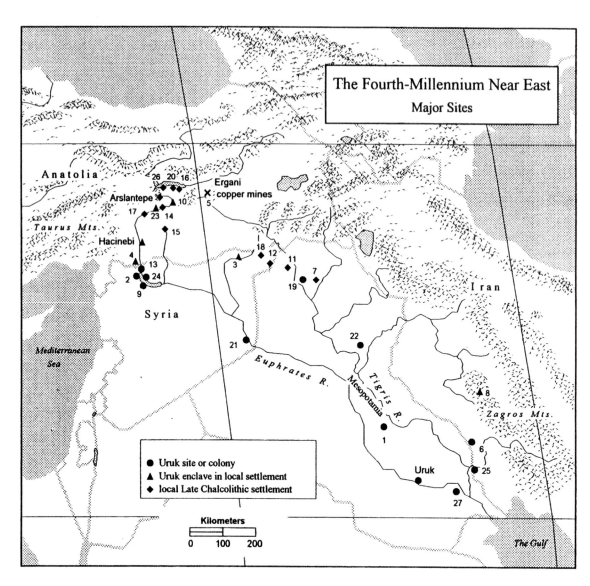

Figure 1: Map of the Fourth Millennium BC Near East, showing Hacınebi, Arslantepe, Uruk, and other fourth millennium sites: 1. Abu Salabikh; 2. Aruda; 3. Brak; 4. Carchemish; 5. Ergani copper mines; 6. Farukhabad; 7. Gawra; 8. Godin; 9. Habuba Kabira; 10. Hassek; 11. Hawa; 12. Hamoukar; 13. Jerablus Tahtani; 14. Karatut Mevkii; 15. Kazane; 16. Korucutepe; 17. Kurban; 18. Leilan; 19. Nineveh; 20. Norşuntepe; 21. Qraya; 22. Rubeidheh; 23. Samsat; 24. Sheikh Hassan; 25. Susa; 26. Tepecik; 27. Ur

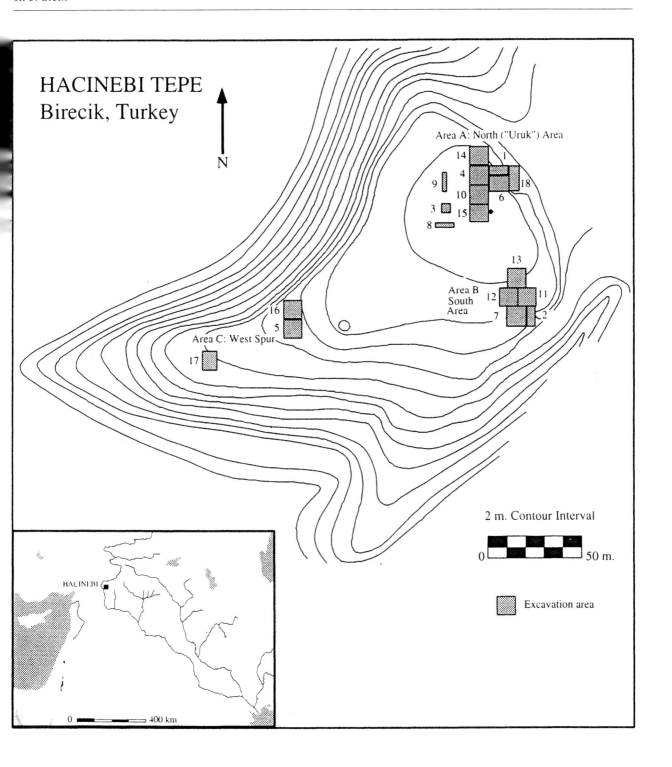

HACINEBI TEPE
Birecik, Turkey

N

Area A: North ("Uruk") Area

Area B
South
Area

Area C: West Spur

2 m. Contour Interval

0   50 m.

Excavation area

HACINEBI

0   400 km

Figure 2: Hacınebi - topographic map showing excavation areas.

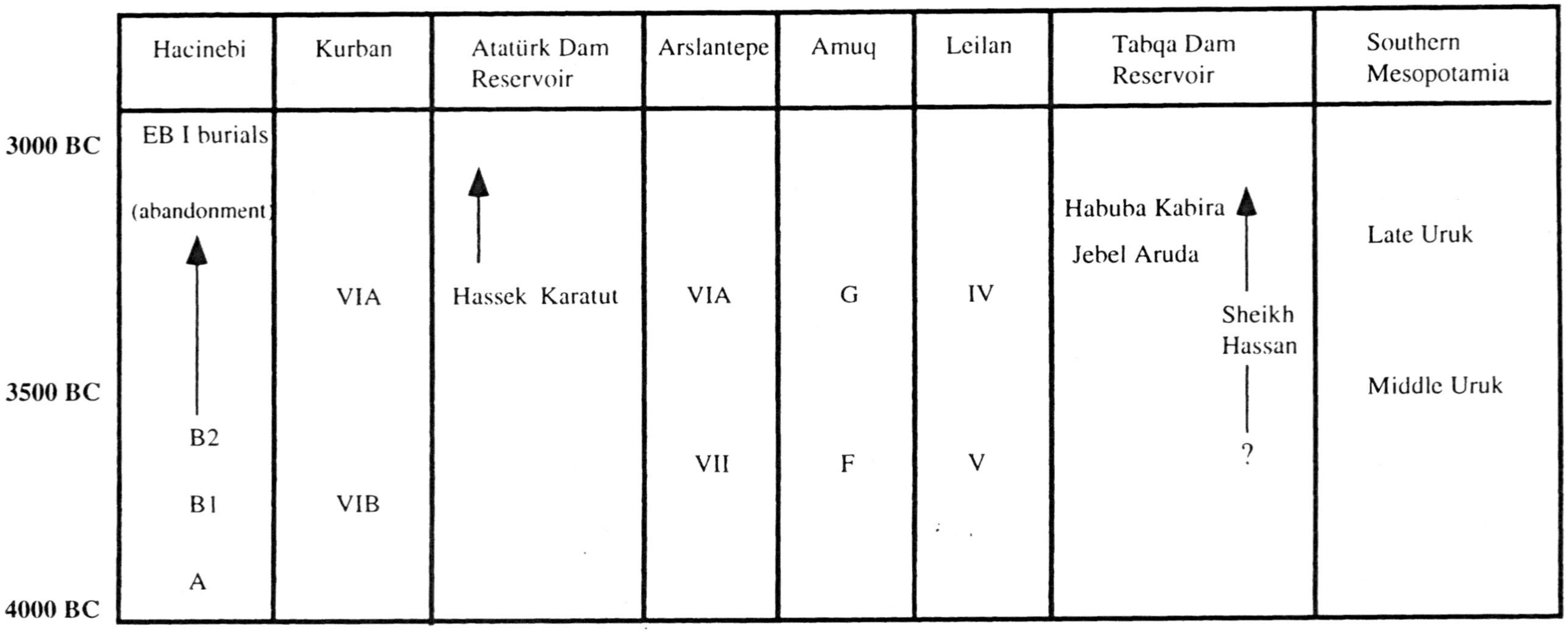

Hacınebi	Kurban	Atatürk Dam Reservoir	Arslantepe	Amuq	Leilan	Tabqa Dam Reservoir	Southern Mesopotamia
EB I burials (abandonment)		Hassek Karatut ←				Habuba Kabira ← Jebel Aruda	Late Uruk
B2	VIA		VIA	G	IV	Sheikh Hassan	
B1	VIB		VII	F	V	?	Middle Uruk
A							

3000 BC

3500 BC

4000 BC

Figure 3a: Hacınebi Fourth millennium chronology.

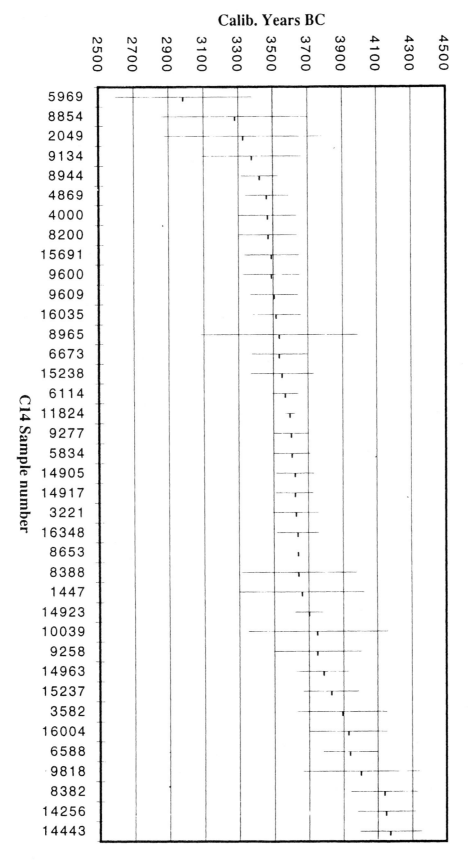

3b: Calibrated radiocarbon dates.

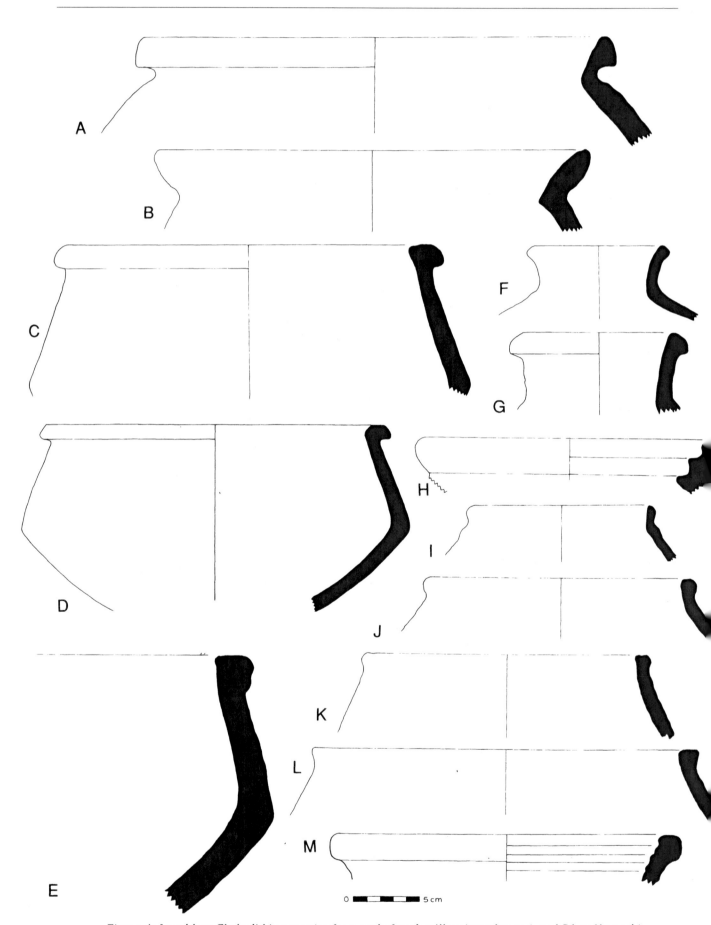

Figure 4: Local late Chalcolithic ceramics from early fourth millennium phases A and B1 at Hacınebi.

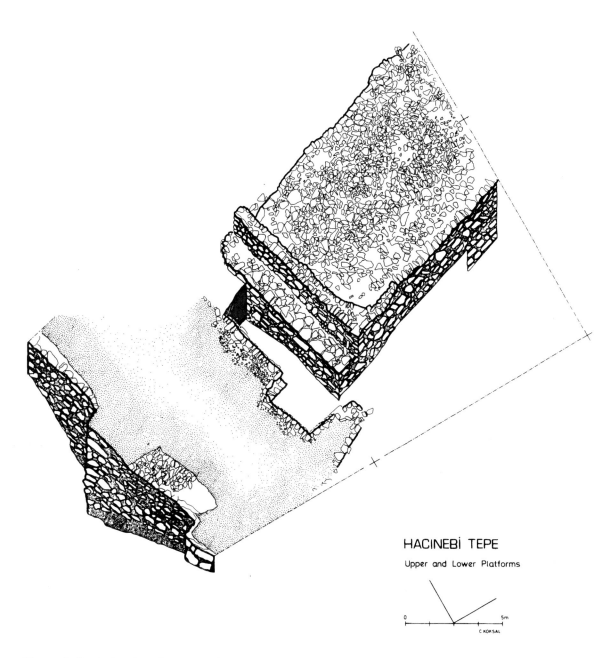

HACINEBİ TEPE

Upper and Lower Platforms

0   5m

C.KOKSAL

Figure 5: Early fourth millennium (phase B1) terrace and platform complex in the northeast part of Hacınebi.

HACINEBİ TEPE

Op.2,7,11,12 Late Chalcolithic
Niched and Buttressed Stone Wall and
Mud Brick Platform

0   1   2   3m

C KÖKSAL

Figure 6: Early fourth millennium (phases A and B1) monumental niched and buttressed enclosure wall, with associated mud brick platform in the south part of Hacınebi.

(Opposite) Figure 7: Early fourth millennium (phase A) possible storage magazines in the west part of Hacınebi.

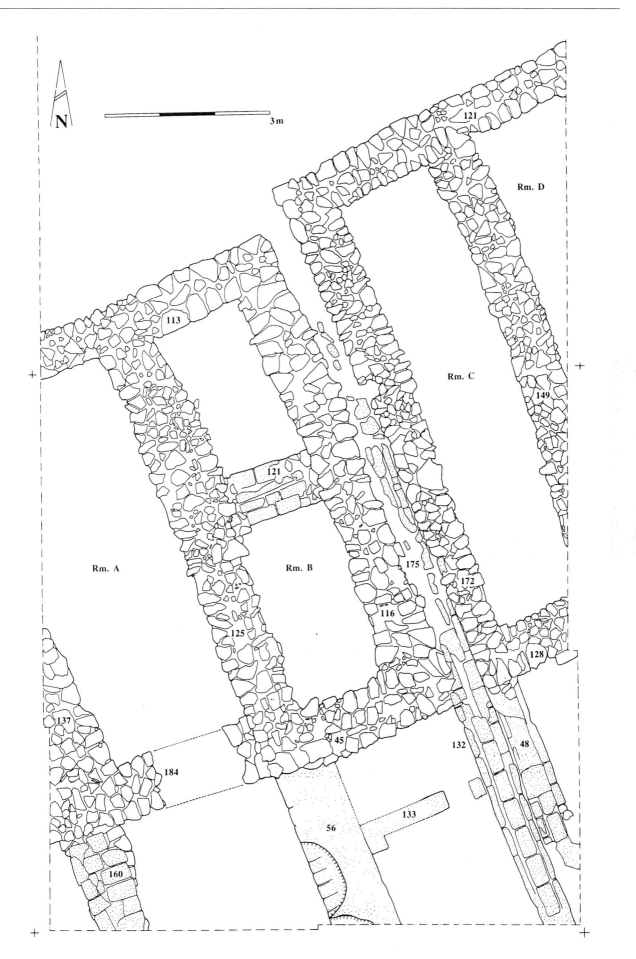

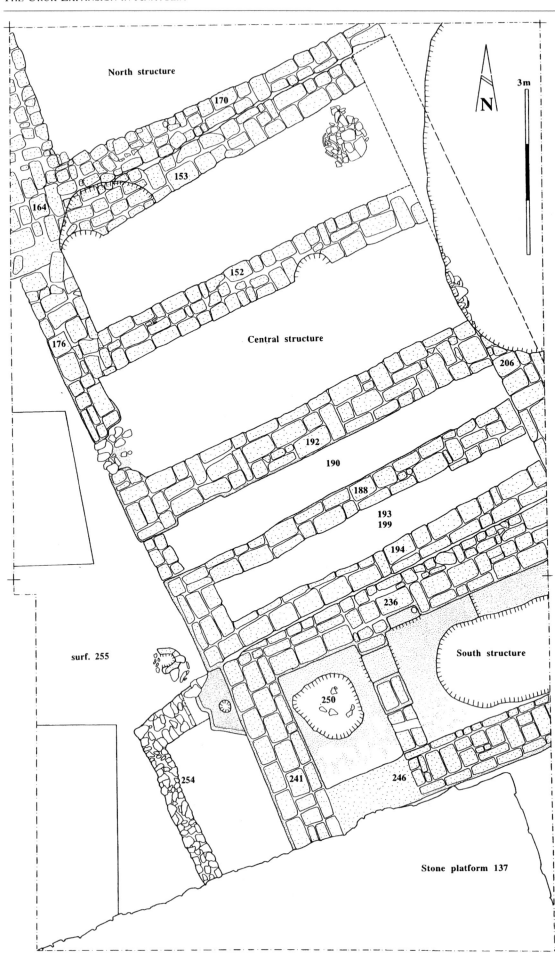

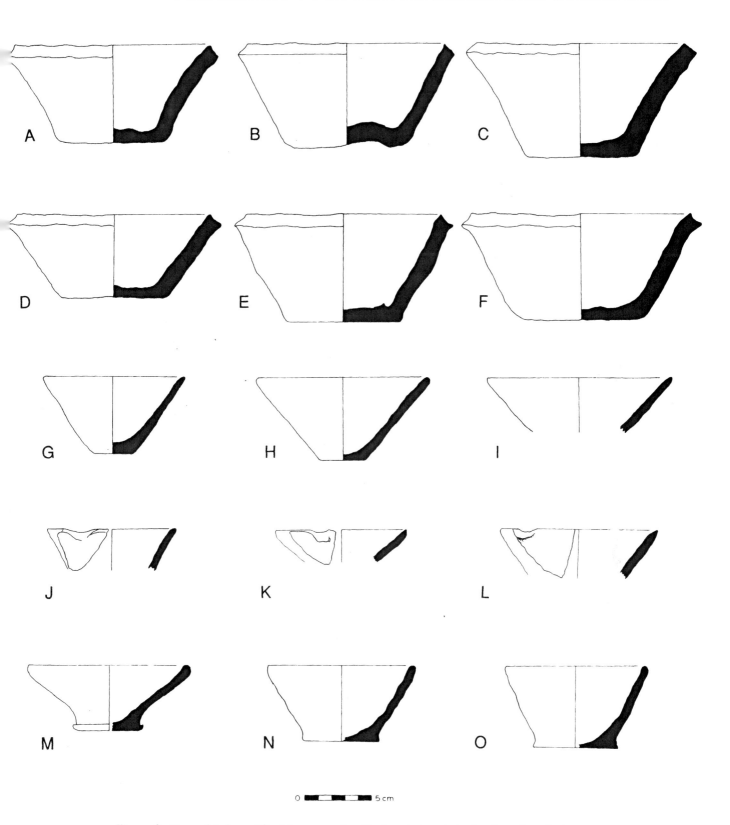

Figure 9: Hacınebi phase B2 - Mesopotamian Uruk style bevel rim bowls and conical cups.

(Opposite) Figure 8: Early fourth millennium (phase A) domestic architecture in the north part of Hacınebi.

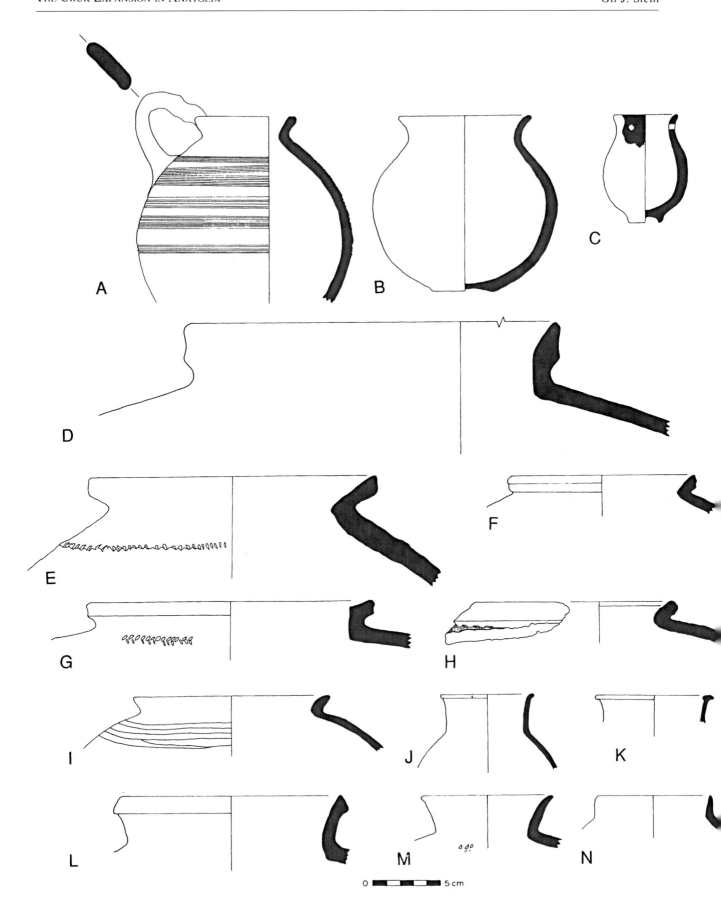

Figure 10: Hacınebi phase B2 - Mesopotamian Uruk style cooking pots and storage jars.

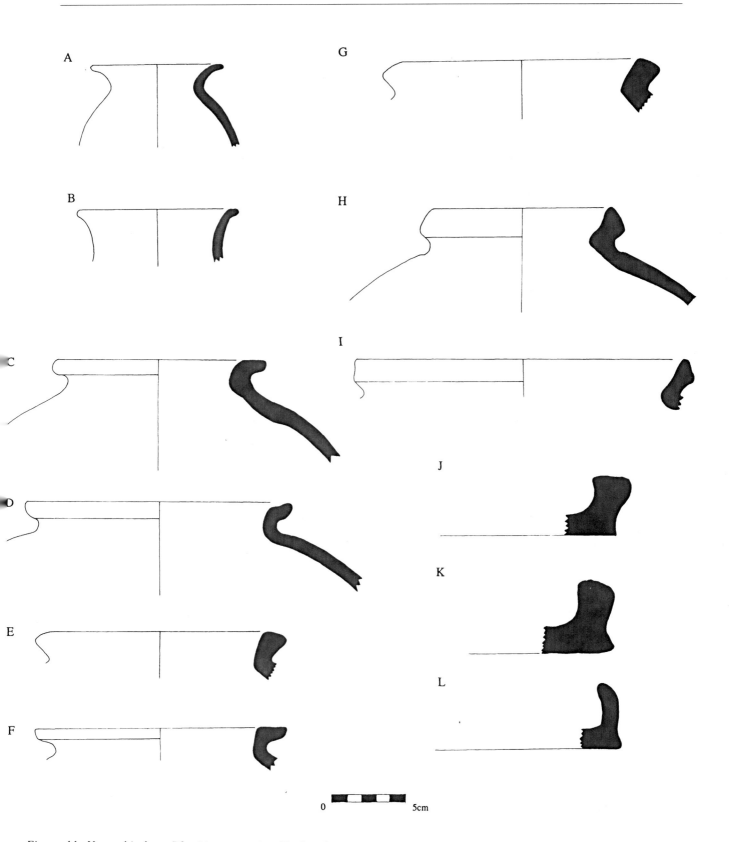

Figure 11: Hacınebi phase B2 - Mesopotamian Uruk style storage jars, trays/platters, and other diagnostic ceramics.

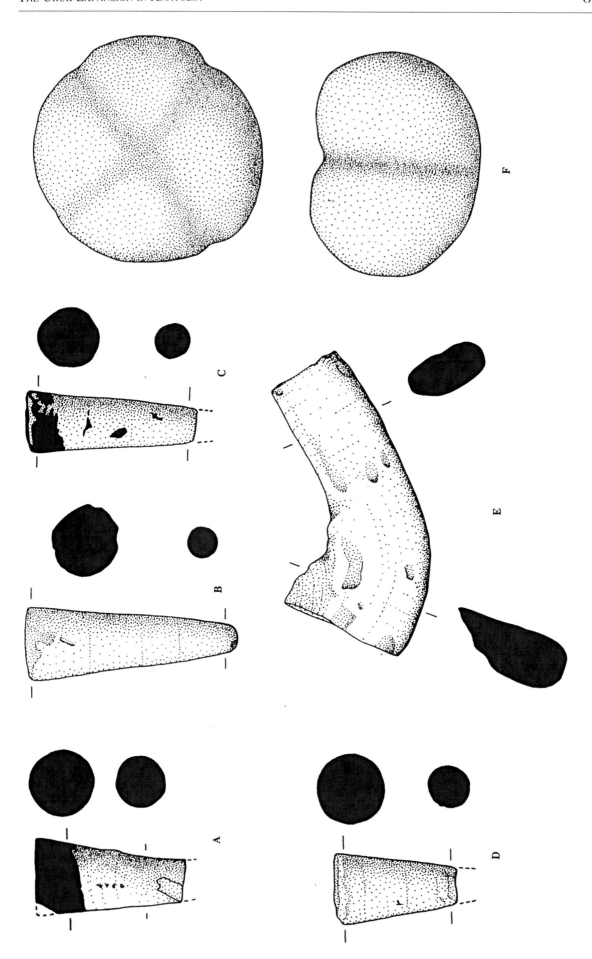

Figure 12: Hacınebi phase B2: Mesopotamian Uruk style items used for architectural ornamentation, subsistence, and exchange: wall cones, clay sickles, and cruciform-grooved stone weight.

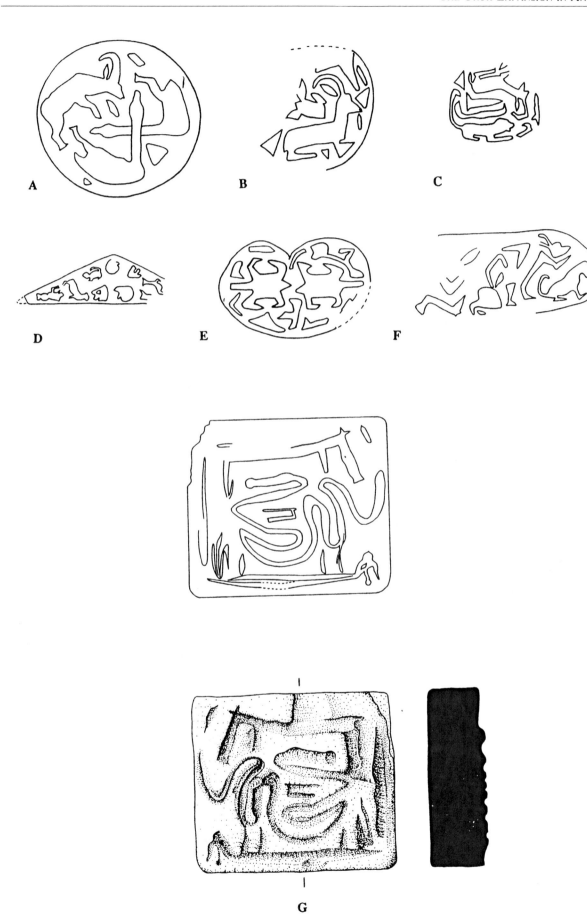

Figure 13: Hacınebi phase B2: Local Late Chalcolithic stamp seal impressions.

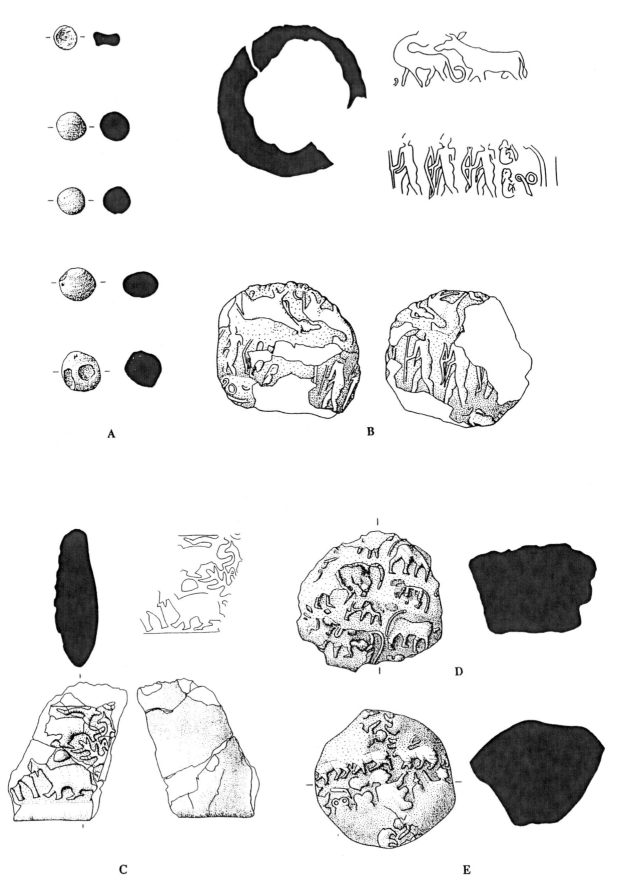

Figure 14: Hacınebi phase B2: Mesopotamian Uruk style cylinder seal impressed administrative artifacts: Bulla/hollow clay ball with tokens, jar stoppers, and seal impressed tablet.

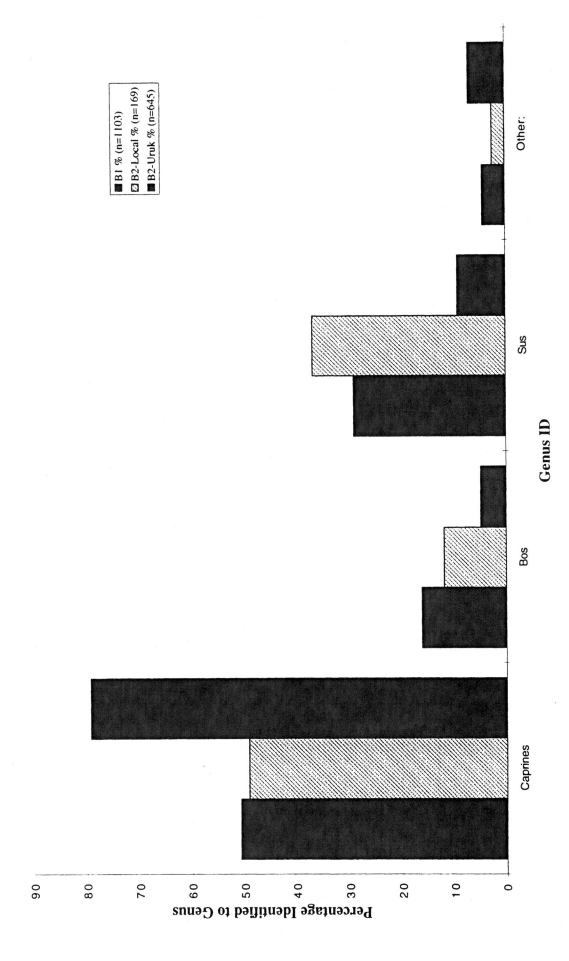

Figure 15: Hacınebi Phase B2 animal use in Uruk and Local contexts, compared with Local patterns of animal use in phase B1 (source- Bigelow 1999: fig.1).

SCIENTIFIC ANALYSES OF URUK CERAMICS FROM JERABLUS TAHTANI AND OTHER MIDDLE-UPPER EUPHRATES SITES

Fiona M. K. Stephen and Edgar Peltenburg

Recent investigations of 4th millennium sites in the Syro-Anatolian Euphrates regions have focused on cultural interactions between indigenous communities in those areas, the local Late Chalcolithic (LLC), and expansive foreign polities of the southern Mesopotamian alluvium, the Uruk. Questions of ethnicity, acculturation, economic interaction and social complexity are critical concepts for understanding the nature of the Uruk phenomenon in this strategic region. Pottery evidence plays a significant role in current debates, especially in identifying discrete cultural and technological traditions, and it has even been used implicitly as a marker of specific population groups (the 'pots equal people' premise). While discussions of the ceramic evidence have largely been based on subjective typological criteria, this paper seeks to contribute to the debate by establishing a thorough scientific analysis of vessel composition.

The paper deals primarily with Uruk ceramics from several key sites in Syria, Turkey and Iraq. The sites were chosen for their geographical location, their distinctive Uruk repertoire of ceramics and the critical role that they play in models of Uruk expansion. From the Tabqa/Tishreen area, these comprise the well-known sites of Jebel Aruda, Habuba Kabira South and Tell Sheikh Hassan. Less well known is Jerablus Tahtani, located beside Carchemish, the site which initially provided pottery for this study. The opportunity will be taken here to introduce aspects of research design that underpin our investigation of the 4th millennium B.C. and some of the relevant discoveries from recent University of Edinburgh excavations at the site. Material from Hacinebi, to the north of the core study area, is also included in the investigation. Ur and Jemdet Nasr in southern Mesopotamia provide a control group. Earlier results of these analyses are considered in Bolger and Stephen, 1999.

MIGRATION, ETHNICITY AND *HABITUS*

There are currently two dominant schools in the debate about the nature of the 4th millennium BC Uruk expansion to the Northwest. Essentially Mesocentric in outlook and world systems theory in approach, the first stipulates that southerners successfully attempted to control procurement of desirable raw materials by occupying parts of the periphery to varying degrees (Algaze 1993). This robust theory has generated diverse responses, but in gen-

eral it is argued that acknowledged expansion keyed into pre-existing socio-political and economic infrastructures in the highland zone and that the latter were more complex, and hence relations more symmetrical, than envisaged in the Mesocentric argument (e.g. Lupton 1996; Stein et al. 1996). Some doubt that the prime mover for expansion was the acquisition of raw materials (e.g. Frangipane 1997).

At the heart of these issues are the vexed problems of archaeological correlates for identification of migration and ethnicity. Difficult concepts in modern times, they are even more challenging for prehistorians aware of many other agents for change and the limitations of evidence for such contingent phenomena. In our case, where southern encroachments are generally admitted, there are additional problems of co-existence and acculturation. These problems may be exemplified by the later situation at Kültepe where, were it not for the durability of the tablets and the discovery of seals, it would have been difficult to conclude unequivocally that there was a *karum* largely occupied by southerners. In other words, there may be circumstances in which migrants possess low archaeological visibility. The Kültepe case also highlights the need to define colonists more closely than has been done since only certain male members of society represented southerners. Problems of identity and archaeological recognition are exacerbated when we have to rely on unquantified mixtures of diacritical markers at individual sites and limitations of survey evidence.

There is an additional reason for attempting to address the question of ethnicity at this critical historical juncture. It has been argued that ethnic identities emerged with the rise of the earliest states and that the pressure of such expansive polities on adjacent groups destroyed previous conceptions of personal identities and mobilised new identities (Bentley 1987; Shennan 1989). The study of interaction between Uruk and native needs to address this issue since it may fundamentally alter our perspectives on acculturation, the pace of change or the whole-hearted adoption of 'Uruk' artefact types and underlying behaviour, and in general the meaning of the material culture record at a time of intense intercultural contact in the 4th millennium.

In outline, our assessment of the Jerablus Tahtani evidence involves the concept of *habitus* to discern group identity. For our purposes, *habitus* (Bourdieu 1977) refers to everyday, mundane activities, the result of evolving social reproduction that supplies a cognitive framework for individuals within their environment and their society (Pearce 1999; Verhoeven 1999; Shennan 1989). The built environment, dress, diet and basic technology are some aspects of learned behaviours that constitute *habitus* and ones that are most readily susceptible to an archaeological approach and further analysis. Note, exotica or foreign symbols imitated in an assertive style, while important, are better treated as instruments deployed by aspiring elites in strategies of legitimation and enhancement. While Jones (1997), for example, concludes that ethnicity and *habitus* are not congruent, the equation gains strength in those historical contexts where there exist confrontations between communities embedded in state organisations and those existing in segmentary societies.

SETTLEMENT VARIATION FROM TABQA TO KARABABA

In terms of models of Uruk contact with Syro-Anatolia, Jerablus Tahtani lies at the southern limit of Algaze's 'Birecik-Jerablus' cluster (Algaze 1993: 29-33; 59) and at the northern margin of Lupton's 'Southern Dominated Area' (Lupton 1996: 66). The cluster appears to be concentrated north of Carchemish, but that is probably an artifice of modern systematic survey which was confined to the prospective dam areas to the north. Since that survey, Uruk pottery has been recognised at a number of sites south of Carchemish, including Chioukh Fouqani and Tell 'Abr (Bachelot 1998: 89-90; Hammade & Yamazaki 1993). To avoid a northern distortion of the scope of this cluster or enclave, therefore, it may be better to refer to it as the Carchemish cluster. Currently, only Jerablus Tahtani and Yarım Höyük provide modern excavated evidence from *in situ* Uruk-related occupation deposits in this area, and the evidence from Yarım Höyük, according to Rothman, is unfortunately inconclusive (Rothman et al. 1998: 66). The closest exposures of similar material to the north are at Hacinebi, to the south in the Tabqa area.

There are marked contrasts between Uruk-related sites in the Karababa and Tabqa areas, ones that suggest that the intermediate Carchemish zone may have formed a critical boundary. To the north are found several types of relationships. There are settlements where indigenous communities adopted only certain traits of the Uruk culture, discrete Uruk occupations are reported to exist within LLC settlements and, according to survey, there are many small sites with exclusive Uruk pottery. According to this characterisation, Hassek Höyük should not be equated with sites like Jebel Aruda (see Frangipane 1997: 47, Fig. 1). To the south, we have the well known series of large colonies and the LLC is notable by its absence. Granted that survey has not been as systematic in the Tabqa zone as in the north, the absence of LLC is strik-

ing and so we should accept the probability that native communities are less archaeologically visible (cf. Lupton 1996: 17; Butterlin 1999: 136). In other words, there existed a greater density of autonomous sedentary populations in the north than in the south. One critical factor that may have promoted such a disparity is the marked decline in mean annual precipitation rates from north to south in the Upper-Middle Euphrates region. Assuming these figures are meaningful for the 4th millennium BC, there is a fall-off from about 550 mm around Hassek Höyük to about 300 mm in the area of Tell Sweyhat (Miller 1997) and 200 mm at Mureybit (Hours et al. 1994). Agricultural settlements in the Tabqa zone, therefore, may only have been sustainable with the support of irrigation farming and long-term settlers probably had alternative subsistence strategies. In the absence of LLC sites, 4th millennium BC autonomous communities here may have concentrated on pastoral lifestyles. To the north, on the other hand, marginal conditions were largely ameliorated and it is here that we find LLC sites suggestive of flourishing agricultural communities (e.g. Stein, this volume). Migrating southerners with their well established irrigation agriculture would have encountered favourable conditions for settlement in the river valley where there was a paucity of extant agrarian groups, but they needed to adopt different settlement policies in the face of well established, sedentary communities. We could expect different types of interaction between Uruk and native in these circumstances. Lying between these two areas, Jerablus Tahtani could provide evidence on sensitive boundary conditions.

FROM NATIVE TO URUK AT JERABLUS TAHTANI

The site of Jerablus Tahtani is an oval, steep-sided mound, 180 x 220 m, rising some 16 m immediately beside the right, that is western, bank of a branch of the Euphrates River (Lat 36° 48'N; Long 38° 1'E). It has been cut to an unknown extent by the Euphrates on its eastern side, and it has an elongated 'head-and-tail' formation with the lower 'tail' located downstream, to the south. This configuration is characteristic of many Tishreen tells and it is due to aeolian and riverine erosion, in our case modified by man. Some 5 km south of Carchemish, the site lies opposite the larger tell site of Shioukh Fouqani. Unlike the latter, which seems to be situated on a Würm gravel terrace, Jerablus Tahtani was founded directly on the active floodplain. Both are the northernmost sites within the Tishreen Dam rescue zone; both yield Uruk pottery.

Woolley was the first to mention Jerablus Tahtani. He referred to it as Tell Alawiyeh, 'the little tell .... on the river front', but apparently he did not work there while conducting the 1911-1920 excavations at nearby Carchemish (Woolley 1921, 38, Pl. 2, Fig. 5). Nor did he report finds from this site as he did from many other sites in the Tishreen zone, including the next major site to the south, Tell Amarna. In the 1970s, Copeland and Moore surveyed our site and in a study of its finds, de Contenson noted the existence of several periods of occupation: Early-Middle Bronze, Roman-Byzantine and Islamic (Sanlaville 1985, 53, 70, Fig. 14). Stein's 1989 survey yielded Uruk pottery (McClellan & Porter n.d.). Our investigations of the site have confirmed the existence of all these periods except the MBA (Peltenburg et al. 1995, 1996, 1997).

In previous reports, we stated that settlers who used Uruk pottery founded the site. That conclusion was based on the evaluation of our eastern soundings where poorly preserved remains on virgin soil were associated with diagnostic Late Uruk wares. Subsequent investigations revealed the existence of very occasional Middle Uruk sherds like those from conical cups with pouring lip spout (cf. Boese 1995: 258, Fig. 1) and local wares, almost exclusively confined to hammerhead bowls (cf. Pollock and Coursey 1995: 135, Fig. 2). As all these came from derived contexts, there was no compelling reason to fundamentally alter our preliminary assessment. Units excavated in the closing week of our 1999 season, however, necessitate reconsideration.

Lying on natural at the base of a 2 x 6m probe in Area III, a probe designed to assess the depth of the Uruk levels, there appeared a thin occupation that contained an exclusive assemblage of hand made wares in complete contrast to the immediately overlying deposits. It will be appreciated that it is too early to provide a detailed appraisal of this assemblage, but the hammerhead bowls, plain rimmed shallow bowls with thick walls and jars with everted plain and flange rims would not be out of place in indigenous ceramic assemblages of the first half of the 4th millennium BC, equivalent with LC 3 in the Santa Fe terminology (cf. Schwartz 1988; Stein et al. 1998). Chaff-faced finishes occur together with a minority of red and brown slipped surfaces, some with pattern burnishing, some with effaced line painting (cf. Bachmann 1998: 64 Fig. 2.8,9). One sherd carries traces of bitumen, a substance that is characteristically found on Uruk wares at Jerablus. The ceramic material is associated with an oven, mudbrick wall and postholes in what appears to be a single phase of occupation. The discovery of this earlier occupation is significant for several reasons, not least because it is of a type hitherto unreported in the Tishreen.

It will be necessary to expand the Area III exposure to obtain a better idea of the occupation and its relationship with the Uruk deposits. In the limited area at our disposal it lies below the Uruk. The paucity of LLC wares in overlying deposits has always struck us, so the difference is sharp, one in which ceramics and other aspects of material culture in the basal occupation played no role. Several large Uruk pits have cut these early levels, and it is from these cuts that the meagre LLC pottery found in overlying levels is probably derived. Preliminary analysis indicates that bevelled rim bowls only enter the Jerablus

Tahtani record together with a suite of other Uruk-type ceramics in the overlying level. The situation, therefore, appears to be different from the Hacinebi record upriver where bevelled rim bowls already occur in B1, before the remainder of the Uruk assemblage appears in B2 (Butterlin 1999, 129-32; Stein and Edens 1999: 168-9). Assuming local reception of the advance wave of Uruk BRB was chronologically uniform, a dangerous assumption, there is a hiatus in the Jerablus Tahtani sequence. There are, however, no macroscopic traces of abandonment between the two phases of occupation to allow for a putative intervening period. The Uruk occupation at Jerablus Tahtani is broadly contemporary with Hacinebi B2, (LC 4 in the Santa Fe terminology) but may carry on a little later.

Bearing in mind the small size of this exposure, we tentatively suggest that the Jerablus sequence may provide a new perspective on the interaction between Uruk and native in the Syro-Anatolian stretch of the Euphrates river valley, one that is still poorly understood in spite of the various models proposed and more recently tested by Stein et al. (1996), Frangipane (1997), Rothman et al. (1998) and others. The reason for this suggestion is that there are no other secure cases of such thorough and seemingly abrupt intra-settlement replacement of indigenous material cultures. In most instances, Uruk affinity sites are new foundations on a substantial (Jebel Aruda, Tell Sheikh Hassan, Habuba Kabira South) or small scale (Algaze 1993: 29-33), medium sites with Uruk occupation in one sector (Hacinebi) or smaller sites with mixed ceramics (Kurban Höyük). The stratified sequence at Jerablus Tahtani indicates that other modes of interaction existed and that perhaps we need to re-examine arguments for the co-existence of discrete areas of Uruk and native on single sites where the evidence is predominantly spatial rather than stratigraphic (cf. Butterlin 1999 and comments by Stein and Edens 1999).

The Jerablus Tahtani sequence may be understood in the context of the intra-regional variation described above, one in which the Tishreen interface corresponds with the broadly defined southern limit of readily sustainable dry farming. In these conditions, the Carchemish cluster of Uruk related sites may have been located in a zone where there was more native sedentary population than to the south and this would have led to different processes of transformation, adaptation and acculturation. For example, southern expansion in the frontier zone may have required more forceful acquisition of territory (although we found no evidence of destruction in these levels) or there may have been other types of contact with the indigenous site hierarchy that we have not yet begun to explore. We plan to examine the nature of the changes in Area III more fully in the future.

As just mentioned, *in situ* Uruk occupation was located immediately above these deposits, in a 70 m^2 exposure. The most informative level comprised part of a building, complex 2185 (Fig. 1), an external flat surface strewn with pottery and ecofactually rich midden material, and a secondary burial. Innovations reveal a profoundly altered way of life. The highly distinctive multi-coloured bricks of the building are made and laid in a way that indicates a new building tradition. While it has been shown that wheel-made pottery was known amongst local groups (Stein et al. 1998: 164-7), the repertoire of shapes indicates new methods of transport, storage and perhaps cuisine. Manufacturing techniques have changed to include scrapers made of pottery. Locally produced bevelled rim bowls (see below) were secondarily used in bitumen processing. Geochemical analyses suggest that the bitumen itself was probably imported from a number of sources in South Mesopotamia and Southwest Iran (Schwartz et al. 1999). Textile preparation saw the introduction of delicately made whorls. Discard behaviour also seems to change, with far greater quantities of pottery per cubic meter of soil than previously. Clearly, it remains to be seen if these observed changes are representative, but preliminary evaluation indicates significant changes in *habitus,* ones with specifically southern characteristics. While low status technological changes may be locally adopted when they are perceived as advantageous in terms of efficiency, increased output or reduced risk, these are so pervasive that they are best equated with altered identity.

The assemblage of smaller objects also includes high status items of more questionable value for recognising group identity. Thus, the community was familiar with the administration of goods, as attested by a sealing of unbaked clay bearing the impression of spirals (Fig. 2), perhaps arranged as a quadruple as at Jebel Aruda (cf. van Driel 1983: 53.35). It seems to have come from a finer, smaller object than the conical and mushroom-shaped clay stoppers found in this level for the first time (cf. Boese 1995: 249, Fig. 6c). Containers requiring intensive, and perhaps specialised, labour include fragments from an alabaster jar decorated with a cross-hatched band like those on nose lug jars at Tell Sheikh Hassan (cf. Boese 1995: 126, Fig. 7) and polished stone bowls with beaded rim like that at Hacinebi (Stein et al. 1998: 187, Fig. 14B). Another instance of specific down river connections is a flattened oval white stone bead(?) with axial incision, exactly like one from Tell Sheikh Hassan (cf. Boese 1995: 225, Fig. 11h). The lower part of what was probably an eye-figure has more widespread links in Uruk and LLC contexts, from Arslantepe to Gawra, and in our part of the river valley, at Hacinebi (Stein et al. 1997: 120, 161, Fig. 12) and Tell Sheikh Hassan (Boese 1995: 74, Fig. 11a; 224, Fig. 10e). In general, the Late Uruk community seems to have many connections with the Tabqa colonies, and this view is supported by the ceramic groupings discussed below which show pervasive links to the south, few to the north. The exception is Red Slip which we may consider special status pottery either for itself or distinctive contents.

The inventory of luxury or high status artefacts raises questions about the role of settlements near alleged

enclaves like Carchemish. The repertoire from the small sampled part of Jerablus is consistent with what might be expected from a trading site, and indeed, it is positioned low on the floodplain beside the Euphrates, well situated for riverine communications. We do not know its overall size since an unknown part was washed away, but it does not seem to have been large. For example, we have not recovered clay cones or cylindrical drain pipes indicating the existence of public structures. Our evidence suggests that some smaller Uruk establishments were closely associated with trade rather than simple agricultural villages whose purpose was to sustain the enclaves like the alleged example at nearby Carchemish.

It is uncertain whether the Uruk occupation ceased as a result of flooding or if we have an unbroken sequence into the EBA. On the east of the site, beside the Euphrates, most Uruk levels terminate in bedded flood deposits, perhaps the result of poorly dated mid-Holocene inundations attested at other sites, during a time of stable alluvial environmental conditions (Oguchi & Oguchi 1998; Wilkinson 1999). Flood deposits are conspicuous by their absence on the west of the site in Area III, suggesting that they were low-magnitude, localised intrusions. It is possible, therefore, that we have an unbroken Area III occupation into the EBA and this will be important for evaluating post-Uruk 'collapse' developments.

ANALYTICAL METHODOLOGY AND RESULTS

Previous studies of Uruk ceramics have concentrated on typological aspects and seldom on the more scientific areas. This study aims to shed light on the Uruk phenomenon and its cumulative effect on the Upper Euphrates River valley area. The aim is to distinguish locally made ceramics from those which might be imported from other areas in North Syria or South Mesopotamia. To obtain the most useful and informative results on such a contested subject, the importance of a multi-faceted investigation incorporating chemical and physical analyses of these ceramics cannot be overestimated. This paper will discuss some of the preliminary results which form part of a much larger study to be presented as a Ph.D. in due course.

Selection Procedure

Seven sites were selected for investigation. They exhibit classic Uruk or Uruk-related ceramics amongst their other distinguishing features. The sites are, Jerablus Tahtani, Hacinebi, Tell Sheikh Hassan, Jebel Aruda, Habuba Kabira, Ur and Jemdet Nasr. The total study set comprised in excess of 500 samples amongst which were diagnostic shapes for each site, including conical cups, bevelled rim bowls, lugged jars, droopy spouts, red slip and incised wares.

Sample Preparation

Selected sherds were washed in distilled water and dried overnight in an oven. A sample was then removed for

>etrographic analysis. The surface of the remainder was braded with a diamond drill until the surface was clear rom slip and decoration (Rice 1987:324). The sample vas rewashed and dried and then drilled at four separate ocations on the sherd to ensure a representative collec-ion. This was then ground to a fine powder and was eady for the chemical analyses.

X-RAY DIFFRACTION

This is a well established technique (Zussman 1977) that is often used in conjunction with X-Ray Fluorescence. The sample is finely ground and mixed with acetone to form a thin film on a glass disc. A scintillation counter then scans the sample through a range of diffraction angles each reflection resulting in a peak on the chart. The peak positions are determined by standard tables and thus identification is a simple matter. This technique is a good choice where samples are at a premium and also results can help determine the direction of subsequent analysis due to the speed and clarity with which they appear. XRD gives a very good overview and starts the process of division amongst the sample set.

Results

Results are displayed in graph form. The X-axis displays the recognisable diffraction angle and the Y-axis displays the intensity. Fig. 3 shows the graphical representation of calcite- and quartz-rich samples, with peaks at $29 \times 2\theta$ and $26 \times 2\theta$ respectively. Samples in this group were mostly from Jerablus Tahtani, Habuba Kabira and Tell Sheikh Hassan with no real distinction between shapes. Fig. 4 shows the calcite-rich graph, with the major peak at $29 \times 2\theta$. Samples in this group were mostly from Jebel Aruda and Hacinebi, again with no real distinction between shapes. Fig. 5 shows the quartz-rich graph, with the major peak at $26 \times 2\theta$. Samples in this group were a mixture from Jerablus Tahtani and Habuba Kabira. Fig. 6 shows the diopside-rich graph, with the major peak at $35 \times 2\theta$. Samples in this group were mostly from the southern control sites, Ur and Jemdet Nasr.

Conclusions

It is clear from the preliminary work done with XRD that there are divisions apparent between the sites with regard to the basic constituents of the samples. There did not appear to be any distinction between shapes at this stage and while samples did seem to cluster mostly under one of the four headings discussed above, there were discrepancies. These results indicated that further chemical analysis was necessary.

X-RAY FLUORESCENCE

X-Ray Fluorescence, or XRF, is one of the principal techniques employed in the study of archaeological ceramics (Bertin 1978: Norrish and Chappell 1977). Up to eighty of the ninety-two naturally occurring elements present in major, minor and trace quantities may be detected by XRF. The sample is irradiated with X-rays and resultant changes within the atoms of the material cause secondary X-rays to be emitted. These wavelengths can then be analysed and elemental concentrations can be ascertained.

Several techniques for the analysis and representation of data from XRF are available of which Principal Component Analysis (PCA) (Shennan 1988, 245-62) is one of the most common. PCA envisages the individual samples as points in a geometrical space whose axes are defined by the variables and which therefore has as many dimensions as there are variables. The space is rotated to a new set of axes so that the observations are as spread out as possible in the directions of the first few axes. This enables them to be plotted in a low number of dimensions while preserving as much as possible of the original structure of the data. The benefits are twofold. Primarily, we can see a picture of as much of the relationship between the original observations as can easily be plotted in two dimensions and secondly, since the new axes can be related mathematically to the old ones, we can see which variables contribute most to the differences between the observations.

The equation reads as:

$$\underline{Z} = \underline{A}.\underline{X}$$

i.e.

$$z_1 = a_{1,1}x_1 + a_{1,2}x_2 + a_{1,3}x_3 + ...$$
$$z_2 = a_{2,1}x_1 + a_{2,2}x_2 + a_{2,3}x_3 + ...$$

X = measured data
Z = principal component vector
A = eigenvectors of covariance matrix.

Results

Results are displayed in graph form. There is a Principal Component for each measurement. For each illustration there are two images. The first displays the scatter and the second shows the plot with the mean portrayed as a symbol and the standard deviation shown with the error bars. The size of the cross relates to the standard deviation and therefore indicates the spread of the data. The standard deviation equates to two-thirds of the spread in each direction. The spread of the data outside this standard deviation produces an overlap which gives an indication of the degree of relationship. Fig. 7 displays the results for elemental analysis by site. This presents a very good summary graph. We can see that Hacinebi (HA) appears as a distinct group as does Tell Sheikh Hassan (TSH). Jebel Aruda (JA) and Habuba Kabira South (HKS) show a large spread of variability. Ur (UR) has a very remote relationship with Jerablus Tahtani (JT). Fig. 8 displays the results from Bevelled Rim Bowl analysis. Samples were only available from four of the selected sites. Hacinebi (HA) appears as a distinct group but the relationship between the remaining three sites makes it impossible to separate them. They are best described as subsets of each other as there is a considerable degree of overlap evident. Fig. 9 displays results from the Clay analysis. Three very distinct clays seem to be in evidence. Of particular interest from this graph is the fact that the local Jerablus clay sample provides an almost perfect match for the Bevelled Rim Bowls from the same site. This is a close relationship with almost complete overlap and seems conclusive. Fig. 10 displays the results from Conical Cup analysis. From this graph Hacinebi appears as a distinct group, whereas the remaining sites have considerable degrees of overlap. Two possible sets emerge with the first containing Jerablus and Habuba and Tell Sheikh Hassan. The second group is composed of Ur and Jebel Aruda. The relationship is extremely close and complex. Fig. 11 displays the results from Incised Wares analysis. From Fig. 11 the southern sites of Ur and Jemdet Nasr have a more remote relationship with the remaining sites than seen in the previous graph. There is some degree of overlap with Jebel Aruda and from there we see the varying relationship continue to include firstly Jerablus, Tell Sheikh Hassan and then Habuba Kabira. Fig. 12 displays the results from Red Slip analysis. This presents a very interesting picture. Hacinebi remains a distinct group but is closer to the others than in the previous graph. This is due to the large spread of variability particularly from Jerablus Tahtani and Jebel Aruda. Two other subsets are visible from the graph with the first containing samples from Jerablus and Habuba Kabira and the other from Jebel Aruda, Ur and Jemdet Nasr. The latter do show some considerable degree of overlap on more than one level indicating a closer relationship, not only with each other but also incorporating Tell Sheikh Hassan on a slightly less complex level.

Conclusions
The XRF results have provided a good deal of information to expand that already gained via XRD. It is clear that the relationship for the total sample set cannot be assessed in terms of site alone and that investigation of the specific shapes is vital. The nature of these relationships is much more complex than could have been imagined. Particularly of interest are the finer wares where the degree of similarity between the northern and the southern groups is intensified. This fact alone provokes the necessity for analysis on a more minute scale where individual minerals may pinpoint a source beyond question. The application of petrographic techniques was the necessary final step.

PETROGRAPHIC ANALYSIS
This technique is one which has had an enormous impact and has become the principal method for identifying minerals in archaeological pottery studies. Applying geological petrographic techniques to ceramics (Williams 1983) is a logical procedure as ceramics share features with both rocks and sediments and so many of the same tools and methodologies can be applied. Examination of thin

sections through the petrographic microscope provid advantages over analysis of the clay composition as mi erals in a thin section will often give valuable clues abo the origin of the clay or filler. Some combinations c indicate that the clay derives from a very specific type geology and the thin section can be regarded as a type fingerprint. Over 400 thin section samples have be taken from the study set. Some samples were too small permit thin sectioning and the decision was made to u them for other analytical procedures to gain the ma mum information. The data provided by these thin se tions is on a very great scale and each sample deserv individual attention. Clearly this is not possible in a pap such as this and so a small selection is included to pr voke further discussion. Samples selected here inclu bevelled rim bowls from Jerablus, Tell Sheikh Hass and Jebel Aruda. Red slip samples selected here are fro Habuba Kabira, Jebel Aruda and Jerablus. Finally, waster from Habuba Kabira South is compared to *i* incised jar from the same site to assess the degree of si ilarity.

Results
From Fig. 13a the bevelled rim bowl from Jerablus co tains volcanic material and the quartz grains are angul and coarse. This is in contrast to Fig. 13b from Jeb Aruda where there is no volcanic material and the grai appear more rounded. From Fig. 14a and Fig. 14b respe tively, Habuba Kabira and Jebel Aruda seem very simil with a small grain size and similar mineralogy which much more ferric compared to Fig. 14c from Jerabl where the grain size is different and we see the inclusio of shell fragments and mica. Fig. 15a from Habut Kabira shows a waster from the site which has a ver glassy background with ferric compound which is simil in mineralogy to Fig. 15b which shows the image from a incised jar from the same site and might provoke argu ment for local production of certain types.

Conclusion
Petrographic techniques have determined differences nc only between the sites and shapes but also, at a mor involved level, similarities between certain types fro different sites reinforce the concept that there was a com plex relationship with regard to these ceramics that fa outweighs previous considerations.

DISCUSSION
The combined results of the analyses presented in thi paper show that we see differences between the sites fo certain shapes and similarities for others, particularly th finer wares, such as Red Slip and Conical Cups. What i certainly clear is the emergence of three geographica areas of interest which have varying degrees of interac tion. The validity of this combined analytical investiga tion cannot be in doubt as the cumulative effect of th results argue most emphatically the case for heterogene

ity of clay sources and thus a multi-centric production of pottery vessels. As more information emerges from the petrographic analysis it is hoped that an accurate picture will develop whereby the separation of samples will finally determine the issue of local as opposed to imported ceramics.

ACKNOWLEDGEMENTS
We are most grateful to the Syrian Ministry of Culture, Directorate General of Antiquities and Museums, for permission to carry out investigations at Jerablus Tahtani and for the active support and advice of its staff. We would like to thank the following for their kind donation of time and samples to the project: Dr J. Boese for samples from Tell Sheikh Hassan, Dr. G. van Driel for samples from Jebel Aruda, Dr. P.R.S. Moorey for samples from the Jemdet Nasr collection in the Ashmolean Museum, Professor G. Stein for samples from Hacinebi, Dr E. Strommenger for samples from Habuba Kabira South, Dr. P. Watson for samples from the Ur collection in Birmingham City Art Museum. Thanks also go to the Geology Department at Edinburgh University, especially to Dr. Dodie James and Mr. Geoff Angell for their assistance with the analyses of the samples. Excavations and studies were made possible by support from the British Academy, the British Museum, the Council for British Research in the Levant, the Jenny S. Gordon Foundation and the National Museums of Scotland. Warm thanks are also due to the project staff who so assiduously and skilfully executed fieldwork.

REFERENCES

Algaze, G., 1993. *The Uruk World System. The Dynamics of Expansion of Early Mesopotamian Civilization.* Chicago.

Bachelot, L., 1998. Tell Shioukh Faouqani 1996, *Chronique archéologique en Syrie* 2: 89-98.

Bachmann, F., 1998. Ein 'Habuba-Kabira-Süd-Horizont' am Tell Sheikh Hassan?, *MDOG* 130: 51-67.

Bentley, G., 1987. Ethnicity and practice, *Comparative Studies in Society and History* 29: 24-55.

Bertin, E.P., 1978. *Introduction to X-Ray spectrometric analysis.* New York.

Boese, J., 1995. *Ausgrabungen in Tell Sheikh Hassan I. Schriften zur Vorderasiatischen Archäologie* Saarbrücken.

Bolger, D. and F. Stephen, 1999 Scientific Analysis of Uruk Ceramics from Sites of the Syrian and Southeast Anatolian Euphrates: Preliminary Results, in G. del Olmo Lete and J.-L. Montero Fenollis (eds.), *Archaeology of the Upper Syrian Euphrates, The Tishrin Dam Area, Aula Orientalis-Supplementa* 15, pp. 301-310. Barcelona.

Bourdieu, P., 1977. *Outline of a theory of Practice.* Cambridge.

Butterlin, P. 1999 Les modalités du contact: chronologie et espaces de l'expansion urukénne dans le secteur de Birecik, *Paléorient* 25/1: 127-38.

Frangipane, M., 1997. A 4th Millennium Temple/Palace Complex at Arslantepe, Malatya. North-South Relations and the Formation of Early State Societies in the Northern region of Greater Mesopotamia, *Paléorient* 23: 43-73.

Hammade, H., Y. Yamazaki, 1993. Some remarks on the Uruk levels at Tell al 'Abr on the Euphrates, *Akkadica* 84-5: 53-62.

Hours, F. et al., 1994. *Atlas des Sites du Proche Orient (14000 - 5700 BP).* Lyon.

Jones, S., 1997. *The Archaeology of Ethnicity: Reconstructing Identities in the Past and the Present.* London.

Lupton, A., 1996. *Stability and Change. Socio-political development in North Mesopotamia and South-East Anatolia 4000 - 2700 B.C.* (BAR-IntSer 627). Oxford.

McLellan, T. & A. Porter (n.d). Archaeological surveys of the Tishreen Dam zone, *AAAS*.

Miller, N., 1997. Farming and Herding Along the Euphrates. Environmental Constraints and Cultural Choice (Fourth to Second Millennium BC), in Zettler *et al.* 1997: 123-32.

Norrish, K., and B. W. Chappell, 1977. X-Ray fluorescence spectrometry, in J. Zussman (ed.), *Physical methods in determinative mineralogy*, 2nd ed.: 201-72. London.

Oguchi, T. & C. T. Oguchi, 1998. Mid-Holocene Floods of the Syrian Euphrates Inferred from 'Tell' Sediments, in G. Benito et al. (eds.), *Palaeohydrology and Environmental Change.* London. Pp. 307-315.

Pearce, J. 1999 Investigating Ethnicity at Hacinebi: Ceramic Perspectives on Style and Behavior in the 4th Millennium Mesopotamian-Anatolian Interaction, *Paléorient* 25/1: 35-42.

Peltenburg, E., S. Campbell, P. Croft, D. Lunt, M. Murray & M. Watt, 1995. Jerablus-Tahtani, Syria, 1992- 4: Preliminary Report, *Levant* 27: 1-28.

Peltenburg, E., D. Bolger, S. Campbell, M. Murray and R. Tipping, 1996. Jerablus-Tahtani, Syria, 1995: Preliminary Report, *Levant* 28: 1-25.

Peltenburg, E., S. Campbell, S. Carter, F. M. K. Stephen and R. Tipping, 1997. Jerablus-Tahtani, Syria, 1996: Preliminary Report, *Levant* 29: 1-18.

Pollock, S. & C. Coursey, 1995. Ceramics from Hacinebi Tepe: Chronology and Connections, *Anatolica* 21: 101-141.

Rice, P.M., 1987. *Pottery Analysis.* Chicago.

Rothman, M. et al., 1998. Yarım Höyük and the Uruk Expansion (Part I), *Anatolica* 24: 65-87.

Sanlaville, P. (ed.), 1985. *Holocene Settlement in North Syria* (British Archaeological Reports, International Series 238). Oxford.

Schwartz, G., 1988. Excavations at Karatut Mevkii and Perspectives on the Uruk/Jemdat Nasr Expansion, *Akkadica* 56: 1-41.

Schwartz, M., D. Hollander, D. and G. Stein 1999. Reconstructing Mesopotamian Exchange Networks in the 4th Millennium BC: Geochemical and Archaeological Analyses of Bitumen Artifacts from Hacinebi, Turkey, *Paléorient* 25/1: 67-82.

Shennan, S.J., 1988. *Quantifying Archaeology.* Edinburgh.

Shennan, S., 1989. Introduction, in S. Shennan (ed.), *Archaeological Approaches to Cultural Identity.* London. Pp. 1-32.

Stein, G. and C. Edens 1999. Hacinebi and the Uruk Expansion: Additional Comments, *Paléorient* 25/1: 167-71.

Stein, G. et al., 1996. Uruk Colonies and Anatolian Communities: An Interim Report on the 1992-1993 Excavations at Hacinebi, Turkey, *AJA* 100: 205-60.

Stein, G. et al., 1997. Excavations at Hacinebi, Turkey - 1996: Preliminary Report, *Anatolica* 23: 111-71.

Stein, G. et al., 1998. Southeast Anatolia before the Uruk Expansion: Preliminary Report on the 1997 Excavations at Hacinebi, Turkey, *Anatolica* 24: 143-93.

Van Driel, G., 1983. Seals and Sealings from Jebel Aruda 1977-1978, *Akkadica* 33: 34-62.

Verhoeven, M., 1999. *An archaeological ethnography of a Neolithic community. Space, Place and Social Relations in the Burnt Village at Tell Sabi Abyad, Syria.* Istanbul.

Wilkinson, T., 1999. Holocene Valley fills of Southern Turkey and Northwestern Syria: Recent geoarchaeological contributions, *Quarterly Science Reviews* 18: 555-71.

Williams, D.F., 1983. Petrology of ceramics, in D. R. C. Kempe and A. P. Harvey (eds.), *The petrology of archaeological artefacts*, 301-29. Oxford.

Woolley, C.L., 1921. *Carchemish II. The Town Defences.* London.

Zettler, R. et al., 1997. Subsistence and Settlement in a Marginal Environment: Tell es-Sweyhat, 1989-1995 Preliminary Report, *MASCA Research Papers in Science and Archaeology* 14. Philadelphia.

Zussman, J., 1977. X-Ray diffraction, in J. Zussman (ed.), *Physical methods in determinative mineralogy*, 2nd ed., 392-473. London.

Fig. 1. Area III, Period I, complex 2185. 2m. scales.

Fig. 2. Sealing JT 2250, from Area III, Period I.

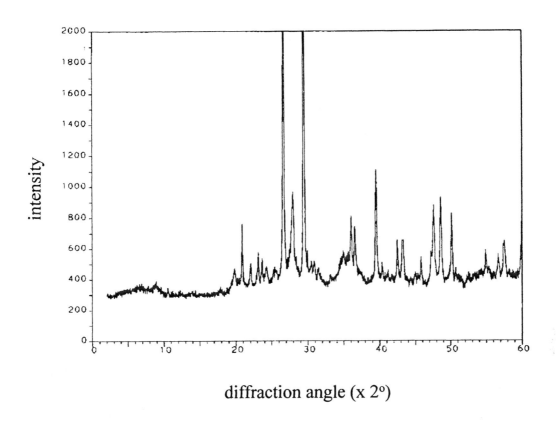

diffraction angle (x 2°)

Fig. 3. X-ray diffraction results for calcite- and quartz-rich group.

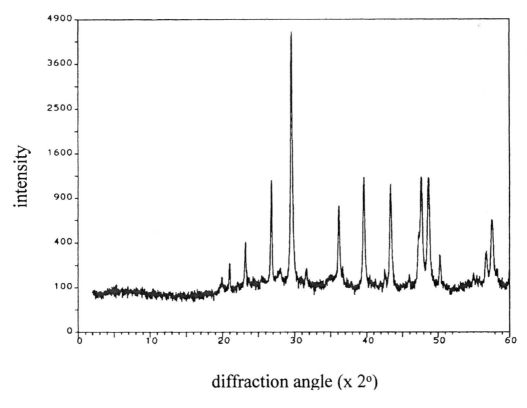

diffraction angle (x 2°)

Fig. 4. X-ray diffraction results for calcite-rich group.

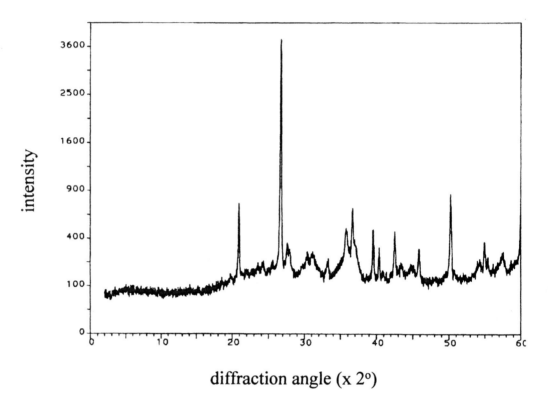

Fig. 5. X-ray diffraction results for quartz-rich group.

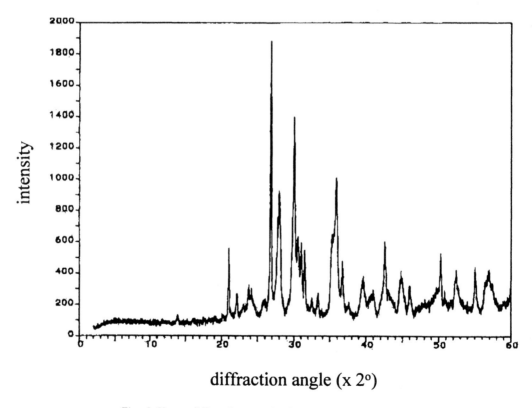

Fig. 6. X-ray diffraction results for diopside-rich group.

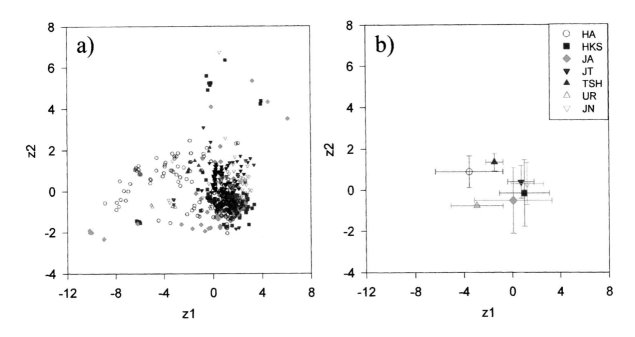

Fig. 7. Principal Components by sites showing a) all data and b) mean (symbol) and standard deviation (error bar).

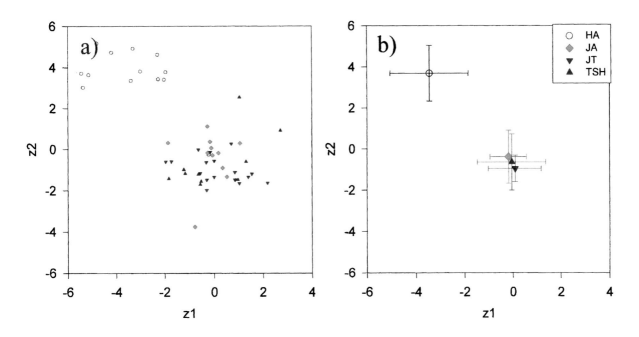

Fig. 8. Principal Components by site for BRB showing a) all data and b) mean (symbol) and standard deviation (error bar)

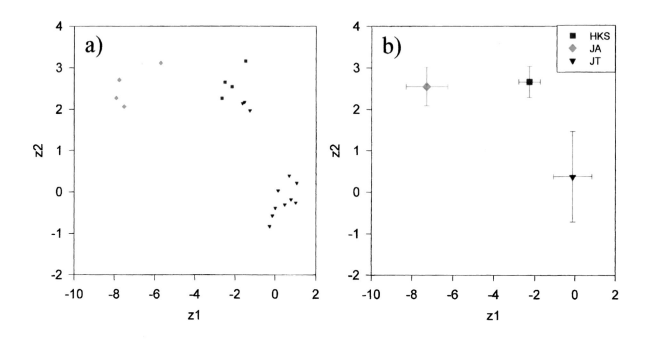

Fig. 9. Principal Components by sites for clay showing a) all data and b) mean (symbol) and standard deviation (error bar).

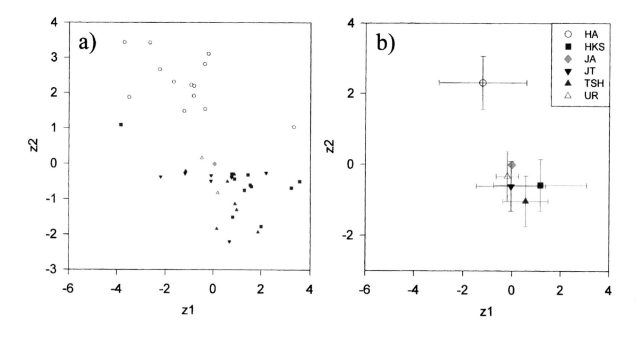

Fig. 10. Principal Components by sites for Conical Cups showing a) all data and b) mean (symbol) and standard deviation (error bar).

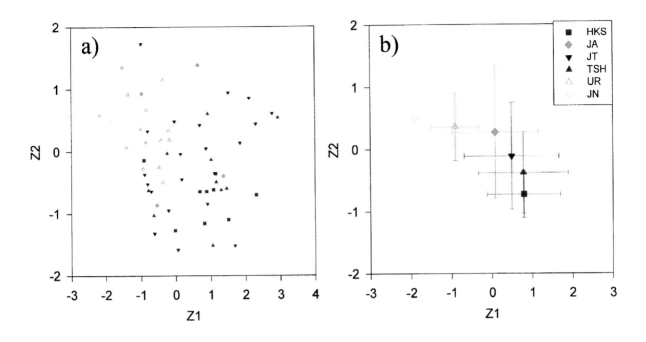

Fig. 11. Principal Components by sites for Incised Wares showing a) all data and b) mean (symbol) and standard deviation (error bar).

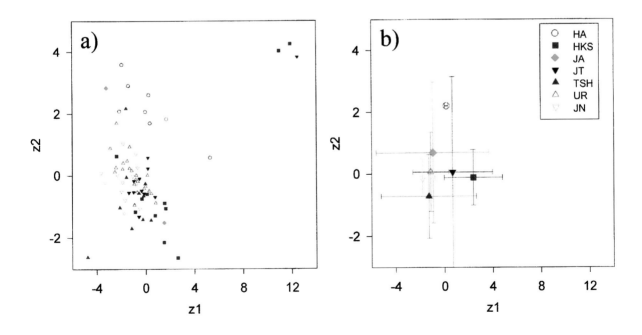

Fig. 12. Principal Components by sites for Red Slip showing a) all data and b) mean (symbol) and standard deviation (error bar).

Fig. 13a. Thin section of bevelled rim bowl from Jerablus.

Fig. 13b. Thin section of bevelled rim bowl from Jebel Aruda.

Fig. 14a. Thin section of red slip sample from Habuba Kabira.

Fig. 14b. Thin section of red slip sample from Jebel Aruda.

Fig. 14c. Thin section of red slip sample from Jerablus.

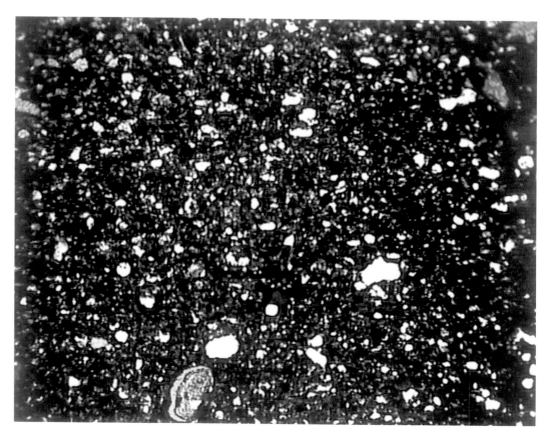

Fig. 15a. Thin section of waster from Habuba Kabira.

Fig. 15b. Thin section of incised sample from Habuba Kabira.

JEBEL ARUDA:
VARIATIONS ON A LATE URUK DOMESTIC THEME

G. van Driel

This contribution will be confined to signalling certain aspects of material culture and its variation between the ten households excavated on Jebel Aruda between 1974-1982.[1] After years of slowly sorting and refitting the sherds from this site, the final publication does at long last appear to be within view, so no more than an outline is offered here.

DATE, DEVELOPMENT AND FUNCTION OF THE SITE

This is not the place for a detailed discussion of the date: suffice it to say 'Late Uruk', contemporary with Habuba and just after Tell Sheikh Hassan. There is fundamentally one settlement period, though this is not to deny development of the initial lay-out, primarily visible in the restructuring of the central Temple area, and also noticeable in the reconstruction of certain houses. The time scale of these changes remains guesswork and could be set anywhere between a century and a decade.

The function of the settlement and the reasons for its construction on this particular spot remain obscure. Jebel Aruda is a notable landmark and the numinous associations evidenced by the modern shrine on the summit can, perhaps, be projected into the more distant past without too much hesitation. Some claim to see a defensive purpose, but a consideration of essential aspects, such as the lack of water on the site, the way in which the settlement is overlooked by very much higher ground and the lack of a clear line of view to either the south or the west, makes this highly unlikely. The settlement is, furthermore, entirely open and any defence system would have to encompass the surrounding higher ground. A possible role as some kind of citadel connected to a settlement on the margins of the river valley must remain speculative.[2] In a relatively recent period, the Euphrates flowed along the foot of the Jebel, destroying any evidence of possible occupation there, but sherds scattered on the lower slopes were all Islamic, belonging to the Ta'as complex. I would consider the most reasonable explanation for the situation of the settlement was its function as a subsidiary service centre to a major sanctuary on the summit of Jebel Aruda. The settlement is thus primarily a sign of the depth of the Late Uruk implantation in the area and is unlikely to have fulfilled any specific role in regional administration or long distance trade networks.

The settlement consists of two areas of occupation which cannot be connected stratigraphically. In the north, however, the Temple Complex[3] is linked to the final occupation phase of the domestic structures by the plaster on the outer face of the final terrace, which can be followed across the intervening alley and up the walls of the adjacent houses (NA and NB). Nevertheless, there is no reason to assume that the Northern Houses were not also contemporary with the earlier temple phases. In the first phase, the Red Temple was located within a low wall with two gate houses and later on the Red and the Grey Temples stood side by side on an open terrace. Apart from the 'kitchen buildings', containing ovens, the area between the temples and the Northern Houses was kept open in this period. Only in the final phase was the terracing extended northwards, leaving no more than a narrow alley between it and the houses.

In the southern area, the central saddle is filled by a group of three well-proportioned houses, with additional space created for a fourth by digging away the lowest part of the slope of the long ridge which runs out from the main body of the Jebel, protecting the settlement from the prevailing south wind. The extracted material was used to make high quality, chalky 'mud bricks', and at first, provision of building material seems to have been more important than provision of space, since the edge of the cut had to be modified when house S IV was constructed. This is not so much planning, as adapting to an existing situation. Additional houses were eventually also built up against, and partially terraced into, the steep slope of the ridge, each adapting to the shape of the terrain available. Access is awkward, courtyard floors tend to slope and room arrangement is complicated by situation on different levels and the necessity for stairways. Erosion has damaged structures (and hence the room contents), especially on the slope adjacent to houses IV and VIII. In the northern part of the settlement, house NF similarly makes the impression of being awkwardly squeezed into an empty spot on the edge of the wadi.[4]

Despite the lack of a direct stratigraphic link, the conviction that both parts of the settlement are contemporary is supported by the essential similarity in construction and planning, the material culture and comparable processes of growth and decline in both areas. Both areas were entirely abandoned following a violent and very

191

thorough conflagration and it is stretching credulity to regard this fact as the result of separate, unrelated incidents.

The central area is dominated by an outcrop of rock and the Temple Complex adjoining it to the north. Initially constructed as a single temple, the complex underwent two major reconstructions, with some smaller alterations at various stages. Contrary to the ordinary houses, the Temple Area was open to view from all sides. The entire area was kept meticulously clean and prior to the encapsulation in the final mud brick terrace, the structures were emptied of virtually all their contents. Though massively constructed, the interior rooms are poky and stand in no relation to the size of the structures. The fittings, especially in the Red Temple which contains both a built-up hearth and a podium of three-quarters of a man's height, contribute to the cramped and awkward use of space: these are definitely not dwellings.[5] As these structures do not directly contribute to insights into Late Uruk material culture, they will not figure in the following discussion.[6]

The gradual expansion of the settlement up the southern ridge, the infilling of open space with houses such as NF, together with the definite phases discerned in the evolution of the temple area are clear indications for the passage of time, though the actual time scale is difficult to assess. Similar pottery in the burnt houses and sealed in the pits below them suggest a relatively short period of occupation, while even the massive rebuilding and terracing activities in the Temple Complex could have followed one another in quite rapid succession.

Some depth of time is also suggested by the building material used. The first houses in the North and on the central saddle were laid out in brick made from the white, chalky topsoil of the original surface. Red subsoil material, providing equally excellent chalky 'mud bricks' was provided by the terracing cuts in the ridge to the south of the saddle and was also extracted from pits dug in the subsoil in the same area. This material obviously became increasingly difficult to obtain as the settlement expanded, although some of the pits situated in empty spaces, such as courtyards, may have been dug after the houses were in place and were immediately filled in with rubbish. Later constructions as well as repairs are carried out in the soft, friable, sandy, greyish clay brought up from the river valley. This material is markedly second rate and lacking in cohesion. It was used in a fairly wet state for the final terracing in the temple area. Though we would not use the building material to impose a strict chronology of successive building stages, its changing nature does suggest a certain progression over a period of time. House ND, which replaced the white brick house NE and is the only case of complete rebuilding in the houses areas on the Jebel, is completely made of the grey mud bricks.

The development of the central temple area, the building materials used and the general layout of the settlement suggest a degree of growth and expansion. But by the time of the destruction of the settlement, there are

equally clear signs of contrary developments. Evidence of decline and abandonment, though also discernible in the southern area, are particularly noticeable in the north, where they seem to be directly related to the excessive over-development of the Temple complex. Both the over-development and the ensuing decline may be related aspects of a more general decline in the importance of the settlement.

In the North the decline was obvious, even though from the outset the houses there looked distinctly poorer than those on the saddle in the South, with NC as a partial exception. Four of the northern houses, NA, NB, NC and ND lost their free-standing reception room. These imposing rooms, with triple entrances in the particularly thick courtyard walls, had, by the end of the occupation, all either been converted or become roofless and abandoned. The rooms were empty, ovens had been built into the former reception rooms of NC and ND, while that of NB was partitioned into two smaller rooms presumably used for manufacturing purposes.

There are indications that the houses next to the Temple Terrace had become more or less uninhabitable, due to water seeping through and under the rubble foundations of the terraces, over the narrow street and into the houses. There were clear indications of a mud flow through the door between the street and courtyard N 36, which contained a paved area and a carefully constructed duct to the wadi. Though this may in part be related to activities in the courtyard, the drain still effectively diverted rainwater from the wall footings when re-opened during the excavation. The wall between courtyards N 36 and N 18 had been pushed over into N 18, where it overlay an array of small ovens and kitchen utensils. The terracing of soft greyish mud brick on a loose rubble footing, with only a thin plaster facing, must have constituted a direct hazard after the first heavy downpour. Where excavated, the lower part of the terracing showed few signs of erosion and it seems safe to assume that the end of the settlement came soon after the work on the terrace encapsulating both the Red and the Grey Temple had ended.

This is perhaps a classic example of systems collapse following ill-considered expansion, itself perhaps stimulated by perception of declining importance or effectiveness.

Reconstructions in the south are less marked, but changes in function can be discerned in some of the houses. Although situated awkwardly from the outset, house S II is the largest single construction on the Jebel and it is also notable in that it has no secondary buildings or a courtyard of its own. It was particularly well built with the thickest and most carefully modelled plaster noted, but from the outset it almost certainly functioned in conjunction with S I. The two buildings were separated by a corridor, which was later roofed over and closed off at the end by the re-construction of a bathroom belonging to S I which entailed other changes. The reconstruction, for which grey river valley mud brick was used, altered access routes within S II, while the insertion of a stair leading to a small additional room, partitioned from the former corridor, at some point provided access between the two houses. The narrow passage was later closed again by a flimsy partition of which only traces of the plaster remained. It is obvious that S II lost its original function, potentially that of the guest house for the entire settlement, though dependent on S I, the stone lined drains from which ran along both its sides. Towards the end, S II became a storehouse, where most of the category 33 storage jars were located (Fig. 6). It had burnt fiercely locally, completely pulverising the wall plaster and the outer skin of the bricks, and the jars most probably contained oil. But there may also have been other valuables, as a pit, filled with a slow accumulation of dust, had been dug along one of the walls down to floor level. It narrowly missed a metal knife, but other items may well have been extracted not long after the destruction.

Another sign of change in at least four houses is the notable concentration of domestic equipment in a single store room, usually one of the secure, back rooms of the living quarters. Typical cases are N 45 in NA, N 100 in NH, S 64 in S III and room S 89 belonging to an eroded house on the (natural) southern terrace. Other cases are less pronounced, but possibly similar, like concentrations of objects in the badly eroded house NF. The storing away of household utensils does indicate the expectation of return, and certainly does not imply complete cessation of occupation, since low level activity can be discerned in most of these houses. In the South S VI and VII were probably locked up, while in S V only a separate craftsman's workshop was to all likelihood in use.

This might be regarded as remarkably similar to the preparations made in modern villages in the region as the majority of the population packs up to follow the flocks into the Jezira in spring, leaving only the old and the sick behind with a few prominent families who can employ herdsmen. It is of course dangerous to project modern practice onto the past and I would in any case regard it unlikely that the inhabitants of this particular settlement could have been heavily involved in animal husbandry or in any form of agriculture which could necessitate seasonal movement. The concentrated storage of goods makes the identification of activity areas hazardous, and means that artefact distributions must be interpreted with great caution. Furthermore, the finds spectrum is likely to be distorted under such conditions, since portable items may well have been removed.

Other signs of rebuilding and change will not be discussed here, as sufficient has been said to show that the settlement should not be regarded as static in functions or status.

ROOM CONTENTS

The first houses to be excavated revealed satisfactory scenes of major destruction. Rooms packed with smashed and burnt household goods, sealed by charred roof beams

and fallen walls. The whole settlement had gone up in flames. The material culture in both settlement areas is identical, and it is pushing coincidence too far to explain this as the result of a series of unrelated events. This represents a very deliberate destruction involving the entire settlement, but it does not mean that the scatter of individual groups or types of objects is uniform. Contemporaneity does, however, allow the recognition of individual variation and choice within the available repertoire of material goods.

The first house excavated, S I, contained the evidence of sudden and unexpected destruction: someone running with tablets and small valuables from the inner store (S 2) had spilled some of them in the race to the nearest door. But this is the only indication of panic. There were no bodies under the fallen roof beams, and even more telling is that there is very little in the way of valuables. Sometime after the destruction people returned to dig through the rubble at very specific points, certain corners and at thresholds for instance, presumably to retrieve valuables known to be hidden under the floors. One such cache was not retrieved and we found it more or less by chance when cleaning revealed a thin greenish line where a group of copper adzes had been hidden under the floor.

The inhabitants may have taken to safety the more valuable contents of the houses or otherwise the settlement may well have been looted of portable valuables, but the nature of the conflagration in certain rooms indicates that textiles, oil or other highly combustible material such as kindling fire wood (not to mention straw) were left and contributed to the conflagration. Considering the extent of the excavations there is very little metal, little more than the odd forgotten or lost pin. There is virtually no inlay work which might have adorned furniture. Stone vessels are virtually all broken and were probably being used as raw material, but there is an awful lot of pottery, which has taken years to stick together. It is this pottery which reveals something of the changing fortunes of individual rooms and complexes. But it must be kept in mind that not all material excavated was found where it was actually being used.

If the interpretation of the Red and Grey buildings in the central part of the settlement as temples is accepted, and if the settlement is regarded as a kind of service area for something on the top of the Jebel, much of the storage and the food preparation for which there is such abundant evidence in pottery, tools and equipment, was presumably related to cult requirements.[7] Jebel Aruda should not therefore be regarded as entirely typical for Late Uruk period settlement and material culture in its Northern Euphrates valley version.

FEMALE OCCUPATIONS

The spindle whorl should be a very sensitive indicator of activity. Assyriologists need to be reminded that there are no texts on spinning even though this is the essential preliminary process to textile production. The reality is that women will have been spinning all the time. There were spindle whorls in almost all of the houses (Fig. 1). But attention to the context suggests a differing pattern. Some of the whorls were clearly in store (S 99, N 47, N 100 and possibly S 94). In three rooms (S 126, S 74 and S 90) the association between soapstone whorls, fragmentary soapstone vessels, rope weights and polishing stones suggests that the whorls were made here and do not, therefore, provide direct evidence for the presence of women spinning.

Thus probably the only spindle whorls actually being used were those in NC, NG and the kitchen courtyard S 7 of house S I. With the otherwise attested low level of occupation in NA the single whorl is not surprising.

There are no indications for weaving, but flat looms would leave no trace other than a peg hole in the ground anyway.

Complete sets of saddle querns occur widely: curiously there are strong indications that they stood on the roof, often in pairs (Fig. 2). In analysing the structure of the settlement, therefore, the importance of rooftop circulation needs to be taken into account, particularly in the area built up the steep southern slopes. On the other hand, in some areas, the querns are represented solely by smashed fragments, raising the suspicion that they were being re-used. Worn or broken base stones continued to be used with massive pebble pounders and certain other basalt items - a ring weight and a heavy bowl for instance - were possibly made from smashed stones.

The lack of milling facilities in the area of S I/VIII is particularly striking in view of the big bread ovens situated here in a special area overlooking the river. Grinding flour and baking bread seem to have been spatially separated activities, though not invariably. The breakage of basalt grinding stones around houses NB and NC is perhaps due to the depredations of early 20th century AD inhabitants, but several querns seem to have been located in the same courtyard as the large bread oven. NA and NC had more extensive facilities for the preparation of food than a simple household would require and we can only suppose that these facilities served the temple, presumably in a developed stage of the settlement, when the earlier temple kitchens had been covered by the terracing.

STONE TOOLS

Flint, or rather chert, tools abound. Often these are no more than opportunistic flakes selected from smashed pebbles, and working is, on the whole, minimal. A few, better finished specialist types do occur, such as the thick tabular flakes or fan-scrapers. The type is virtually confined to the houses of the high Southern terrace, and it is, therefore particularly regrettable that their function is so elusive (Fig. 3). Large numbers of snapped Canaanean blades were scattered all over the site. Traces of wear on these long blades seem to be consistent with wood working, but there is no trace of the products.[8]

Unmodified stones gathered from the river valley were used in large numbers as pounders, smoothers, work surfaces, pestles and palettes. Occasionally more specialist uses can be suspected. There are three anvil-shaped stones suggestive of fine metal working. Working of copper or precious metals does not leave much in the way of archaeologically recognisable debris. One of the store rooms contained lumps of material which are probably raw lapis lazuli or copper-containing rock, but the evidence of their working remains elusive.

Stone vessels are relatively common, steatite, alabaster and a fine grained dark sandstone were used. But it is a curious fact that many of the complete examples are re-worked, more are fragmentary, some even displaying saw marks, while small chips left from bowls are widespread. There are no definite lumps of raw material. So if vessels were being made it can only have been a finishing process, though to judge by the cut-up vessels it is more likely that stone was being re-cycled, in much the same way as was suspected for some of the basalt querns. Rope weights, generally two together, and drill hand guards point to some form of stone working. This need not leave much in the way of recognisable debris, since spindle whorls could be cut from cores and most of the fashioning will have been carried out by laborious scouring and filing, as the marks on the surviving vessels show only too clearly.

POTTERY

The *in situ* household inventories on Jebel Aruda provide some insight into the extent of differentiation within the same basic Late Uruk pottery spectrum which was in use throughout the settlement (Figs. 4 and 5). Examples of most of these types, including some of the more unusual ones, also occur in the series of pits under houses S IV and S VIII, thus emphasising the relatively short period of occupation.

Within this scala, however, there is notable evidence for individual 'preferences', with certain types virtually confined to a single house or a particular room location. This observation clearly carries implication for the interpretation of pottery complexes taken from soundings scattered over the surface of a tell, especially when detailed chronological sequences are constructed from such material. The extent of such differentiation can only be recognised in a fully excavated series of adjoining houses.

On the one hand we have functional differentiation, such as the occurrence of spouted 'tea pots', if these could indeed be functionally associated with the evidence for stone drilling in the rooms S 90/2 (Fig. 4, top right). On the other hand differences in access are exemplified by the unequal distribution pattern of the torpedo-shaped vessels of cat. 33, which may have been used to store oil (Fig. 6). Generally, their capacity varies from 20 to 40 litres, but the metrological system which we had hoped to reconstruct starting from this large group of very similar vessels failed to materialise: the potting techniques simply do not allow such standardisation.[9] Most cat. 33 vessels weigh between 10-12 kg, but this is the result of rigorous scraping, both inside and out, reducing the clay from an original lump of around 15 kg. With almost all the larger pottery types, it is generally the poorly controlled scraping of the interior which is the major cause of fluctuation in capacity.

The main storage depot of the torpedo vessels cat. 33, was house S II, which was controlled by S I. Other houses seem to have been supplied with just one or two for immediate use. Differential access between the northern and southern areas is clearly marked: despite the very extensive evidence for food processing in the north just a single example was possessed by only three of the houses.

The relative poverty of the northern area is further emphasised by the distribution of the large decorative Uruk Red vessels (cat. 14). There is a notable concentration in three of the southern houses: S III with 5, S V with 6 and S VI with 3. They were usually stacked in the inner secure store, also in NH, which underlines the fact that these vessels served no immediate practical purpose. The absence from the North is striking, though broken specimens had been used in the courtyard paving of NA, perhaps a reminder of pottery used in the heyday of the house. The Uruk Red vessels vary considerably in quality, from a fine thin fabric with a hard glossy red surface, to thick, soft friable fabric with a thin reddish wash which rubs off rather easily. Diatom analysis of certain sherds indicates that the clay of the finer vessels incorporates maritime diatoms, suggestive of import from Southern Mesopotamia.[10]

More individual choices, though perhaps still based on functional criteria are revealed in the distribution of two highly specific categories of pottery.

Cat. 35, dubbed 'rolly-bins', have very characteristic features and a peculiar concentration (Fig. 7). These large vessels with a capacity of up to 90 litres have heavy strap handles, which enable the vessel to be rolled onto its side, presumably to make it easier to scoop out the contents. A prominent air hole between the handles indicates that usage required ventilation. What the commodity was is unknown, but a connection with the brewing of beer has been suggested on the basis of residual analysis elsewhere.[11] With the exception of a single example in house NF and an incomplete example in the soak-away of a drain in S I, all specimens come from house S III, most from room S 52 (or its roof?). One other specimen comes from the refuse pit behind the house. Why only house S III utilised this type of vessel is not clear if it was used for

such a common purpose as brewing, nor why the vessels should, apparently, be stored on the roof of this house alone.

Equally obscure is the reason why the cooks working in courtyard N 18 of house NC should have preferred a very special, narrow necked cooking pot, cat. 19 (Fig. 8). These chaff-faced, hand made vessels with heavy organic temper are red in colour with a black core. Unused examples had a whitish 'slip' on the exterior. The sherds are extremely friable when soaked, but become very hard when dry. This type of vessel is concentrated in the one area, though there are two strays, both from cooking areas.

Most of the pottery on Jebel Aruda has a simple sand temper, special cooking vessels with calcite temper are rare, but there is one category of organically tempered vessel which deserves mention, if only because only the most dedicated of pottery menders will manage to entirely restore one. Single examples of cat. 29 occur infrequently but widely scattered and must have served a very specific function. It is a distinctive globular vessel, characterised by an extremely hard, brittle fabric, organically tempered and often greenish and over-fired, with marked ribs on the surface suggesting slow rotation. Especially notable are the air bubbles in the fabric which raise blisters on the surface, leading to flaking, which makes these vessels difficult to re-assemble. The capacity lies between 35-60 litres. The distribution over the site is not helpful in explaining their particular purpose (Fig. 9).

Occasionally, functional sets of pottery can be discerned, such as a re-occurring group of goblets together with a spouted bottle. One such set had been sealed into the terracing in front of the Red Temple and was instantly recognisable to our workmen as a guest-set for tea or coffee. But another set, with a little flask of only 20 cm, suggests a somewhat stronger tipple (Fig. 10).

Even more enigmatic are the exceptional vessels, which, when seen in context, betray truly individual choices. What are we to make of a collection of no fewer than three specially formed hedgehog vessels in House S I?

In all this a combination of the functional and the personal may be discerned and no doubt other individual preferences would emerge if variants within categories were examined more closely. The element of personal choice which still speaks through the household inventories is one of the most significant results of the time-consuming re-fitting of the sherds recovered from this excavation.

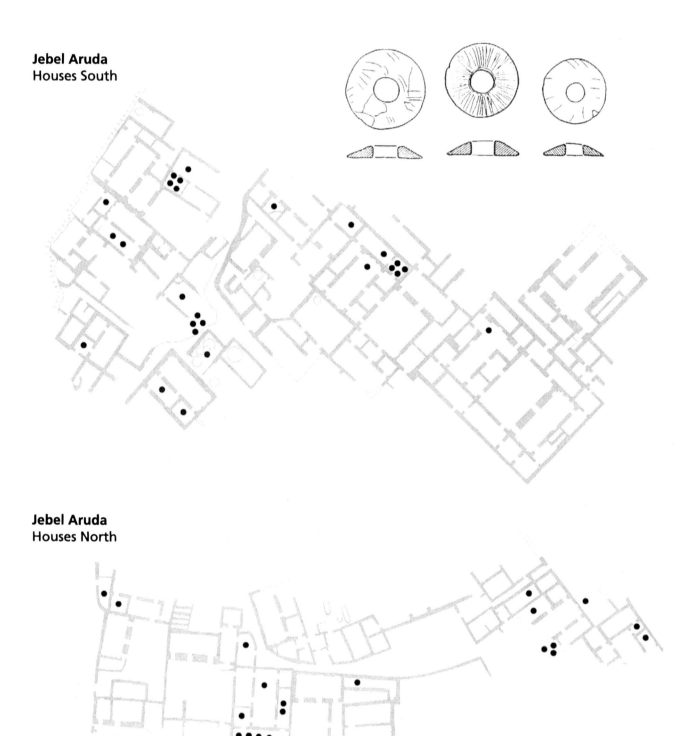

Jebel Aruda
Houses South

Jebel Aruda
Houses North

Spindle whorls soapstone

*Fig. 1. Distribution of spindle
whorls*

Jebel Aruda
Houses South

Jebel Aruda
Houses North

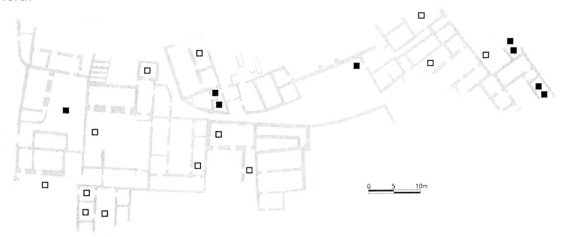

Basalt querns
■ set
□ fragment

Fig. 2. Distribution of saddle querns

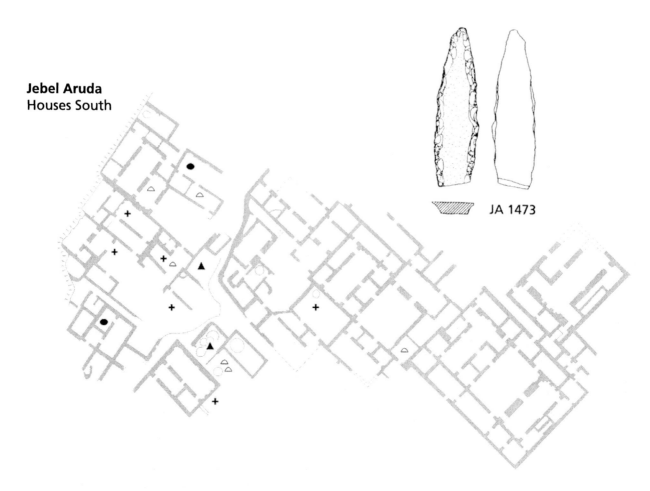

Jebel Aruda
Houses South

JA 1473

Jebel Aruda
Houses North

+ broken
● fan
△ scraper
▲ triangular

Fig. 3. Distribution of tabular flakes.
Fig. 4 (opposite). Small pottery, not all to the same scale.

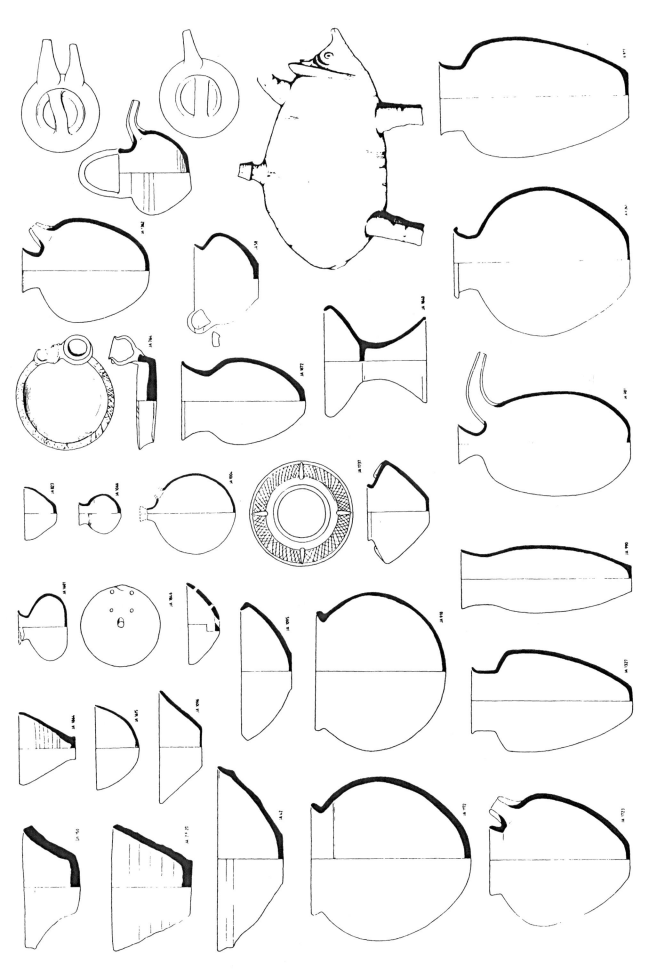

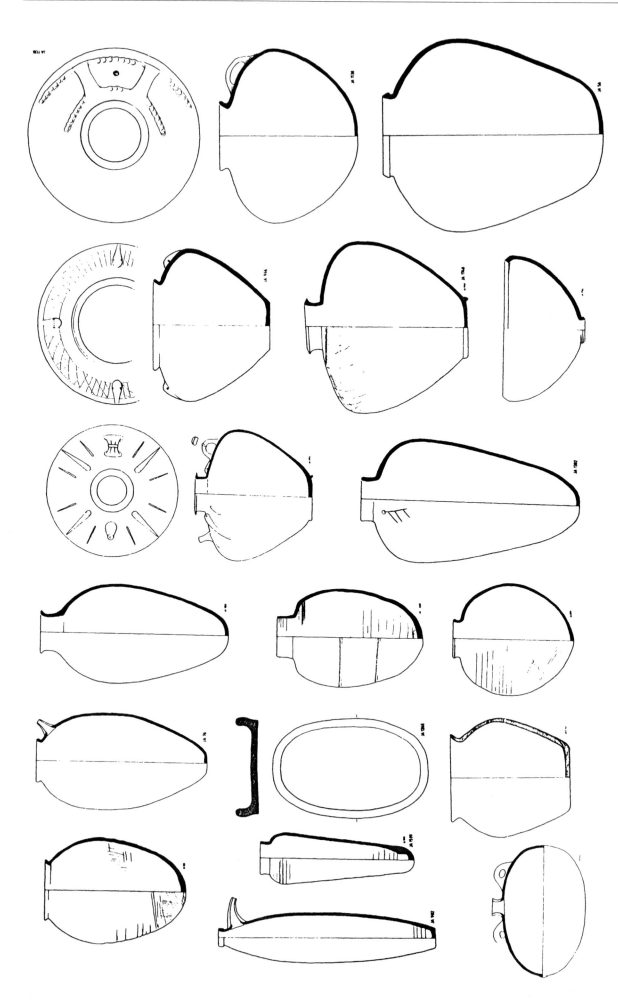

Fig. 5. Large pottery, not all to the same scale

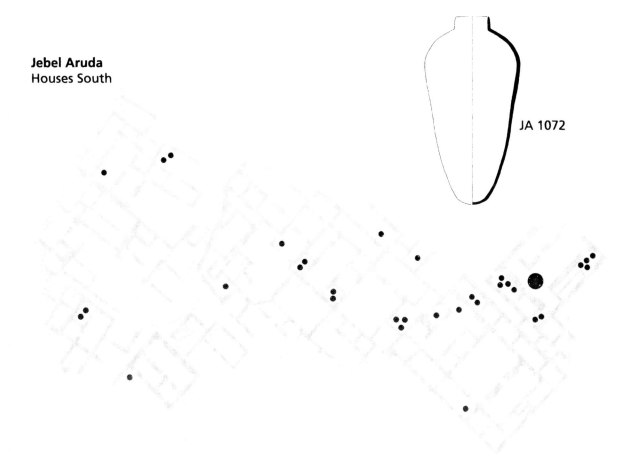

Fig. 6. Distribution of Cat. 33, torpedo-shaped vessels

Jebel Aruda
Houses South

JA 1072

Jebel Aruda
Houses North

Cat 33
- 1
● 40

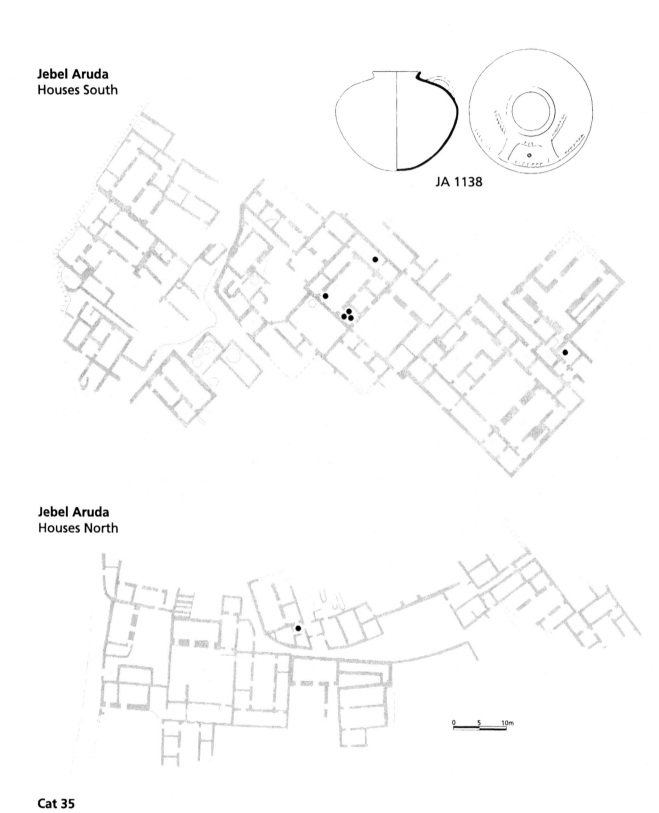

Fig. 7. Distribution of 'rolly-bins'

Jebel Aruda
Houses South

JA 1138

Jebel Aruda
Houses North

Cat 35

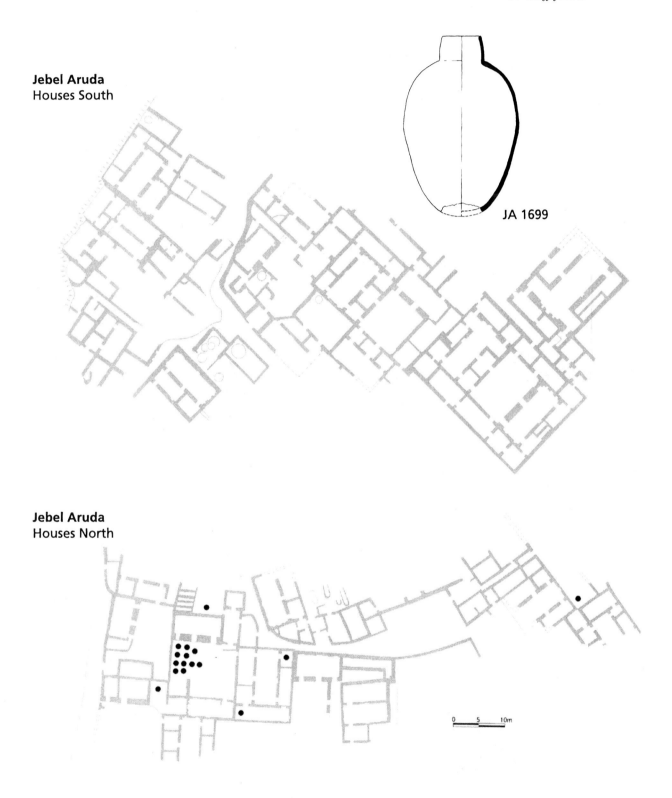

Fig. 8. Distribution of Cat. 19 chaff-faced.

Jebel Aruda
Houses South

JA 1699

Jebel Aruda
Houses North

Cat 19

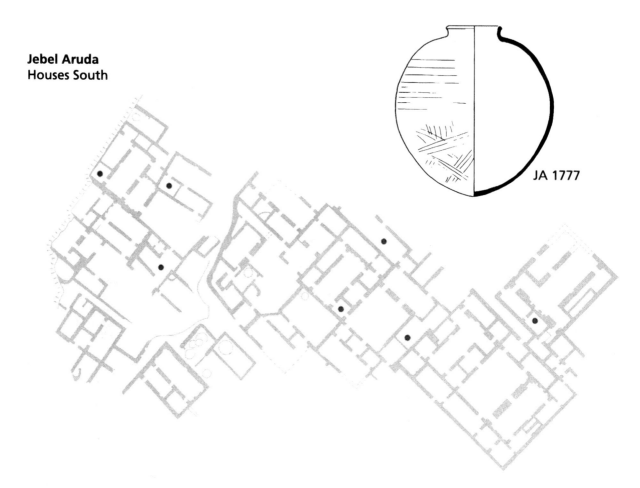

Fig. 9. Distribution of Cat. 29 chaff-faced.

Jebel Aruda
Houses South

JA 1777

Jebel Aruda
Houses North

Cat 29

●

Fig. 10. Set consisting of goblets and bottle from room S 23, scale 1:4

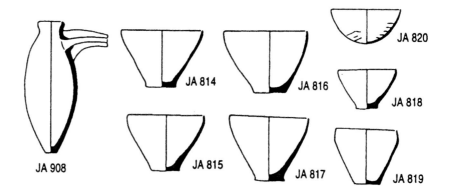

[1] Cf. the plans published in G. van Driel & C. van Driel-Murray, 'Jebel Aruda 1977-1978', *Akkadica* 12 (1979) pp 2-28, after p. 28 for room numbers in the South, and G. van Driel & C. van Driel-Murray, 'Jebel Aruda 1982. A preliminary report', *Akkadica* 33 (1983) pp. 1-26, after p. 24 for the North Houses and the Southern Terrace.

[2] Mud brick brought up from the river valley contained both Ubaid and Late Uruk sherds. The latter may have come, like the Ubaid material, from a now lost settlement in the valley, or they may have been incorporated during brick making.

[3] The term 'temple' is used here in respect of buildings which are out of the ordinary as regards situation, shape, construction, architectural treatment and (lack of) contents, serving some exceptional purpose other than that of domestic occupation. However, each phase of these 'buildings with a specific purpose' possessed a 'kitchen' containing ovens. I regard the suggestion of a specific secular use even less justified than the generic term 'temple'.

[4] The present contour of the entire spur between wadi and river valley is much the same as in Uruk times, thus allowing little leeway for speculation on a more regular shape for houses such as NF. Here, the ash from its ovens still clothes the slope down into the wadi, indicating little change in contour. Only the end of House S II was extended to the very edge of the wadi with a shallow stone terracing.

[5] Nor would I like to contemplate the spectacle of some dignitary clambering onto the podium to harangue the assembled local or regional worthies in the main room of the Red Temple, as has been implied by one recent interpretation of the function of the building.

[6] For the development of the temple area cf. the preliminary reports in *Akkadica* mentioned in note 1.

[7] That is in activities related to the buildings called 'temples', which possessed kitchens.

[8] Unpublished report by Mrs Dr. A. L. van Gijn, Institute of Archaeology, UL.

[9] It is fitting here to thank Ing. P. Borgmeyer, who, voluntarily over many years, drew all the reconstructed pottery and calculated the individual capacities, work which forms the basis of the categorisation of the pottery from the site.

[10] Unpublished report by Drs. M. Jansma, formerly IPP, UVA.

[11] During the conference Ms V. Badler kindly reminded me of the use of these vessels in brewing, as she, incidentally, had done years earlier in Leiden.

CONTACTS BETWEEN THE 'URUK' WORLD AND THE LEVANT DURING THE FOURTH MILLENNIUM BC: EVIDENCE AND INTERPRETATION

Graham Philip

1. INTRODUCTION

One of the most striking aspects of the so-called Uruk expansion is the contrast between the large quantities of material of south Mesopotamian style documented at fourth millennium BC sites across north Mesopotamia, northern Syria and southeastern Anatolia (Algaze 1993; Lupton 1996; Frangipane 1997; Oates and Oates 1997)

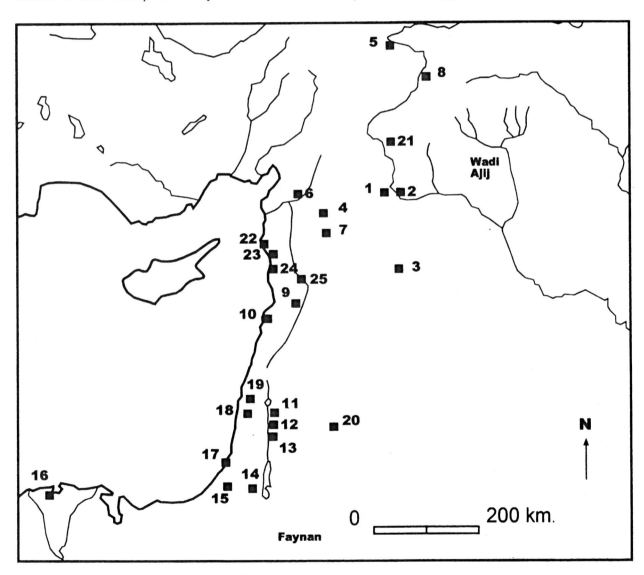

Fig. 1. Sites mentioned in the text.

1. Habuba Kabira / Jebel Aruda, 2. Tell Sheikh Hassan, 3. El-Kowm, 4. Tell Afis, 5. Arslantepe, 6. 'Amuq sites, 7. Tell Mardikh, 8. Hassek Höyük, 9. Tell Nebi Mend, 10. Byblos, 11. Tell esh-Shuna, 12. Tell Abu Hamid, 13. Tell Um Hammad, 14. Arad, 15. Wadi Beersheba, 16. Tell el-Fara'in, 17. Afridar, 18. 'Ain el-Assawir, 19. Yiftah'el, 20. Jawa, 21. Hacinebi, 22. Ras Shamra, 23. Tell Sukas, 24. Qal'at ar-Rus, 25. Hama.

and the far more limited evidence reported from the area west of the Euphrates and along the Mediterranean coast (Algaze 1993: 72; Schwartz 1998). Clearly if the Uruk phenomenon in the north is viewed primarily as indicative of the south Mesopotamian interest in resources such as metals which were unobtainable in the southern alluvium (e.g. Algaze 1993), the limited interest in the Levant may be self-explanatory; the region had little to offer that could not be obtained along major riverine routes into southeast Anatolia. That said, the location of both Middle and Late Uruk settlements in the Tabqa region of the Euphrates Valley can be read as indicating some interest in the Aleppo region and areas to the west (Lupton 1996: 99).

More recently, researchers have tended to view the Uruk phenomenon as the combined product of a range of processes operating in rather different local contexts. These include emulation, sustained economic interaction, the establishment of small-scale southern 'implants' within indigenous communities, and the operation of parallel processes in both north and south (Frangipane 1993, 1997; Lupton 1996; School of American Research Advanced Seminar 1998). In the light of this wide range of mechanisms, there may well be a need to ask why none of these appear to have had a significant impact on the Levant. The situation is made even more anomalous by the evidence for the influence of Mesopotamian ideas upon developments in Egypt during the late fourth millennium BC (Wilkinson this volume). Moreover, if, as Sherratt (1993: 15) has suggested, the Uruk network constituted the core of a fourth millennium BC 'world system' linking Europe and southwest Asia, the absence of the east Mediterranean basin from this system appears even more striking.

In fact, the apparent disengagement of communities in the Levant from the Uruk world appears to conflict with (at least) three other aspects of the evidence.

1. Chaff-tempered pottery is characteristic of local fourth millennium Cal. BC ceramic assemblages across a large swathe of north Mesopotamia, northeast Syria, southeast Anatolia and northwest Syria (Frangipane 1993: 154; Lupton 1996: 19, fig. 2.4; Mazzoni 2000: 98). The evidence of shared ceramic styles and technology implies links between all four regions, but connections with southern Mesopotamia are well documented in only the first three areas (Algaze 1993; Lupton 1996; Schwartz 1998). In the light of the communication of ceramic information, it is not easy to explain the limited evidence for Mesopotamian contacts with western Syria as the result of either distance or cultural isolation.

2. The influence of Mesopotamian ideas and imagery upon the development of the early Egyptian state in the late fourth millennium BC is now widely acknowledged, with contact generally understood as having been mediated via the Euphrates Valley and the Levant coast (Moorey 1990; Joffe 2000; Wilkinson this volume, p. 244). However, this situation appears at odds with the

limited archaeological evidence for connections between the Levantine littoral and southern Mesopotamia.

3. There is good evidence for substantial connections between the Levant, and both Anatolia and Mesopotamia during the first half of the third millennium BC. Instances include; the spread of Red-Black Burnished Ware (RBBW) (Philip 1999; Mazzoni 1999: 113; Frangipane 2000: 444-50), political and administrative developments at Ebla showing clear Mesopotamian influence (Mazzoni 1991; Dolce 1998), and the growth of communications in the east Mediterranean involving Cyprus, the Levant and the Anatolian coast (Sherratt and Sherratt 1991: 367-8; Knapp *et al.* 1994: 419-20; Peltenburg 1996: 23-5; Webb and Frankel 1999: 38-40, fig. 27). These phenomena imply a significant interchange of ideas, technology and social practices within and between these regions before the mid-third millennium BC. Such a development is most easily understood if envisaged as building upon pre-existing networks of communication.

If we wish to square the circle, we appear to have two options. The first is to argue for a degree of contact between the Mesopotamian world and the Levant during the fourth millennium Cal. BC, but accept that in the present state of our knowledge, the archaeological evidence required to demonstrate this point is simply not available. This position follows the old maxim that 'absence of evidence is not evidence of absence'. The second is to take the archaeological data at face value and accept that there were connections between predynastic Egypt and Uruk societies in the Euphrates Valley but that these were mediated in such a way as to have had little or no impact upon the intervening communities of the Levant, which therefore remained relatively isolated from wider social and economic developments. In order to evaluate these two alternatives, it will be necessary to examine in some detail the data relating to the fourth millennium Cal. BC from the 'Amuq to the Nile Delta. However, this is more easily said than done, as any such attempt will require the analyst to work across the traditional disciplinary boundaries between the archaeology of Mesopotamia, and that of the Levant.

The continued existence of these boundaries is illustrated by the fact that published discussions of developments in the fourth millennium BC have generally fallen into three groups. Papers of the first kind have considered the material from the perspective of a particular site or very localised region (e.g. Dunand 1973; Levy 1987; Rothman 1993; Frangipane 1993; Boese 1995; Oates and Oates 1997; Braun 1997; Epstein 1998; Stein *et al.* 1998). Of course, other discussions have taken a broader perspective, but these can be readily divided into studies focused upon an axis linking Mesopotamia with southeast Anatolia (e.g. Algaze 1993; Lupton 1996; Frangipane 1997), or those rooted in the southern Levant (Helms 1987; van den Brink [ed.] 1992; Joffe 1993; Levy 1995). I am not aware of a recent publication which covers the entire area of interest in this case. Such are the limitations of the data in fact, that recent works which have dealt with sites in both regions have generally concentrated upon the correlation of site and regional sequences, and have paid less attention to analysis and interpretation (Thuesen 1988: 180-87; Ben-Tor 1989; Schwartz and Weiss 1992).

The ground rules for the present paper are largely determined by changes to the nature of the dataset in the last decade, which warrant a reconsideration of the evidence for inter-regional connections — improved radiocarbon chronologies, recently published excavation data, and a revised understanding of the relationship between southern Mesopotamia and north Mesopotamia-Syria (see below). These developments have facilitated a reconsideration of the evidence in terms of past socio-economic structures and relationships. As a result it is now possible to attempt to understand the archaeological record in terms of the social practices through which it was generated (Barrett 1994), albeit in a flawed and partial manner.

THE URUK PHENOMENON

Until recently the majority of accounts of the development of complex societies in north Mesopotamia, Syria and Anatolia viewed this as a secondary process driven by contact with more advanced 'pristine' civilizations in south Mesopotamia, and which could be assigned to the latter part of the fourth millennium BC (Sürenhagen 1986; Algaze 1993; Oates 1993). However, recent discussions have highlighted several key issues in this regard, which appear germane to the situation in the Levant.

1. The so-called 'contact period' is now seen as a long-term, multi-staged process, which in the case of the Euphrates Valley area was underway by 3700-3600 Cal. BC (Boese 1995: 256, Abb. 15; Stein 1998, this volume,

p. 149; Pearce 2000: 121, figs. 18, 19). As a result, the evidence from sites such as Habuba Kabira and Jebel Aruda (see Fig. 1 for site locations), once deemed central to the discussion, is now understood as pertaining only to a relatively late stage of this process, termed Local Late Chalcolithic 5 (LC5) according to the Santa Fe scheme.

2. Recent work in Syria and Anatolia has revealed the existence in these areas of societies showing complex organizational characteristics (e.g. monumental architecture, formal administrative systems, mass produced ceramics) during the first half of the fourth millennium Cal. BC, i.e. preceding the documentation of regular contacts with the southern Uruk world (Frangipane this volume, p. 124; Trufelli 1994; Lupton 1996; Oates this volume p. 119; Stein *et al.* 1998).

3. It is increasingly clear that the nature and degree of participation in Uruk-related networks by communities in northern Syria and southeast Anatolia were highly diverse. North-south contacts could take a variety of forms including the implantation of whole southern communities, the establishment of spatially delimited southern 'enclaves' within indigenous settlements, the adoption and the exploitation of southern practices and symbols by local elites in order to enhance their own power, or simple non-participation (Frangipane 1993: 156-7, fig. 13; this volume p. 126; Rothman 1993, this volume p. 49; Lupton 1996: 68-72; School of American Research Advanced Seminar 1998). There is no reason to see involvement in the wider system as constituting a 'default option'. In practice, the form and degree of engagement by any particular community with the Uruk world would have been dependent upon a range of factors (Frangipane this volume, p. 125-6; Rothman this volume, p. 49). Among these would have featured the perceived gains and risks entailed by the various potential responses, with the key decisions made by local elites, where such existed.

2. FOURTH MILLENNIUM BC CHRONOLOGY

Southern Levant Terminology	Approx. dates (Cal. BC)	Santa Fe Terminology
Chalcolithic (Ghassulian)	Late Fifth millennium-3600	LC2-LC3
Early Bronze Age I (early)	3600-3400/3350	LC4
Early Bronze Age I (late)	3400/3350-3100/3000	LC5
Early Bronze Age II[1]	3100-3000-2800/2700	LC5/post-Uruk[2]

Table 1. Comparative calibrated radiocarbon chronology for the fourth millennium BC in the southern Levant and North Syria/North Mesopotamia (dates after Joffe and Dessel 1995; Carmi and Segal 1998; Fischer 1998; in press; School of American Research Advanced Seminar 1998; Philip and Millard 2000; Baird and Philip n.d.).[3]

According to the chronological framework proposed by the recent Santa Fe meeting (School of American Research Advanced Seminar 1998), the period of Uruk contact termed LC 4-5 begins no later than c. 37/3600 Cal. BC, and continues until c. 3000 Cal. BC. Thus in

terms of the south Levant chronology, the Uruk period is contemporary with the very end of the Chalcolithic, the whole of Early Bronze Age (EBA) I and the beginning of EBA II, the latter part of which is contemporary with the post-Uruk (Table 1).

The increasing recourse to radiocarbon dating by researchers working in southwest Asia allows a correlation between developments in the Euphrates Valley and the southern Levant, in spite of the great differences in the material cultures of the two regions. In particular the existence of an independent chronological control permits discussion to extend to aspects of the data — raw materials and technological innovations for example — which lie outside those considered under typology-based analyses. However, fine-grained analysis on a Levant-wide scale is held back by the paucity of reliable radiocarbon evidence from western Syria and Lebanon. Here, local relative chronologies remain dependent upon traditional ceramic typology, often using material derived from fieldwork undertaken in the first half of the 20th century.

In absolute terms, the period of interest appears well-defined. In terms of the 'Amuq sequence, it post-dates the _floruit_ of Ubaid-related pottery ('Amuq E), and precedes the impact of RBBW ('Amuq H). However, the lack of radiocarbon dates combined with the unsatisfactory excavation and recording characteristic of many older projects, and our limited grasp of inter-site ceramic diversity (see below), means that although general correlations have been established between the stratigraphic sequences of the 'Amuq, Hama, and Ras Shamra (de Contenson 1979, 1982; Thuesen 1988; Schwartz and Weiss 1992: 187, fig. 3), many problems remain.

IMPLICATIONS

In the absence of radiocarbon dates, the absolute dating of the 'Amuq sequence was established with reference to the chronology of sites in north Mesopotamia. Thus Watson (1965: 82-83) linked 'Amuq E and F with the later Ubaid and the Uruk periods respectively, and placed the transition around 3600 BC, a position maintained until quite recently (e.g. de Contenson 1982: 97, table 1), though others have noted that Phases E and F as defined in the 'Amuq do not run in strict succession, but are separated by a local stratigraphic break (Braidwood and Braidwood 1960: 512-13; Mazzoni 1998: 22; Helwing 2000: 146). However, the evidence from Hacinebi Phase A and Arslantepe VIII (Pearce 2000: 114; Frangipane 2000: 440) indicates that the production of Ubaid-style pottery had ceased in the Euphrates Valley by the end of the fifth millennium Cal. BC. Regardless of the likelihood of a break in the sequence between phases E and F in the 'Amuq, this still requires us to either raise the date for the disappearance of Ubaid pottery in west Syria, which would require major adjustments to the current chronology, or accept that 'Ubaid-related' painted ceramics remained in production there for many centuries after they had been superseded further north.

On the basis of the evidence from Tell Afis, Mazzoni (1998: 18; 2000: 100) favours the second explanation. However, its acceptance has significant implications for other aspects of our interpretation of the evidence from western Syria.

1. We need to be more cautious regarding our use of the term 'Ubaid' with respect to the painted pottery traditions of west Syria (see also Thuesen 1990: 435-6; below).

2. The continued use of painted pottery well into the fourth millennium Cal. BC in western Syria, should alert us to the fact that painted and chaff-tempered ceramics do not always indicate distinct successive chronological units — a point of great importance for the interpretation of survey data.

3. If we are continue to place faith in pottery as a means by which to construct reliable interregional synchronisms, we will need to be far more rigorous in our definitions of ceramic styles and/or wares than has been the practice to date. The continued application of terms coined long ago to the present rich and complex dataset, may have resulted in a significant degradation of its information potential (Campbell 2000: 55-6; Philip and Baird 2000: 3-4).

The existence of real differences between patterns of ceramic development at fourth millennium BC communities (Lupton 1996: 37; Frangipane 2000: 441; Mazzoni 2000: 98) undermines the view that in the various regions producing 'chaff-faced' pottery there existed 'a surprising degree of material culture homogeneity — over an exceedingly broad area' (Algaze 1993: 92). Such diversity might lead us to ask whether divergences in ceramic production might not suggest that the northern Levant differed from areas to the north and east in other

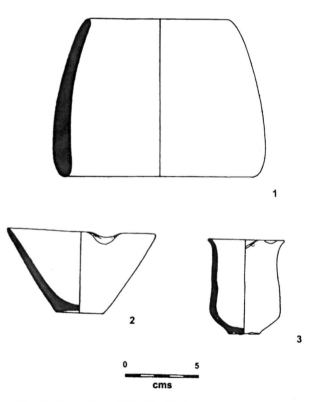

Fig. 2. Examples of Middle Uruk ceramic forms from El-Kowm also documented at Tell Sheikh Hassan (see Table 2 for details).

aspects of its social, economic and political structure. It is in this direction that we must go if we are to attempt to explain the limited evidence for an 'Uruk' impact on the former region. The first step however, is to review the evidence for 'Uruk' contact with the west.

3. THE ARCHAEOLOGICAL EVIDENCE FROM THE LEVANT IN THE FOURTH MILLENNIUM

THE SYRIAN STEPPE ZONE

The recent publication of ceramics and radiocarbon dates from Tell Sheikh Hassan on the middle Euphrates (Boese 1995; Bachmann 1998) has clarified the chronological position and cultural relationships of the assemblage from El-Kowm 2 - Caracol located in the Syrian steppe some 100 km northeast of Palmyra. Many ceramic forms (see Table 2, Figure 2) and a stone eye idol from this site (Cauvin and Stordeur 1985: 205, fig. 8. 1) have clear parallels with material from Middle Uruk contexts in the Euphrates Valley (Boese 1995: 74, abb. 11a).

The absence at El-Kowm of particular forms characteristic of the earlier part of the Middle Uruk at Tell Sheikh Hassan, and the presence of goblets which are restricted to the late Middle Uruk at the latter site (Table 2, Figure 2.3), would place the El-Kowm material in the late Middle Uruk, i.e. around the 34th century Cal. BC. This is in broad agreement with the excavators' assignation of the occupation to 'une phase evoluée mais non finale de la culture d'Uruk' (Cauvin and Stordeur 1985: 195).

Discussion

However, the El-Kowm assemblage does not constitute a simple extension of the Mesopotamian ceramic province into the steppe; it also includes forms less well documented in south Mesopotamia such as small globular jars with everted rim and conical pot stands (Cauvin and Stordeur 1985: 194, figs 4.3, 4.4; Figure 2.1 here). These Boese (1995: 255, abb. 13, 14) believes to be specific to the 'Uruk' culture of north Syria.

Furthermore, the El-Kowm assemblage includes a

Vessel Form	El-Kowm (Cauvin and Stordeur 1985: 194-95)	Tell Sheikh Hassan (Boese 1995: 255)	Date in terms of Tell Sheikh Hassan sequence (Boese 1995)
Wheelmade, sharply carinated bowls, some with spout	Not reported	Abb. 2	Early Middle Uruk
Thin-walled ovoid jar with inner ledge-rim, surface bears burnished white slip	Not reported	Abb. 13	Early Middle Uruk
Bowl with thickened rim, often with white or red slip.	fig. 4.7	Abb. 12 top	Middle Uruk
Conical pot-stand	fig. 4.4; Fig. 2.1 here	Abb. 14	Middle Uruk
Conical bowls, including a form with a lip on the rim	fig. 6.2; Fig. 2.2 here	Abb. 1	Middle Uruk
Globular jar with short neck everted rim and tubular spout.	fig. 7.3	Abb. 4	Middle Uruk
Jar with single handle 'squashed' centrally in cross-section; some bear horizontal bands of fine incised decoration	fig. 6.6	Abb. 3	Middle Uruk
Jar with four horizontally pierced lugs, incised decoration and appliqué pellets on vessel shoulder	fig. 5.2	Abb. 7, 8	Middle Uruk
Goblet	fig. 4.1; Fig. 2.3 here	Boese (1995: 226 Abb.12. a-c)	Late Middle Uruk

Table 2. Presence/absence at El-Kowm of Middle Uruk ceramic forms documented at Tell Sheikh Hassan.

significant proportion of chaff-tempered vessels, including bevelled-rim bowls (BRBs) but also globular jars and conical bowls (Cauvin and Stordeur 1985: 193-95, fig. 6). The use of chaff-temper in this context however, should not automatically be equated with the chaff-tempering tradition of north Syria, as good parallels for some of these vessel forms are documented at Tell Sheikh Hassan. In the case of the conical bowls however, the examples from Tell Sheikh Hassan were made from well-fired, relatively fine, mineral-tempered fabrics containing a low proportion of organic matter (Bachmann 1998: 195, abb. 7d-7k), i.e. quite different from the coarse, friable, dark-cored fabric in which such vessels occur at El-Kowm (Cauvin and Stordeur 1985: 193). It is clear therefore that despite formal similarities, there were significant differences in the pottery used at the two sites, suggesting a degree of variability in what constituted 'Middle Uruk' within north-central Syria. Overall, however, El-Kowm appears to show far stronger connections with sites in the Middle Euphrates (Boese 1995; Geyer and Monchambert 1987) than with those of western Syria.

In contrast to the situation at El-Kowm, the pottery reported from Uruk-period steppe sites in the Wadi Ajij north of the Euphrates, is predominantly mineral-tempered (Bernbeck 1993: 46-7, table 16). Clearly, all 'Uruk' steppe assemblages were not the same. Algaze (1993: 53, 58, table 1) suggested that El-Kowm represented an 'outpost' on a route linking Mesopotamia and western Syria. However, the absence there of both permanent structures, and the administrative apparatus generally associated with Uruk 'enclaves' renders this unlikely. In fact, the predominance of tabular flint scrapers in the chipped stone assemblages from both El-Kowm and the Wadi Ajij sites (Cauvin and Stordeur 1985: 195; Bernbeck 1993: 54-5), suggests rather a common connection with animal herding, and that the former site represented the southwestern edge of a steppe-based component of Middle Uruk activity.

INLAND WEST SYRIA: CERAMIC EVIDENCE

As discussion has traditionally been couched in ceramic terms, I will deal with this first, before considering other classes of material. The fourth millennium BC pottery of west Syria is dominated by chaff-tempered bowls and jars which are generically related to wider fourth millennium chaff-tempered ceramics of southeast Anatolia and north Mesopotamia (Algaze 1993: 86-91; Frangipane 1993: 155; Lupton 1996: 19). In the north, this development is generally seen as reflecting the replacement of Ubaid painted traditions by undecorated, mass produced, chaff-tempered pottery, a shift involving a reorganization of ceramic production, and consistent with the increasingly complex nature of the societies concerned (Akkermans 1988: 127; Trufelli 1994: 247; Frangipane this volume, p. 125). In Syria east of the Euphrates just such a change is evident in LC 1-2 (c. late fifth-early fourth millennium Cal. BC), which witnesses the appear-

ance of 'Coba bowls'. These are succeeded in LC 3 by Chaff-faced simple ware (Schwartz 1998). The crucial question is whether a similar process can be documented at contemporary sites west of the Euphrates.

The 'Amuq

The 'Amuq sequence is clearly problematic in that Phase F, as represented at the key JK sequence of Tell al-Judeideh, consists of but two floors (Braidwood and Braidwood 1960: 226-27), and can encompass only a very brief part of the fourth millennium BC. Moreover, as this was not directly stratified over Phase E remains, there may well exist a gap between Phases E and F as published (Mazzoni 1998: 22). Therefore, in the absence of radiocarbon dates, the exact chronological position of the initial Phase F deposits within the fourth millennium BC remains uncertain.

The following points appear important to obtaining a general understanding of the 'Amuq in the fourth millennium BC.

1. The earliest Phase F floor, JK22 produced very little grit tempered pottery, although this reached 13-18 % in the subsequent floor 21 (Braidwood and Braidwood 1960: 228, 264, table III).

2. The ceramic assemblage from Floor 21 was similar to those from Floors 20-18, which were assigned to Phase G by the excavators. However, the latter saw a substantial increase in the relative proportion of mineral tempered pottery (Braidwood and Braidwood 1960: 264). The apparent continuity between these deposits has led both Tadmor (1964: 257-58) and Algaze (1993:92) to class the first few Phase G floors as late Chalcolithic. Other material from Phase G however, shows clear links with EBA I as known at Hassek Höyük (Gerber 2000: 208), and clearly dates to the early third millennium BC.

3. Recent work at Tell al-Judeideh has provided two radiocarbon dates (Table 3). These come from deposits sealing a destruction which produced material estimated by the excavators to be transitional between 'Amuq F and G (Yener *et al.* 1996: 70). These dates provide a *terminus ante quem* for the 'Amuq F/G transition, some time around the end of the fourth millennium BC (Table 3). The implication would appear to be that most of JK 21-18 ought to fall late in the fourth millennium Cal. BC.

4. Physical evidence for 'Uruk' contact with the 'Amuq is sparse. The few published BRBs assigned to 'Amuq F contexts actually came from Çatal Höyük W16 floor 6 (Braidwood and Braidwood 1960: 234 n.10, figs. 174.17, 175.1) which was noted as a contaminated deposit (Braidwood and Braidwood 1960: 4-5). The only example from the JK sounding at Tell al-Judeideh came from Floor 20, as did the small number of other Uruk shape-parallels, such as fragments of droop spout bottles. On the evidence above these should be placed late in the fourth millennium Cal. BC. Hemispherical bowls bearing reserved slip spiral decoration on the interior are reported in 'Amuq F deposits (Braidwood and Braidwood 1960: 232, fig. 173. 12-14),

and should also fall within the same chronological horizon.

In summary, the ceramic evidence for 'Uruk' connections with the 'Amuq is both limited in quantity and appears consistent with LC 5 in the SAR scheme (see Table 1), indicating a relatively late fourth millennium BC date. There is presently no evidence upon which to see the 'Amuq as involved in Middle Uruk activity.

Tell Afis
The situation in the 'Amuq is broadly confirmed by the recently published fourth millennium BC sequence from Tell Afis from which no diagnostic Uruk material has been reported, despite the presence of BRB fragments in secondary contexts at nearby Tell Mardikh (Mazzoni 2000: 100). Although limited in area, the Tell Afis sounding spanned 7 stratigraphic phases (18-26), of which three produced clear architecture (Mazzoni 1998; Gianessi 1998: 102). 'Coba bowls' are frequent throughout the Tell Afis Late Chalcolithic (Mazzoni 1998: 17) which has also produced a variety of what Mazzoni terms 'Late Ubaid Painted wares' (1998: 11-12). Both of these are absent from the Phase F deposits at Tell al-Judeideh, a fact which has led Mazzoni (2000: 99) to place the Afis assemblage between 'Amuq E and F in chronological terms. While the absence of BRBs might therefore be attributed to chronological factors, the presence of reserved slip ware in phase 20 and of RBBW from phase 20 onwards (Mazzoni 1998: 20-21, figs 11.7, 9.9) suggests that later occupation is certainly present at Tell Afis.[4] The difficulty is that without radiocarbon dates we cannot be sure whether the contrasts between the ceramic data from the 'Amuq and Tell Afis represent chronological, regional or even functional differences — both soundings were of limited dimensions. However, the presence of at least some later fourth millennium occupation is indicated at Tell Afis suggesting that the lack of Uruk material is not entirely attributable to temporal factors.

Tell Nebi Mend
The evidence from Tell Nebi Mend (TNM) is of particular importance because the site's carefully excavated fourth and third millennium BC sequence may span as much as 1000 years (Mathias and Parr 1989; Mathias in press). However, the material described below, although termed 'Early Bronze Age' by the excavators (Mathias and Parr 1989; Mathias 2000: 411), begins some way before 3000 BC.

The 'EBA' sequence from TNM comprises four successive ceramic phases, the latest of which, Phase 4, can be equated with EBA IVA, and thus provides a *terminus ante quem* of c. 2500 BC for the three previous phases. Three radiocarbon dates come from contexts deemed stratigraphically early within ceramic Phase 2 (Table 3). While the standard deviations of two of the dates are rather wide, both appear compatible with the narrower range provided by the third date. Taken together the dates suggest that the occupation of Phase 2 falls within the last few centuries of the fourth millennium Cal. BC, providing a *terminus ante quem* for Phase 1, which might accordingly be placed no later than the third quarter of the fourth millennium Cal. BC.

Table 3. Radiocarbon dates from Tell al-Judeideh, and Tell Nebi Mend 'Early Bronze Age' Phase 2 (Yener et al 1996: 68-69; Mathias 2000: 413). Calibration after OxCal v2.18 (Stuiver M. and R.S. Kra eds. 1986).

Site	Lab. No	Date BP	Calibrated 2 s.d.
Tell al-Judeideh	Beta 88281	4270±70BP	3100BC (0.63) 2850BC 2820BC (0.35) 2660BC 2640BC (0.02) 2620BC
Tell al-Judeideh	Beta 88280	4390±50BP	3310BC (0.11) 3230BC 3180BC (0.02) 3160BC 3140BC (0.87) 2910BC
Tell al-Judeideh	Beta 88280	4400±50BP	3310BC (0.14) 3230BC 3180BC (0.02) 3160BC 3140BC (0.84) 2910BC
TNM	BM 2934	4460±45BP	3340BC (0.91) 3020BC 2990BC (0.09) 2930BC
TNM	BM 2036R	4440±160BP	3650BC (1.00) 2600BC
TNM	BM 2039R	4400±130BP	3500BC (1.00) 2650BC

The ceramic evidence from TNM is of considerable significance for the interpretation of the less well controlled sequence from Hama. Ubaid-related material has not been reported from the site, and the fourth millennium BC occupation was terraced into earlier Ceramic Neolithic remains, suggesting that TNM EBA Phase 1 (Table 4) provides a *terminus ante quem* for the disappearance of Ubaid-related painted pottery from the upper Orontes Valley. According to Mathias (2000: 419), two fabrics are represented in Phase 1 (Table 4). Fabric C occurs in bowl and jar shapes which are comparable to examples from both the smooth and chaff-faced simple wares of 'Amuq F, and which have more specific parallels in shape IIIA from Hama. The fabric A vessels are broadly comparable to 'Amuq F cooking pots (e.g. Braidwood and Braidwood 1960: fig. 175: 3-4), and in particular to shape VA from phase K at Hama (see Thuesen 1988: fig. 59). Only with Phase 2, i.e. late in the fourth millennium Cal. BC, does wheel-made pottery appear at TNM (Table 4), and then only as an addition to the existing fabrics A and C. Neither of the wheel-made wares provide shapes which are readily comparable to the published forms from Phase G in the 'Amuq, although closer parallels are documented at Hama (Mathias 2000: 425-6), suggesting a degree of regionalism within the upper Orontes Valley. Phase 3 sees the appearance of hard-fired sherds with pattern combing typical of Ras Shamra and Tell Sukas Phases L2 and L1 (Mathias 2000: 423) and large shallow bowls with inturned rim which resemble the platter forms of coastal EBA II/III suggesting a date in the first half of the third millennium BC.

The evidence from TNM clarifies several important points.

1. There is no evidence for the presence of Uruk-related material at the site.

2. The Phase 1 pottery from TNM appears to represent a local variant of the chaff-tempered tradition. Evidence for the use of the fast wheel appears only with Phase 2, i.e. in the last quarter of the fourth millennium BC, and its use appears to be restricted to specific fabrics. The adoption of the wheel at TNM thus appears to lag several centuries behind developments at sites such as Arslantepe where wheel-made ceramics are documented in level VII contexts (Trufelli 1994, 1997; Frangipane this volume, p. 125), and at Hacinebi where wheel-production is documented as early as Phase A, i.e. the beginning of the fourth millennium BC (Stein *et al.* 1998: 165-66).

3. TNM reveals no equivalent to the Painted Simple Ware which is documented right through the sequence at Tell Afis. While this might be explained by regional factors, the sharpness of the contrast does reinforce Mazzoni's (1998: 18) concerns regarding the extent of residuality in the pottery from the Afis sounding. This point has obvious implications for the apparent frequency of other types such as Coba bowls at the latter site. Painted pottery appears to have disappeared from the Homs area by at latest the third quarter of the fourth millennium Cal. BC.

4. The absence during Phases 1 and 2 of red-slipped and burnished finishes, high-necked jugs, ledge and strap handles and holemouth jar forms suggests that during the fourth millennium BC, the Orontes Valley remained isolated from the traditions of both the coastal and the southern Levant.

Overall, the fourth millennium ceramics from TNM are best interpreted as an essentially domestic assemblage

Table 4. Summary of Early Bronze Age ceramics from Phases 1 and 2 at Tell Nebi Mend (after Mathias 2000).

Fabric	Forms	First appearance
Fabric A hand-made, dark-red heavily grit tempered, unslipped.	Globular and sub-globular jars with short everted rims.	Phase 1 (Mathias and Parr 1989: fig 7. 1-7, 9).
Fabric C hand-made, soft, low fired orange-buff, often with a grey core. Temper: shell, quartz grain and some organic material, latter appears burnt out on the surface. Traces of a fugitive red slip in some cases.	Thick walled bowls, including both deep and shallow, platter-like forms, frequently with slight carination.	Phase 1 (Mathias and Parr 1989: fig 7. 8, 10-15).
Fabric B wheel-made showing often rilling outside buff-light red to white, bears white slip or wash, mineral tempered with fine vegetable matter	Medium-sized round-based globular or ovoid jars with round base, short neck and rolled-over rim.	Phase 2 (Mathias and Parr 1989: fig 11. 60-67).
Fabric E wheel-made, fine clay with few inclusions. Vessels show vertical burnish on a cream-buff slip	Small jars with flaring necks and rolled or beaded rim and vertical burnish strokes on exterior, and shallow bowls with round base, often with radial burnish strokes inside.	Phase 2 (Mathias and Parr 1989: fig 11. 68-81).

which utilized only a limited range of vessel forms, suggesting a fairly unsophisticated ceramic industry. Comparison with material from the 'Amuq and Arslantepe, highlights the diversity among those fourth millennium BC sites whose ceramic industries fall under the general archaeological term 'chaff-faced'.

Hama
While Phase L was essentially characterized by a local 'Ubaid-related' repertoire, the succeeding Phase K which comprised more than 4.5 m depth of deposit is generally believed to span much of the fourth and the first half of the third millennia BC (Thuesen 1988: 186, table 30).

The evidence for 'Uruk' connections consists mainly of the presence of BRBs (Thuesen 1988: 112). However, a terracotta eye-idol (Thuesen 1988: 172-73, Pl. 34.9) in Phase K contexts has been seen as evidence for Middle Uruk contact with the Orontes Valley (Helwing 2000: 150). This view can be discounted for two reasons. Firstly, eye idols have been recovered from 'pre-contact' deposits at Hacinebi (Stein *et al.* 1997: 120), indicating that they are not a specifically 'Uruk' tradition. Secondly, in a recent review of these artefacts, Breniquet (1996: 35) observes that the examples from Hama are both relatively large and made from fired clay. On that basis she assigns them to her Type 2 'large spectacle idols', which she believes represent not 'idols' at all, but artefacts used in the spinning of thread (Breniquet 1996: 51, fig. 7). The distribution of these objects is concentrated in fourth millennium BC sites in Syria and north Mesopotamia (Breniquet 1996: 43, fig.1, 48 tab. 1).

Given the problems arising from the methods of excavation and recording (Thuesen 1988: 11), and the potentially unrepresentative nature of the published ceramic data (Thuesen 1988: 109), it seems inappropriate to interpret the evidence from other sites in terms of the Hama sequence. All that can be said with safety is that Hama reveals a local variant of the chaff-tempered ceramic tradition, alongside which were found several fragments of BRBs, made in a distinctive fabric (Thuesen 1988: 112; Table 6 here). The details of the Hama ceramic sequence are not entirely clear (Thuesen 1988: 112, table 30). However, as far as can be gauged from the publication, BRBs first appeared in K8-9, and continued through to K2-3. However, the appearance of RBBW in K5-7, only one major phase later than BRBs, suggests that the former appeared at Hama late in the fourth millennium BC.

Lacking other 'Uruk' style material, and without contextual and petrographic studies, we have no way in which to assess the significance of the presence of BRBs at Hama. These may be indicative of the presence of a small non-local population at the site, as has been argued in the case of Hacinebi (Stein this volume). However, it is also possible that the BRBs were local copies of a foreign vessel style. In that case they may have been incorporated within the social practices of Hama in a way

which was quite different from the manner in which they were deployed at Uruk sites in the Euphrates Valley. We should not assume that similarity of form implies the operation of a single set of social processes in each case (Thomas 1996: 78-82).

The ceramic 'wares' from Hama as described by Thuesen (1988: 111-13) appear to include both a light buff and a darker coarse ware which appear broadly comparable with the two hand-made wares defined at TNM Phase 1, as well as finer, well fired mineral-tempered fabrics, probably used for wheel-made vessels.

Fine wares make little impact prior to K5-7, suggesting that, as at TNM, wheel-made wares appeared relatively late in the fourth millennium BC. Once again we can identify very little material held in common with the south Levant. Of particular interest is the absence from the Orontes Valley (where basalt is readily available) of any equivalent to the fine basalt bowls which are such a characteristic feature of fourth millennium sites in Palestine and Jordan (Braun 1990, Philip and Williams-Thorpe 1993, 2001).

Bowls which have undergone the removal of slip from the interior occur in Phases K5-7 (Thuesen 1988: 113).[5] The distribution of these vessels — the Orontes Valley and coastal Syria (Table 5) — does not indicate a connection with the Uruk world. Rather the form appears characteristic of late fourth millennium BC ceramic production of the northern Levant.

The situation in west Syria is that Uruk-type material appears only at a very late stage of the fourth millennium BC, is concentrated at inland sites and even then is sparsely represented (Table 6). The ceramic assemblages from the Orontes Valley appear particularly conservative and show little evidence of external influence, specialized production or technical innovation prior to the last quarter of the fourth millennium BC. There is little here to suggest that contacts between Mesopotamia and Egypt ran *via* the Tripoli-Homs gap, and hence to Byblos.

COASTAL SYRIA: CERAMIC EVIDENCE
The presence of Uruk-related material in Egypt is now generally viewed in terms of maritime contact rather than connections around Arabia (Moorey 1990; Wilkinson this volume, p. 244; Joffe 2000). However, the mechanisms through which contact between western Asia and Egypt, and more specifically between the Euphrates Valley area and the Mediterranean coast, was mediated remain unclear.

a. Cilicia can be ruled out as a likely point of contact (Steadman 1996: 152-55).

b. There is little evidence for a significant 'Uruk' impact on inland west Syria, yet this would seem to be a prerequisite for the involvement of Byblos (see above, below).

c. The Nile Valley apart, no clearly Mesopotamian-type material has been reported from locations south of Hama (see below and Table 6).

By default then, we are directed towards the northern section of the coast of modern Syria — in particular the region around Ras Shamra.

Ras Shamra
The excavator of Ras Shamra (RS) (de Contenson 1979; 1982; 1992: 196) has argued that the site was unoccupied for the greater part of the fourth millennium BC. This view is based upon the fact that deposits producing Khirbet Kerak Ware (KKW), generally dated to the early third millennium BC (RS IIIA1), are directly superimposed upon the uppermost of a long sequence of levels characterized by Ubaid-related painted wares (Ras Shamra IIIB). While this statement has been widely accepted in the literature (e.g. Thuesen 1988: 186, table 30; Schwartz and Weiss 1992: 187, fig. 3), de Contenson's view appears to be based upon the apparent absence at Ras Shamra of particular ceramic wares deemed characteristic of phases F and G in the 'Amuq (Curvers 1989: 174), a position which takes no account of the probable existence of a distinct local fourth millennium BC coastal assemblage. A degree of regional ceramic diversity within western Syria during the fourth millennium BC is clearly attested by the evidence from the Orontes Valley (above). Moreover, Mazzoni (1998: 23) has suggested that clear evolutionary stages of the kind which scholars seek, may be less evident at coastal sites, where fourth millennium BC ceramic assemblages reveal considerable continuity through time.

The recent publication of the key sounding from Ras Shamra (de Contenson 1992) has provided more detail on this part of the sequence, termed Ras Shamra IIIB. Ubaid-related painted wares are present throughout (de Contenson 1992: table 27) and appear to have provided the key criteria for dating (de Contenson 1992: 196), despite the fact that some of this material may be residual.[6] Some pottery from RS IIIB appears to resemble

material published from the Hama K and TNM 'Early Bronze Age' deposits, in particular two low-fired wares (de Contenson 1992: 182) with what is described as '*surface griffée*', which appear comparable to the bowls and chaff-faced wares found on inland sites (Mazzoni 2000: 99).[7] Additional support for the presence of a significant body of mid-late fourth millennium BC material within RS IIIB comes from de Contenson's (1992: 196) claim that the chipped stone assemblage is characterized by 'Canaanean' technology (see discussion of dating below). Mazzoni (1998: 23) has also observed that examples of red-slipped platters and bowls, and 'metallic' ware jars occurred in the RS IIIB sequence but were dismissed by de Contenson (1992: 182) as intrusive. However, these are broadly comparable to material which first appears at Byblos and the southern Levant, around or a little way before 3000 Cal. BC. While there is no ceramic evidence for Uruk connections with the Syrian coast in the later fourth millennium BC, it appears possible that RS was occupied during the critical period. In particular, the appearance around the end of the fourth millennium BC of a coastal ceramic assemblage, linking Ras Shamra, Byblos and the Palestinian littoral, implies an increasing level of maritime communication. Such a structure might have provided the context within which the transmission of 'Uruk' imagery and practices to Egypt was made possible (see below).

Other sites on the Syrian coast
Bowls with reserved slip decoration (called Early Reserved Slip by Ehrich 1939) occur in Layers 19-17 at Qal'at ar-Rus (Table 5). Here they are contemporary with a range of hemispherical and carinated bowl forms in so-called natural burnished and unburnished wares (Ehrich 1939: 10-13, pl. 5, figs. II, III), which include both chaff- and mineral-tempered fabrics. Yener *et al.* (1996: 70, fig. 7J) have recently drawn attention to parallels between

Site	Phase	Absolute date(*)	Reference
Tell al-Judeideh	Phase F, floor 22, debris 21	Late 4th millennium Cal. BC	Braidwood & Braidwood 1960: 230-32, fig. 173. 12-15; Trentin 1993: 103, note 17
Hama	K7-5		Thuesen 1988: 113, fig. 45, 5, 7, 9
Tell Nebi Mend	Phase 2	c. 3250-3000 Cal. BC	Mathias in press
Qal'at ar-Rus	19-17		Ehrich 1939: 6, pl. V.1, XII.1
Tell el-Fara'in/Buto	Str. IIIa-b/c	After 3250 Cal. BC	Köhler 1998: 37, fig. 68. 1-6, pl. 74, 46, table 9

Table 5. Presence of bowls with reserved slip decoration on the interior
*(*where this can be established through non-ceramic evidence)*

material from the transitional 'Amuq F/G deposits from Tell al-Judeideh discussed above, and dated to the late fourth millennium BC on radiocarbon evidence (above, Table 3), and what are termed Red Rim Pithoi at Qal'at ar-Rus (Ehrich 1939: 14-15, pl. VI, fig. IV). These were particularly concentrated in Layers 18-16 at the site (Ehrich 1939: 50). The late fourth millennium Cal. BC date for these layers suggested by the 'Amuq radiocarbon evidence appears consistent with their association with bowls bearing reserved slip decoration (Table 5).

Noteworthy is the apparent temporal overlap between both of the above ceramic forms and red-slipped and burnished material which is first documented in Layer 18 (Ehrich 1939: 50). This surface treatment was applied to hand-made vessels in both chaff and mixed tempers, and extended to jar and bowl forms, the latter including examples with a vertical rim (Ehrich 1939: 18-19, pl. 6, fig. VI); bowls with inverted rims appeared only with Layer 16 (Ehrich 1939: 18). The contemporaneity of these ceramic styles suggests that they formed the most recognizable parts of a late fourth millennium BC coastal ceramic assemblage. In particular, the red-slipped and burnished pottery detailed above was noted as quite distinct from the harder-fired, red-grey wares termed 'Stone ware' (Ehrich 1939: 27-9, pl. VIII) which first appeared in Layer 13 and which resemble the 'metallic' fabrics first securely documented in the southern Levant around 3000 BC (Greenberg and Porat 1996).

Phases M1 and L4 at Tell Sukas were broadly equated by Oldenburg (1991: 63, table 8) with Layers 19-17/16 at Qal'at ar-Rus. Phase M1 sees the appearance of red slipped and burnished pottery including bowls with slightly inverted rims (Oldenburg 1991: 19-20, fig. 15. 13). Shape parallels from early 'Amuq G contexts (Oldenburg 1991: 20) indicate that these deposits date around end of

fourth millennium BC, although the presence of a sherd with combed surface treatment (Oldenburg 1991: 22, fig. 14. 26) casts some doubt on the stratigraphic integrity of the sample. Here too we appear to see a coastal assemblage of the late fourth millennium BC, featuring red-slipped and burnished ceramics but without hard fired 'metallic' pottery. The latter which appears in classic third millennium forms — tall necked jugs and platter-bowls with inturned rims — occurs in quantity only in Phase L2, although the fabric is first documented in the preceding Phase L3 (Oldenburg 1991: 36, 59, table 1).

The evidence from Tell Sukas and Qal'at ar-Rus appears to confirm Mazzoni's suggestion cited above, that the coastal ceramic assemblage characteristic of the late fourth millennium BC was the product of a gradual evolution, with clear chronological stages less readily discernible than in the 'Amuq (Mazzoni 1998: 22). It thus supports the idea that the late fourth millennium BC 'gap' at Ras Shamra may be in part methodological, and that the key site of Ras Shamra should not be ruled out as a potential point of contact between the 'Uruk' world and the communities of the Levantine littoral. That said, however, it remains the case that no coastal sites have, to date, provided clear ceramic evidence for 'Uruk' connections. At this stage we need to look beyond ceramics to consider other aspects of the data.

THE NORTH LEVANT: NON-CERAMIC EVIDENCE
Glyptic
Despite evidence for their use in Middle Uruk contexts in both the Euphrates Valley and in northeastern Syria (Boese 1995: 95-6, 104 fig. 8; Oates and Oates 1997: 291), cylinder seals are not documented in the 'Amuq before Phase G (Braidwood and Braidwood 1960: 331-3, fig. 254. 1-5). In the case of the examples from Hama,

Site	Earliest BRBs from sites in the Levant (see text for references)
'Amuq	Phase G or F/G transition
Tell Mardikh	Secondary contexts only
Hama	Phase K8-9
Tell Afis	Not reported
Tell Nebi Mend	Not reported
Ras Shamra	Not reported
Tell Sukas/Qal'at ar-Rus	Not reported
Byblos	Not reported
Southern Levant	Not reported

Table 6. Presence/absence of bevelled-rim bowls at key sites in the Levant

both stylistic comparanda (Matthews 1997: 70-1) and the presence of KKW in associated deposits, support a third millennium BC date for their appearance. At present then, there is little in the glyptic evidence from western Syria to indicate significant contact with the economic practices of the Uruk world prior to the end of the fourth millennium BC.

On the other hand, the presence of gable-shaped seals bearing zoomorphic decoration in Phases F through H in the 'Amuq, and in Hama K9-8 (Braidwood and Braidwood 1960: 253-4, 256, fig. 191. 331, 337, fig. 253. 8-9, 11-12, 388, fig. 297. 4; Thuesen 1988: 177, pl. 36. 17) provides evidence for the participation of these sites in a Syro-Anatolian glyptic tradition quite distinct from that of Mesopotamia (Mazzoni 1980; 1992). This point is reinforced by the presence of a gable seal at Tell Mardikh (Mazzoni 1980: 55, fig. 14, 15), albeit out of context.

Glyptic evidence may also bear on the dating of the RS IIIB occupation. While the three of the four fourth-third millennium cylinder seals from Ras Shamra appear on stylistic grounds to date some way into the third millennium (Amiet 1992: 10; Matthews 1997: 98), the fourth (RS 7.011), which depicts a procession of horned animals arranged tête-bêche, was believed by Amiet (1992: 10, Cat. No. 1, fig. 2.1), to be an actual import dating to the Uruk period. This view is supported by Matthews (1997: 59) who places the seal within his 'Aleppo series: Uruk period' and assigns it to a group described as 'seals whose designs are indistinguishable from the Late Uruk glyptic of Habuba Kabira and Jebel Aruda', arguing that 'it is unlikely that such perfect stylistic conformity could have survived for long after the end of the Uruk system'. While its context is not secure (Mazzoni 2000: 103), the very presence of such a seal on the coast should remind us that the degree of inter-community connections should not be reckoned on ceramic grounds alone.[8]

The paucity of fourth millennium BC glyptic evidence from western Syria indicates that Uruk-period bureaucratic practices, to which cylinder seals were central (Nissen this volume, p. 11-12), had made little impact on the Levant. Moreover, the third millennium BC Levantine practice of using seals to mark the shoulders of jars, has been suggested by Mazzoni (1984: 19, 1992) to derive from an indigenous tradition documented at Byblos Enéolithique, rather than from that of Mesopotamia. Thus, the eventual adoption of cylinder seals in the Levant would appear to represent the adaptation of new technical possibilities within the framework of traditional practices (Mazzoni 1992: 98). In Mazzoni's opinion (1984; 1992), the glyptic traditions of northwest Syria and Cilicia shared many features, and were closely linked to the mobilization of local agricultural products, and thus to traditional systems of economic management. In contrast, developments in the Euphrates Valley and northeastern Syria were more clearly linked to Mesopotamian traditions (Mazzoni 1992: 129).

Chipped Stone
The appearance of 'Canaanean' blade technology is of particular interest, as blades of this form are documented in Phase A (early fourth millennium Cal. BC) contexts at Hacinebi (Stein *et al.* 1998: 155) but, on present evidence, appear no earlier than c. 3600 Cal. BC in the southern Levant (Rosen 1997: 140-41). They are characteristic of the Late Chalcolithic sequence at Tell Afis (Mazzoni 1998: 25-6), Tell al-Judeideh Phase F (Braidwood and Braidwood 1960: 247), Phase K at Hama (Thuesen 1988: 145-6), and according to de Contenson (1992: 196) of period IIIB at Ras Shamra. The latter deposits are therefore unlikely to be earlier than c. 38-3700 Cal. BC. The important point here is that as in the case of glyptic, we can detect common technical features linking inland Syria, the Levantine littoral and Anatolia, but preceding evidence for an Uruk presence in the Euphrates Valley.

BYBLOS AND THE SOUTHERN LEVANT
Byblos
The occupation of Byblos contemporary with the Uruk expansion is mainly that termed Byblos II or the Enéolithique récent which was dated by the excavator (Dunand 1973: 213) to c. 3700-3200 BC. However, Dunand's dates were established without reference to radiocarbon evidence, and should be viewed as no more than estimates. The terminal date of 3200 BC was derived from parallels between pottery from the beginning of the Early Bronze Age at Byblos (Saghieh's [1983], Phase KI) and Levantine ceramic finds from 1st Dynasty Egyptian tombs (Dunand 1973: 216). According to Saghieh (1983: 105, 108) the best Palestinian parallels for this material fall within Kenyon's EBA I period, equivalent to the beginning of EBA II as understood by most scholars today (Esse 1984).[9] On the basis of the current Egyptian and Palestinian chronology Phase KI should begin around 3050-3000 Cal. BC (Wilkinson 1999; Fischer 2000: 228; Joffe 1993:30, fig. 5) which suggests that the Enéolithique récent did not extend much after 3100 BC. Ultimately the effective limits on the use of the Byblos data are set by problems arising from methods of excavation and recording, and the incomplete state of publication.[10]

Despite its largely local character, sufficient parallels can be drawn between the architectural and ceramic evidence from Byblos Enéolithique récent and Early Bronze Age I Palestine (Miroschedji 1971: 96-7, fig. 25. 1-13; Prag 1986: 63; Ben Tor 1989: 46-50) to indicate that the period spans much of the second half of the fourth millennium Cal. BC. However, other ceramic forms are more obviously related to those of Chalcolithic Palestine,[11] suggesting that the period encompasses part of the earlier fourth millennium and begins prior to 3600 Cal. BC (Table 1). Also present are a number of flat-based, straight-sided bowls, some with a red painted band around the rim (Dunand 1973: fig. 151); one of these appears to show evidence of wheel-production (Dunand 1973: pl. CXLIX. 23114). These appear to be related to the v-shaped bowls familiar from the later stages of the Palestinian Chalcolithic (see below). A violin-shaped stone figurine (Dunand 1973: pl. CLXII. 34966) also has good parallels in Chalcolithic Palestine (e.g. Alon and Levy 1989: 185-9, table 6, fig. 7). Clearly, Dunand's Enéolithique récent overlaps both the later Chalcolithic and the EBA I of Palestine and must therefore span a large part of the fourth millennium Cal. BC. However, the ceramic connections of Byblos Enéolithique are predominantly with the south, and there is little evidence for close parallels with fourth millennium sites in the Orontes Valley or the Syrian littoral.

While the very different material culture of EBA Byblos has been held to be intrusive (Dunand 1945: 59; Saghieh 1983: 88), its point of origin is by no means clear. In fact, the continuity in glyptic practices observed by Mazzoni (1992), and the existence of local stratigraphic breaks at a number of key excavation areas (Saghieh 1983: 88) suggest that the population change may be more apparent than real. Rather, the widespread appearance of new styles of red-slipped and burnished pottery along the east Mediterranean littoral beginning in the late fourth millennium BC appears to confirm the growing integration of communities in the region. It is likely that the observed differences in material culture between the Enéolithique and Early Bronze Age periods at Byblos are related to this process, and thus to changes to social and economic organization at the site around the end of the fourth millennium BC.

Contacts between Egypt, Byblos and the Levant

As the evidence for Mesopotamian influence upon late Predynastic Egypt is clear (Wilkinson this volume), and that for contact between the northern Levant and Egypt is limited, one might wonder whether Byblos, which had well documented connections with Dynastic Egypt, might have fulfilled the role of intermediary. However, the lack of ceramic evidence for connections between Byblos and Syria argues against this. Moreover, despite the well-documented contacts between Byblos and Egypt during the third millennium BC, there is less evidence for significant connections during the fourth millennium BC. Prag's (1986: 66-72) suggestion that a number of the portable objects from Enéolithique récent graves at Byblos were of Egyptian origin is open to dispute (e.g. Saghieh 1983: 104-05; Ward 1991: 13, note 2), while her argument that the silver found at Byblos was of Egyptian origin has now been rejected (Köhlmeyer 1994: 43; Rehren *et al.* 1996: 6-7), as has the notion of a significant fourth millennium BC trade in timber with Egypt (Ben Tor 1991: 4).

Saghieh (1983: 105, and note 45) observes that in addition to the absence of Early Dynastic material from Byblos, there is/are;

a. A number of ceramic forms which occur in both Egypt and Palestine but which are absent from Byblos,

b. Little in the way of pottery that is particularly characteristic of Byblos and which is also common in late fourth millennium BC Egypt,

In fact, on current evidence the sheer scale of Egyptian involvement in southern Palestine during the later part of the fourth millennium BC (van den Brink [ed.] 1992; Harrison 1993; Levy *et al.* 1995; 1997) suggests that connections with Byblos would have been of marginal significance by comparison. There is therefore no evidence upon which to assign Byblos a significant role in the transmission of 'Uruk' traits to Egypt. The presence of occasional items of Egyptian origin at Byblos is best seen in the context of generic coastal contacts, linking, perhaps indirectly, areas from the Nile Delta to Syria. In fact, when material other than pottery is considered, it is clear that while there is good evidence to indicate the existence of such coastal contacts during the fourth millennium Cal. BC, there is no particular reason to see these as in any way related to the 'Uruk' world.

Silver

Byblos has produced a significant number of silver objects, mostly from tombs dating to the later fourth millennium BC (Prag 1978: 36). A number of contemporary silver objects are also known from the southern Levant and Egypt (Philip and Rehren 1996; Rehren *et al.* 1996). It has recently been argued (Rehren *et al.* 1996) that the presence of gold in the silver from both Tell esh-Shuna and in artefacts from Predynastic Egypt (Gale and Stos-Gale 1981: 113) suggests either common recycling practices in both areas, or access to the same metal 'stock', through the transport and exchange of recycled metal. Such a development would appear consistent with the existence of a complex inter-regional procurement system in the east Mediterranean. It would be valuable in this light to examine a sample of silver artefacts from Byblos in order to ascertain whether they too contained gold. Whatever the case, the silver itself was almost certainly acquired in the first instance from sources in the north, where silver processing is documented in fourth millennium BC contexts at Habuba Kabira (Pernicka *et al.* 1998) and late Chalcolithic Arslantepe (unpublished data cited by Hess *et al.* 1998: 65).

Copper

The presence at Byblos of a number of copper objects provides a second strand of evidence for contacts with the north. In the absence of analytical data it is not possible to rule out the use at Byblos of copper from sources in the southern Levant, although this would seem unlikely. However, copper containing around 2 wt% arsenic and nickel, thus quite distinct from the low-impurity metal typical of the Faynan ores of southern Jordan (cf. Hauptmann *et al.* 1992; 21-2, table 6; Hauptmann *et al.* 1999: 9-10, table 3), was used at the late fourth millennium Cal. BC site of Tell esh-Shuna in the north Jordan Valley (Rehren *et al.* 1997). Copper of similar composition is documented at sites like Hassek Höyük and Arslantepe in the fourth millennium BC (Schmitt-Strecker *et al.* 1992: 111, fig. 3; Palmieri *et al.* 1993) where it appears to indicate the smelting of polymetallic ores of Anatolian origin. Thus a northern origin for the copper from Tell esh-Shuna appears likely (Rehren *et al.* 1998). The use of copper derived from complex Anatolian ores is documented in Chalcolithic Palestine (Tadmor *et al.* 1995), demonstrating that the supply of metal from northern sources to the southern Levant was established well before the Uruk impact upon Syria. Taken together then, the evidence for the distribution of copper and silver argues for the existence of long-established, if low volume, supply networks which made raw materials originating in Anatolia available to fourth millennium BC communities in the coastal and southern Levant. There is, at present, no particular reason to see this as directly connected with the 'Uruk' world.

However, the repertory of Levant-wide connections extends beyond that of raw material acquisition, to encompass aspects of shared technology such as prismatic blades, wheel-made bowls and glyptic traditions.

Chipped Stone
While traditionally understood as a distinctive element of the EBA of the southern Levant (Rosen 1997: 60), it is now clear that the prismatic flint blades often termed 'Canaanean' belong to a wider technological tradition documented in fourth millennium BC contexts throughout north Syria and north Mesopotamia (Oates this volume, p. 115). Examples observed in 'pre-contact' contexts at Hacinebi Tepe date to the early fourth millennium Cal. BC (Stein *et al.* 1998: 155-56), clearly preceding their appearance in the southern Levant where they are first securely documented in deposits dating to the beginning of EBA I at Tell esh-Shuna (Baird pers. comm.).[12] As in the case of the metals, the presence of Canaanean blades in early fourth millennium BC contexts in southeast Anatolia, argues against either the development or the spread of this technology having any particular link to the Uruk world. Rather, the wide adoption of prismatic blade technology should be viewed in terms of a widespread positive response to a technological innovation which offered worthwhile efficiency gains within a key element of the subsistence economy.

Wheel-made ceramics
Another technological innovation reported from both Anatolia and the Levant, well in advance of Uruk connections is the potter's wheel. At Arslantepe conical bowls with string-cut bases are first documented during Phase VII, where they appear alongside flint-scraped bowls (Trufelli 1997: 16, fig. 7.2). These were produced in a fairly coarse chaff-tempered ware (Trufelli 1994: 263, 272). The presence of large numbers of mass pro-

duced bowls in a Phase VII monumental building, in association with numerous clay sealings, suggests that these were involved in administrative activities, perhaps related to the distribution of food (Frangipane 1997: 66, 2000: 442-43). The potter's wheel is also documented at Hacinebi from the early fourth millennium Cal. BC onwards, where it was employed in the production of a range of small, fine-ware bowls (Stein *et al.* 1998: 165-66, fig. 17).

Further south, Chalcolithic sites in the Wadi Beersheba and the Jordan Valley dated c. 4000 Cal. BC (Commenge-Pellerin 1987, 1990; Roux and Courty 1997: 26) have produced evidence for the presence of wheel-made, v-shaped bowls. Many examples from the Jordan Valley were made from Negev clays suggesting that production was to some extent specialised and concentrated in the former area (Roux and Courty 1997: 34-5, table 1). It is possible that the adoption of this technique in both Anatolia and the southern Levant may be connected as bowls with string-cut bases have been reported from what appear to be very early EBA I contexts at Afridar in coastal Palestine (Braun 2000: 122), and also from Byblos Enéolithique récent (Dunand 1973: Pl. CXLIX.23114). The observation by Roux and Courty (1997: 26) that macroscopic evidence for wheel production is often obscured by the finishing of the vessel, and that string-cut bases are actually very rare, even among wheel-made bowls from Tell Abu Hamid (Roux and Courty 1997: 39), suggests that the use of the fast wheel may have been rather more common in the southern and coastal Levant than has been recognized hitherto. Thus while production *may* have been concentrated in the Negev, it seems more likely that, as with prismatic blade technology, fast wheel technology was adopted at a number of locations along the Levantine littoral during the fourth millennium BC. Thus fast wheel technology joins prismatic blades, copper and silver as evidence for a consistent pattern of long range contacts between the Levant and southeast Anatolia during the fourth millennium Cal. BC.

The evidence from both the northern and southern sites suggests that in its early stages wheel production was particularly associated with bowls. The highly specific skills required suggest that this represented a specialist craft activity (Roux and Courty 1997: 33). While at Arslantepe mass produced bowls may have been bound up with aspects of the local political economy — food distribution systems in particular — (Frangipane 2000: 443), there are no such indications from sites in the south, where bowls occur in domestic, mortuary and cultic contexts (Roux and Courty 1997: 40). Thus the evidence suggests that while the technology was held in common, it was employed in a manner consistent with specific local social and economic organization.

Against this background the lack of evidence for the use of the potter's wheel in Phase L at Hama or at Tell Nebi Mend prior to the last quarter of the fourth millennium (Thuesen 1988: 54; Mathias 2000: 419) is striking.

It might be concluded on this basis that, until the late fourth millennium BC at least, the upper Orontes Valley remained somewhat peripheral to inter-regional networks focused upon southeast Anatolia and the east Mediterranean coast.

THE NILE DELTA

At this point it is worth reviewing briefly the evidence for northern connections from the site of Tell el-Fara'in / Buto during the fourth millennium BC, as this site has played an important part in recent, and often controversial, discussions of contacts between Egypt and Mesopotamia (von der Way 1993: 67-75; 1997). Contacts between the Nile Delta and southern Palestine during the later fourth millennium BC are now well documented (van den Brink [ed.] 1992; Harrison 1993; Levy *et al.* 1995; Levy *et al.* 1997). Moreover, evidence for contact during the earlier part of the fourth millennium BC includes the presence of locally produced v-shaped ceramic bowls in Buto Stratum I (Faltings and Köhler 1996: 104-106, Abb. 7), a fragment of a basalt vessel of a form common in Chalcolithic Palestine (von der Way 1997: 109, Taf 50.1, 110, note 623) and the recovery at various sites in the Delta of tabular scrapers imported from the southern Levant (Schmidt 1992; 1993). These long-established contacts provide the background against which connections between Buto and the northern Levant in Stratum III should be understood.[13]

In Stratum III the only material which appears to be of Syrian origin is thirteen sherds in a distinctive fabric, which accord with the shape and style of decoration typical of bowls with reserved slip decoration found in late fourth millennium BC contexts in western Syria (Table 5 here, Köhler 1998 Taf. 68. 1-6; colour pl. 74). All examples come from deposits equated with Buto III a-b/c, that is Naqada IId2/IIIa1 (Köhler 1998: 46, table 9), and should, according to Wilkinson (this volume, p. 242), be dated no earlier than 3250 Cal. BC. This date accords well with that indicated by the evidence from Syria (Table 5).

These bowls are documented at a number of sites in west Syria (see above; Trentin 1993: 182-3), many of which have produced little evidence for 'Uruk' contacts, and so should be considered as a west Syrian form. Moreover, given recent scholarly caution regarding the initial identification of a number of objects from the site as Uruk-style clay cones or nails used in architectural decoration (Teitge 1997: 233; Wilkinson 1998a, 1998b), the evidence does not now appear to indicate specific and strong 'Uruk' connections with the Delta. As Wilkinson (this volume, p. 242) has made clear, material with Mesopotamian ideological connections, such as cylinder seals, is concentrated at the major centres of the Nile Valley, where the evidence indicates the development of powerful regional elites (Spencer 1993; Wilkinson 1996). The evidence from the Delta appears qualitatively quite different, and might represent simply its participation in

developing coastal networks towards the end of the fourth millennium BC. This suggestion is reinforced by the heavy bias towards connections with the southern, rather than the northern Levant, documented at Buto.[14]

JAWA AND THE STEPPE

The argument so far has emphasized interaction among communities along the Mediterranean coast. However, it is also appropriate to consider Helms' (1984; 1987), observations concerning the potential evidence for contacts with the Uruk world noted at the EBA site of Jawa, located in the basalt harra of eastern Jordan. Such links would appear to imply contact across the arid eastern steppe presumably mediated by mobile groups (Joffe 1993: 55).

The settlement of Jawa is presented as representing a short-lived occupation (Betts [ed.] 1991: 13). The excavators have dated it to the early part of EBA I on the basis of ceramic parallels from the stratified sequence at Tell Um Hammad in the Jordan Valley (Betts [ed.] 1991: 54), that is within the period 3600-3350 Cal. BC (see Table 1). Thus Jawa would be contemporary with the Middle Uruk occupations at Tell Sheikh Hassan and El-Kowm, although little of the very distinctive Middle Uruk repertoire from these sites is readily comparable to the Jawa ceramics (see Fig. 3). Some, (Braemer 1993: 285; Philip 1995) have suggested that the Jawa assemblage is a palimpsest arising from multiple occupations over an extended period of time, a position given support from the presence at the site of twelve distinct ceramic fabrics (Betts [ed.] 1991: 106, table 4), a figure well in excess of the number present within any single phase of the large EBA I site of Tell esh-Shuna in the Jordan Valley (Rowan pers. comm.), and substantially more than are present at Chalcolithic sites in the Negev (Levy 1987; Commenge 1990).

Several types which the excavators have considered as evidence for connections with the north warrant further discussion. Jars of Genre D (Fig. 3. 1) are characterized by high indented shoulders, short neck and round base; they constitute only 1% of the assemblage (nine examples), and occur in a fabric exclusive to this group (Betts [ed.] 1991: 62, 106-08, 272, table 6, fig. 135). While there are parallels from Habuba Kabira for this style of vessel (Sürenhagen 1974/75: 84, taf. 12. 78,79), the bodies of the Jawa examples are described as coil built (Betts [ed.] 1991: 62) in contrast to those from Habuba Kabira which are wheel-made (Sürenhagen 1974/75: 84). Furthermore, examples from Habuba Kabira feature a distinctive corrugation on the outer surface in the upper two thirds of the vessel, and are often white slipped; neither feature is reported in those from Jawa. Thus the common element may amount to little more than indented shoulders, presumably indicative of a specific technique for attaching the neck to the body.

As regards dating, Trentin (1993: 182) sees this vessel form as related to a group of white-slipped jars,

221

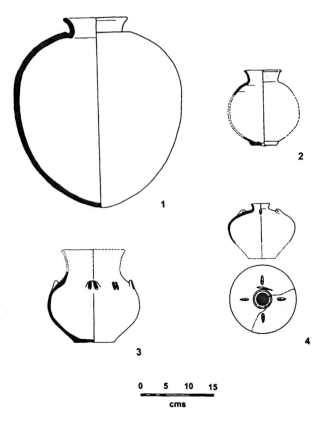

Fig. 3. Ceramic forms from Jawa believed to show northern affinities. 3.1 Genre D (after Betts [ed.] 1991 fig. 135. 329); 3.2 Genre CC (after Betts [ed.] 1991 fig. 130. 259); 3. 3 Genre BA (after Betts [ed.] 1991 fig. 122. 162); 3. 4 Genre EE (after Betts [ed.] 1991 fig. 139. 392).

generally produced in chaff-tempered fabrics and which appeared 'no later than the late fourth millennium BC', a date confirmed by examples from Hassek Höyük (Behm-Blancke 1984: 118, fig. 13.6) and Tell Nebi Mend (Mathias 2000, Fig. 23.4, no. 56). Confirmation that this material may post-date the Middle Uruk by some way is provided by parallels from Hama which span almost the entire period K occupation (Betts [ed.] 1991: 87), and various instances from early third millennium BC contexts in Syria and north Mesopotamia (McLellan and Porter 1995: fig. 10. 17-19).

Genre C jars (Fig. 3. 2), the second most common form at Jawa, have high shoulders, an everted rim, and are generally pattern burnished, often over a red slip. Larger vessels were made on a tournette, the smaller ones on a wheel. Most examples are in one of two chaff-tem-

pered fabrics, one of which is unique to the genre (fabric 09). However, chaff-tempering is atypical both of classic Uruk ceramics and those of the southern Levant. The parallels cited among the material from Habuba Kabira (Betts [ed.] 1991: 86) concern individual features such as indented shoulders (Sürenhagen 1974/75: Tab. 16: 98), or the use of a distinctive style of ring base in which the bottom of the vessel body bulges below the top of the ring (Sürenhagen 1974/75: Taf. 6. 63) rather than whole vessel forms (see also now Boese 1995: 270, fig. 13 bottom). In fact, the closest of the parallels cited by Helms (1987: 60-5, fig. 21. 3-7) for the smaller-sized Jawa Genre C vessels come from early third millennium BC contexts in northern Syria and north Mesopotamia, while ring bases appear more characteristic of 'Amuq G than of F (Braidwood and Braidwood 1960: cf. 'Amuq F p. 231 and 237, and comments on Plain Simple Ware p. 274).

Five fragments are ascribed to Genre BA, a distinctive group of jars with everted and grooved rim produced in fabric 02 (Fig. 3. 3). Two examples reveal the presence of four pushed-up lug handles with paired seal impressions, in one case on lugs and the shoulders, in the other only on shoulders in between the lugs. Suffice it to say here that these vessels find their best northern parallels in early third millennium BC contexts at sites such as Hacinebi (EBA I) and Arslantepe Phase VIB2 (Lupton 1996: 77-8, fig. 4.4E, F; Stein *et al.* 1997: 130, fig. 19D; Frangipane 2000: 449-50, fig. 13. 8, 9), while the form is characteristic of the earliest third millennium BC phases at sites in the Syrian Jezireh (Lebeau 2000: 175, table V). Much the same range of parallels could be applied to the unique example of Genre EE (Fig. 3.4) a small necked jar with horizontally pierced lugs on the shoulder (Betts [ed.] 1991: 91, fig. 139: 392). While it has good shape parallels at Habuba Kabira (e.g. Sürenhagen 1974/75: 109 taf. 18, 124), these have a red slip, which is not the case in the Jawa example.

Taken as a whole, the wide range of parallels for the Jawa pottery among 'post contact' assemblages in the north (McClellan and Porter 1995: 54-5, figs. 12), suggests that the evidence for the site's northern connections should be dated around 3000 Cal. BC rather than in the middle of the fourth millennium. Thus the Jawa data cannot be used to argue for links between the Badia and the Uruk sites of the Euphrates. If anything, the evidence might better support the idea of intermittent, cross-steppe contacts with the north over a period spanning the late fourth and earlier third millennia BC. However, the evidence appears slight in comparison to that for contact along the coast described earlier.

4. DISCUSSION

Before proceeding to wider discussion, it is worth reiterating several key points that have emerged from the reconsideration of the data, and the significance of which appears to have largely escaped comment in the literature to date.

1. There are marked regional differences in the ceramic repertories within the Levant during the fourth millennium Cal. BC. This extends not just to contrasts between northern chaff-tempered and southern Ghassulian/EBA I mineral-tempered traditions, but

includes quite significant distinctions between regions within the north itself.

2. We can see towards the end of the fourth millennium, the development of a distinctive coastal ceramic tradition, linking northern and southern parts of the littoral which had previously demonstrated quite distinct ceramic repertoires, and which differs in various respects from contemporary assemblages from inland sites.

3. At present, the ceramic evidence for Uruk connections from the area west of the Euphrates is restricted to a subset of inland sites — the 'Amuq, Tell Mardikh and Hama — and takes the form of small numbers of sherds, mostly BRBs. Moreover, the evidence indicates that these connections can be dated to the last few centuries of the fourth millennium Cal. BC, in effect LC 5. The significance of the presence of this material is not clear, but in the absence of glyptic evidence for contemporary Uruk-style administrative systems, we should not assume that it indicates the adoption of Mesopotamian organizational or social practices. It may indicate sporadic, rather than systematic contact.

4. There is presently no ceramic evidence to indicate a significant Uruk impact on communities either on the coast, or the upper reaches of the Orontes Valley.

5. In contrast however, the distribution of certain raw materials and the transmission of technological innovations provide clear evidence for the existence of regular contacts between parts of the Levant and southeast Anatolia. New radiocarbon evidence indicates that these connections go back to the early part of the fourth millennium Cal. BC, *at least*, and thus predate the impact of Middle Uruk settlements in the Euphrates Valley, and have no specific relationship to the 'Uruk' phenomenon. It is possible that these networks represent simply a continuation of earlier maritime interactions, as evidenced in particular by the circulation of obsidian (Cauvin and Chataigner 1998). In the absence of evidence for wheel-made bowls at Tell Nebi Mend in the mid-fourth millennium BC (Mathias 2000), we might speculate that communications were particularly focused upon the Levantine coast, and that the Orontes Valley was of less importance as a channel of communication at this point.

6. The site of El-Kowm-Caracol is far more closely related to Middle Uruk communities in the Euphrates Valley than to contemporary sites to the west or south, and might be viewed as representing the southwestern edge of 'Greater Mesopotamia'.

7. There is presently no evidence for direct connections between the Nile Delta and the Uruk world. Contacts were almost certainly mediated through pre-existing networks connecting communities along the Levantine littoral with each other, and with inland areas. Such a mechanism would have provided a means through which knowledge of Uruk material and ideas could have reached Egypt; the possibility of contact by sea reduces considerably the effort of long range communication (Anthony 1997: 24). However, this raises the question of why communities in much of the Levant appear to have remained impervious to 'Uruk' ideas which were, however, developed in Egypt, while simultaneously remaining responsive to innovations in other areas. In terms of the ceramic data, part of the answer is obvious. The evidence for ceramic production at fourth millennium BC sites in the Levant indicates that its manufacture was for the most part highly localized, and frequently organized at household level (Braun 1997; Baird and Philip [eds.] 2000). Given ceramic organization of this nature, the limited impact in the Levant of Uruk ceramic styles, which were generally associated with mass production, appears less surprising.

THE NATURE OF FOURTH MILLENNIUM BC COMMUNITIES

By touching upon the relationship between the transmission of specific innovations and practices, and aspects of community organization, we highlight a weakness of general contact models (e.g. Algaze 1993), which do not take adequate account of the highly contingent nature of relationships between different regions and communities. We must now consider to what extent the organizational characteristics of fourth millennium Cal. BC communities in the Levant and southeast Anatolia / north Syria were in fact comparable, and to what extent any differences which can be identified might have contributed to the differential impact of the 'Uruk' phenomenon in each case.

Societies dating to the first half of the fourth millennium Cal. BC in northern Syria and Anatolia have produced a range of evidence for complex organizational characteristics — monumental architecture, formal administrative systems for the circulation of goods and precious metals, and the mass production of ceramics (Frangipane 1993: 139; 2000; 440-43; Trufelli 1994, 1997; Lupton 1996; Oates and Oates 1997; Oates this volume, pp. 118-9; Stein *et al.* 1998;). Frangipane (1993: 159-60) has argued that these developments were facilitated by important organizational changes in the late Ubaid period, and that the Uruk impact upon the north constituted but one stage within the integrated development of the northern and southern areas of what she terms 'Greater Mesopotamia' (Frangipane 1997: 46). Both regions shared common Ubaid roots (Oates 1993), and this common history and the existence of parallel structural features, may have increased the ability of communities in the north to undergo the far-reaching organizational changes documented during the later fourth millennium BC (Frangipane 1997: 48). Thus the existence of incipient elites in the north meant that they were able to exploit the possibilities provided by increased contacts with southern societies, to broaden and consolidate their control over major aspects of the local economy.

In contrast, the Chalcolithic of the southern Levant constituted a distinct regional entity with few material indications of direct connections with the Ubaid traditions of the north (Thuesen 1988: 91). It appears to have lain outside the common developmental framework which Frangipane (1997) terms 'Greater Mesopotamia'. Although the data is limited, there are archaeological indications which support the notion of major differences between the organization of communities in Greater Mesopotamia' and the Levant[15] during the fourth millennium BC.

1. There is presently no published evidence from the Levant (Braidwood 1937; Matthers 1981; Esse 1991; Joffe 1993; Marfoe 1995) for anything equivalent to the large fourth millennium BC settlements documented in north Mesopotamia (Algaze 1993: 92-9; Wilkinson and Tucker 1995: 45; Lupton 1996: 24-5; Oates this volume). It is quite possible that comparable large sites simply did not exist in the Levant.

2. Frangipane (1997: 49) has pointed out that the extensive public buildings of Arslantepe VIA would have left only a limited area on the main mound for domestic occupation. Her observation may have significant implications for developments in the Levant where large horizontal exposures at Enéolithiqe Byblos (Dunand 1973; Ben-Tor 1989: 44) and EBA II Arad (Amiran *et al.* 1978; Amiran and Ilan 1996) have revealed not numerous public buildings, but large expanses of essentially homologous residential structures. Arslantepe and the walled EBA I and II settlements of the southern Levant, may represent quite different categories of site — elite residential and administrative centres on the one hand, and extensive agglomerations of domestic units on the other (see Philip in press).

3. While Byblos Enéolithique récent has produced several burials which appear rich by the standards of the fourth millennium BC Levant (Prag 1978), these must be seen against the excavation of more than 2000 fourth millennium BC burials in total. In fact, the evidence for 'wealth' at Byblos is in no way comparable to the conspicuous consumption witnessed in late fourth millennium BC burials at Arslantepe (Frangipane 2000: 450-51, figs 15, 16, 17.6-19), or those of late Predynastic and Early Dynastic Egypt (e.g. Spencer 1993: 50-53, 71-89). Neither have the mortuary records of Palestine or Jordan (Joffe 1993, Philip in press) produced evidence for the kind of conspicuous consumption generally associated with the existence of political elites. Thus architecture, settlement and burial all appear to indicate important organizational differences between communities in the Levant and other areas.

4. The large scale use of stamp seals within a system designed to control the distribution of commodities is well documented at Arslantepe (Frangipane 1994; Ferioli and Fiandra 1994), while Tell Brak provides evidence for the use of cylinder seals in early fourth millennium BC contexts (Oates and Oates 1997: 291). In contrast, there are no comparable data from sites in the Levant. There is evidence from Enéolithique Byblos for the application of seals to the handles of large storage jars (Dunand 1945:

25-58, pl. 2-6: 1973: 329, fig. 204), but their reuse as containers for inhumations indicates that the jars were intended for on-site storage only, and that the glyptic system functioned merely to mark commodities in storage, and not to facilitate the control and monitoring of access.

In fact, Mazzoni (1980; 1992) has suggested that the jars from Enéolithique Byblos were marked using gable-shaped seals, themselves part of a wider Syro-Cilician, pre-Uruk glyptic tradition, and which, if correct, would add yet one more strand of evidence for pre-Uruk interaction around the Levant. Following suggestions made by Joffe (in press) and Teissier (1987), Levantine glyptic in the EBA can be viewed as involving the haphazard and decontextualised employment of motifs of Mesopotamian and Iranian origin. This indicates not the adoption of a system of economic organization, but the reworking of a poorly understood concept to suit the more limited demands of the simpler system of commodity management current in the southern Levant.

To sum up, despite extensive excavations undertaken in the southern Levant, there is currently no evidence to suggest the presence there during the most of fourth millennium BC, of the kind of complex political and economic structures which existed in contemporary north Mesopotamia and southeast Anatolia. Here surely lies the key to the limited impact of Uruk developments upon the region. South Levantine communities lacked those critical elements which might have encouraged the adoption of Mesopotamian styles, symbolism, and administrative practices. In the absence of complex economies and self-aggrandizing elites, features of Uruk material culture which were intimately connected with elite lifestyles and consumption, and structures of bureaucratic control, would have been of little relevance.

We can now reconsider the nature of the strands of evidence for interaction between the coastal Levant, and Local Late Chalcolithic societies of the north. One point which stands out in the light of the discussion above, is that there was a clear concentration upon materials and techniques concerned with subsistence technology, the storage of agricultural produce and craft production. With the possible exception of silver, which appears only in very small quantities, none of these innovations concern aspects of organization which have any necessary link to elites. However, all of the above would have been of clear and obvious value to a society consisting of substantial, if largely unstratified, agricultural communities. Thus the selective adoption of particular components from a larger range of innovations, appears to confirm our earlier suggestions concerning the organizational basis of south Levantine societies in the fourth millennium Cal. BC.

THE SOUTHERN LEVANT AROUND 3000 BC
In the southern Levant the late fourth millennium BC witnessed increased settlement size, the initial appearance of public architecture, and the development of a more spe-

cialized ceramic repertory (Joffe 1993: 50-3; Philip in press). This ceramic repertoire has clear parallels at more northerly coastal sites such as Byblos and Ras Shamra, although connections with the Orontes Valley are less apparent. These developments are broadly contemporary with the settlement expansion and construction of public architecture which characterized the 'urbanization' of Byblos, and which is generally dated around the early third millennium BC (Saghieh 1983: 129-30; Joffe 1993: 58). This development, which takes place rather later than comparable processes in southeast Anatolia can be viewed as one stage in the growing participation of Byblos in wider regional networks, and which led eventually to the establishment of political relations with Egypt around the end of the 2nd Dynasty (Wilkinson 1999: 161).

Late EBA I Palestinian ceramic forms, vessels with bent spouts in particular, may ultimately have derived from Uruk forms. Examples have been reported from sites in northern Palestine (Amiran 1969: 43, photo 24, 25, 1992: 427, fig. 2.3-4; Yannai 1996: fig. 4. 7, 9-10, 12-14). Those from 'Ain el-Assawir appear to date quite close to 3000 BC, as they occur in tombs alongside what appear to be genuine northern imports of early third millennium BC types (Yannai and Grosinger 2000: 161). However, it should be borne in mind that the increasing ceramic evidence for north-south contacts along the Levant, observed towards the end of the fourth millennium Cal. BC may represent simply the first manifestation in this form of the contacts previously evidenced through the supply of raw materials and shared technologies. The sheer visibility of pottery should not lead us to overstate its actual significance as an indicator of contact. I would also suggest that the development of elements of a coastal 'koine' by c. 3000 BC would have provided the structure through which the rapid dissemination of KKW in the early third millennium BC was facilitated (Philip 1999: 50).

EGYPT

The reason for the contrast between the palpable Mesopotamian impact upon societies in the Nile Valley close to the end of the fourth millennium BC (Joffe 2000; Wilkinson this volume) and the minimal evidence for an equivalent influence on the Levant is now clear. In the Egyptian case elements of the Uruk symbolic vocabulary were adopted and reworked in a region in which elite-dominated states were in the process of emerging (Wilkinson this volume). The fact that cylinder seals were employed in 1st Dynasty Egypt as administrative devices, i.e. to seal jar stoppers and on bullae as in Mesopotamia, rather than to mark the shoulders of jars during their production as in the Levant (Joffe 2000: 116) is instructive in this regard. The evidence suggests that in Egypt a selected range of Mesopotamian practices were adopted by an indigenous elite of a kind which simply did not exist in the contemporary Levant. This may reflect the sheer scale of the ideological effort required to sup-

port the major political developments taking place in Egypt around the end of the fourth millennium BC. When understood in this light, we can also eliminate the 'problem' of the locus of contact between Egypt and the Mesopotamian world. Rather than seeking a single point of contact somewhere along the Levant coast, we need to accept that knowledge of ideas and organizational practices originating in 'Greater Mesopotamia' may have been quite widely disseminated among communities involved in east Mediterranean networks. However, these were irrelevant, and perhaps poorly understood, within most such societies. They only assumed concrete form, generally through the modification of traditional practices, in the few locations where local social or political circumstances were favourable to their adoption, such as the Nile Valley.

THE NORTHERN LEVANT

On present evidence the Middle Uruk presence in the Euphrates Valley appears to have had little impact upon developments in western Syria. Certainly the contrast between the few BRBs reported from the riverine site of Hama, and the much larger Uruk component at the small steppe site of El-Kowm some 150 km to the east, indicates that in the mid-fourth millennium Cal. BC the western limit of the 'Mesopotamian' world lay well to the east of the Orontes Valley.

The position of communities in the northern Levant with regard to the two different organizational forms outlined above is difficult to assess on current evidence. While similarities between the Ubaid-related ceramics of Phase E in the 'Amuq, Hama L, and Ras Shamra IIIB are well documented (de Contensón 1982; Thuesen 1988: 91-2, Schwartz and Weiss 1992: 231-32), there has been less discussion of the degree of relationship between this material and the better-known Ubaid pottery of Mesopotamia, nor of the likely significance of 'Ubaid-related' material in terms of wider connections between the northern Levant and societies to the north and east (but see Thuesen 1990). In the fourth millennium BC western Syria clearly belongs to the general chaff-tempered ceramic tradition. However, it is clear that despite the sharing of certain technical procedures over a wide area, there also existed significant variations within this tradition (Lupton 1996: 20), presumably indicative of differences in social and economic organization of the various communities concerned. Pertinent examples include the much longer duration of painted pottery in the Levant than elsewhere, the regional nature of certain vessel forms — note the absence of so-called 'casseroles' and the late adoption of the potter's wheel at Tell Nebi Mend (Mathias 2000), and the existence of a distinct coastal ceramic region.

Parts of western Syria provide little evidence for the shift towards ceramic mass production which is documented in southeast Anatolia by the middle of the fourth millennium BC. Moreover, there is little published evidence that is clearly indicative of the existence of powerful political elites in this area prior to the third millennium BC. Despite the clear morphological distinctions between the ceramics of the northern and southern parts of the Levant during the fourth millennium BC, and the obvious northern connections evidenced by the use of chaff-temper in west Syria, it remains quite possible that societies in the latter region were more akin to those of the southern Levant in terms of scale and organization, than to communities in 'Greater Mesopotamia'. While little more than a speculative observation at present, this suggestion does point up issues to be addressed by future research.

AFTERTHOUGHT

If nothing else, this paper should have served to broaden perspectives on developments in the fourth millennium BC, to embrace regions outside 'Greater Mesopotamia'. I have also used a consideration of the non-ceramic evidence to demonstrate the existence of connections that would not be detectable through pottery alone, a point

which suggests that the 'Uruk' system was far from being the only network of inter-regional contacts in existence during the fourth millennium BC. That done, I have sought to explain the uneven nature of the evidence for 'Uruk' connections in the east Mediterranean as resulting from the varied social and political circumstances prevailing within potential recipient communities. This in turn, has raised interesting questions concerning possible differences between fourth millennium BC communities located in the Levant, and in the northern part of 'Greater Mesopotamia'. More tentatively, I hope that I have brought into question the status of communities in western Syria *vis-à-vis* those to the north and east, and the south, although I can offer no definite answers at present.

ACKNOWLEDGEMENTS

I wish to thank Douglas Baird, Tim Harrison and Toby Wilkinson for their kindness in reading and commenting on a draft of this text. Naturally they bear no responsibility for the remaining errors which are entirely attributable to my own ineptitude.

[1] Note that Kenyon's (1960; 1965; 1979) Proto-Urban period is equivalent to EBA I as used here, while the material which she termed EBA I is now generally equated with the early part of EBA II (Esse 1984).

[2] The 'Post-Uruk' phase is broadly equivalent to the later part of 'Amuq G and is characterized by 'Late Reserved Slip Ware'and sinuous-sided bowls (Schwartz 1998).

[3] Table 1 highlights the problems inherent in using the term 'Chalcolithic' to designate fifth millennium BC village communities of Ubaid Mesopotamia and Ghassulian Palestine and the altogether more complex late fourth millennium BC societies of Syro-Mesopotamia.

[4] Frangipane (2000: 444-45) has recently confirmed the appearance at Arslantepe of a little RBBW in final Phase VII contexts, but notes that it appears in quantity within Phase VIA, that is after c. 3300 Cal. BC. The date of its initial appearance in western Syria however, remains uncertain in the absence of good radiocarbon dates.

[5] This is quite different from the Reserved Slip ware discussed by Trentin (1993), and which appears at Habuba Kabira, 'Amuq G and Arslantepe VIA, and where the technique is applied mainly to the exterior of large jars and, on occasion, bowls.

[6] More than 80% of the painted pottery was recovered from the first four of the seven phases identified within RS IIIB (de Contenson 1992: table 27).

[7] These are 'poterie jaunâtre à noyau gris' and 'poterie blanchâtre à surface griffée'. The first often bears a red slip and occurs as bowls with recessed rim, including some with relatively thin walls (de Contenson 1992: fig. 229. 1-2). The second was employed for vessels with relatively thick sections including hemispherical and carinated bowls, jugs or bottles with everted rim, and jars (de Contenson 1992: fig. 229. 3-10, 230, 231. 1-2). Unfortunately it is not possible to examine the distri-

bution of these wares throughout the sequence as they are absent from the tabulation of pottery from level IIIB (de Contenson 1992: table 27), which appears to concentrate upon the painted material.

[8] The excavation notebooks as quoted by Amiet (1992: 10) suggest that the seal was found on the slopes of the acropolis in an area where painted pre- and proto-historic potsherds of level III type were eroding out, and it was concluded that according to 'le contexte archéologique et la position stratigraphique, le cylindre remonte au Ve millénaire'. This seems highly unlikely. However, the records may indicate that the seal came from deposits equivalent to the latter part of the RS IIIB sequence, and that the painted sherds refer to something akin to the 'Ubaid-related' material, which is characteristic of much of this sequence.

[9] Note that Saghieh's (1983) reanalysis of the EBA material from Byblos employs Kenyon's periodization of the Early Bronze Age when discussing the Palestinian data.

[10] For example, Dunand (1950: 599-600) argued for a gap of some fifty years between the end of the Enéolithique récent and the beginning of the subsequent Phase III, which was itself seen as transitional between the Enéolithique récent and the Early Bronze Age proper (Phase KI). However, Saghieh (1983: 129) has cast doubt on the very existence of Byblos III as a distinct stratigraphic phase. Under such circumstances it would be foolish to assign Byblos a key role in any detailed chronological argument.

[11] Examples include a churn, in this case used for the inhumation of a child (Dunand 1973: 292, fig. 170. 32258), and the use of a pedestal foot on bowls, including examples with and without fenestrations (Dunand 1973: fig. 149. 19514, fig. 158. 19767).

[12] The rarity of these blades at early EBA I Yiftah'el (Rosen and

Grinblat 1997: 139), in contrast to their presence at the contemporary site of Tell esh-Shuna may be related to differences in the subsistence practices of the two sites, or that Shuna being a much larger site than Yiftah'el, participated in a wider range of activities and long-range contacts.

[13] The initial identification of sherds from Stratum I as representing Syrian reserved slip bowls, has now been rejected (Faltings and Köhler 1996: 98-99).

[14] Evidence for a growing 'koine' along the east Mediterranean littoral at the end of the fourth millennium BC includes the presence in Tell el-Fara'in Str. III of a range of both Palestinian imports, and 'Palestinian' forms produced locally in the Nile Delta (Porat 1997: 231). The latter includes two sherds from red burnished 'Abydos' jars (Porat 1997: 225-26, table 2).

[15] As the evidence from west Syria comes mainly from small soundings, discussion will, of necessity, concentrate upon Byblos and the southern Levant.

[16] Commentators are generally rather vague as to the specific correlates of 'urbanism' as the term is applied to EBA Byblos.

REFERENCES

Akkermans, P.M.M.G., 1988. An Updated Chronology for the Northern Ubaid and Late Chalcolithic Periods in Syria: New Evidence from Tell Hammam et-Turkman. *Iraq* 50: 109-45.

Algaze, G., 1993. *The Uruk World System: The Dynamics of Early Mesopotamian Civilization.* Chicago: University of Chicago Press.

Alon, D. and T.E. Levy, 1989. The archaeology of cult and the Chalcolithic sanctuary at Gilat. *Journal of Mediterranean Archaeology* 2: 163-221.

Amiet, P., 1992. *Corpus des cylindres de Ras Shamra-Ougarit II Sceaux-cylindres en hématite et pierres diverses.* Ras-Shamra-Ougarit IX. Paris: Éditions Recherche sur les Civilisations.

Amiran, R., 1969. *Ancient Pottery of the Holy Land.* Jersualem: Masada Press.

Amiran, R., 1992. Petrie's F-ware. In E. C. M. van den Brink (ed.), *The Nile Delta in Transition: 4th-3rd Millennium BC,* 427-32. Jerusalem: Israel Exploration Society.

Amiran, R., U. Paran, Y. Shiloh, R. Brown, Y. Tsafrir and A. Ben-Tor, 1978. *Early Arad: The Chalcolithic Settlement and Early Bronze Age City I. First-Fifth Seasons of Excavations 1962-1966.* Jerusalem: Israel Exploration Society.

Amiran, R., and O. Ilan, 1996. *Early Arad II: The Chalcolithic and Early Bronze IB Settlements and Early Bronze II City: Architecture and Planning. Sixth to Eighteenth Seasons of Excavations 1971-1978, 1980-1984.* Jerusalem: Israel Exploration Society.

Anthony, D.W., 1997. Prehistoric migration as social process. In J. Chapman and H. Hamerow (eds.), *Migrations and Invasions in Archaeological Explanation.* BAR International Series 664, 21-32. Oxford: British Archaeological Reports.

Bachmann, F., 1998. Das keramische Inventar eines urukzeitlichen Gebäudes in Tell Sheikh Hassan / Syrien. *Subartu* IV/2: 89-129.

Baird, D.W. and G. Philip, n.d. *Excavations at Tell esh-Shuna, Jordan 1991-1994.*

Barrett, J., 1994. *Fragments from Antiquity: an Archaeology of Social Life in Britain, 2900-1200 BC.* Oxford: Blackwell.

Behm-Blanke, M.R., 1984. Hassek Höyük. Vorläufiger Bericht über die Ausgrabungen in den Jahren 1981-1983. *Istanbuler Mitteilungen* 34: 31-149.

Ben-Tor, A., 1978. *Cylinder Seals of Third Millennium Palestine.* Bulletin of the American Schools of Oriental Research, Supplement Series No. 22. Cambridge MA: American Schools of Oriental Research.

Ben-Tor, A., 1989. Byblos and the Early Bronze Age I of Palestine. In P. de Miroschedji (ed.) *L'urbanisation de la Palestine à l'âge du Bronze ancient. Bilan et perspectives des recherches actuelles,* 41-52. British Archaeological Reports Int. Series. 527. Oxford: British Archaeological Reports.

Ben-Tor, A., 1991 New light on the relations between Egypt and southern Palestine during the Early Bronze Age. *Bulletin of the American Schools of Oriental Research* 281: 3-10.

Bernbeck, R., 1993. *Steppe als Kulturlandschaft: das 'Agig-Gebiet Ostsyriens vom Neolithikum bis zur islamischen Zeit.* Berliner Beiträge zum Vorderen Orient Ausgrabungen Bd. 1. Berlin: Dietrich Reimer.

Betts, A.V.G. (ed.), 1991. *Excavations at Jawa 1972-1986.* Edinburgh: Edinburgh University Press.

Betts, A.V.G. (ed.), 1992. *Excavations at Tell Um Hammad: The Early Assemblages (EB I-II).* Edinburgh: Edinburgh University Press.

Boese J., 1995. *Ausgrabungen in Tell Sheikh Hassan I Vorläufige Berichte über die Grabungskampagnen 1984-1990 und 1992-1994.* Schriften zur vorderasiatischen Archäologie, Band 5. Saarbrücken: Saarbrücker Druckerei und Verlag.

Braemer, F., 1993. Review of A.V.G. Betts Excavations at Jawa 1972-1986. *Syria* 70: 283-286.

Braidwood, R.J., 1937. *Mounds in the Plain of Antioch.* Oriental Institute Publications No. 48. Chicago: Chicago University Press.

Braidwood, R.J. and Braidwood, L.S., 1960. *Excavations in the Plain of Antioch I: The Earlier Assemblages, Phases A-J.* Oriental Institute Publications No. 61. Chicago: Chicago University Press.

Brandl, B., 1992. Evidence for Egyptian Colonization in the Southern Coastal Plain and Lowlands of Canaan during the EB I Period. In E. C. M. van den Brink (ed.), *The Nile Delta in Transition: 4th-3rd Millennium BC,* 441-76. Jerusalem: Israel Exploration Society.

Braun E., 1990. Basal Bowls of the EB I Horizon in the southern Levant. *Paléorient* 16.1: 87-96.

Braun, E., 1997. *Yiftah'el : salvage and rescue excavations at a prehistoric village in Lower Galilee, Israel* Jerusalem: Israel Antiquities Authority Reports No. 2.

Braun, E., 2000. Area G at Afridar, Palmahim Quarry 3 and the Earliest Pottery of Early Bronze Age I: Part of the 'Missing Link'. In G. Philip and D. Baird (eds.), *Ceramics and Change in the Early Bronze Age of the Southern Levant*, 113-28. Sheffield: Sheffield Academic Press.

Breniquet, C., 1996. Du fil a retordre: réflexions sur les "idoles aux yeux" et les fileuses de l'époque d'Uruk. In H. Gasche and B. Hrouda (eds.), *Collectanea Orientalia histoire, arts de l'espace et industrie de la terre. Etudes offerts en hommage à Agnès Spycket*, 31-53. Civilisations de Proche-Orient Serie 1 Archéologie et Environnement 3. Neuchâtel: Recherches et Publications.

Campbell, S., 2000. Questions of definition in the Early Bronze Age of the Tishreen Dam. In C. Marro (ed.), *Chronologies des pays du Caucase et de l'Euphrate aux IVème-IIIème millénaires*, 53-63. Institut Français d'etudes anatoliennes d'Istanbul. Varia Anatolica XI. Paris: Boccard.

Carmi, I. and Segal, D., 1998. 14C Dates from Chalcolithic Sites in the Golan. In C. Epstein *The Chalcolithic Culture of the Golan*, 343-45. Israel Antiquities Authority Reports No. 4. Jerusalem: Israel Antiquities Authority.

Cauvin, J. and D. Stordeur, 1985. Une occupation d'époque Uruk en Palmyrène: le niveau supérieur d'el Kowm 2 - Caracol. *Cahiers de l'Euphrate* 4: 191-205.

Cauvin, M.-C. and C. Chataigner, 1998. Distribution de l'obsidienne dans les sites archéologiques de Proche et Moyen Orient. In M.-C. Cauvin, (ed.), *L'obsidienne au Proche et Moyen Orient: du volcan à l'outil*, 325-50. British Archaeological Reports International Series No. 738. Oxford: Archaeopress, 1998

Cecchini, S.M. and S. Mazzoni, 1998. *Tell Afis (Siria) Scavi sull'acropoli 1988-1992. The 1988-92 Excavations on the Acropolis*. Richerche di Archeologia del Vicino Oriente 1. (Tell Afis 1) Pisa: Edizioni ETS.

Commenge-Pellerin, C., 1987. *La poterie d'Abou Matar et de l'Ouadi Zoumeili (Beershéva) au IVe millénaire avant l'ére chrétienne*. Les cahiers du Centre de recherche français de Jérusalem No. 3. Paris: Association Paléorient.

Commenge-Pellerin, C., 1990. *La poterie de Safadi (Beershéva) au IVe millénaire avant l'ère chrétienn*. Les cahiers du Centre de recherche français de Jérusalem No. 5 Paris: Association Paléorient.

Contenson, H. de, 1969. Les couches du niveau III au sud de l'acropole de Ras Shamra. In C.F.A. Schaeffer (ed.), *Ugaritica* VI, 43-89. Paris: Geuthner.

Contenson, H. de, 1979. Nouvelles données sur la chronologie du Bronze Ancien de Ras Shamra. *Ugarit Forschungen* 11: 857-862.

Contenson, H. de, 1982. Phases préhistoriques de Ras Shamra et de l'Amuq. *Paléorient* 8: 95-106.

Contenson, H. de, 1992. *Préhistoire de Ras Shamra. Les sondages stratigraphiques de 1955 à 1976*. Ras Shamra — Ougarit VIII. Paris: Éditions Recherche sur les Civilisations.

Curvers, H.H., 1989. The Beginning of the Third Millennium in Syria. In O.M. Haex, H.H. Curvers and P.M.M.G. Akkermans (eds.), *To the Euphrates and Beyond. Archaeological Studies in Honour of Maurits N. van Loon*, 173-193. Rotterdam: Balkema.

Dessel J.P. and A. H. Joffe, 2000. Alternative Approaches to Early Bronze Age Pottery. In G. Philip and D. Baird (eds.), *Ceramics and Change in the Early Bronze Age of the Southern Levant*, 31-58. Sheffield: Sheffield Academic Press.

Dolce, R., 1998. The Palatial Ebla Culture in the Context of North Mesopotamian and North Syrian Main Powers. *Subartu* 4/2: 67-81.

Dunand, M., 1945. *Byblia Grammata Documents et recherches sur le dévelopment de l'écriture en phénicie*. Beirut: Direction des Antiquités.

Dunand, M., 1950. Chronologie des plus anciennes installations de Byblos. *Revue Biblique* 57: 583-603.

Dunand, M., 1973. *Fouilles de Byblos* V. Paris: Paul Geuthner.

Ehrich, A.M.H., 1939. *Early Pottery of the Jebeleh Region*. Philadelphia: The American Philosophical Society.

Eisenberg, E., 1996. Tel Shalem — Soundings in a Fortified Site of the Early Bronze Age IB. *'Atiqot* 30: 1-24.

Epstein, C., 1998. *The Chalcolithic Culture of the Golan.* Israel Antiquities Authority Reports No. 4. Jerusalem: Israel Antiquities Authority.

Esse, D.L., 1984. A Chronological Mirage: Reflections on Early Bronze IC in Palestine. *Journal of Near Eastern Studies* 43: 317-330.

Esse, D. L., 1991. *Subsistence, Trade and Social Change in Early Bronze Age Palestine.* Studies in Ancient Oriental Civilisation, 50. Chicago: University of Chicago

Faltings, D. and Köhler, E.C., 1996. Vorbericht über die Ausgrabungen des DAI in Tell el-Fara'in Buto 1993 bis 1995. *MDIK* 87-114.

Ferioli, P. and E. Fiandra, 1994. Archival Techniques and methods at Arslantepe. In P. Ferioli, E. Fiandra, G. G. Fissore and M. Frangipane (eds.), *Archives Before Writing*, 149-161. Roma: Scriptorium.

Fischer, P.M., 1998. Tell Abu al-Kharaz. The Swedish Jordan Expedition 1997. Eighth Season Preliminary Excavation Report. *Annual of the Department of Antiquities of Jordan* 42: 213-223.

Fischer, P.M., 2000. The Early Bronze Age at Tell Abu al-Kharaz, Jordan Valley: A Study of Pottery Typology and Provenance, Radiocarbon Dates, and Synchronism. In G. Philip and D. Baird (eds.), *Ceramics and Change in the Early Bronze Age of the Southern Levant*, 201-32. Sheffield: Sheffield Academic Press.

Frangipane, M., 1993. Local Components in the Development of Centralized Societies in Syro-Anatolian Regions. In M. Frangipane, H. Hauptmann, M. Liverani, P. Matthiae and M. Mellink (eds.), *Between the Rivers and Over the Mountains*, 133-161. Rome: Università di Roma 'La Sapienza'.

Frangipane, M., 1994. The record function of clay seal-ings in early administrative systems as seen from Arslantepe. In P. Ferioli, E. Fiandra, G. G. Fissore and M. Frangipane (eds.), *Archives Before Writing*, 125-36. Roma: Scriptorium.

Frangipane, M., 1997. A 4th-Millennium Temple/Palace Complex at Arslantepe-Malatya. North-South Relations and the Formation of Early State Societies in the Northern Regions of Greater Mesopotamia. *Paléorient* 23/1: 45-74.

Frangipane, M., 2000. The late Chalcolithic/EB 1 Sequence at Arslantepe. Chronological and Cultural Remarks from a frontier site. In C. Marro (ed.), *Chronologies des pays du Caucase et de l'Euphrate aux IVème-IIIème millénaires*, 439-71. Institut Français d'etudes anatoliennes d'Istanbul. Varia Anatolica XI. Paris: Boccard.

Gale, N. and Stos-Gale, Z., 1981. Ancient Egyptian Silver. *Journal of Egyptian Archaeology* 67: 103-115.

Genz, H., 1994. Zur Datierung der Frühbronzezeit in Ras eš-Šamra. *Zeitschrift des Deutschen Palästina Vereins* 110: 113-124.

Gerber, C., 2000. Bermerkungen zur Stratigraphie von Tell Judaidah (Amuq Phase G). In C. Marro (ed.), *Chronologies des pays du Caucase et de l'Euphrate aux IVème-IIIème millénaires*, 205-09. Institut Français d'études anatoliennes d'Istanbul. Varia Anatolica XI. Paris: Boccard.

Geyer, B. and J.-Y. Monchambert, 1987. Prospection de la moyenne vallée de l'Euphrate: rapport prélimi-naire. *Mari Annales de Recherches Interdisciplinaires* 5: 293-344.

Giannessi, D., 1998. Area E1 Late Chalcolithic, Early, Middle and Late Bronze I Ages Architecture and Stratigraphy. In S. Mazzoni (ed.) *Tell Afis*, 101-21.

Greenberg, R. and Porat, N., 1996. A Third Millennium Levantine Pottery Production Center: Typology, Petrography and Provenance of the Metallic Ware of Northern Israel and Adjacent Regions. *Bulletin of the American Schools of Oriental Research* 301: 5-24.

Harrison, T.P., 1993. Economics with an entrepreneurial spirit: Early Bronze Age trade with late Predynastic Egypt. *Biblical Archaeologist* 56: 81-92.

Hauptmann A., F. Begemann, E. Heitkemper, E. Pernicka and S. Schmitt-Strecker, 1992. Early Copper Produced at Feinan, Wadi Araba, Jordan: The Composition of Ores and Copper. *Archaeomaterials* 6: 1-33.

Hauptmann A., F. Begemann and S. Schmidt-Strecker, 1999. Copper objects from Arad — their composition and provenance. *Bulletin of the American Schools of Oriental Research* 314: 1-17.

Helms, S.W., 1984. Land Behind Damascus: Urbanism during the 4th Millennium in Syria/Palestine. In T. Khalidi (ed.), *Land Tenure and Social Transforma-tion in the Middle East*, 15-31. Beirut: American University of Beirut.

Helms, S.W., 1987. Jawa, Tell um Hamad and the E.B.I/Late Chalcolithic Landscape. *Levant* 19: 49-81.

Helwing, B., 2000. Regional variation in the composition of Late Chalcolithic pottery assemblages. In C. Marro (ed.), *Chronologies des pays du Caucase et de l'Euphrate aux IVème-IIIème millénaires*, 145-64. Institut Français d'etudes anatoliennes d'Istanbul. Varia Anatolica XI. Paris: Boccard.

Hess, K., A. Hauptmann, H. Wright and R. Whallon, 1998. Evidence of fourth millennium BC silver production at Fatmali-Kalecik, East Anatolia. In T. Rehren, A. Hauptmann and J.D. Muhly (eds.), *Metallurgica Antiqua In Honour of Hans-Gert Bachmann and Robert Maddin*, 57-67. Der Anschnitt Beiheft 8. Bochum.

Joffe A.H., 1993. *Settlement and Society in the Early Bronze I and II Southern Levant*. Sheffield: Sheffield Academic Press.

Joffe, A.H., 2000. Egypt and Syro-Mesopotamia in the 4th millennium: implications of the new chronology. *Current Anthropology* 41: 113-123.

Joffe, A.H., in press. Early Bronze Age Seal Impressions from the Jezreel Valley and the Problem of Sealing in the Southern Levant. In S. Wolff (ed.), *Douglas Esse Memorial Volume*. Studies in Ancient Oriental Civilization. Chicago: The Oriental Institute.

Joffe, A.H., n.d. Slouching toward Beersheva: Chalcolithic Mortuary Practices in Local and Regional Context.

Joffe A.H. and J.-P. Dessel, 1995. Redefining chronology and terminology for the Chalcolithic of the Southern Levant. *Current Anthropology* 33: 507-17.

Knapp, A.B., S.O. Held and S.W. Manning, 1994. The prehistory of Cyprus: problems and prospects. *Journal of World Prehistory* 8: 377-453.

Köhler, E.C., 1998. *Tell el-Fara'in Buto III. Die Keramik von der späten Naqada-Kultur bis zum frühen Alten Reich (Schichten III bis VI).* Deutsches Archäologisches Institut Abteiling Kairo Archäologische Veröffentlichungen 94. Mainz am Rhein: Verlag Philip von Zabern

Kohlmeyer, K., 1994. Zur frühen Geschichte von Blei und Silber. In R. Wartke (ed.), *Handwerk und Technologie im Alten Orient*, 41-48. Mainz: von Zabern.

Lebeau, M., 2000. Stratified archaeological evidence and compared periodizations in the Syrian Jezierah during the third millennium BC. In C. Marro (ed.), *Chronologies des pays du Caucase et de l'Euphrate aux IVème-IIIème millénaires*, 167-92. Institut Français d'etudes anatoliennes d'Istanbul. Varia Anatolica XI. Paris: Boccard.

Levy, T.E., 1987. *Shiqmim I — Studies Concerning Chalcolithic Societies in the Northern-Negev Desert, Israel (1982-1984).* British Archaeological Reports, International Series No. 356. Oxford: British Archaeological Reports

Levy, T.E., 1995. Cult, Metallurgy and Rank Societies - Chalcolithic. In T.E. Levy (ed.), *Archaeology of Society in the Holy Land*, 226-243. Leicester: Leicester University Press.

Levy, T.E., E.C.M. van den Brink, Y. Goren and D. Alon, 1995. New light on King Narmer and the Protodynastic Egyptian presence in Canaan. *Biblical Archaeologist* 58: 26-36.

Levy, T.E., D. Alon, P. Smith, Y. Yekutieli, Y. Rowan, P. Goldberg, N. Porat, E.C.M. van den Brink, A.J. Witten, J. Golden, C. Grigson, E. Kansa. L. Dawson, A. Holl, J. Moreno and M. Kersel, 1997. Egyptian-Canaanite interaction at Nahal Tillah, Israel (ca. 4500-3000 BCE): an interim report on the 1994-95 excavations. *Bulletin of the American Schools of Oriental Research* 307: 1-51.

Lupton, A., 1996. *Stability and Change: Socio-political development in North Mesopotamia and South-east Anatolia.* Oxford. British Archaeological Reports Int. Series 627. Oxford: British Archaeological Reports.

McClellan, T. L. and A. Porter, 1995. Jawa and North Syria: In *Studies in the History and Archaeology of Jordan* V, 49-65. Amman: Department of Antiquities of Jordan.

Marfoe, L., 1995. *Kamid el-Loz 13. The Prehistoric and Early Historic Context of the Site.* Saarbrücker Beiträge zur Altertumskunde Bd. 41. Bonn: Rudolf Habelt.

Mathias, V.T., 2000. The Early Bronze Age Pottery of Tell Nebi Mend in its Regional Setting. In G. Philip and D. Baird (eds.). *Ceramics and Change in the Early Bronze Age of the Southern Levant*, 411-27. Sheffield: Sheffield Academic Press.

Mathias, V.T. and P.J. Parr, 1989. The Early Phases at Tell Nebi Mend: A Preliminary Account. *Levant* 21: 13-29.

Matthers, J. (ed.), *The River Qoueiq, northern Syria, and its catchment: studies arising from the Tell Rifa'at Survey 1977-79*. British Archaeological Reports. International Series 98. Oxford: British Archaeological Reports.

Matthews, D.M., 1997. *The Early Glyptic of Tell Brak. Cylinder Seals of Third Millennium Syria*. Orbis Biblicus et Orientalis, Series Archaeologica 15. University Press Fribourg, Göttingen: Vandenhoeck and Ruprecht.

Matthews, R.J., 2000. Fourth and third millennia chronologies: the view from Tell Brak, north-east Syria. In C. Marro (ed.), *Chronologies des pays du Caucase et de l'Euphrate aux IVème-IIIème millénaires*, 65-72. Institut Français d'etudes anatoliennes d'Istanbul. Varia Anatolica XI. Paris: Boccard.

Mazzoni, S., 1980. Sigilli a stampo protohistorici di Mardikh I. *Studi Eblaiti* 2/4-5: 53-80.

Mazzoni, S., 1984. Seal-Impressions on Jars from Ebla in EB IVA-B. *Akkadica* 37: 18-40.

Mazzoni, S., 1991. Ebla e la formazione della cultura urbana in Siria. *La Parola del Passato* 46: 163-93.

Mazzoni, S., 1992. *Le Impronte su giara eblaite e siriane nel Bronzo Antico*. Materiali e Studi Archeologici di Ebla - 1. Missione Archeologica Italiana in Siria. Roma: Università degli studi di Roma 'La Sapienza'.

Mazzoni, S., 1999. Tell Afis and its Region in the Late Chalcolithic Period. *Annales Archéologiques Arabes Syriennes* 43: 97-117.

Mazzoni, S., 2000. From the Late Chalcolithic to Early Bronze I in North-West Syria: Anatolian Contact and Regional Perspective. In C. Marro (ed.), *Chronologies des pays du Caucase et de l'Euphrate aux IVème-IIIème millénaires*, 97-114. Institut Français d'etudes anatoliennes d'Istanbul. Varia Anatolica XI. Paris: Boccard.

Mellaart, J., 1981. The Prehistoric pottery from the Neolithic to the beginnings of EB IV. In J. Matthers (ed.), *The River Qoueiq, northern Syria, and its catchment: studies arising from the Tell Rifa'at Survey 1977-79*, 131-326. British Archaeological Reports. International Series 98. Oxford: British Archaeological Reports.

Miroschedji, P. de, 1971. *L'époque préurbaine en Palestine*. Cahiers de la Revue Biblique 13. Paris: Gabalda.

Miroschedji, P. de, 2000. La céramique de Khirbet Kerak en Syro-Palestine: état de la question. In C. Marro (ed.), *Chronologies des pays du Caucase et de l'Euphrate aux IVème-IIIème millénaires*, 255-78. Institut Français d'etudes anatoliennes d'Istanbul. Varia Anatolica XI. Paris: Boccard.

Moorey, P.R.S., 1990. From the Gulf to the delta in the fourth millennium BC: the Syrian connection. *Eretz Israel* 21: 62-9.

Nocera, G.-M. di, 2000. Radiocarbon dating from Arslantepe and Norsuntepe: the fourth and third millennium absolute chronology in the upper Euphrates and Transcaucasian region. In C. Marro (ed.), *Chronologies des pays du Caucase et de l'Euphrate aux IVème-IIIème millénaires*, 73-93. Institut Français d'etudes anatoliennes d'Istanbul. Varia Anatolica XI. Paris: Boccard.

Oates, J., 1993. Trade and Power in the Fifth and Fourth Millennia BC. New Evidence from Northern Mesopotamia. *World Archaeology* 24: 403-422.

Oates, D. and J. Oates, 1997. An open gate: cities of the fourth millennium (Tell Brak 1997). *Cambridge Archaeological Journal* 7: 287-97.

Oldenburg, E., 1991. *Sukas IX: The Chalcolithic and Early Bronze Periods*. Publications of the Carlsberg Expedition to Phoenicia 11. Copenhagen: Munksgaard.

Palmieri, A., K. Sertok and E. Chernykh, 1993. From Arslantepe Metalwork to Arsenical Copper Metallurgy in Anaolia. In M. Frangipane, H. Hauptmann, M. Liverani, P. Matthiae and M. Mellink (eds.), *Between the Rivers and Over the Mountains*, 573-600. Rome: Università di Roma 'La Sapienza'.

Pearce, J., 2000. The Late Chalcolithic sequence at Hacinebi Tepe, Turkey. In C. Marro (ed.), *Chronologies des pays du Caucase et de l'Euphrate aux IVème-IIIème millénaires*, 115-43. Institut Français d'etudes anatoliennes d'Istanbul. Varia Anatolica XI. Paris: Boccard.

Peltenburg, E.J., 1996. From isolation to state formation in Cyprus, c. 3500-1500 B.C. In V. Karageorghis and D. Michaelides (eds.), *The Development of the Cypriot Economy from the Prehistoric Period to the Present Day*, 17-43. Nicosia: Bank of Cyprus.

Pernicka, E., T. Rehren and S. Schmitt-Strecker, 1998. Late Uruk silver production by cupellation at Habuba Kabira, Syria. In T. Rehren, A. Hauptmann and J.D. Muhly (eds.), *Metallurgica Antiqua In Honour of*

Hans-Gert Bachmann and Robert Maddin, 123-34. Der Anschnitt Beiheft 8. Bochum.

Philip, G., 1999. Complexity and Diversity in the Southern Levant During the Third Millennium BC: the Evidence of Khirbet Kerak Ware. *Journal of Mediterranean Archaeology* 12: 26-57.

Philip, G., in press. The Early Bronze I-III Ages. In R. Adams, P. Bienkoswki and B. MacDonald (eds.), *The Archaeology of Jordan.* Sheffield: Sheffield Academic Press.

Philip, G. and O. Williams-Thorpe, 1993. A provenance study of Jordanian basalt vessels of the Chalcolithic and Early Bronze Age I Periods. *Paléorient* 19/2: 51-63.

Philip, G. and T. Rehren, 1996. Fourth millennium BC silver from Tell esh-Shuna, Jordan: archaeometallurgical investigation and some throughts on ceramic skeuomorphs. *Oxford Journal of Archaeology* 15: 129-150.

Philip, G. and D. Baird, 2000. Early Bronze Age Ceramics in the Southern Levant: an Overview. In G. Philip and D. Baird (eds.), *Ceramics and Change in the Early Bronze Age of the Southern Levant*, 3-29. Sheffield: Sheffield Academic Press.

Philip, G. and A.R. Millard, 2000. Khirbet Kerak Ware in the Levant: the implications of radiocarbon chronology and spatial distribution. In C. Marro (ed.), *Chronologies des pays du Caucase et de l'Euphrate aux IVème-IIIème millénaires:* 279-96. Institut Français d'etudes anatoliennes d'Istanbul. Varia Anatolica XI. Paris: Boccard.

Philip, G. and O.Williams-Thorpe, 2001. The production and consumption of basalt artefacts in the southern Levant during the 5th-4th millennia BC: a geochemical and petrographic investigation, 11-30. In A.R. Millard (ed.), *Archaeological Sciences 1997*. Oxford: Oxbow Monograph.

Porat, N., 1997. Petrography and Composition of the Pottery. In T. von der Way, *Tell el-Fara'in Buto I. Ergebnisse zum frühen Kontext Kampagnen der Jahre 1983-89*, 223-231. Deutsches Archäologisches Institut Abteilung Kairo Archäologische Veröffentlichungen 83. Mainz am Rhein: Verlag Philip von Zabern.

Prag, K., 1978. Silver in the Levant in the Fourth Millennium B.C. In P.R.S. Moorey and P.J. Parr (eds.), *Archaeology in the Levant: Essays for Kathleen Kenyon*, 36-45. Warminster: Aris and Phillips.

Prag, K., 1986. Byblos and Egypt in the Fourth Millennium BC. *Levant* 18: 15-74.

McClellan, T. L. and A. Porter, 1995. Jawa and North Syria. In *Studies in the History and Archaeology of Jordan* V: Amman: 49-65.

Rehren, T., K. Hess and G. Philip, 1996. Auriferous silver in Western Asia: ore or alloy? *Historical Metallurgy* 30/1: 1-10.

Rehren, T., K. Hess and G. Philip, 1997. Fourth millennium BC copper metallurgy in northern Jordan: the evidence from Tell esh-Shuna. In H.-G. Gebel, Z. Kafafi, and G.O. Rollefson (eds.), *The Prehistory of Jordan, II. Perspectives from 1997. Studies in Early Near Eastern Production, Subsistence, and Environment* 4: 625-40. Berlin: ex oriente.

Rosen, S. and M. Grinblat, 1997. The Chipped Stone Assemblages from Yiftah'el. In E. Braun, *Yiftah'el. Salvage and Rescue Excavations at a Prehistoric Village in Lower Galilee, Israel,* 133-54. Israel Antiquities Authority Reports No. 2. Jerusalem: Israel Antiquities Authority.

Rosen, S.A., 1997. *Lithics After the Stone Age. A Handbook of Stone Tools from the Levant.* London: Altamira.

Rothman, M.S., 1993. Another Look at the 'Uruk' Expansion from the Tigris Piedmont. In M. Frangipane, H. Hauptmann, M. Liverani, P. Matthiae and M. Mellink (eds.), *Between the Rivers and Over the Mountains*, 163-76. Rome: Università di Roma "La Sapienza".

Roux, V., and M.-A. Courty, 1997. Les bols elaborés au tour d'Abu Hamid: rupture technique au 4e millénaire avant J.-C. dans le Levant-sud. *Paléorient* 23/1: 25-43.

Saghieh, M., 1983. *Byblos in the Third Millennium.* Warminster: Aris and Phillips.

Schmidt, K., 1992. Tell el-Fara'in/Buto and Tell el-Iswid (south): The Lithic Industries from the Chalcolithic to the Early Old Kingdom. In E.C.M. van den Brink (ed.), *The Nile Delta in Transition: 4th-3rd Millennium BC, 441-76.* 31-42. Jerusalem: Israel Exploration Society.

Schmidt, K., 1993. Comments to the Lithic Industry of the Buto-Maadi Culture in Lower Egypt. In L.Krzyzaniak, M. Kobusiewicz and J. Alexander (eds.), *Environmental Change and Human Culture in the Nile Basin and Northern Africa until the Second Millennium BC.* Poznan: Poznan Archaeological Museum.

Schmitt-Strecker, S., F. Begemann and E. Pernicka, 1992. Chemische Zusammensetzung und Bleiisotopenverhältnisse der Metallfunde vom Hassek Höyük. In M.R. Behm-Blancke (ed.), *Hassek Höyük. Naturwissenschaftlich Untersuchungen und lithische Industrie,* 108-123. Istanbuler Forschungen Bd. 38. Tübingen: Ernst Wasmuth Verlag.

School of American Research Advanced Seminar 1998 [online]. Accessed at http://www.science.widener. edu/ssci/mesopotamia. on 21st Sept. 1999.

Schwartz, G. and H. Weiss, 1992. The Chronology of Syria to 2000 B.C. In R. Ehrich (ed.), *Chronologies in Old World Archaeology,* 3rd ed., 221-243. Chicago: University of Chicago Press.

Schwartz, G., 1998 Syria and the Uruk expansion [online]. Accessed at http://www.science.widener. edu/ssci/mesopotamia. on 21st Sept. 1999.

Sherratt, A., 1993. What would a Bronze-Age world system look like? Relations between temperate Europe and the Mediterranean in later prehistory. *Journal of European Archaeology* 1.2: 1-58.

Sherratt, A., and E. Sherratt, 1991. From Luxuries to Commodities: The Nature of Mediterranean Bronze Age Trading Systems. In N. H. Gale (ed.), *Bronze Age Trade in the Mediterranean,* 351-86. Studies in Mediterranean Archaeology 90. Jonsered: Aströms Förlag.

Spencer, A.J., 1993. *Early Egypt: the rise of civilisation in the Nile valley.* London: British Museum Press.

Stager, L.E., 1992. The periodization of Palestine from Neolithic through Early Bronze times. In R.W. Ehrich (ed.), *Chronologies in Old World Archaeology,* 3rd ed. 22-41. Chicago: University of Chicago Press.

Steadman, S., 1996. Isolation or interaction: prehistoric Cilicia and the fourth millennium Uruk expansion. *Journal of Mediterranean Archaeology* 9: 131-165.

Stein, G.J., 1998. Uruk expansion with indigenous complex societies of southeast Anatolia, evidence from Hacinebi, Turkey [online]. Accessed at http://www. science.widener.edu/ssci/mesopotamia. on 21st Sept. 1999.

Stein, G.J., K. Boden, C. Edens, J.P. Edens, K. Keith, A. McMahon and H. Özbal, 1997. Excavations at Hacinebi, Turkey — 1996 preliminary report. *Anatolica* 23: 111-71.

Stein, G.J., C. Edens, J. Pearce Edens, K. Boden, N. Laneri, H. Özbal, B. Earl, A.M. Adriaens, H. Pittman, 1998. Southeast Anatolia before the Uruk expansion.: preliminary report on the 1997 excavations at Hacinebi, Turkey. *Anatolica* 24: 143-93.

Stuiver M. and R.S. Kra eds., 1986 Calibration issue. Proceedings of the 12th International 14C conference. *Radiocarbon* 28 (2B): 805-1030.

Sürenhagen, D., 1974/75. Untersuchungen zur keramikproduktion innerhalb der Spät-Urukzeitlichen Siedlung Habuba Kabira-Süd in Nordsyrien. *Acta Praehistorica et Archaeologica* 5/6: 43-170.

Tadmor, M., 1964. Contacts between the 'Amuq and Syria-Palestine. *Israel Exploration Journal* 14: 253-269.

Tadmor, M., D. Kedem, F. Begemann, A. Hauptmann, E. Pernicka and S. Schmitt-Strecker, 1995. The Nahal Mishmar Hoard from the Judean Desert: Technology, Composition, and Provenance. *'Atiqot* 27: 95-148.

Teitge, W., 1997. Die 'Grubenkopfnägel' aus den Schichten des 3 Jahrtausends. In T. von der Way, *Tell el-Fara'in Buto I. Ergebnisse zum frühen Kontext Kampagnen der Jahre 1983-89,* 232-38. Deutsches Archäologisches Institut Abteilung Kairo Archäologische Veröffentlichungen 83. Mainz am Rhein: Verlag Philip von Zabern.

Teissier, B., 1987. Glyptic evidence for a connection between Iran, Syro-Palestine and Egypt in the fourth and third millennia. *Iran* 25: 27-53.

Thomas, J., 1996. *Time, Culture and Identity: an Interpretative Archaeology.* London: Routledge.

Thuesen, I., 1988. *Hama I The Pre and Proto-Historic Periods.* Fouilles et Recherches de la Fondation Carlsberg. 1931-38. Copenhagen.

Thuesen, I., 1990. Diffusion of 'Ubaid pottery into western Syria. In E. Henrickson and I. Thuesen (eds.), *Upon this Foundation - The 'Ubaid Reconsidered,* 419-37. Kobenhavn: Museum Tusculanum Press.

Trentin, M.G., 1993. Early Reserved-Slip wares Horizon of the Upper Euphrates Basin and western Syria. In M. Frangipane, H. Hauptmann, M. Liverani, P. Matthiae and M. Mellink (eds.), *Between the Rivers and Over the Mountains,* 177-199. Rome: Università di Roma 'La Sapienza'.

Trufelli, F., 1994. Standardisation, Mass Production and Potter's Marks in the Late Chalcolithic Pottery of Arslantepe (Malatya). *Origini* 18: 245-89.

Trufelli, F., 1997. Ceramic correlations and cultural relations in IVth millennium eastern Anatolia and Syro-Mesopotamia. *Studi micenei ed egeo-anatolici* 39/1: 5-53.

Van den Brink, E.C.M. (ed.), 1992. *The Nile Delta in Transition: 4th-3rd Millennium BC.* Jerusalem: Israel Exploration Society.

Ward, W., 1991. Early contacts between Egypt, Canaan, and Sinai: remarks on the paper by Amnon Ben Tor. *Bulletin of the American Schools of Oriental Research* 281: 11-26.

Watson, P.J., 1965. North Mesopotamia and Syria In R.W. Ehrich (ed.) *Chronologies in Old World Archaeology,* 2nd ed. Chicago, 61-100.

von der Way, T., 1993. *Untersuchungen zur Spätvor - und Frühgeschichte Unterägyptens.* Studien zur Archäologie und Geschichte Altägyptens. Bd. 8. Heidelberger Orientverlag.

von der Way, T., 1997. *Tell el-Fara'in Buto I. Ergebnisse zum frühen Kontext Kampagnen der Jahre 1983-89.* Deutsches Archäologisches Institut Abteilung Kairo Archäologische Veröffentlichungen 83. Mainz am Rhein: Verlag Philip von Zabern.

Webb. J. and D. Frankel, 1999. Characterizing the Philia facies: material culture, chronology and the organization of the Bronze Age in Cyprus. *American Journal of Archaeology* 103: 3-43.

Wilkinson, T.A.H., 1996. *State Formation in Egypt: Chronology and Society.* British Archaeological Reports, International Series 651. Oxford: Tempus Reparatum.

Wilkinson, T.A.H., 1998a. Review of T. von der Way, *Untersuchungen zur Spätvor- und Frühgeschichte Unterägyptens. Bibliotheca Orientalis* 55: 110-13.

Wilkinson, T.A.H., 1998b. Review of T. von der Way, *Tell el-Fara'in Buto I. Ergebnisse zum frühen Kontext Kampagnen der Jahre 1983-89. Bibliotheca Orientalis* 55: 764-8.

Wilkinson, T.A.H., 1999. *Early Dynastic Egypt.* London: Routledge.

Wilkinson, T.J. and D. Tucker, 1995. *Settlement in the north Jazira, Iraq: a study of the archaeological landscape.* British School of Archaeology in Iraq and the Department of Antiquities and Heritage, Baghdad, Iraq Archaeological Reports 3. Warminster: Aris and Phillips.

Yannai, E., 1996. A Tomb of the Early Bronze I Age and Intermediate Bronze Age near Tel Esur (Assawir) *'Atiqot* 30: 125 (1-16 Hebrew).

Yannai, E. and Z. Grosinger, 2000. Preliminary Summary of Early Bronze Strata and Burials at 'Ein Assawir — Israel. In G. Philip and D. Baird (eds.), *Ceramics and Change in the Early Bronze Age of the Southern Levant,* 153-64. Sheffield: Sheffield Academic Press.

Yener, K.A., T.J. Wilkinson, S. Branting, E.S. Friedman, J.D. Lyon, C.D. Reichel, 1996. The Oriental Institute Amuq Valley Projects 1995. *Anatolica* 22: 49-84.

URUK INTO EGYPT:
IMPORTS AND IMITATIONS

Toby A.H. Wilkinson

Egypt's relations with Mesopotamia have a long and complex history. The inspiration that early Egyptian royal art derived from Mesopotamian iconography is well known, and is a subject that has been discussed over the years by many scholars. This paper focuses instead on the artefactual evidence for contact between Uruk Mesopotamia and Predynastic Egypt, and on the underlying factors behind such exchange. To understand the dynamics of this contact, the chronological and social context within which it took place must first be appreciated.

CHRONOLOGY

The Uruk period in Mesopotamia is broadly contemporary with the Predynastic period in Egypt: more specifically, the three phases of the Upper Egyptian Predynastic sequence termed Naqada I, Naqada II and Naqada III. These phases are named after the site of Naqada, located some 30 km north-north-east of the modern tourist town of Luxor. Together with the towns of This (near modern Girga) and Hierakonpolis (15 km north of Edfu), Naqada emerges as a leading centre of Predynastic Egypt. Here, Flinders Petrie excavated extensive cemeteries dating to the Predynastic period (Petrie and Quibell 1896). The material from these cemeteries, especially the pottery, enabled Petrie (1901) and subsequent generations of Egyptologists to establish a relative chronology for the Predynastic period.

Naqada I is dated very broadly between c. 4000 and c. 3600 BC; Naqada II spans the period from c. 3600 to c. 3200 BC. Naqada III, although strictly speaking a period defined by a cultural assemblage, is generally used to refer to the span of time separating the end of Naqada II (defined in cultural terms) and the formation of the Egyptian state (a political event), in other words c. 3200 to c. 3050 BC (cf. Wilkinson 1996: 9-15). While the transmission of iconographic motifs - and perhaps also the distinctive style of niched, mudbrick architecture termed by Egyptologists 'palace-façade' - seems to have occurred most intensively during the late Uruk period or Naqada III, the artefactual evidence for contacts between Egypt and Mesopotamia is concentrated in the Naqada II period. Since Petrie's pioneering excavations, studies of cemetery material have enabled scholars to subdivide the principal periods of the Upper Egyptian Predynastic

sequence (Kaiser 1957; Hendrickx 1996; Wilkinson 1996). Hence, Naqada II is now split into four shorter phases, termed IIB, IIC, IID1 and IID2 (following Hendrickx 1996; phase IIa, as identified by Kaiser, is now generally recognised as belonging at the end of the preceding Naqada I period). In absolute terms, these phases may be dated very approximately as follows.
- Naqada IIB 3600-3500 BC
- Naqada IIC 3500-3300 BC
- Naqada IID1 3300-3250 BC
- Naqada IID2 3250-3200 BC

In Mesopotamia, the third quarter of the fourth millennium BC seems to be characterised by the first expansion of the Uruk heartland (presumed to be the southern alluvium) into its northern periphery (Rothman, this volume), as attested at Tell Sheikh Hassan on the Upper Euphrates (Boese 1995), Tell Brak (Oates, this volume) and Hacinebi Tepe (Stein, this volume).

THE SOCIAL CONTEXT: UPPER EGYPT IN NAQADA II

The third quarter of the fourth millennium BC was a period of significant socio-political and economic development in Upper Egypt, just as it was in Mesopotamia. Recent archaeological discoveries make it clear that, by the end of the Naqada I period (about 3600 BC), the ideology and institution of kingship were already emerging at a few key centres in Upper Egypt. To judge from the mortuary record, This (its necropolis was situated at nearby Abydos), Naqada and Hierakonpolis led the way in such developments. By Naqada IIC, all three centres had probably become the capitals of larger, regional polities (Kemp 1989: fig. 8). At each site, the local rulers were buried in high-status, mudbrick-lined tombs. At Naqada (Kemp 1973: 38-42) and Hierakonpolis (Adams 1996), these were situated in élite cemeteries, separated from the burial-grounds serving the general population. In one famous instance, the burial of a local ruler was made yet more distinctive, in a unique fashion: the interior walls of the mudbrick-lined tomb were plastered and decorated with ritual scenes. This is the Painted Tomb (T100) at Hierakonpolis, believed to have been the tomb of a ruler of the Hierakonpolis region (Quibell and Green 1902: 20-3, 54; Case and Payne 1962; Payne 1973). It is dated to Naqada IIC (c. 3400 BC). The Hierakonpolis Painted

Fig. 1. Sherd from Badari Cemetery 3800 (Spur 16). Petrie Museum of Egyptian Archaeology, London (UC 9796).

Tomb provides a good starting point for this discussion of 'Uruk into Egypt', because one of the elements in the decorative scheme is the well-known motif of dominance termed 'the master of the beasts'. Although present in an Egyptian tomb, this motif is clearly derived from Mesopotamian iconography (Smith 1992: 235-8). In fact, some of the closest parallels come from Susa (Amiet 1980: pl. 14.239). It is not intended to repeat discussion of such iconographic borrowings here. What is interesting, for the purposes of the present paper, is the social context in which such borrowings took place. This context has implications for the artefactual evidence as well.

The regional élites of Naqada II Upper Egypt were engaged in a concerted programme of status demarcation and status display. Iconography served to display status through the medium of art (Wilkinson 1999: 31-4); the conspicuous consumption of prestige commodities, especially imported goods, achieved just the same. One of the most distinctive types of pottery indicative of a Naqada IIC date is the wavy-handled jar (Bourriau 1981: 132-3). Vessels of this form were made by Egyptian potters, but were, in origin, imitations of imported Palestinian vessels. Only a few certain Palestinian imports have been excavated, for example at Naqada (Payne 1993: 130-1). Yet the impact that such imports had on the status- and fashion-conscious Upper Egyptian élites can be gauged by the fact that imitations of the Palestinian jars gave rise to a whole new class of Egyptian pottery.

IMPORTS AND IMITATIONS: POTTERY VESSELS

Imports from Mesopotamia reaching Upper Egypt may have resulted in a similar phenomenon. In the Naqada II period, pottery was clearly more than a utilitarian product. It could also serve to display or reinforce status, when placed in the grave of a deceased person. In particular, this seems to have been the case with more elaborate types of pottery. Piriform jars of marl clay, decorated in red ochre with complex natural or ritual scenes, and provided with triangular lug-handles for suspension, may have been produced in a few specialist workshops, for an élite market. Spouted jars of red-polished, Nile clay have likewise been found in a limited number of graves and may represent another type to which access was restricted. In both cases, the Egyptian potters seem to have been copying foreign imports (contra Hendrickx and Bavay, forthcoming), not in these cases from Palestine, but from Mesopotamia.

Four-lugged jars

The impact that imported four-lugged jars must have made on the tastes of the Upper Egyptian élites can be seen clearly in the archaeological record. Although by no means common, decorated vessels with triangular lug-handles are nevertheless one of the diagnostic types for a late Naqada II (IID1-IID2) date in Upper Egypt (cf. Kaiser 1957: pl. 23, centre). As in the case of the

Palestinian wavy-handled jars which were subsequently copied by Egyptian potters, we have very few examples of the imported Mesopotamian four-lugged jars that may have provided the inspiration for Egyptian decorated ware vessels. To date, only two such imports have been positively identified.

Both examples were found in the Badari region of Middle Egypt. The first instance of a Mesopotamian import was found in the Predynastic Cemetery 3800, situated on Spur 16 of the low desert near the village of Badari itself (Brunton and Caton-Thompson 1928: pl. XL). The sherd was collected from the surface debris, so had probably been thrown out from a nearby, plundered grave. The other graves in the cemetery suggest a date of mid-Naqada II, probably IIC. The sherd is now in the collection of the Petrie Museum of Egyptian Archaeology at University College London (UC 9796). It is one of the clearest examples of an Uruk artefact found in Egypt (Fig. 1). The fabric is dense and hard, with mineral inclusions. The colour of the break is pale grey-buff, changing to pinkish-buff at the edges. The vessel is coated with a red slip, quite different from the micaceous haematite slip so common on indigenous Egyptian Predynastic pottery. The slip on the Badari sherd is duller, and more of a pinkish-red. It has been polished with uneven strokes, giving a rather crude finish. An incised cord pattern runs around the neck of the jar; once again, this has been rather hastily executed. Small relief studs have been applied in a line beneath this pattern. Both the incised decoration and the line of applied studs are interrupted by triangular lug-handles. Close parallels for the Badari sherd are known from a number of Mesopotamian sites. A vessel from Choga Mish (III-477), dated to the 'Protoliterate' or late Uruk period, shows a similar red wash and smoothed surface (Delougaz and Kantor 1996, II: pl. 120.C); while a red-slipped four-lugged jar with incised hatched band and appliqué studs from the Ninevite IV level at Nineveh (Gut, this volume, p. 39, Fig. 17:9) provides perhaps the closest parallel for the Badari sherd. Other vessels of the same type have been found at Susa level 18 (Delougaz and Kantor 1996, I: table 8) and Tello (Mark 1998: fig. 15.B, after Genouillac 1934: pl. 25.2), among other sites.

The second imported four-lugged jar was excavated a short distance to the north of Badari, in the Predynastic Cemetery 1600-1800 at Mostagedda. Grave 1837 contained just one vessel, a small jar with four lug-handles and a line of incised notches below the neck (Fig. 2; Brunton 1937: pl. 32.2). It is now in the Egyptian Museum, Cairo (Journal d'Entrée 52848). The excavator described the ware as 'brown with a thick cream slip' (Brunton 1937: pl. 35.24). Because the grave contained just this one artefact, it is impossible to date the context precisely. However, the burials in the vicinity suggest a date of mid-Naqada II (perhaps IIC or IID1). The site of Choga Mish provides close parallels for this vessel as well, including a jar (III-401) with traces of cream slip (Delougaz and Kantor 1996, II: pl. 114.C). Perhaps more

Fig. 2. Four-lugged jar from Mostagedda grave 1837. Egyptian Museum, Cairo (JdE 52848) (after Brunton 1937: pl. 35.24)

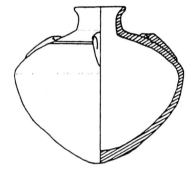

Fig. 3. Four-lugged jar from Habuba Kabira (after Mark 1998: fig. 15.A, itself after Sürenhagen 1977: pl. 18.124)

significant for the question of Egyptian-Mesopotamian contacts is a parallel for the Mostagedda vessel found at Habuba Kabira, the Uruk 'colony site' on the Upper Euphrates (Fig. 3; Mark 1998: 29, fig. 15.A, after Sürenhagen 1977: pl. 18.124). Once again, the Mesopotamian parallels are dated to the 'Protoliterate' or late Uruk period.

In discussions of foreign imports from Predynastic Egypt, a third four-lugged jar is often cited (e.g. Kantor 1992: 15), namely a vessel from grave 5112 at Matmar, a Predynastic site which lies a few kilometres to the north of Mostagedda. The vessel is now in the British Museum (EA 63689). Despite its un-Egyptian appearance (Brunton 1948: pl. 12), first-hand study indicates that it is a locally-made imitation of a Mesopotamian form. It is hand-made from a very rough, brown ware of alluvial clay, heavily chaff-tempered. The fabric is soft and very friable, and the manufacture is crude: the mouth of the vessel is far from circular, the body colour varies widely (indicating uneven firing conditions), while the base shows some large cracks where the clay has contracted during drying or firing. Contrary to the excavator's comments (Brunton 1948: pl. 12; followed by Kantor 1992: 15), the simple, hole-mouth vessel never had a neck: the upper part shows no signs of breakage. It seems highly unlikely that such a vessel would - or could - have been transported over a long distance. Nevertheless, it indicates the appeal that Mesopotamian ceramic forms had in Predynastic Egypt. A vessel from Choga Mish (III-226) provides a good parallel for the shape (Delougaz and Kantor 1996, II: pl. 120.D), as does an example from level VI of the Eanna sequence at Uruk (Delougaz and Kantor 1996, I: table 8). Ironically, the Matmar vessel

Fig. 4. Spouted jar from Mostagedda Cemetery 1600-1800. British Museum, London (EA 63003).

comes a securely-dated archaeological context (unlike the genuine imports found at Badari and Mostagedda). Grave 5112 at Matmar is dated to Naqada IIC-D1 (Hendrickx 1993; Wilkinson 1996), and belonged to a child. Other artefacts found in the burial included a cowrie shell, galena and malachite (Brunton 1948: pl. X). Inherited status was clearly a feature of Predynastic society in the mid-Naqada II period, even in a place like Matmar, comparatively remote from the centres of developing political and economic power.

The four-lugged vessels from Badari and Mostagedda prove that genuine imports from Mesopotamia were reaching Middle Egypt during the middle of the fourth millennium BC. The locally-made imitation from Matmar suggests that, if genuine imports were unavailable or beyond one's limited means, a poorly-made copy was the next best thing.

Spouted jars

Spouted jars are a comparatively rare, but distinctive form of Upper Egyptian Predynastic pottery, found in graves dated to Naqada II and early Naqada III. Although, until the present study, none of the examples from Egypt had been positively identified as a Mesopotamian import, the likelihood that the form derived from Uruk antecedents was clear to scholars (but

note Hendrickx and Bavay, forthcoming, for an alternative view). As one leading scholar commented, 'it seems unlikely that such a specific form would have been invented independently in Egypt' (Kantor 1992: 14) when it is a well-known element of the late Uruk ceramic repertoire. Now, the 'missing link' between the Uruk antecedents and the Egyptian imitations may have come to light. First-hand inspection of a spouted jar in the British Museum (EA 63003) suggests that it is a true import (Fig. 4). Like the other vessels of confirmed Mesopotamian origin, it comes from the Badari region of Middle Egypt. It was found on the surface next to a plundered grave in Cemetery 1600-1800 at Mostagedda. Although the original context is lost, the general date of the burials in the cemetery spans the Naqada II period.

Three factors point to a likely foreign origin: fabric, technology and shape. The fabric looks decidedly un-Egyptian. It is hard, dense and non-porous; both the surface and the break show small fragments of limestone and a few particles of mica. The break is salmon pink in colour, while the exterior surface ranges from grey-buff on the spout to salmon pink on the base. In contrast to vessels of hard pink ware made in Egypt, the spouted jar from Mostagedda shows a high degree of chaff temper. Chaff marks are very noticeable on the surface and are also visible in the break. In terms of technology, the vessel shows distinct signs of turning in the area of the junction between the main body and the neck. The neck was formed separately and was clearly turned. The spout is hand-made, and was shaped by scraping with a knife, as was the main body of the vessel. The surface has been very well smoothed, and there are traces of a red slip. The burnishing strokes are horizontal above the waist, more vertical or diagonal on the lower part of the vessel. The shape seems to have been designed to keep the contents cool and prevent excess evaporation. Hence the vessel walls are thick, and the spout has only a narrow channel for pouring. The neck is very narrow and the rim flares outwards. This shape contrasts with clear Egyptian examples of spouted jars where the neck is usually wider and the walls much thinner. Mesopotamian parallels for the Mostagedda spouted jar have been found at Choga Mish (III-692, Delougaz and Kantor 1996, I: fig. 12) and, perhaps more significantly, at Habuba Kabira (Strommenger 1975: 163, fig. 6); both contexts are dated to the late Uruk period.

The shape of imported spouted jars — or, perhaps, the status associations of the commodity they contained — clearly inspired Egyptian potters to produce imitations. The copies are usually of standard Upper Egyptian polished red ware, made from Nile clay (which is rather porous) and coated with a micaceous haematite slip. The distribution of Egyptian-made spouted jars is telling. Of the fifteen examples with known provenance, five come from graves in the Badari region, three from graves in the Abydos region, and seven from the single site of Naqada (see Appendix 1). Significant is the concentration of examples in two of the leading centres of Predynastic Upper Egypt: both the Abydos region and Naqada were at the forefront of socio-political and economic developments in Naqada II.

IMPORTS AND IMITATIONS: ARTEFACTS OF COMPLEXITY

During the course of the Predynastic period, the process of political and economic centralisation gathered pace in Upper Egypt. The archaeological evidence suggests that, at the beginning of the process in late Naqada I, the three regional centres of This, Naqada and Hierakonpolis were fairly evenly balanced in terms of importance and influence, with Hierakonpolis perhaps enjoying a small advantage. At the end of the process, marked by the formation of the Egyptian state, the Abydos region emerged supreme, and the rulers of This became the first kings of Egypt. However, between these two points, in Naqada IIB-IIC, there is at least some evidence that the site of Naqada and its rulers were temporarily in the ascendant (Wilkinson, forthcoming). The reason for this probably lies in the fact that the town of Naqada controlled access to the gold reserves in the eastern desert (Trigger et al. 1983: 39; Wilkinson 1999: 37). Indeed, the ancient Egyptian name for Naqada was Nubt ('the golden'). Exploitation of these gold reserves must have made the

rulers of Naqada prosperous and powerful, especially when Egypt was drawn into the system of high-value international exchange. The international exchange network which had existed in the Near East from at least Neolithic times (Sherratt 1998) must have been stimulated by the first Uruk expansion into northern Mesopotamia and south-eastern Anatolia, itself a phenomenon which seems to have been driven by a desire to gain access to sources of precious commodities. It is telling that the rise of Naqada, as attested by the earliest burials in the élite Cemetery T, coincides with the first Uruk expansion; moreover, in both cases, the key seems to have been access to metals. Within this context of socio-economic development, it should come as little surprise that the cemeteries of Naqada provide the most abundant evidence for foreign influences during this period. Hence, it is at Naqada that we see the earliest imported Palestinian wavy-handled jar, the most numerous Mesopotamian-inspired spouted jars, and the earliest examples of imported artefacts of complexity: cylinder seals.

Cylinder seals

Cylinder seals are rare in Predynastic Egypt, with only 17 examples known. Of these, only four are certain imports; the rest are probably locally-made Egyptian imitations. Two of the imported cylinder seals come from secure archaeological contexts at Naqada; a third is probably from Naqada too, although it was bought on the Luxor antiquities market a couple of years after Petrie had excavated at Naqada. The remaining import was excavated at Matmar.

The cylinder seal from Naqada grave 1863, dated by its pottery to Naqada IIB-IIC, is now in the Petrie Museum at University College London (UC 5374). The seal is carved from brown limestone, and the incised decoration consists of lentoid shapes with curved lines above and below (Fig. 5; Boehmer 1974: Abb. 1). One of the lentoid shapes has two small projections at the back, which resemble a fish-tail. The other lentoid shape could also be interpreted as a fish. Hence, the design as a whole seems to suggest fish swimming in water. Parallel designs are known from a number of Mesopotamian sites, including Susa, Tello, Tepe Gawra, Ur and Tell Brak.

The second cylinder seal from Naqada was found in

Fig. 5. Cylinder seal from Naqada grave 1863. Petrie Museum of Egyptian Archaeology, London (UC 5374) (after Boehmer 1974: Abb. 1).

 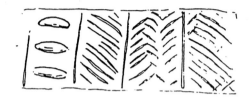

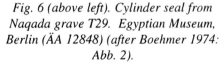

Fig. 6 (above left). Cylinder seal from Naqada grave T29. Egyptian Museum, Berlin (ÄA 12848) (after Boehmer 1974: Abb. 2).

Fig. 7 (above right). Cylinder seal from Upper Egypt, probably Naqada. Egyptian Museum, Berlin (ÄA 15388) (after Boehmer 1974: Abb. 10).

Fig. 8 (left). Cylinder seal from Matmar grave 3039. Ashmolean Museum, Oxford (1932.901) (after Payne 1993: fig. 72).

grave T29, dated to Naqada IIC. The seal is also of limestone, and its decoration is very similar to that of the seal from Naqada grave 1863 (Fig. 6; Boehmer 1974: Abb. 2). Unfortunately, the present location of the cylinder seal from Naqada grave T29 is not known. It was formerly in Berlin (ÄA 12848), but is now lost. The context in which it was found is highly significant when considering the circumstances in which artefacts of complexity were imported from Mesopotamia into Egypt during the middle of the fourth millennium BC. As stated above, Cemetery T at Naqada was an élite cemetery, reserved for the interments of the local rulers. The establishment of separate élite cemeteries marks a crucial stage in the development of political structures in Upper Egypt. Grave T29 is one of the earliest burials in Cemetery T. Its owner not only expressed his status by the location of his tomb, but also by its contents. The cylinder seal found in T29 identifies the tomb owner as an administrator, someone with access to the mechanisms and artefacts of rule.

A third cylinder seal imported from Mesopotamia is unprovenanced but most probably came from Naqada, too. It is now in Berlin (ÄA 15388). Carved from light grey limestone, the seal bears an incised design of lentoid shapes with curved lines above and below, alternating with groups of fish (Fig. 7; Boehmer 1974: Abb. 10). Close parallels have been found at Susa, dated to the late Uruk period.

A cylinder seal of cream limestone was among the artefacts found in grave 3039 at Matmar (Brunton 1948: 18), dated to Naqada IIC-D1. The seal, now in the Ashmolean Museum (1932.901) measures 2.3 cm in height and 1.7 cm in diameter. The incised design is arranged in four vertical panels: two are cross-hatched, one is filled with a herring-bone pattern, and the fourth with three lentoid shapes (Fig. 8; Brunton 1948: pl. XV.5; Boehmer 1974: Abb. 4; Payne 1993: fig. 72). There has been some dispute about the provenance of the seal. Boehmer (1974: 513) found no specific Mesopotamian parallels for the design and identified the seal as an

Egyptian imitation, but Payne (1993: 203) was clear in identifying it as a genuine import. The material of the seal - limestone - certainly points to a foreign origin, since most early Egyptian cylinder seals were carved from steatite, ivory or ebony.

A cylinder seal of blue-green glazed composition (Boehmer 1974: Abb. 15), acquired on the antiquities market by Borchardt in 1911 and now in Berlin (ÄA 20099) has been cited as an import (most recently by Pittman 1998). However, given the material and the execution of the design - three rows of recumbent lions - the seal is almost certainly an Egyptian imitation (Boehmer 1974: 505-6).

Like the four-lugged jars and spouted jars, cylinder seals imported from Mesopotamia were copied by Egyptian craftsmen. The Egyptians adapted the original designs to suit their own tastes, and eventually produced seals with entirely Egyptian designs. Like the style of niched mudbrick architecture borrowed from Mesopotamia, cylinder seals eventually became a standard component of Early Dynastic Egyptian élite culture. Why were cylinder seals adopted and adapted, whereas most of the Mesopotamian motifs found in early Egyptian iconography were abandoned after they had served their purpose? The answer must lie in the administrative practice that cylinder seals represented. As we have seen, Upper Egypt in Naqada II was undergoing a process of rapid socio-political and economic change. Political and economic power were becoming increasingly concentrated in the hands of a few élites. They displayed and reinforced their status, inter alia, by means of prestige artefacts, often imported. But the maintenance of political and economic power also requires administrative mechanisms: controlling peoples' lives means controlling their livelihoods. To put it simply, economic control requires documentation. In the sphere of documentation, especially accounting, Mesopotamia had an early lead over Egypt. Throughout its long history, Egyptian culture was adept at borrowing ideas from abroad if they were useful, and adapting them to its own needs. This is particularly true of cylinder seals, and the concepts of ownership and economic control which they embodied. As an artefact of administration, the cylinder seal was exceptionally effective. With the emerging Egyptian élites intent upon securing their own power, the whole-hearted adoption and survival of the cylinder seal was guaranteed.

Stamp seal

The cylinder seals deposited in graves at Naqada and elsewhere were not the earliest artefacts of complexity to find their way from Mesopotamia to Egypt. A stamp seal from grave 7501 at Naga ed-Deir (Lythgoe and Dunham 1965: 318-19, fig. 142.e; Podzorski 1988: 262-3, fig. 3; Mark 1998: fig. 25), now in the Lowie Museum of Anthropology at the University of California (UCLMA 6-3919), may be seen as an early fore-runner. The cemetery of Naga ed-Deir lies on the opposite bank of the Nile from Abydos. It seems to have alternated with Abydos as the cemetery serving the Predynastic town of This (Wilkinson 1999: 354-5). Grave 7501 at Naga ed-Deir can be dated by its pottery to Naqada IIB or IIC, roughly contemporary with grave 1863 at Naqada which yielded an imported cylinder seal. Grave 7501 was the burial of a mature woman, unremarkable except for one artefact, a hemi-spheroid stamp seal of hard, shiny white limestone.

It is pierced through, and the underside bears an abstract design of 22 small circular pits, in the shape of the letter 'e' (Fig. 9). The pits were produced by drilling. There can be no doubt that this seal was imported from Mesopotamia, and probably from eastern Mesopotamia (cf. Podzorski 1988: 263). Close parallels, both in shape and decoration, have been found at Tepe Gawra, Tepe Giyan, Nuzi (Fig. 10), and Choga Mish (Delougaz and Kantor 1996, II: pl. 41.J). The examples from Nuzi (Homès-Fredericq 1970: nos 416-18, 421) were previously dated to the Jemdet Nasr period, but Pittman (1998) has pointed out that this dating should now be revised to the late middle Uruk, contemporary with Naqada IIB in Upper Egypt. The appearance of drilled seals in the late middle Uruk period may mark the introduction of a new drilling technology (Pittman 1998).

To date, the Naga ed-Deir artefact is the only example of a Mesopotamian stamp seal found in Egypt. Its presence at Naga ed-Deir is not entirely surprising, since the Abydos region was one of the three main centres of socio-political developments in the Predynastic period. Other aspects of the find, however, are more puzzling. The inclusion of an artefact of administration in an otherwise unremarkable burial of a mature woman raises important questions. By the time it was buried, the seal may perhaps have become a treasured family possession, disassociated from its original function; or it may never

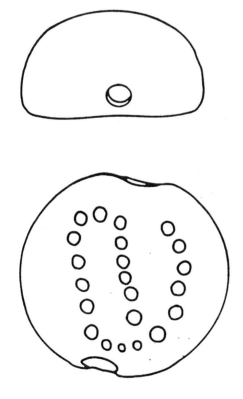

Fig. 9. Stamp seal from Naga ed-Deir grave 7501. Lowie Museum of Anthropology, University of California (UCLMA 6-3919) (after Mark 1998: fig. 25.A, itself after Podzorski 1988: fig. 3).

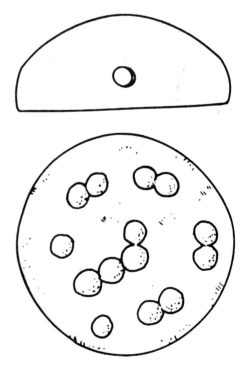

Fig. 10. Stamp seal from Nuzi (after Mark 1998: fig. 25.B, itself after Starr 1937: pl. 40A).

have served as an administrative artefact within Egypt. It may simply have been viewed as a curio, an exotic object to be valued for its rarity.

Tokens?

The Mesopotamian cylinder seals found in Egypt represent not just the importation of exotic baubles for conspicuous display, but the adoption of a complex administrative system. Clay tokens constituted another important mechanism of economic administration and accounting used in Mesopotamia in the Uruk period. Tokens have been recovered from the Uruk 'colony sites' at Tell Brak, Habuba Kabira and Jebel Aruda, and in the Amuq Plain (Schmandt-Besserat 1992: 39). It is not entirely implausible that such tokens may have reached Egypt in the Naqada II-III periods, together with other artefacts of complexity and influences from Mesopotamia. Indeed, excavations of Predynastic mortuary and settlement contexts in Egypt have occasionally unearthed small, cone-shaped objects of fired clay, some examples with traces of red pigment (e.g. three cones from Abadiya tomb B101, Ashmolean E.942-4, Payne 1993: cat. nos 1948, 1949, 1950). Such objects have usually been identified as gaming pieces (Payne 1993: 235); this was also the case in early site reports of Mesopotamian excavations, where 'authors who risked an interpretation identified the tokens as amulets or game pieces' (Schmandt-Besserat 1992: 8). It is possible that the same mis-identification may have plagued Egyptologists as well. It is also probable that, as in the Mesopotamian case before tokens were recognised, similar objects from Egyptian excavations may have been 'mostly ignored' (Schmandt-Besserat 1992: 195). There are good Mesopotamian parallels for the enigmatic objects found in Egyptian contexts. A cone-shaped token covered in red pigment, like the examples from Abadiya, is known from Arpachiyah; and tokens are attested as grave goods both here and at Tepe Gawra (Schmandt-Besserat 1992: 106-7).

There is good reason to suppose that the practice of economic administration represented by cylinder seals spread from Mesopotamia to Egypt. It is certainly possible that a mechanism of accounting followed the same route.

ROUTE OF TRANSMISSION

There has been considerable debate about the route Mesopotamian imports and influences followed to reach Egypt. Some scholars (e.g. Rice 1990; Smith 1992) have favoured a southern route around the Arabian peninsula, up the Red Sea and along the Wadi Hammamat to Upper Egypt. Others (Moorey 1990) have argued for a northern route via the Uruk outposts in Syria, and thence by land or sea to the Nile Delta. There is no question that the latter, northern route is the shorter by far. Moreover, the Uruk colony sites in northern Mesopotamia and southern Anatolia provide staging posts for a route linking Khuzistan and southern Mesopotamia to Egypt. By con-

trast, the southern, round-Arabia route has very little archaeological evidence to support it. Two main points have been advanced in support of a southern route. First, rock-cut pictures in the Wadi Hammamat itself show high-prowed boats of supposedly 'Mesopotamian' form. However, the identification of these boat glyphs as Mesopotamian craft is by no means universally accepted. Second, the frequency of Mesopotamian imports and influences in Upper Egypt, particularly at the site of Naqada (which seems to have commanded access to the Wadi Hammamat), is highlighted.

There are powerful answers to this latter point. First, We should expect to find most evidence of Mesopotamian influence in Upper Egypt, since that is where the concentration of political and economic power associated with the rise of social complexity was most advanced. An iconography of power, employing some motifs borrowed from Mesopotamia, was being developed by the rulers of Predynastic Upper Egypt, not by their Lower Egyptian counterparts, if such figures even existed. We should also assume that the rulers of the Abydos and Naqada regional polities were the intended recipients of most of the artefacts of complexity imported from Mesopotamia. Upper Egyptian rulers needed administrative mechanisms to maintain their authority. Hence, it should come as no surprise to find an imported stamp seal in the Abydos region, and the earliest cylinder seals at Naqada.

Second, recent excavations at Buto in the northwestern Delta have provided definitive evidence for contacts between Egypt and northern Syria at the end of Naqada II, in the form of a few sherds of spiral reserved slip pottery (Köhler 1998: pl. 68, photographic pl. 11). Such pottery is characteristic of the ceramic repertoire of the Amuq Plain, itself a region in close contact with the Uruk sites on the Upper Euphrates. The discovery of these sherds at Buto indicates that a northern, possibly maritime, trade route was in existence during the third quarter of the fourth millennium BC. As we have seen, all the examples of Uruk imports found in Egypt come from funerary contexts. Prestige, exotic objects were highly valued, and were interred in graves to express the status of the deceased. To date, no burials dating to the period of either Uruk expansion have been located at Buto; excavations here have uncovered only settlement remains. The fourth millennium BC graves at Buto, if they exist, may well contain further evidence of Egyptian-Mesopotamian contacts.

Third, the discovery of Mesopotamian imports - one seal and three pots - in Middle Egypt more-or-less proves a northern route of transmission. It shows that objects were travelling upstream towards the courts of Predynastic Upper Egypt. It also argues strongly against a southern, round-Arabia route. If trade was following the Red Sea route, we would not expect to find Mesopotamian vessels in Middle Egypt.

The Badari region

The peculiar concentration of imports in this politically insignificant region of Egypt is noteworthy. Although never a leading region for socio-economic or political developments, the Badari region seems nevertheless to have prospered throughout the Predynastic period. Communities like Matmar and Mostagedda survived the vicissitudes of political and economic change, leaving a continuous sequence of burials over a period of some two millennia. A key factor favouring this region may have been its geographic location.

As well as commanding a wide expanse of alluvial floodplain, Matmar is situated at a point where the cliffs of the eastern desert approach close to the river, in other words a natural constriction in the course of the Nile. This may have given it a strategic advantage in controlling riverine trade. Goods travelling from sites in the Delta (like Buto) southwards to the courts of Predynastic Upper Egypt had to travel by river, and they had to pass through the Badari region. This seems the best explanation for the unexpected concentration of Mesopotamian imports in this part of Egypt.

CONCLUSION

As we have seen, artefacts imported from Mesopotamia and their imitations fall into two categories, pots and seals. The distribution of these two categories is highly significant. All three imported vessels come from the Badari region of Middle Egypt, comparatively remote from the process of state formation; while three out of four imported seals of known provenance and most of the Mesopotamian-inspired pottery (whether decorated, four-lugged jars or spouted jars) come from important Upper Egyptian sites at the heart of this process.

The first Uruk expansion happened to coincide with the rise of complex society in the Nile valley. The exploitation of gold reserves in Egypt's eastern desert drew the polities of Naqada II Upper Egypt into the wider, international trade in low-weight, high-value commodities (Sherratt 1998). Participation in this exchange network brought imports and ideas from an advanced civilisation (Uruk Mesopotamia) to Egypt at a time when Egypt's own rulers were particularly receptive to such influences. A re-appraisal of the evidence for contacts between Egypt and Mesopotamia suggests that the Near East in the fourth millennium BC was a dynamic melting pot of ideas, characterised by significant cross-cultural exchange. Importation, imitation, emulation: these were the hallmarks of early Egypt's relations with other advanced cultures of the Near East. The artefacts of the Uruk found in Egypt represent merely the archaeologically visible tip of the iceberg, the surviving material manifestations of a much broader phenomenon.

ACKNOWLEDGEMENTS

First, I should like to thank Nicholas Postgate and Stuart Campbell for inviting me to speak at the conference 'Artefacts of complexity: tracking the Uruk in the Near East'. Thanks are also due to the British School of Archaeology in Iraq for generously paying the speakers' expenses. The paper, as presented here, has benefited from discussions and correspondence with a number of colleagues, including Mitchell Rothman, Holly Pittman and Alexander Joffe. The suggestion that some of the small clay cone-shaped objects from Egyptian excavations may represent tokens was first made by Baruch Brandl at an international conference held in Jerusalem in April 1998. The sherd in Fig. 1 is illustrated here by kind permission of the Petrie Museum of Egyptian Archaeology, University College London. The pot in Fig. 4 is illustrated by kind permission of the Trustees of the British Museum. My research at the University of Durham was supported by the Leverhulme Trust through a Special Research Fellowship.

APPENDIX 1: EGYPTIAN-MADE PREDYNASTIC SPOUTED JARS OF KNOWN PROVENANCE

site	context	probable date	publication	present location
Matmar	grave 3110	IID2	Brunton 1948: pl. XII.9	Cairo JdE 57428
Matmar	grave 3128	IIC-D1	Petrie 1921: pl. XVIII	Cairo JdE 57435?
Qau	Cemetery 200	?	Brunton and Caton-Thompson 1928: pl. XXXVIII	?
Badari	Cemetery 3800	?	Brunton and Caton-Thompson 1928:pl. XXXVIII	?
Badari	Cemetery 4600	?	Brunton and Caton-Thompson 1928:pl. XXXVIII	?
Mahasna	grave H123	IID2-IIIA1	Ayrton and Loat 1911: pl. XXXVIII	?
Mahasna	grave H131A	IID2	Ayrton and Loat 1911: pl. XXXVIII	?
Hu	grave U 187A	IIIA1	Petrie 1921: pl. XVIII	Petrie UC 10849
Naqada	grave 145	?	-	Ashmolean 95.397
Naqada	grave 421	IIC	Payne 1993: cat. no. 1043	Ashmolean 95.396
Naqada	grave 1069	?	Petrie 1921: pl. XVIII	Petrie UC 5742
Naqada	grave 1108	?	Petrie 1921: pl. XVIII	Chicago OIC 858
Naqada	grave 1211	IIC	Petrie 1921: pl. XVIII	Petrie UC 5741
Naqada	grave 1619	?	Petrie 1921: pl. XVIII	Petrie
Naqada	grave 1886	IIC-D1	Payne 1993: cat. 704	Ashmolean 95.768

REFERENCES

Adams, B., 1996. Elite graves at Hierakonpolis, in J. Spencer (ed.) *Aspects of Early Egypt*, 1-15. London: British Museum Press.

Amiet, P., 1980. *La glyptique mésopotamienne archaïque*. Paris: CNRS.

Boehmer, R.M., 1974. Das Rollsiegel im prädynastischen Ägypten, *Archäologischer Anzeiger* 89: 495-514.

Boese, J., 1995. *Ausgrabungen in Tell Sheikh Hassan. I: Vorläufige Berichte über die Grabungskampagnen 1984-1990 und 1992-1994*. Saarbrücken: Saarbrücker Druckerei und Verlag. Schriften zur vorderasiatischen Archäologie 5.

Bourriau, J., 1981. *Umm el-Gaab. Pottery from the Nile valley before the Arab conquest*. Cambridge: Cambridge University Press.

Brunton, G., 1937. *Mostagedda and the Tasian Culture. British Museum Expedition to Middle Egypt, first and second years 1928, 1929*. London: Quaritch.

- 1948. *Matmar. British Museum Expedition to Middle Egypt 1929-1931*. London: Quaritch.

Brunton, G. and G. Caton-Thompson, 1928. *The Badarian civilisation and Predynastic remains near Badari*. London: British School of Archaeology in Egypt.

Case, H. and J.C. Payne, 1962. 'Tomb 100: the decorated tomb at Hierakonpolis', *Journal of Egyptian Archaeology* 48: 5-18.

Delougaz, P. and H.J. Kantor, edited by A. Alizadeh, 1996. *Choga Mish, Volume I. The first five seasons of excavations 1961-1971*, Parts I-II. Chicago: The Oriental Institute of the University of Chicago. Oriental Institute Publications Volume 101.

Genouillac, H. de, 1934. *Fouilles de Telloh, I: époques présargoniques*. Paris: Paul Geuthner.

Hendrickx, S., 1993. 'Relative chronology of the Naqada culture', paper presented at the colloquium 'Early

Egypt', British Museum, London, 22 July 1993. Manuscript on file with the author.

- 1996. 'The relative chronology of the Naqada culture. Problems and possibilities', in J. Spencer (ed.), *Aspects of early Egypt*, 36-69. London: British Museum Press.

Hendrickx, S. and L. Bavay, forthcoming. 'The relative chronological position of Egyptian Predynastic and Early Dynastic tombs with objects imported from the Near East and the nature of interregional contacts', in E.C.M. van den Brink and T.E. Levy (eds.), *Egyptian-Canaanite relations during the 4th through early 3rd millennia, BCE*. Leicester: Leicester University Press. New Approaches to Anthropological Archaeology.

Homès-Fredericq, D. , 1970. *Les cachets mésopotamiens protohistoriques*. Leiden: E.J. Brill.

Kaiser, W., 1957. 'Zur inneren Chronologie der Naqadakultur', *Archaeologia Geographica* 6: 69-77, pls 15-26.

Kantor, H.J., 1992. 'The relative chronology of Egypt and its foreign correlations before the First Intermediate Period', in R.W. Ehrich (ed.), *Chronologies in old world archaeology*, third edition, volume I: 3-21; volume II: 2-43. Chicago: The University of Chicago Press.

Kemp, B.J., 1973. 'Photographs of the decorated tomb at Hierakonpolis', *Journal of Egyptian Archaeology* 59: 36-43.

- 1989. *Ancient Egypt: anatomy of a civilization.* London: Routledge.

Köhler, E.C., 1998. *Tell el-Fara'în. Buto III. Die Keramik von der späten Naqadenkultur bis zum Alten Reich (Schichten III-VI, Grabungen der Jahre 1987-1989).* Mainz am Rhein: von Zabern. Deutsches Archäologisches Institut, Abteilung Kairo: Archäologische Veröffentlichungen 94.

Lythgoe, A.M., edited by D. Dunham, 1965. *The Predynastic Cemetery N7000. Naga-ed-Dêr Part IV.* Berkeley and Los Angeles: University of California Press.

Mark, S., 1998. *From Egypt to Mesopotamia. A study of Predynastic trade routes.* College Station, Texas/London: Texas A&M University Press/Chatham Publishing. Studies in Nautical Archaeology 4.

Moorey, P.R.S., 1990. 'From Gulf to Delta in the fourth millennium BCE: the Syrian connection', *Eretz Israel* 21: 62-9.

Payne, J.C., 1973. 'Tomb 100. The decorated tomb at Hierakonpolis confirmed', *Journal of Egyptian Archaeology* 59: 31-5.

- 1993. *Catalogue of the Predynastic Egyptian Collection in the Ashmolean Museum.* Oxford: Clarendon Press.

Petrie, W.M.F., 1901. *Diospolis Parva. The cemeteries of Abadiyeh and Hu, 1898-9.* London: Egypt Exploration Fund.

- 1921. *Corpus of prehistoric pottery and palettes.* London: British School of Archaeology in Egypt.

Petrie, W.M.F. and J.E. Quibell, 1896. *Naqada and Ballas.* London: Quaritch.

Pittman, H., oral presentation at Manchester, Nov. 1998.

Podzorski, P.V., 1988. 'Predynastic Egyptian seals of known provenience in the R.H. Lowie Museum of Anthropology', *Journal of Near Eastern Studies* 47: 259-68.

Quibell, J.E. and F.W. Green, 1902. *Hierakonpolis, II.* London: Quaritch.

Rice, M., 1990. *Egypt's making. The origins of ancient Egypt 5000-2000 BC*, London: Routledge.

Schmandt-Besserat, D., 1992. *Before writing, I: from counting to cuneiform.* Austin: University of Texas Press.

Sherratt, A., 1998. Introductory comments delivered at the conference 'Artefacts of complexity: tracking the Uruk in the Near East', University of Manchester, 6 November 1998.

Smith, H.S., 1992. 'The making of Egypt: a review of the influence of Susa and Sumer on Upper Egypt and Lower Nubia in the 4th millennium BC', in R. Friedman and B. Adams (eds) *The followers of Horus. Studies dedicated to Michael Allen Hoffman*, 235-46. Oxford: Oxbow. Memoirs 20/Egyptian Studies Association Publication No. 2.

Starr, R., 1937. *Nuzi*, volume 2: *Report on the excavations at Yorgan Tepa near Kirkuk, Iraq, conducted by Harvard University in conjunction with the American Schools of Oriental Research and the University Museum of Philadelphia, 1927-1931.* Plates and plans. Cambridge, Massachusetts: Harvard University Press.

Strommenger, E., 1975. 'Habuba Kabira-Süd 1974', *Les Annales Archéologiques Arabes-Syriennes* 25: 155-64.

Sürenhagen, D., 1977. 'Untersuchungen zur Keramikproduktion innerhalb der spät-Urukzeitlichen Siedlung Habuba Kabira-Süd in Nordsyrien', *Acta Praehistorica et Archaeologica* 5-6: 43-164.

Trigger, B.G., B.J. Kemp, D. O'Connor and A.B. Lloyd,

1983. *Ancient Egypt: a social history.* Cambridge: Cambridge University Press.

Wilkinson, T.A.H., 1996. *State formation in Egypt: chronology and society.* Oxford: Tempus Reparatum. BAR International Series 651. Cambridge Monographs in African Archaeology 40.

- 1999. *Early Dynastic Egypt.* London: Routledge.

- 2000. 'Political unification: towards a reconstruction', *Mitteilungen des Deutschen Archäologischen Instituts, Abteilung Kairo* 56: 377-95.

Indices

1. Index of sites & geographical names

NB map references are given first in italics; principal discussion of a site is marked in bold. Very frequently recurring names like Syria or Tigris are not taken up.

2. Pottery styles, wares, etc.

251

3. Time spans

4. Persons

5. General